THE BICKERSTETH
DIARIES

BY THE SAME AUTHOR
JOINTLY WITH ROBERT W. DUNNING

*Clerks of the Closet
in the Royal Household*

Alan Sutton 1992

THE BICKERSTETH
DIARIES

1914–1918

Edited by

JOHN BICKERSTETH

Sometime Bishop of Bath and Wells
and Clerk of the Closet to
Her Majesty The Queen

LEO COOPER
LONDON

First published in Great Britain in 1995, re-issued in this format, 1996 by
LEO COOPER
190 Shaftesbury Avenue, London WC2H 8JL
an imprint of
Pen & Sword Books Ltd,
47 Church Street,
Barnsley, South Yorkshire S70 2AS

Introduction © John Terraine, 1995
Foreword © Donald Coggan, 1995
Text © John Bickersteth, 1995

A CIP record for this book is available from
the British Library

ISBN 0 85052 546 2

Designed by Humphrey Stone

Typset in 10½/13pt Linotype Sabon by
Phoenix Typesetting, Ilkley, West Yorkshire

Printed in Great Britain by Redwood Books,
Trowbridge, Wilts

In affectionate and grateful memory
of grandmother and the uncles

CONTENTS

CONTENTS

INTRODUCTION

JOHN TERRAINE

In 1914 all ranks, all ages in the Navy and the Army were 19th Century people, men born in the reign of Queen Victoria: the boy-midshipmen in the boats at Gallipoli, the boy-subalterns who came forward in droves from the public school and grammar school OTCs, Boy First Class Jack Cornwell who won a posthumous VC at Jutland at the age of 16, and a regiment of first-class boys who gave false ages to the Recruiting Officers and lie beside the men in the War Cemeteries – they were all Victorians. The gulf between them and the people of the 1990's is already virtually unbridgeable, and widens every day. Two elements, above all others, separate the 1914–1918 people from ourselves: patriotism and religion.

The patriotism is unmistakable, even across the great gulf that divides us. The first five months of the War (August to December 1914) witnessed the extraordinary phenomenon of 1,186,357 voluntary recruits for the Regular Army and Territorial Force; by the end of 1915 the total had risen to 2,466,719. The high peak of recruiting was September 1914, when the realization dawned on the British people that all was not well at the Front, and that a long, hard war was in prospect: 462,901 men volunteered during that month. It has also been reliably stated that 'nearly half those who filled [the Army's] ranks between August 1914 and November 1918 were volunteers'[1]. It is not difficult to find fault with the Voluntary Principle on which the recruitment of the British Army had always been based – it has been bitterly renamed 'The Principle of Unequal Sacrifice'; the vivid patriotic instinct which marked its last manifestation is nevertheless not open to doubt.

The Bickersteth family well illustrates the powerful motive forces both of patriotism and religion, but nationally the religious element is certainly harder to assess. The family represents what must at all times have been a small section of the nation; an upper-middle-class fraction, with close Public School and University connections, and a strong ecclesiastical thread running from generation to generation, liberally decorated with bishops. There was no significant military tradition, but the call of duty would be readily heard. Canon Sam Bickersteth of Leeds had six sons, all grown up in 1914, two already in Holy Orders; five of them served in or for the Army, one in the War Office, the other four on the Western Front. They obeyed the call unhesitatingly, one of them coming from as far away as Melbourne, Australia, to do so. One did not return – killed on 1 July 1916 on the Somme, the worst day in the British Army's history.

It is the letters – the extraordinarily detailed and graphic letters from the Front, intended to be circulated throughout the family, to keep all its close-knit members in touch with each other – written by the third and fourth brothers, Julian and Burgon, that constitute the 'pith and marrow' of this book. They contain some astonishing material: yet more revealing descriptions of the Western Front, to add to the vast existing archive, revelations also of the particular dilemmas and problems of that interesting, influential, dedicated social group from which they sprang.

Burgon himself illustrates the duality of all their characters. He was not ordained; he was a cavalryman, proud to serve in the senior regiment of the Cavalry of the Line, the 1st (Royal) Dragoons[2] – but so intense was his religious feeling, and presumably his expression of it, that in the Regiment he attracted the nickname 'Bishop', which seemed to stick to him, without any ill-feeling or hint of denigration. By 1918, he was as respected as any regular soldier; three years of trench warfare had been bad for the self-respect of the cavalry, but in the final offensive in 1918 they found opportunities of vindication which he was as eager as any of them to grasp.

The coming of war found Julian in Melbourne, chaplain of the city's renowned Grammar School. From that position he was able to observe Australia's enthusiastic but at times somewhat disorderly entry into the War. It is interesting to note that in 1914 he was disposed to attribute the patriotic reaction of Australia (summed up in the words of the Prime Minister, Sir Joseph Cook, 'If the Old Country is at war, so are we') to what he calls 'the better classes', while thanks to 'Socialist legislation', the 'working classes, who form of course the great majority here . . . have been taught to think only of themselves and their own wages and gains'. The reader will perceive that this early critique would require considerable modification as the War continued[3] – and Julian's own views would change drastically.

As 1915 wore on, he became increasingly restless on the other side of the world, while his brothers gathered for the great European fray. He made up his mind that he must become a chaplain to a front-line unit, and this was formally agreed in July, but the rest of the year would pass before his ambition bore fruit. He arrived in France on 22 February, 1916, and was posted to the 56th Division, otherwise known as the 1/1st London, a Territorial Force formation consisting entirely of sub-units of the London Regiment, referred to in the Official History as 'some of the best infantry in the Armies in France'.[4] Julian's particular charge was the 1/12th London (The Rangers) in the 168th Brigade, and for the rest of the war his special private attachment was to them.

So Julian joined a select (though not universally admired) group of men, the padres, the front-line chaplains, whose task proved to be his personal métier, something he was able to do extremely well, setting a standard which it would be difficult to surpass. Who and what were these 'men of peace' in uniform, 'men of God' working in godless scenes according to their lights? When war broke out in August 1914, there were 117 of them in the British Army, by November 1918 there were 3,475, all still volunteers. They divided as follows:

Church of England	1,985
Roman Catholic	649
Presbyterian	303
Wesleyan	256
Baptists, Congregationalists, Methodists	251
Jewish	16
Welsh Calvinists	10
Salvation Army	5

During the war, 172 of them lost their lives, of whom eighty-eight were Anglican; four were awarded the Victoria Cross. Some of the clergy who volunteered were not up to the task, and Julian says as much, more than once. Nevertheless, magnificent work was done and, rightly, there are tributes to many heroes. Many more remain unsung.[5]

In both brothers, in the early days, the flame of patriotism was fierce. It became a commonplace that fire-eating attitudes multiplied and gained intensity, the further their possessor was from the Front. It is therefore not entirely surprising to find the most ferocious expressions of anti-German feeling coming from Julian, in far-away Melbourne. He writes in May 1915 (in the wake of the first gas attack on the Western Front):

As to the Germans! May God help them! We shall win this war because God cannot allow such scum to exist. . . . How can the Kaiser possibly reconcile such things as asphyxiating gases and slaughter of innocents with his reputed Christianity? He and Tirpitz[6] and others responsible must be tried for murder after the war, and if proved guilty, hanged, and may God have mercy on their souls.

Julian was a school chaplain, a Christian priest; but this was 1915, a year of delusions and horrible awakenings – and Melbourne was a long way away. . . .

Burgon, with time on his hands (which he much resented[7]), and very near to the action that he craved but could not share, was already by early 1916 beginning to take a less straightforward view of the war itself – 'Fighting seems incessant, and the whole business a hopeless nightmare'. Nevertheless, he still retains a stiff measure of his earlier simple enthusiasm:

an extremely healthy feeling that will welcome the next opportunity of sending as many Boches as possible hurtling to eternity.

Both brothers – and one could say, the bulk of the British people – were about to undergo a profound change of mind and heart which, while not fatally damaging their resolution to go on until victory, stripped away many of the crudities of wartime propaganda and jingoism and raised questions they had never asked before. In Julian and Burgon, and more slowly as awareness dawned in the people behind them, the turning-point was to be that terrible day, 1 July 1916, when the British Expeditionary Force suffered 57,470 casualties, of whom 993 officers and 18,247 other ranks were killed. Among the 993 officers was Morris Bickersteth, aged twenty-five, an acting company commander in the 15th Battalion The West Yorkshire Regiment (31st Division). To a close-knit family, his death came as a heavy blow, not lessened by his own clearly-expressed belief that 'dying for one's country is a magnificent thing'. For the Bickersteth brothers (and many others besides) the war was never to be viewed in quite the same way again.

The Battle of the Somme continued into November 1916, by which time well over a million men, German, British and French, had become casualties in it, and a nightmare landscape had been created. The painter Paul Nash said that:

no pen or drawing can convey this country. . . . Evil and the incarnate fiend alone can be master of this war, and no glimmer of God's hand can be seen anywhere. . . . It is unspeakable, godless, hopeless . . .[8]

Lord Chandos, then a Guards officer who had fought over it, wrote:

this country stinks of corruption . . . it is all dead, and God has utterly forsaken it.[9]

In September, 1916, Burgon Bickersteth wrote:

I think after the war I shall write a book, and in it I shall put everything that is filthy and disgusting and revolting and degrading and terrifying about modern warfare – and hope thereby to do my bit towards preventing another.

But it was Julian, in daily close contact with the (often unidentifiable) dead, the mortally wounded, the maimed survivors, the burial parties, and twice with poor devils awaiting execution, who seems to have been most affected by the increasing ferocity of the war. Also in September, 1916, with two more months of this battle, and two more years of war to go, he wrote:

This war may bring out some of the good qualities in man, but the evil it does is incalculably greater. The whole thing is utterly devilish and the work of all the demons of hell. It will take generations to eradicate the evils done to civilization by it. I feel that our whole moral outlook is being systematically lowered . . .

1917 brought the Third Battle of Ypres ('Passchendaele'), fought in a landscape of squalid evil fully matching that of the Somme. It was a battle of hope constantly deferred, which, as Julian says, was most depressing:

and perhaps takes from one the power of preserving an even judgment; but this appalling carnage and ever-increasing losses of splendid men, without material success to show for them, makes me think that to continue this war much longer will be more wicked than to stop it. To beat Germany on land seems well-nigh impossible.

At the end of the year Julian permits himself a cri-de-coeur, reminiscent of the poems of Wilfred Owen and others:

My nostrils are filled with the smell of blood. My eyes are glutted with the sight of bleeding bodies and shattered limbs, my heart wrung with the agony of wounded and dying men.

He has come a very long way from the clear-cut, unquestioning patriotism of 1914, and Burgon has come with him. By 1918 they are both socialists at heart.

For Burgon the final offensive, with its restoration of the war of movement at last, brings some consolation (and decoration); Julian is also decorated, but unconsoled. To him must go the last word from the Front, in late August, as the crumbling of Germany into defeat begins to be apparent, but difficult for the truly war-weary to perceive:

The cry goes up, 'How long, O Lord, how long?' Forgive this outburst of weary bitterness, but 'my heart is heavy, my heart is heavy'.

The Bickersteth Diaries constitute a remarkable document, valuable to military and social historians alike, and containing an impetus which will carry along the general reader too. What we perceive here, only faintly recognized by the writers, is the undermining of the middle class, especially of one of its most influential, opinion-forming sections. One senses the shock of involvement in a world far removed from the closed circle, or circles, in which the Bickersteths had been reared. These may be viewed as four concentric rings, isolating them and their peers from the main stream of British life: they were, first of all, the privileged prisoners of their class, its traditional upbringing and frames of mind; those who went to public schools were then imprisoned by their system and its codes and its limitations (Julian came to recognize that 'the knowledge of the world of the ordinary public school is extraordinarily limited'); the two great universities, towards which they automatically gravitated, added their own limitations and seclusion; and finally, their chosen vocation of lay or ordained ministry within the Church, set the vast majority of them even further apart from the ordinary man and woman. It came as a serious shock to appreciate how deep and wide this segregation was, and with the shock came a demoralization whose effects were far-reaching.

The loss of morale of the British middle class was without doubt one of the most serious results of the War. Their sense of collective blundering, of having, in effect, betrayed a trust, by blindness and sheer error, badly diminished their confidence during the first critical decades of peace, with consequences that we know too well. All the seeds of future disaster were planted on those ghastly battlefields – unimagined, unimaginable, but soon to be hideously exceeded – which Julian and Burgon Bickersteth here delineate with such astonishing precision.

FOREWORD

THE RIGHT REVEREND AND RIGHT HONOURABLE
DONALD COGGAN · ARCHBISHOP OF
CANTERBURY 1974 – 1980

I knew only one of the Bickersteth brothers, Burgon; of that more in a moment. Julian I never met, although I heard much of him when we came to live in Canterbury. This last sentence however needs to be qualified, for in a real sense I have 'met' Julian as I have read this book, itself a greatly reduced version of the vast original.

What a man to 'meet'. A born leader, he showed the quality of his leadership in his four years of service as an army chaplain, in the thick of it at its very worst, hating the bloodshed and the mud, but glorying in the camaraderie which war somehow seems to generate and encourage. He consistently magnified his office as a priest in the Church of God; for example, when in a single day he was burying seventy mangled bodies, mostly of men that he knew, and thinking while he was doing it carefully and reverently for each one: 'these men are living, not dead'. In time of peace that leadership found ample outlet in the headmastership of two great schools, St Peter's, Adelaide, and Felsted; and then in full-time service to the Church of England as Residentiary Canon of Canterbury, Treasurer of the Cathedral and Archdeacon of Maidstone. A man – he richly deserved his mention in dispatches, that Military Cross, and his promotion to Senior Chaplain. A man of God – first and last.

Burgon I knew – not very intimately – in his Canadian days when we lived next door to what is indeed his lasting memorial, Hart House, Toronto. Walking to his work in the University, Burgon would pick up the toys which our infant daughter had thrown from her pram on the campus grass and pursue his way to encourage the growth of that centre of culture and creativity, which was his pride and joy and of which he was the heart and soul for twenty-five years.

It was later, during his Canterbury years, that Jean and I came to know him well, eventually to visit him when he was dying, and to speak at his funeral. I would call on him in his home in the Canterbury Precincts. Often before such a visit, he would have made out a list of subjects which he wanted to discuss, and we would go through the items together. They covered a range which was world-wide. His knowledge of men and affairs was extensive; and his interest in humankind, in all its vicissitudes, never slackened. I would tease him that his two main interests were Canadians and criminals for, after his war-service, in which he was twice awarded the Military Cross, and after the important years in Canada, he spent much time on prison-visiting and in following up the prisoners when they came out into freedom. There were senior people at his funeral who spoke of him as the doyen of the prison visitors of England.

This book is valuable for the truly terrible picture it gives of war and its agonies. We should never be allowed to forget them. But it does much more than that. It reminds us of what might become (if it has not already done so) a lost art – the art of letter-writing. The two uncles wrote and wrote, even when under the severest pressures of war, and their mother kept those letters. Such letters, in the intimacy of their detail, have preserved for us a vivid picture of a particular period of history which is of the greatest value.

They have shown to us other things, two of which I must mention. First, the stability of family life as exhibited in the persons, senior and junior, of the Bickersteth tribe. How those sons loved their parents! How those parents loved their sons! – including Morris, who died in action. There was nothing sloppy in this. Here was love at its sincerest.

The other thing which emerges from page after page of those letters is the centrality of the Christian faith as the foundation of their lives and actions. Julian and Burgon might criticize the Church of England in which they had been reared, but of their loyalty to it and their service within it there could be no shadow of doubt.

I welcome this book. Labour of love by their nephew it obviously is; he knew and loved his uncles, and the diarist, his grandmother, too. The months of studying and working on all this material have meant much to him. What is offered to us in these pages will stand out among the millions of words written about the First World War.

Donald Coggan

PROLOGUE

There are two complete sets of the Bickersteth War Diary containing thousands of newspaper cuttings and some 7,000 typescript pages. Eleven fat cloth-bound volumes, some of them three inches thick, cover the First World War, its aftermath, and then various continental journeyings made by members of the family between the wars. The Second World War fills seven more, rather less bulky, volumes. Both sets belong to my brother, Ted Bickersteth, the elder son of the eldest son of the diarist. In 1988 he gave the first set, under a long loan arrangement, to Churchill College, Cambridge. They were very keen to have it, having been long encouraged to do so by the military historian, the late Stephen Roskill, who knew our family. My wife and I house the second set, simply because we have a little more room in our small house than my brother has in his even smaller one.

The diarist of all eighteen volumes was our grandmother, Ella Bickersteth. She was the only daughter of Sir Monier and Lady Monier-Williams of Oxford; he was then Professor of Sanskrit in the University. In 1881, Ella married Samuel Bickersteth, one of the sixteen children of Edward H. and Rosa Bickersteth; Edward was Bishop of Exeter from 1885-1900, after having been Vicar of Christ Church, Hampstead, for thirty years. Sam and Ella had six sons. The growing family lived in vicarages in Belvedere and Lewisham in Kent, and then Leeds in Yorkshire where, with his ten curates, Sam was the incumbent at the outbreak of the Great War in 1914. By then all the boys were grown up.

The eldest, Monier, a priest, had been married in 1911 to Kitty, one of the daughters of Canon and Mrs George Jelf, a Residentiary Canon of Rochester. Monier and Kitty became the parents of Sam and Ella's first grandchild, another Ella, shortly before the war. Three more children, of which I was the youngest, were later born to them. By 1914 our father was Rector of Castle Bromwich, which was then in the country outside Birmingham.

The second son was Geoffrey. After Charterhouse and Oxford he taught at Marlborough, and then went out to Heidelberg to continue his academic studies. Later an internationally-known Dante scholar (he held the chair of English at Aberdeen University for 20 years), he had by 1914 published his first work on the Italian poets. But that July he ran it so fine getting out of Germany that all his books had to follow him home after war was declared, by a circuitous route through Switzerland.

Julian was Sam and Ella's third son. Like his eldest brother, he too was a priest, trained, as Monier had been at Wells Theological College after Christ Church, Oxford. He then had a year in India. A curacy at Rugby (he knew the parish from having been a boy at Rugby School) led him to become Chaplain to Melbourne Grammar School in 1912. He soon made a mark there, among other innovations taking in 1913 the first-ever Australian boys cricket side touring abroad, to what was then Ceylon.

Burgon came next, named to his later mild annoyance after Dean Burgon of St Paul's Cathedral, a distinguished Victorian ecclesiastic. He captained Charterhouse at Association Football, and went on to do the same for Oxford University. From there, immediately after taking his Finals in 1910, he crossed the Atlantic to answer a call from the Archbishops of Canterbury and York. In February of that year they appealed in The Times for help, both lay and ordained, from England for the Canadian Church in its ministry to the hundreds of men flooding the western parishes to build the second railway line through the Rocky Mountains. Burgon had two adventurous years as a lay missionary there, publishing his letters home in a book he called 'The Land of Open Doors' in 1913. He then had a year in France at the Sorbonne (his French in consequence was always very good). He had just secured a post at the University of Alberta in Edmonton; so he was about to start work in Canada again, as the storm clouds gathered over Europe during the peerless days of that 1914 summer.

Morris, the fifth son, had gone out to stay for some months with his brother in Melbourne after coming down from Oxford. By midsummer 1914 he was on his way home, touring South Africa, and not at all sure what he was going to make his life's work.

It was Ralph, the youngest, still only nineteen, who was the first of the brothers into uniform. At Oxford, like all his brothers, he had been at Christ Church (five of the six of them had the same rooms in succession from 1900-1914 – Peckwater Quad 5.6; my brother Ted had them in the 1930s; I in the 1940s; and two of our sons in the 1970s and '80s). Ralph belonged to the University Training Corps, and so found himself going to camp in his home district with the West Yorkshire Regiment on the very day that war was declared.

*   *   *

The Bickersteth War Diary began because Burgon, very soon in that August, urged his mother 'to share with Julian, stuck out in Australia, these momentous happenings which are affecting all of us'. She agreed to do what she could, having no idea of course that she would be hard at it for four and a half years; still less that, encouraged in 1939 by her five surviving sons and by her grandchildren (including myself, I am reminded by an entry that September in Vol.1), she would take up her pen again at the age of eighty to do a similar task for the whole of the Second World War, in her, by then, greatly extended family.

The result of all the trouble she took may well be, as Burgon was later to write, 'a unique account of how war affects an average English family'. 'Middle-class' ought properly to have been added as a qualifying factor. In 1988 when, for the first time, I began to read right through the Diary, I soon discovered what a very mixed bag it was. Much of what was there had lost the appeal it had had to the family and to friends, at the time. In particular, the seven volumes of the Second World War mostly made rather turgid reading; the diarist was after all over eighty when she collated the contents. I say this even though I contributed an account of my tiny part in the invasion of France in June 1944! There are also much more dramatic letters from my cousin Tony, who had a very dangerous war with the Gurkhas in Burma.

But it was the letters of the First World War from Julian and Burgon which stood out as being of commanding and still immensely vivid quality. I decided, on the advice of a London publisher friend, the late Jock Murray, to test the waters by sending a particularly moving excerpt to the Spectator. The editor rang at once to say he wanted to publish it complete, and not only did he do that but also at the end of that year (1991) included the whole passage in the Spectator Annual.

This success prompted me to go further, but on a limited scale to the extent on the one hand of only working on the first set of diaries, and on the other of singling out from everything else the contributions of the third and fourth brothers, Julian the padre and Burgon the cavalry officer; with the connecting thread of the diarist's own writing.

So I started on my ruthless pruning to reduce three thousand pages to manageable proportions. The uncles' long letters home, mostly written in pencil it must be remembered, (biros did not exist) and sometimes put together in extremely hazardous conditions, contain plenty of material emphasizing the boredom of army life in wartime, with only a little which brings out the excitements and the miseries of actual battle. I have felt it right to include enough of both elements to convey what I hope is a realistic balance. Certainly what they wrote makes it clear enough that there is no glamour and glory in war any more, if indeed there ever was. Only the triumph of the human spirit and the comradeship of shared experiences, funny or sad or just terrible, are good. Very evident also is the natural determination of the brothers to go on enjoying themselves despite everything – without that, they and millions like them would surely have been broken as the war dragged on.

But I resist further philosophizing. This is not my book. The uncles' own soliloquys are in the text, eloquent still after nearly three generations.

I pay tribute to my wife Rosemary and a Canadian scholar, Norah Moorhead, for between them gallantly committing my messy manuscript to the typewriter, after which a computer-wise friend in the neighbourhood, Derek Phillips, tidied up the pages for the publisher.

Both personally, and as a family, we are most grateful to Lord Coggan and to John Terraine, for their perceptive and very different contributions; to three friends, David Edwards, Geoffrey Rose, and Cecil Humphery Smith for their help in the Epilogue; to Humphrey Stone for his meticulous design skills; and finally to Leo Cooper himself, whose readiness to publish the diary in the first place, and then his continued patient enthusiasm for the whole project has made several years' work on it an infinitely worthwhile pleasure.

JOHN MONIER BICKERSTETH

VOLUME I

JULY 1914 – FEBRUARY 1915

———

The outbreak of war – Burgon and Ralph join up – Julian is kept informed
of affairs at home and describes Australia's growing commitment to
the war – an accident to Burgon delays his posting to France –
the Germans shell Scarborough.

*Since 27 July, 1914, Canon and Mrs Bickersteth had been on holiday in
the west country with two of their sons, Burgon and Geoffrey. The
weather was perfect, but the international news increasingly bad.*

*They were in Exeter on Tuesday 4 August, staying at the Royal
Clarence Hotel; the evening papers said that the war between England
and Germany could not be delayed many hours. 'Next morning', wrote
Burgon, Wednesday 5 August, 'we opened our papers and found the
great flaring words we expected, written right across the principal sheet
"War declared between England and Germany".'*

*'It was impossible to suppress a sigh of relief. At any rate we had been
true to our obligations. We were entering the great struggle with
Germany under the best conditions, and in our heart of hearts we had
not the least doubt about the successful issue of the war'. The party
returned to Leeds at once.*

*On Monday 10 August Burgon went to London by train for an
appointment with three University professors (from Canada), 'who I
knew were in the UK. They were most kind and said that they spoke
for the President of the University when they said that I might certainly
consider myself free from the contract to take up my work in Edmonton
at the end of September, on the condition that there was a real need for
men and that there was reasonable prospect of my being able to get to
the Front. They also promised – which from my point of view was
essential – that my post at the University of Alberta would be open to
me whenever I applied for it'.*

*Next morning he went to the headquarters of the Inns of Court
Squadron in Lincoln's Inn (he had been attached to the regiment while*

I

in the Cavalry of the Officers Training Corps at Oxford), signed on again and went through his medical. 'When the MO, who had been tipped the wink that my eyesight was not brilliant, examined me, he merely pointed to a large Oxo advertisement on the hoarding the other side of the road and, without batting an eyelid, asked me if I could read it. "Yes", I answered, and read it straight off. Anyone half blind could have done so, but I was through, and thus took the King's Shilling'.

The next fortnight he spent trying both in London and Yorkshire for an interpretership or a commission, but his attempts, despite string-pulling (including an interview with Sir Herbert Plumer[1], and with Lord Grey[2]) were not immediately successful. He reflects on the remarkable patriotism he was hearing in his news from Canada:

The Dominion Government is preparing to send a force of 20,000 men to Europe and maintain them in the field; if necessary, it will send 100,000. Double the number of men needed have volunteered. The Federal Government is also sending 1,000,000 bushels of wheat. Alberta is sending 500,000 bushels of oats. Winnipeg wishes to raise and equip a regiment. Ontario is giving money and wheat. Rich men are giving their yachts, or are raising and equipping regiments, or giving a battery of quick-firing guns.

On the morning of 13 August Burgon was walking with a friend across Horse Guards Parade, 'which presented a most unusual appearance. In the middle were three large marquees – and a huge queue waiting to pass through the barriers into the tents, where the names of the men were taken; they were then medically examined. The crowd was large but orderly. Men in top-hats stood in the queue with rough working-men and seedy-looking clerks'.

On 22 August Burgon and his parents were week-end guests of the Archbishop of York[3] at Bishopthorpe. Ralph was in camp with the West Yorkshire Regiment on York racecourse, 'and we walked over to the camp. Ralph met us and showed us what there was to be seen. We all four went back to tea at Bishopthorpe, where several officers of Ralph's battalion joined us. The Archbishop told Father (a Territorial Force chaplain and attached to the West Yorkshire Regiment) to bring as many officers as he liked to tea, and has given him leave to show the house to the Tommies. Accordingly Father showed over parties of fifty to one hundred every night. Father told me:

The Archbishop was quite in favour of my trying to get to the front, but he lost patience with those who had gone and should have remained at their posts at home, e.g., Dick Sheppard, who was in charge of Grosvenor Chapel and has just been appointed to St Martin-in-the-Fields. Lady Dudley had begged him to come as Chaplain to the Field Hospital she was taking to Belgium, and Dick had accepted. Neville Talbot, who fortunately just happened to be free, having left his work at Balliol and not yet gone to India, has gone as Chaplain to his old regiment, the Rifle Brigade, with whom he served as an officer in the South African war. 'He snorted like an old war horse when he donned his khaki once again', said the Archbishop. Ted Talbot has also gone to the front as Chaplain. The Bishop of London's announcement that he intended going with the London Rifle Brigade for six months, wherever they were ordered, was looked upon as a piece of rather dramatic playing to the gallery.'

*   *   *

The news of the recently-landed British Expeditionary Force was not good – they were having to retreat from Mons, and by 26 August 2,000 British casualties had been announced. 'Our troops apparently fought magnificently against terrific odds', the Diary records.

Morris was in South Africa when war was declared, having been going around the world for some months. He got a passage at once in the P&O liner Borda *and arrived in England after exactly three weeks. 'His voyage from the Cape had been highly exciting – there were no lights at night, and the horizon was anxiously scanned all day for the smoke of a German cruiser'.*

Two days before Morris' arrival, Burgon had seen a letter from Lord Helmsley in the Yorkshire Post 'saying he had been authorized to raise a foreign service corps [ie. for service overseas] of the Yorkshire Hussars, and appealing to ex-yeomen and others used to riding and the management of horses, to enrol. I thought this looked as if it might do for me and decided to return to Leeds in the afternoon and possibly go over to Scarborough, their headquarters, the next day'.

'I did exactly this and saw Lord Helmsley at the Grand Hotel. He was at first rather against gentlemen joining the ranks, but finally said that he did not see any real reason why I should not. It was quite possible that there might be other gentlemen joining, and in any case this was quite common in time of war'.

'So on September 2nd', begins the diarist, taking up the tale which Burgon had been writing till then:

Burgon went off to Malton to join the Yorkshire Hussars. We are all ourselves a little sorry that he has not managed to get a commission, but he himself seems quite happy to be a simple trooper. He is still perfectly free to accept either a military interpretership or a commission, should either be offered to him.

In his first letter as a private soldier, Burgon writes:

Yorkshire Hussars, A Squadron, Place Newton, Wintringham
Nr. Malton. 6 September 1914.

My dear Mother,

I can now give you some little idea of life here. The first night I arrived all the men were sleeping in three marquees, so the crush was very great – we were like sardines. I was posted to a sergeant and a squadron temporarily – given a palliasse, which I filled with straw, a mackintosh sheet and a blanket. I slept tolerably well, finding a corner near two very decent fellows from Middlesboro'.

On Thursday morning we did rifle drill on foot – just the recruits. The trained men went out on horseback. Then shortly before dinner they brought their horses in and we had to ride them round in a circle, walking, trotting, etc., just to see if we could ride. After dinner we did more rifle drill and of course had to help at morning and evening stables – all old work for me. There was not much to do, as there were really as many recruits as trained men. Last night, however, about fifty more horses arrived from Scarboro', and I and a few other recruits from A Squadron were told off to get a horse. I pitched on a fairly good animal – the choice had to be made in about three minutes, so it was difficult, but I think he will turn out all right if he is up to my weight; at any rate it is good to have a horse to look after. I also have a complete set of saddlery – which is lucky because we are really short of everything. On the whole they are a very good set of horses; numbers come from big estates round here – for instance, on Friday, Lord Furness sent about ten of his hunters, and ten of his grooms as troopers. They are typical small boys – all magnificent riders, but how they will mount these big horses quickly and with their rifles and accoutrements on, I don't know. Furness is Master of the Bramham Moor, and they have sent some good horses, so our lines look well.

My relationship with the officers is rather amusing. Helmsley (who to the regiment of course is a very big man) came up one day outside the orderly tent and said, 'Hello Bickersteth, you've turned up all right. How are you?' And then I told him about the Inns of Court and we had

4

quite a chat – rather to the astonishment of some of the men who were there. Still more amusing was Lascelles[4] yesterday. He runs the machine-gun section and by the men is cordially hated. Indeed he always does seem rather the la-di-da-dy lord, effeminate and affected – and the average trooper in the regiment thinks him a d——d fool and says so, only in much stronger language. He is considered very standoffish and offensive. Last night when I was grooming my horse, up he comes and says, 'Hello Bickersteth, very sporting of you to have joined. What sort of horse have you got?'. I jumped to the salute, which I think slightly disconcerted him, as the last time we met I was in a tail coat and top hat, and we lunched with the Harewoods in London. However, he really was very decent, as it was a much more difficult position for him than me. We had quite a long talk. All this much surprised the men and not a few of the officers . . .

We get morning and evening papers here, so are as well up with the news almost as you. I do hope the counter stroke, which surely must have been planned to cut off the German army, will soon be carried out. They are getting perilously near Paris. There are several of my Charterhouse contemporaries in the second list of officers' casualties.

I write to you on the grass in our marquee – with all the sides down and a glorious view beyond the horse lines and the park – but a number of the men are gambling in one corner and others are singing and talking, so excuse the discursive character of this letter. Mrs Davidson[5] writes that she and the Archbishop think I have done absolutely right. I do not think it is any good your coming over here. I have very little time – can show you no hospitality – nor is there any accommodation. I am extremely busy and very happy. I feel I am doing something in this crisis, if only in a humble way, and I think we have a good chance of getting abroad to France or Belgium or Germany sometime. I don't think I shall take a commission.

Barely ten days after receiving that letter, Burgon's mother and father and two brothers were going against his expressed wish of 'No visiting'; maybe there had been some telephone conversations. At all events he gave them a great welcome that Saturday evening; his mother writes about it in almost holiday mood as a family-outing-to-see-their-soldier-son:

No more beautiful spot could be imagined than that selected for the encampment – grass, river and woodland with sheltering hills on every side. We drove up through the park grounds almost as far as the horse lines. Then Burgon conducted us through the camp, first of all showing us the horses, all of which are good – some of them being really valuable animals, commandeered from private stables or freely given by their owners. Burgon's quarters and food are certainly rough in the extreme, but he did not seem to mind, and as they are there under war conditions nothing else was to be expected. The men among whom he is thrown he described as being of a thoroughly good sort, though certainly not remarkable for the refinement of their manners and language.

But his days in the ranks were numbered:

On Wednesday September 23rd (just three weeks since I had joined the Yorkshire Hussars in the camp at Wintringham) I was out as usual all the morning doing squadron drill. The regiment came in about noon and a telegram was put into my hands. It read:

War Office. Sept. 22nd, 1914
I am directed to inform you that you have been appointed to the 5th Cavalry Reserve Regiment quartered at York. You are to join for duty as soon as possible.

The orderly officer was just entering the tent to put the usual question 'Any Complaints?'. I waited for him outside, saluted, and asked him to read the telegram; he did so, smiled, congratulated me and said he would take it up to Lord Helmsley who would be at lunch.

I felt certain I ought to take the commission, my only hesitation being, would the new job take me to the Front? Lord Helmsley felt I should accept. While we were talking, a grey taxi came dashing along over the park. Father jumped out, and walked towards us, beaming all over his face. He had in his hand the letter from the War Office. Still more important from my point of view was that he had 'phoned that morning from Leeds to Sir Herbert Plumer, who was delighted I had got the commission and said it meant getting to the Front with absolute certainty, after I had gone through the proper cavalry training.

That decided me, and while Father talked to Lord Helmsley, I rushed back to the tent to pack my kit. My saddlery, blankets and all other regimental kit I was ordered to hand over to my squadron Sergeant-Major; I walked into the Sergeants' mess – in itself rather a bold act! – and asked for Sergeant-Major Roberts. He came out, surprised at being disturbed, and was still more so when I told him why I wanted him. The

6

Regimental Sergeant-Major, who is a very important person and treats one as the dirt beneath his feet, rather altered his talk.

I packed my stuff, handed over saddlery etc., to Roberts, gave my tin mug and plate to someone who wanted to buy them, said good-bye to two or three pals, and was back within a quarter of an hour at the officers' lines. Father and I said good-bye to Helmsley, got into the taxi and drove off. Thus ended somewhat suddenly my experiences as a trooper in the Yorkshire Hussars; they had lasted less than a month.

The end of September saw the inclusion in the diary of Julian's first letter from Melbourne about the war:

Church of England Grammar School, Melbourne. Aug. 2 1914.
I cannot say if this letter will ever reach you. The terrible news that has come through all too slowly from Europe in the last four days has filled everyone with anxiety.

Tonight we only know that Russia and France are both fighting Germany. This afternoon, although it was Sunday, the evening papers brought out extra editions, which were bought at three pence each. These contained the news of the declaration of war by Germany against Russia, that England was isolated from the continent and that Italy is asking to remain neutral.

The question on every one's lips is 'Will England join in?' Most people seem to think that she will never get such another opportunity of smashing the German fleet, and it will give us a chance of crippling her commerce for generations. There are only, I believe, three old and nearly obsolete German Warships in the Pacific, which any one of the ships of the Australian fleet could completely destroy.

It is expected here that there will be a partial mobilisation of the troops in Australia, with the object of drafting them to India, so as to set free British regiments there which might be needed at home.

Monday, 3 August
I preached last night to a large crowd in Chapel on the war. Late editions of the evening papers came out far into the night. This morning the school assembled in a great state of excitement. As each edition came out, it was pinned on to the notice board and besieged by a struggling mass of boys. A boy appeared at the interval, carrying a rifle from his study to the armoury and was immediately cheered and cheered

again. The opinion here is that Great Britain will have great difficulty in keeping herself neutral, and that if Germany refuses to respect Belgium's neutrality, she will not wait but attack the German fleet at once.

4 August, 1914

At 1.30 p.m. the Headmaster posted an edition of the '*Argus*' containing the news of the Declaration of War made by England against Germany. So the die is cast. Pray God we save our coasts from invasion!

I suppose now that we shall be cut off from direct communication by letter from Europe. Ordinary mail-boats will have to go very carefully to avoid capture. I do hope I shall get news from you.

Will Burgon delay his departure? Will Ralph volunteer? What will Geoffrey do? Where is Morris, and can he get home to England or will he try for a job in South Africa? You can well imagine how I long to be able to answer these questions. Separation will be difficult now as never before, but it will after all really be a very small thing to bear, compared to the hardships and trials of our sailors and soldiers, and I am well content to suffer even this little amount for my country.

Australia is mobilising 20,000 men on a war footing instantly. Today a German merchantship tried to escape out of Port Phillip Bay, but was brought back by having two shots fired across her bows from the Greenscliff Fort. This shot is supposed to be the first shot ever fired in warfare in Australia – quite an historic occasion.

18 August, 1914

The first contingent of the Expeditionary Force paraded some 2,000 strong at the Vidona Barracks in St Kilda Road, and marched through the city on their way to camp some twelve miles outside Melbourne. They were most of them in mufti, and a strange heterogeneous crowd they looked. The men were physically fit enough, the authorities having rigorously excluded all the weaklings of course, but also every man whose chest measurement was not over 34, or who had corns or defective teeth.

But this force seemed hardly disciplined enough to face German quick-firers. However, three weeks in camp, and uniforms and rifles will doubtless effect a great change, though I should say Australians would always be better at irregular work rather than a disciplined advance on a position.

The School was personally interested in this first contingent because it contained many Old Boys and two of our staff. A third member of the School, the School Captain, Billy Hughes, has also gone. I suppose he is universally admitted to be the finest captain of the School we have ever possessed here. He was to have entered Christ Church, Oxford, in October of this year. Feeling it his duty, and really for no other reason, he volunteered. There was a special assembly of the School called to bid him good-bye. He received a great ovation from the School, and made a manly speech in reply.

Burgon, meanwhile, still on leave, had got his officer's uniform and put it on after dinner and was duly admired. The diarist writes:

It certainly suited him better than the trooper's tunic, though we did not get quite all the straps right, and he is still without his cavalry sabre. But booted and spurred, he jingled down the stairs in a very martial and military manner. He went off to York by train in great state in a first-class compartment, looking very different indeed from Trooper Bickersteth of a few days ago.

A week later Burgon was writing home:

I think I shall much enjoy life here. If only (as everyone says) they push us through in two months, it will be splendid. Today we did a lot of riding without stirrups and soon began riding merely on blankets (no saddle). Eventually we jump like this! There is a great difference from the Yeomanry. Everything has to be done correctly, and done quickly or there is a row. Riding such as we have to do can only be described as exhausting, at any rate at this stage. One of the most tiring things we do is to receive the order to vault from the horse we are riding and to jump on to the one in front of us. To vault (without stirrups) on to a sixteen-hand horse is difficult, and to do it about a dozen times in the space of a quarter of an hour is tiring, especially when in between one has to ride the horse which one has never seen before, which may be extremely rough and difficult, with only a blanket on its back.

At 11.30 we go to stables. I have half a troop to look after, about sixteen men and horses. One walks up and down superintending every horse and man, asking questions, getting to know one's own men, and at the proper times telling them to water, hay-up, feed, bed down etc.

He describes the rest of his hard-working day which is not over

till 7.00 when it is time to go to one's rooms, shout for one's servant
(for all the world like Oxford and one's scout) and have a hot bath and
change, and return at 8.00 for Mess.

We have a very good dinner, five or six courses. Drinks of course
for all meals are extra, and are expensive. For instance, port at
dinner costs 1/-, whether one has one or six glasses. Messing account
per day is 5/3. Tea 4d extra – share of messing expenses about 9d per
day, often more. I think messing will be on average 7/- a day, if
not 7/6.

Both my servants are good, especially my groom, Johnson, who is a
groom in civilian life and takes tremendous care of one's horse. My first
servant or body-servant is Cameron, very Scotch [sic], anxious to
please, but not trained at valeting. There is really very little for the first
servant to do, and of course they take the job because it is a soft one.
On the strength of it they get off all morning parades.

This morning there were four different Church Parades, two
Presbyterian, one R.C. and one Church of England. I was ordered to go
with C Squadron to the Church of England, and marched my men up
to the appointed place after inspecting them! There were not more than
70 Church of England men altogether out of the whole barracks, so
strong is the Presbyterian element.

The parson did not strike us as very attractive. The officers sat in the
second row, and in front of us sat Plumer and his wife and daughter
and a red-moustached A.D.C. The church was full because there were
many infantrymen; (these of course, don't count!!!).

One mid-October Sunday he writes:

This morning I went to the Minster. I was too tired to go early but stayed
after the 10.30 service to the mid-day Celebration. The chancel was very
full and the service beautiful, though I do not think the choir touches
ours[6]. The only other officer who was at the Celebration was the
Colonel, Lord Basing, and we went back to the barracks and lunched
together. I liked him immensely. When we are all there he seems shy and
reserved, but he talked away like anything with me about the war. He
is of course very patriotic and not in the least pro-German, but as a
soldier he has a profound admiration for the way in which the Germans
are conducting the war. He does not hold that the secret preparations

for war on their part were wrong. Any nation in their position would have done the same, and with regard to secret intelligence every nation is the same.

About this time a letter from Julian in Melbourne says:

Tonight we hear that New Zealand troops have taken Samoa, quite a useful little colony, and we expect soon to hear of the fall of German New Guinea.

The news from Northern France, however, is anything but re-assuring. The Germans seem to be willing to sacrifice immense numbers of men in order to reach Paris. The British seem to have borne the brunt of the fighting. The casualty list must be enormous. It is strange to think of county cricket matches going on now, as if there was no European war going on.

A second expeditionary force is now being prepared here. 20,000 men are sailing in three weeks' time, but many of these are not at all well trained; some have never had a rifle in their hands at all, and certainly can't shoot. There has been considerable difficulty in making up the numbers – all of which shows how absolutely cut off we are here from the world.

The war fever lasted only a week or so, and we are now going to have a General Election next Saturday, whereas every other part of the Empire has sunk all political differences for the nonce. I think this shows not a lack of patriotism but an inability to realise the serious position in which the Empire would be placed if Germany defeated both France and Russia on land. Many of the volunteers who have joined the Expeditionary Force are mere boys – quite unfit to be pitted against trained German soldiery who, in spite of all their vile barbarities, seem to be wonderfully brave fighters.

I am supposing that Burgon will be leaving for Canada this week. I see in today's paper that the Canadian Expeditionary Force has been delayed owing to the expected presence in the Atlantic of German cruisers. So he may have an exciting voyage.

Burgon realised that his brother must be sad at being cut off. In a note home on 21 October, he says:

Please send him on this scrap so that he may hear of me every week.

And then on quite another tack:

All cavalry regiments in future are to have bayonets as well as cavalry swords and carbines, so really we shall be armed to the teeth.

But always the urge to get to the scene of action is evident:

Yesterday a draft of twenty men and one subaltern was sent to the front. The men had a great send-off at York station, it being a Saturday afternoon. Drums and bagpipes accompanied them, and large crowds.

Julian's letters were taking about six weeks:

Here we are a little disturbed because the departure of an Expeditionary Force has been postponed owing, it is said, to the presence of some of the German Pacific Fleet in Australian waters. How far this is a mere rumour and how far fact, no one but the authorities knows.

On Friday last, the Victorian contingent of the Australian Expeditionary Force had a ceremonial march through the streets. They certainly have come on tremendously with six weeks' training; they were very steady and looked the picture of health and determination. The Light Horse seemed a thoroughly fine lot of men, though I was not over-impressed with the horses. They are taking 1,000 horses from Victoria alone, and all the troop-ships have given up large spaces on their main decks to horse-boxes. Five thousand men in all marched through the streets, and there were enormous crowds who displayed quiet enthusiasm.

Julian was certainly never far from Burgon's thoughts (9th November):

I write you a short letter so that it may go out to Julian. I have been trying to keep him posted with more or less one letter a week.

There are over thirty subalterns here, and a list has today been put up of those 'who should possess all necessary kit for active service'. I am not on this list; it is full of the younger men who mean to make the Army their profession, including three or four boys of only 18 to 19 who really have only just left school, but have had part of a year at Sandhurst. On the face of it, it seems that one's experiences of knocking about, and the 'Varsity and so on, do not fit one for all the wear and tear of war, and the leading of men and the ability to make up one's mind.

But then, more cheerfully:

I am hunting again tomorrow with the York and Ainsty which will be great fun.

*   *   *

The diarist records a speaker at the Leeds Parish Church Mothers' Union telling of a chaplain at the front who says the French soldiers are 'most impressed by the piety of the English soldiers'. The Frenchmen stand round bareheaded while our chaplains are holding a service:

In a hospital in Paris, the English and French were in two adjoining wards. The French were very much impressed by the English soldiers' attitude to dying. One Frenchman said to his English nurse, 'Your English soldiers are wonderful; when they are about to die they send at once for the chaplain and the barber, the chaplain for the needs of their souls, the barber that their bodies may appear before their Maker smart and trim as a soldier should be'.

Burgon had to go to hospital at this crucial stage of his training because of a horse's kick. Out on exercise the horse in front of him suddenly let fly and caught his knee with its full force: The diarist writes:

He tumbled off and lay on the ground in great agony. A stretcher was sent for and he was taken in a taxi to the Military Hospital. He hopes nothing is broken, but cannot tell yet. Poor fellow! The disappointment is keen because any injury to the knee must take some time and will quite prevent his going to the Front for many weeks, which is the one thing he has been living for.

Next day, his mother visits him in hospital:

I found Burgon very brave but desperately disappointed.

Burgon himself writes on 23 November that there is not much progress yet. He does not sleep well, nor has 'a sleeping draught' made much difference 'so far'.
   He writes to his mother a week later:

I confess to feeling thoroughly depressed today. There has been a sudden clearance of subalterns at the barracks; eight are leaving this

13

afternoon, and that brings me third on the list for General Service, which practically means 1st, 2nd or 3rd Life Guards. I think there can be little doubt that had I been fit, I should now have gone any time within the next three or four weeks, very possibly sooner, almost certainly before Christmas. It is however equally possible that this accident will completely prevent me from being able to take my turn. However, there is no knowing, and I must look on the best side of things. You will have me home for Christmas now, which you would not have done before.

It certainly seems curious one should be laid aside just now. On reviewing my life pretty carefully I can think of no period in it (with the exception of the weeks leading up to the 'Varsity match in the year of my captaincy) when I would more than now have given worlds to be absolutely and entirely fit; and until this thing happened, I had been so extraordinarily well.

Meanwhile Julian's comments on the Australian scene continue unabated:

Of the patriotism among the better classes there is no doubt whatsoever, but the working classes, who form of course the great majority here, are too much inclined to think of their own pockets and their probable losses. You see under Socialist legislation they have been taught to think only of themselves and their own wages and gains. The Empire doesn't mean much to them beyond some kind of far-away abstract idea, which very few of them realize alone enables them to enrich themselves and be prosperous, and legislate free of outside interference. It will take a very long time to teach them anything higher and nobler.

I believe it is true to say that the authorities nearly all realize now that without the Empire, Australia is a 'goner', i.e. wouldn't be able to hold up her head alone for a week.

It is, I believe, therefore slowly dawning upon the Government that to talk of 'cutting the painter' is sheer nonsense, and so we may have already learnt, among those who rule us here and among all thinking Australians, that England is our own safeguard.

Gradually, very gradually, Australians will realize what they owe to England. How all my English blood courses through my veins when I read of England's responses to the great call! It is true of course that Australians are joining the colours here, but the majority are either of the well-to-do or middle class, or else recent emigrants.

His brother Burgon saw that letter at once and comments to his mother:

Military Hospital, York 9th December.
Julian's letter was delightful. I felt sure he would appreciate the Diary. . . . I am not certain he of all the family is not doing the finest or most self-denying of work for our Empire.

My knee was X-rayed again this morning. The bone has completely healed across, and I got out of Dr Bateman who does all the X-ray and electrical work, that electricity would probably do the knee a considerable amount of good in about a week or ten days. In any case it can do no harm to try it. We must get the water away as soon as ever possible. I bend it a good deal now.

. . . Did you know that shrapnel is so called because it was invented by a Colonel Shrapnel in 1803?

He has heard a story 'which would be good for the Diary':

All the socks, mufflers etc. sent out by The Queen (Queen Mary) to those at the front have a card attached to them on which is written, 'From Mary and the women of the Empire'. An officer in the trenches received one of these parcels, opened it, read the card, looked puzzled, scratched his head and at last was heard to remark, 'Well that's funny; I know all the women at the Empire, but I'm d——d if I can remember which Mary is!'[7]

For Julian there was at this time, despite the departure of the Expeditionary Force, a general air of 'life being absolutely normal here':

The papers are eagerly read, of course, and small groups constantly gather outside the newspaper offices to read the cablegrams which are also put up for passers-by to see. People are planning summer holidays just the same. Henley-on-Yarra last Saturday, in spite of a temperature of 100 degrees Fahrenheit in the shade, was as much a social success as ever, the river being crowded with pleasure craft and boats, the houseboats bright with flowers and over-dressed ladies and the racing as keen as ever. I did not go near it.

. . . I have a little hunchback German friend here in Melbourne, long since a neutralised [sic!] British subject but still of course, German in his sympathies, although not, I am glad to say, altogether in his outlook on life. He heartily condemns the German invasion of Belgium and the atrocities, but cannot bear to think of his beloved country going through such an appalling time, nor does he dare to allow himself to think of what the end will be. He is a sincere Christian.

The mails from England are coming in with the utmost regularity, in fact, with no change from peace time except that they take longer to come. This speaks volumes for the naval patrol work. It will be a fine record if the end of the War sees an unbroken mail service to the most distant of the Empire's dominions. I cannot help feeling that our Empire is coming a second time to the birth, and there will be much travail before it is born again. But what possibilities lie ahead with the Imperial Parliament sitting in London. If we can keep open the seas during wartime, we shall find no difficulty in sending representatives from overseas dominions to sit in the Central Parliament and discuss Imperial affairs.

Here our Second Expeditionary Force is rapidly preparing. On the whole it contains a better set of men than the first. I am thankful to say the Labour Minister now in office, Senator Pearce, has forbidden the 'wet' canteen, and no liquors or alcoholic beverages can now be obtained at the Broadmeadows training camp. There were some disgraceful scenes before the First Force left. It is reported on good authority that not one single man of the Tasmanian Expeditionary Force left Hobart sober, and the Military Police failed to find 100 men there on the last night before the contingent sailed, and they had to be left behind. These can't have been deserters; they must have been dead drunk. Of course the majority of those who have volunteered and left for the front are a fine stamp of man, but there is a portion who are simply scum.

In England Burgon's hospital days were unexpectedly enlivened:

16 November
A memorable day on which German shells for the first time have done material damage to an English coast town. You of course know the only facts which are at present common property – that shells began falling in Scarborough about five minutes to eight this morning. At Hartlepool a hundred soldiers and civilians have been killed. At Whitby only a few have been killed outright, while at Scarborough the numbers are unknown though they will probably not amount to more than fifty. If it all results in stimulating conscription and brings home to people here even a small degree what war means, this little raid will have been a great advantage to us, and will easily have compensated the country for a few thousand pounds' worth of damage.

On 22 December Julian was remembered with a cable:

Greetings. Father, Mother, Geoffrey, three soldier sons home for Christmas.

Besides Burgon in uniform (he must have been able to escape from hospital for a few days over Christmas itself), there were Morris and Ralph in different battalions of the West Yorkshire Regiment, and both still training not far away.

By the end of the year, Burgon is 'going out in a bath chair' every morning. His mother gives her New Year comment:

January 1st, 1915.
The year which ended yesterday will be forever memorable in the history not only of the British Empire but of Europe and the world. For five months there has been raging in Belgium and France and over vast regions in the East of Europe the greatest of all the wars of which we have any record. To a lesser extent it has been the same upon the sea, for though the enemy's main fleet has avoided a battle, there have been encounters far and wide which have sent great ships to the bottom, costing some thousands of lives, while the British Fleet has swept the enemy's commerce from the oceans of the world. Some of the German colonies in Africa have been lost; others are threatened; an attempted pro-German rebellion in British South Africa has been put down; and the political connection between Turkey and Egypt, now a British Protectorate, has been cut asunder.

Julian's last letter of the old year came on 12 January. He comments on 'the German spy system':

It has been found to be most complete and far-reaching here. Powerful wireless installations have been discovered in any number of places, even plans for the blowing up of our railways, bridges and dockyards. Apparently they are not going to stick at anything.

Burgon is obviously beginning to get about again by early in the month and writes from London:

On Tuesday morning I had an interesting talk with Dr Parkin, secretary of the Rhodes Trustees[8]. I asked him frankly what he thought about the Canadian contingent on Salisbury Plain. He said that over sixty per cent are definitely English and a great deal of trouble has come through them, though there has also been insubordination among those who are Canadian-born. For instance, sixteen Canadians were so drunk, disorderly and rough at Devizes the other night that they had to be roped together and brought home behind a cart. Of the Canadians, those of the Highland Regiments from Toronto and Montreal have been the worst.

Parkin told me that nearly all the Rhodes Scholars who are members of the British Empire were serving, and to show the spirit of the American Rhodes Scholars, only yesterday one of them walked into his office and asked Parkin if he could get him a commission in the Coldstream Guards. He was a fine specimen of manhood and wealthy, but spoke with a strong American accent, and the Colonel of the Coldstreams to whom Parkin wrote, answered politely that he feared his men would not like to be commanded by an American.

The diarist comments on the air defence of London arising from the nuisance of the Zeppelin raids. There was no danger yet from any other kind of aircraft:

There are about 170 anti-aircraft guns in London. One of the largest is rigged up on a wooden structure in the Green Park which commands a clear view of the area of Buckingham Palace. A powerful searchlight has just been put up on Admiralty Arch and, in fact there is a circle of powerful lights all round this central part of London. Across the Park on the grass are rows of lights put on small pegs, which from the air give the impression of streets. These are moved every night so as to mystify hostile airships, while the streets themselves are made more difficult to recognise through a number of lights being extinguished.

By 17 January Burgon is back in the saddle:

I rode twice yesterday in the morning and afternoon, for a short time on each occasion, and am certainly none the worse for it today. Tomorrow I go to Strensall and shall take a horse and get a quiet ride in the afternoon. I sat next to the Colonel (Lord Basing) last night at Mess. He told me his friend who is Colonel of the Greys much prefers getting older men from here. By age and experience they are much better able to stand the strain than the boys who have just left Sandhurst.

Basing, as usual, was full of admiration for the Germans. They are willing to attack *en masse* and have one or two huge losses; we prefer many small ones. In 1903 he had been a guest of the Kaiser at the autumn manouvres. He had a good deal of talk with the Emperor and told him he thought the huge mass attacks for which the Germans are famous would fail when they were being shot at a mile off. The Kaiser, however, practically said, 'Wait and see', and criticized our open order attacks which, he argued, gave no confidence to the men. Basing said the Kaiser told him he had made a point of mastering as far as possible even the smallest details of military science, and had also done his best to make himself efficient in naval matters, though he himself recognizes he is not a sailor. But Basing says he really is a good soldier, and had a tremendous admiration for England.

The German Navy comes in for comment by Julian that same month:

I had an interesting talk with the Paymaster of the Fleet here the other day. He told me that the defeat and capture of the German Pacific Fleet is imminent, that the *Australia*, our local super-dreadnought, was working in conjunction with two Japanese squadrons which were forming a large semicircle off the west coast of South America, and that a squadron consisting of the *Invincible* and *Inflexible* and other ships was acting as 'beaters' at a shoot, and was coming round the south of South America and hoped to drive the German ships into the net waiting for them.

In the middle of January, Burgon went to Strensall for a week's shooting course:

I shoot with spectacles; no one seems to mind and I do as well, if not better than anybody else.

I really rather like it here and it is a change from York. My knee improves daily, but I expect rapid mounting (not so much dismounting) will be a trouble for some little time.

But he was back in a hurry:

I came in today from Strensall because I heard this morning that Seymour, who has been with us from the first, had left for France and the Scots Greys yesterday. This, I knew, meant a vacant room in Barracks, and I did not intend anyone else to get it if possible. So I wired about it and then followed this up by coming in myself to see it. I found the room empty. I had my name painted on the door, telephoned for a lock, put some of my luggage into the room, fastened the place up and kept the key, so when I come in on Saturday I hope it will be all right.

I think we are all very bored with soldiering. It is difficult to maintain enthusiasm over doing the same things day after day, and this probably strikes those of us who are amateurs more than it does the professional soldier.

VOLUME II
FEBRUARY – JULY 1915

———

Burgon joins the 1st Royal Dragoons in France – the Dardanelles fiasco hits Melbourne hard – Ralph is taken seriously ill in the trenches and sent home – Burgon starts his machine-gun course.

It is late February and Julian's letters continue to be full of comments on the war:

The recruit is drafted at once to Broadmeadows, the big military camp outside Melbourne, where no fewer than 14,000 men are in training. In spite of the departure of 40,000 men to Egypt, this number at the camp is kept the same, fresh batches coming in daily.

Burgon is still in York where a game of football gives him time to think:

The Royals draft came over and shot on Friday morning, and in the afternoon we had a game of football, the officers of the draft against the men of the draft, the horses unsaddled, all tethered by the side of the field behind the goal posts. I refereed, as my knee did not allow me to play. During the match there was a great deal of fun, men yelling at their friends or shouting encouragement to the officers, and officers and men alike charging into each other with the utmost freedom and goodwill. Directly after the match, the order to on-saddle and move off was given, and ordinary discipline immediately returned; I could not help thinking it was a good example of our English way of doing things, both in the Army and as a nation.

The month of February saw the formation of the Welsh Guards. Burgon's colonel's comments are mentioned in the same letter:

Basing, who is always against anything in the way of appeal to senti-ment, thought the formation of the Welsh Guards very unnecessary and unwise. They have had to take trained men from the other Guards regiments to form the nucleus of the raw Welsh battalion.

Morris is stationed on the east coast of Yorkshire in newly-dug trenches and barbed wire, and his mother visiting him there records the rumours of the time:

The whole place is full of spies. For some months before the war broke out, there were a number of Germans who ostensibly were learning agriculture from the farmers on the marshes and were staying at the farms. It is supposed that these men have in some way laid a cable when they were at work in the fields, and it was completed as a submarine cable. There is no doubt that information gets out to the Navy in an extraordinary way, which can only be accounted for by some hidden cable.

. . . The other day the Brigadier was out with the Brigade Major. When not far from Louth, they met a curious wagon, grey, driven by two soldiers in khaki. They observed that on this wagon was an entire wireless apparatus. The soldiers saluted the Brigadier, and it never occurred to him that they were anything but our own men. On talking it over with the Brigade Major, however, they thought it suspicious and on their return to Louth, rang up the various regiments in the neighbourhood and found that none of them owned such a vehicle.

Burgon reverts to the subject of the Welsh Guards:

The formation of the Welsh Guards is generally considered a mistake. The Grenadiers lose two of their best recruiting areas in South Wales thereby. It is said the Prince of Wales is very unwilling to be their Colonel-in-Chief.

The increasing losses at the front are brought home to the diarist, (who now has three of her six sons in the Army) when she goes to see a friend in London:

who has lost her eldest and youngest sons. She has only two other sons remaining and has just sent them off to the Front, saying to us very simply, 'My country has now got the last drop of my heart's blood. I can give no more'.

She continues with a tale about a British officer high in court circles, who had just escaped from being a prisoner-of-war:

He had many adventures, too long to tell here, and when he got back to England, went to see the King, and told him how badly our prisoners are treated. The King was very much moved and walked up and down the room in real anguish of mind. It is believed that the King, after this interview, sent a personal letter to the Kaiser about the treatment of our prisoners. I fear, however, from letters in the papers from friends of prisoners that their treatment is really quite disgraceful. Our Tommies are half starved and are made to do the vilest work of the Camps.

A young friend serving in France, only nineteen years old, sent the diarist some grisly details:

Some things are harder to bear than others. My own friend standing beside me had his head blown off. This was bad enough, but what I felt still more was when I had to take my company to see one of our own men shot because he had been absent from the trenches without leave. It was dreadful to stand by and see it done, and I staggered away feeling really ill.

Burgon writes on 21 March that he has just been lunching with the Archbishop of York at Bishopthorpe. Lang was good with young men, and enjoyed introducing them to interesting people in his beautiful house. It was a large and distinguished gathering for lunch, Burgon, the young subaltern, clearly taking it in his stride:

Afterwards the Archbishop took me down to the Minster in his car and we heard Bach's Passion music. It was a gloriously sunny afternoon and the Minster was flooded with sunlight. The music was most beautiful, and the whole thing struck me as very touching. There must have been many in the huge congregation which filled the nave who had lost those dear to them.

Julian was writing that same week about very different young men, the Australian Expeditionary Force in Egypt where the hospitals are filled with soldiers suffering from VD:

A reporter in the local press says that 2,000 men (that is 10 per cent of the total) are to be sent back as useless to the force. . . . What is to happen to these men on their return, goodness only knows. The cause of this sad state of affairs is not hard to seek. First, the almost total lack of discipline at Broadmeadows, the great Concentration Camp [sic!] for the Australian forces, situated twelve miles outside Melbourne. Secondly, the lack of discipline throughout the country and in the Australian character. Thirdly, lastly and most important of all, the State authorities have tried to teach morals without the aid of religion, the result of course being a hopeless failure. Public opinion is not so high as it ought to be in consequence of this, and the state schools are Godless institutions. . . . The real truth of the difficulty is that these colonial contingents are not officered by the right men. The officers are drawn from a variety of sources, and only a small percentage are public school men, and of course even they have not had half the opportunity which the real public schoolboy in England has had, that of learning how to rule others.

He had been busy at a 'summer camp on a bluff overlooking the ocean, an ideal spot':

The war seemed far away; I wonder if these Australian lads really have much grip on the importance of it all. I spoke at prayers this evening, quite shortly, but I found the war atmosphere very heavy spiritually. Most of the boys had come down to have a good time and intended to enjoy themselves, and the average Australian boy gets but little spiritual influence in his home, so it is all far different from the English camps.

Burgon had not found that organized religion was easy either:

This morning I went on Church Parade to the Presbyterian Church – a big affair with full band and a long march through the streets. I disliked the Presbyterian service extremely.

An unexpected picket duty on the London road was much more fun:

We have been out all night stopping every motor-car, because information has been passed to Zeppelins by motors with powerful headlights, and we have power to arrest anyone in the least suspicious. It is a change, and the men rather like it.

So do the officers:

Curiously enough my post was just outside a large private house. One of the sons had just come back from the Front after Neuve Chapelle where he was wounded. I called and begged sandwiches. They invited me to stay for dinner, so I had an excellent meal; and then the other subaltern with me went up in his turn.

Early in May, the Cunard liner Lusitania *was sunk, not far from the Irish coast, with the loss of 1300 lives including many women and children. 700 people were saved. Lord Rosebery[1] wrote to* The Times *to express the nation's sense of moral outrage:*

The sinking will secure for Germany without any possible competition the title of 'Enemy of humanity and horror of the civilized world'.

In consequence, writes the diarist, there has been in the last few days:

an outbreak of Germanophobia not only in England but throughout the British Empire.

*   *   *

Meanwhile Burgon's chances of getting into the regiment he really wanted, the Royal Dragoons, seemed to be increasing. His Colonel, Lord Basing, said to him:

nothing would give me greater pleasure than to recommend you to the colonel of the Royals. I consider you are a first-class cavalry officer.

He would clearly give anything to be in his youngest brother Ralph's position – in the trenches.
    On 17 May, Ralph had written from billets, just after ten days in:

'a beastly bit of line': (even then) we officers had good breakfasts – porridge, eggs and bacon, potted meats, marmalade, tea and coffee.

It was very much home service for Burgon still:

FEBRUARY – JULY 1915

Sunday, 16 May.
We all paraded to march to the Minster for the annual Military Sunday service. There were several thousand troops and nine or ten bands. The most moving moment was when the drums and trumpets played a fanfare and then the National Anthem crashed out, every man rigidly at attention. The sun shone through the windows of the old Minster, and hanging from the great columns were the war-stained standards of famous regiments. One felt the inspiration of worshipping in a place so full of great memories; if this was to be the last service we should attend before we set off to the war, it could not have been a more perfect setting.

I write this just before Mess on Sunday. Still no definite news from the War Office. It is trying to wait so long before one knows for certain.

But on 20 May, his mother wrote:

He rang from York, and I could tell by the tone of his voice that he had good news. Three minutes before he telephoned, a wire had come from the War Office saying that he and three other officers were to report to the Embarkation Office at Southampton at once. He was evidently very much pleased, and I congratulated him most heartily. We decided to borrow a motor and go over to York next morning.

This they duly did:

We spent an hour helping him sort his things and loading up the motor car with saddles and other belongings which he could not take to the Front. Father then had to say farewell.

Later:

We went to the Academy. It rather reminded us of the old days of filling up time before the train left for school. We then sent our week-end cable to Julian which read: 'Starting France First Royal Dragoons. Ralph well. Morris Ripon. Edward's baptism June 11.

It really mattered to the family that they kept in touch with each other: Geoff was in War Office intelligence in London; Julian was still 12,000 miles away; Ralph, the youngest, was in the trenches, as we have seen; Morris was training in the Vale of York; and Monier, the parish priest,

was having his baby son baptized shortly. After sending the cablegram,
their mother said good-bye to Burgon and he embarked for France at
Southampton a few hours later, crossing to Le Havre uneventfully
overnight:

on board the ordinary Southampton-Le Havre packet, on which there
were about fifty other officers, a detachment of Flying Corps men, some
Marines and a few Belgian and French officers. There were also a
number of civilian passengers, about two hundred of us altogether and
no crowd or rush. I went to bed at 2.00 and woke up at 8.30 . . . We
stepped ashore at the ordinary quay where I have landed many a time.

Next day he was at the huge base camp in Rouen, and was soon
taking part in the exercising of some three hundred horses in the sur-
rounding woods:

You have no idea how perfectly lovely the forest is. You know the type
of French pine woods, miles upon miles of them, with countless bridle-
paths and rides, and then an occasional *Rond Point* where perhaps
sixteen avenues meet. One such place I came to this morning when I
was out for a ride by myself. Far away in the distance one hears all the
noises of a huge camp and the bugle calls; and the shouts of the men
riding their horses re-echo through the glades. It is all most fascinating.
War has many picturesque sides.

By 30 May, that is less than a fortnight after he heard he was going
to France, he was 'within sound of the guns' having travelled up by train
to join his regiment:

Except for occasional visits to the trenches we are in billets, and I have
taken over the Third Troop, with thirty horses to look after, far fewer
than I had in York. Evidently we think a very great deal about what we
eat and drink. Please cancel the weekly 'Times'. We get the proper daily
'Times' the morning after the day it is published, sometimes even the
same day, also the 'Morning Post'. We also have 'Punch', 'Field',
'Sketch', 'Tatler', etc. but I should like the 'Bystander'. We get cream
and milk at this farm. If you could get Tiptree Farm jam in tins it would
be acceptable. Of course it is all very interesting, and the fellows here
are awfully nice, though I must confess I should like to have a 'go' in
the trenches to get it over.

27

On 7 June he writes:

I long to have my first experience of being under fire behind me. I am assured by everybody I shall not have to wait long. It is rather like a prospective visit to the dentist or a surgeon only on a very large scale. The salient at Ypres must be a very unpleasant place, but somehow I long to go there.

Meanwhile he continues to enjoy some good rides:

Our ride back in the evening along the canal banks was most beautiful. The late sun sent long slanting shadows from the poplars across the canal and far over the fields the further side. On our left was a slight ridge, noticeable enough in this flat country, and on its slopes nestled red-roofed hamlets and comfortable farms. Nothing could be more peaceful – and then we came to a lock, and just entering it was one of our gunboats – and always in the distance the sullen roar of guns. 1200 guns are supposed to be bombarding La Bassée simultaneously. We think that there is just a chance we may be sent up to the trenches to give our fellows a rest, but today we have heard that they are probably coming out altogether tomorrow. We do not know anything for certain, but I think my chances of going up this time are very slender. Monier asks in his letter why they continue to put the cavalry in the trenches. The reason is that the cavalry, in spite of losses, still possess a far greater percentage of the original regular troops than any other part of the Army, and they are therefore, I suppose, more reliable. At any rate, it is to the Ypres salient that they are generally sent.

To Monier he spells out his pride in belonging to a great regiment:

There is a spirit in a famous regiment such as the Royals, which is very difficult to describe. It is a great force among the officers and men. I suppose a college or a school *esprit de corps* is the only thing to which it can be compared.

Meanwhile, Julian writes to his mother that Australia has received its first news of the casualties to their Expeditionary Force in the Dardanelles. These are only the first, and there were fifty officers killed, hundreds wounded, and one thousand five hundred men killed:

There are hundreds of mourning homes. Among those who fell is the efficient Captain of our School Corps, Captain Hoggart, who volunteered right at the start of the War. He was quite one of the most popular and deservedly popular masters. For once the School has been quieted. Small groups of boys gathered in the quadrangle at the 11 o'clock break and discussed the sad news. By 12.20 I had arranged a Memorial Service and the Chapel was crammed with the whole school, except the Jews and RCs. All the masters came. It is the first time I have seen them all in chapel. We had one hymn 'Peace, perfect peace'[2], and our organist at the end of the service played the 'Dead March' from 'Saul' superbly. Australia is indeed at last learning the price of war. Rumour has it that a whole battalion, the 5th, has been wiped out and that other heavy casualties are soon to be reported.

In mid-June, Burgon, still not in the Line, writes about his assistants, two-legged and four:

My first servant Wallis is invaluable, by far the best servant I have ever had. The reason is that he has been a servant almost ever since he joined the regiment. He is quite as good as a valet, and looks after one as if one was living under the most ordinary peace conditions. I am told too that in the fighting line he never leaves one and is most faithful. My second servant Hunt is also an old soldier – and up to every trick. Between them, I am extremely well off. My horses number three: (1) a large bay horse, standing a good sixteen hands and large in proportion, an excellent stayer and a jumper, and first-rate for a long trek. He goes by the name of Percy. (2) A small black mare, a South African, came with the regiment from Africa at the beginning of the War, has never been known to have anything wrong with her, can go all day without turning a hair and looks as fit as a fiddle. (3) A pack pony, also a South African, very hardy and strong, and also a good rider if necessary. My second servant rides my second charger and leads my pack pony. He keeps with Echelon B when we are on the move. Echelon B consists of regimental stores in a wagon (i.e. food, saddlery, ambulance and officers' valises).

He goes on, three days later, to describe a visit from the Commander-in-Chief:

The Royal Dragoons. 6th Cavalry Brigade. 18 June, 1915[3]
My dear Father and Mother,

Today under ordinary circumstances the Kaiser sends the Royal Dragoons, of which he is Hon. Colonel, a laurel wreath tied with golden ribbons, and accompanied by a note of good wishes. A century ago we fought side by side with our present enemies and no doubt before another century is up we shall be fighting side by side with them again, and photographs of their Emperor will once more adorn the walls of our mess. So far today, however, there has been no intimation of the arrival of the laurel wreath!!!

This morning we had what I notice '*The Times*' the other day called 'A Pat on the Back', in other words a personal visit from Sir John French[4], who came to thank the three regiments of the 6th Brigade (the Royal Dragoons, the 3rd Dragoon Guards and the North Somerset Yeomanry) for the gallant way in which they had behaved on the occasion of that terrible bombardment on the ill-fated May 13th, and again two weeks ago.

It was a glorious morning and we were all drawn up in a field near a neighbouring village; the three regiments with C Battery of the RHA formed the three sides of a square – in the centre was a cart – three or four packing cases made steps up to it. We waited over an hour standing easy. Then suddenly we heard the hoots of a string of staff motors and our Brigadier's voice yelling, 'Attention', and then as the first large motor drew up on the field and Sir John French stepped from it came the command, '6th Cavalry Brigade – General Salute'.

The Field Marshal walked round the three sides of our square, being introduced to each Commanding Officer by the Divisional General. After inspecting the three regiments of the Brigade, French, who is very short and has a very red face and a white moustache, stood in the middle of the square by himself, and leaning on a large gold-mounted walking stick, addressed us for about ten minutes. He paid special reference to 13 May, and condoled personally with the Royals in the loss of their great Colonel. He made no reference to its having been the last occasion on which the cavalry were to be used in the trenches! And we hear today that quite possibly we shall be for Ypres next week – but nobody knows. As you can gather from this letter, we have not moved. Finally we gave three cheers for the Commander-in-Chief, who stood at the salute, and then he stepped into his motor, followed by various members of his staff and off they went. He was not present more than 20 minutes altogether. From us he went straight to the 8th Brigade, and no doubt made just the same speech.

Burgon goes on to record in a matter of fact way what was, though he could not know it at the time, his introduction to the deadly weapon he was to use for much the rest of his military career:

I have begun my machine-gun course; it is very interesting. The gun in its latest form is a marvel of ingenuity. I have been picking the inside to pieces today. We spend all the morning in the most beautiful little orchard, working away at the murderous instrument.

By contrast, he went shopping next day in Hazebrouck, only 10 kilo-metres away:

It was a lovely sunny afternoon, and the central square, with which all the towns and villages out here, however small, seem to be provided, looked very attractive. The houses are old and very irregular in shape, and with their high-pitched tiled roofs and long dormer windows, have a most picturesque appearance. On one side of the square stands the Town Hall with a somewhat ambitious Greek-looking façade of stone columns. In the centre of the square are parked innumerable motors, all painted grey, all marked with huge white numbers and most of them flying on their bonnets a small flag, lettered or coloured to show to which branch of the Expeditionary Force they belong. Round a band-stand in the middle are a score of cavalry officers' chargers, held by small urchins who run at one directly one rides into any town out here, in order to earn an easy 50 centimes bit. The owners of the chargers are to be found in the shops all round the square, busily summoning their best French in their efforts to lay in provisions for the next few days' Mess. At each of the corners of the square where the main roads enter, stands a Tommy with a red flag, giving information to strangers in the town and controlling the stream of motor traffic, country carts etc., which are continually passing. There are few people in civilian clothes about, a sprinkling of French and Belgian uniforms, but almost every-body is in the King's khaki. The whole scene is one which is ordinary enough out here now, being typical of scores of other small towns in this part of France, but it is nonetheless remarkable and curious if one thinks of it.

Towards the end of the month, his youngest brother, Ralph, had to come suddenly out of the trenches (he was with the West Yorkshire Regiment) for an appendicitis operation – just as Burgon had discovered which part of the line his regiment was in. In two days Ralph was in a Base Hospital on the coast at Le Tréport:

where I am in a ripping bed (think of it, clean sheets!!). The change from those smelly trenches to comfort is incomprehensible.

The operation went well. Burgon in typical fashion, and apparently having no problem about getting the whole Sunday off, decided to ride over to where Ralph's battalion was, 'to see his friends'. He left at 6.00 am.

For the journey I chose my second charger, the little black South African mare, and as I set out on the long trek by myself, there came into my mind days in the Far West when I hit the trail, a long day's travelling before me.

Needless to say, the battalion had moved, but by dint of persistent asking (including riding along a crowded road beside a Brigadier and two Staff Officers who for the first time actually knew precisely where they had moved to) he found himself in:

a particular field whence over the hedge came the sound of a familiar church hymn, and there I saw several officers I knew and a couple of hundred men at Church Parade. The service was being taken by Hood. On the door of a house in a row of small one-storeyed cottages was chalked up 'C' Company, Captain Watson. I shouted, and out came a lad in khaki who informed me everybody was out. Could he give a message? Would I leave my name? I told him my name. 'Beg pardon, Sir, are you a relation to our Mr Bickersteth?' I was forced to admit it. The boy smiled all over. 'I was Mr Bickersteth's servant', he said; 'Will you come in, and should I take your horse?' He took my horse round to the transport and saw her watered, rubbed down and fed, and on my way back I met Watson and Roberts. Such a warm welcome they gave me. We went into the front room of the little cottage – just room for two mattresses on the floor and a few chairs round the table – and had a drink. Soon the Colonel came in, having heard I had arrived, and by degrees pretty well all the officers dribbled in, all anxious to hear how Ralph was. Not once but many times it was said, 'How splendid it would be if only the Vicar[5] could come up and see us'. And certainly I do wish you could. If only it could have been arranged apart from that silly old man Taylor Smith[6]. Michael Furse came out without reference to him. Of course the latter was annoyed, but the chief thing is that Furse got here[7].

Burgon was back in billets:

in time for dinner after an extremely interesting day. They all miss Ralph so much.

The next day was very different, also 'extremely interesting':

Twenty-four men from the Brigade Machine-Gun Sections (i.e. eight each from the Royals, the 3rd DG[8] and the N. Somerset Yeomanry) were selected to go over to Whisques to see the MG entrenchment 6 km west of St Omer. Standing in large grounds is a huge monastery, or, to be more accurate, a huge building originally intended to be a monastery. Till quite recently it stood unused. Then our Government took it over and have established there a Machine-gun School. In the refectory sit khaki-clad British officers, eating very English-looking food cooked by English Tommies. In the chapel lectures are given on all the latest devices for killing the largest number of Germans in the shortest space of time.

We all went over from here in a London motor 'bus, with the driver and the conductor dressed in khaki. When we got to Whisques, we were taken round these modern trenches by a young Lieutenant (who was wearing the white and blue ribbon of the Military Cross on his tunic). This fellow enjoys the reputation of having killed more Germans than any other man in the Army. He has had the East Surrey machine-guns since the beginning of the War and lectured to us in the chapel, in a most self-possessed way, on the part which machine-guns played in the capture of Hill 60. To illustrate what he said he had a large blackboard showing how machine-gun fire was arranged to cross and recross every inch of ground round the hill and even behind it, so as to prevent the bringing up of German reinforcements. I have drawings of the whole thing, and one day, after the silly war is over, I will show them to you.

Round the walls of the chapel hung all the latest devices in machine-gun construction. Of course we are very behind the times. It is only just now that Generals are beginning to realise the value of machine-guns and to enquire into their tactical handling and management. We were also shown a German machine-gun, which is very similar to ours, and

33

the Lewis gun (an American invention) – it is not much larger and roughly the same shape as an ordinary rifle.

But basically the young cavalry officer is bored, and reflecting:

It is extraordinary what a high opinion everyone who has had anything to do with them entertains for the great fighting qualities and sporting instincts of the Canadians. The Royal Canadian Dragoon Guards are in the trenches now. They go in regularly with the rest of their contingent – all their horses were taken from them in England. The other day the Quartermaster of that regiment was walking along the canal towing path, when a young subaltern riding a pushbike overtook him. He stopped and asked the Quartermaster the way to a certain place. The Quartermaster told him and then began to rag him about his bike. 'Say, kid, I guess that ain't much of a cheeval you've got there!'. The Prince of Wales, for it was he, took it in excellent part and stayed to have quite a long yarn with the Canadian.

A letter from the Dean of Christ Church, Oxford[9] cheered him greatly:

Oxford is far more desolate than the Sahara. We have had a gorgeous summer term so far as weather is concerned, but no men were playing about in it. I crossed the High – after a poker as a VC[10] should – on a glorious day in what might have been Eights' Week, and I could see nothing but a bicycle or two, a few wounded soldiers, a motor-bus, and a countryman driving a pig. If it had not been for my respect for the poker, I should have sat down on the kerb and howled. No one would have noticed me – except the poker. To think I should have come to miss the Eights' women.

More of our men go out from day to day, and the anxiety of thinking of them increases.

We have lost thirty-six men, of whom the majority were men who had made the Army their profession, and many of whom joined it in the South African War. I tremble to think what may happen when the new Armies get to work.

I am extremely glad to have heard from you, and I hope it will not be long before I see you again. I pray every day that God may bless and protect you and bring you back soon and safe to all who love you.

After a long gap, there is a letter from Julian, dated 13 May, 1915:

As to the Germans! May God help them! We shall win this war because God cannot allow such scum to exist. A letter written to the paper here deprecated the comparison of Germans to beasts, saying that no beasts ever behaved as badly as they have – it was an insult to the 'brute' or 'beast' creation to mention Germans with them in the same breath – and I agree.

How can the Kaiser possibly reconcile such things as asphyxiating gases and slaughter of innocents with his reputed Christianity? He and Tirpitz and others responsible must be tried for murder after the War, and if proved guilty, hanged, and may God have mercy on their souls!

14 July: A disappointment looms for Burgon:

I regret to say that it is now more than possible that in the near future I shall have to return to the base at Rouen. We are at present much over strength. The C.O. could not have been nicer, but he has no option in the matter; he has to send back any who are not regulars and do not mean to stay in the regiment after the war, before the others.

He goes on to look at the various options, all of which have arisen because the 'powers that be have for the first time ever in the history of warfare, found no real use for the cavalry':

So you will see from all this I am once again all uncertainty. I want with all my heart to stay in the Royals, but I do not want to go to Rouen for some weeks. Altogether it is difficult to know. I wish to goodness the beastly war was over.

But that particular move was cancelled or, at least postponed – no reason was given, but he muses:

Of course if ever we do anything, they will want everybody. I cannot help feeling that we must do something soon.

VOLUME III
JULY 1915 – FEBRUARY 1916

———————

Death of Rupert Brooke – Burgon in Ypres; explores the Front Line – Julian released from his chaplaincy in Melbourne to return home and serve as a chaplain in France – Burgon's first action in the trenches in the infantry role – Julian and Morris meet on the Suez Canal – Julian arrives in England.

In England there was an unending scare of spies. Lord Harewood told the diarist at lunch on 26 July, 1915, that a short time ago an order had been given to all regiments that for three days in London no soldier was to go in either bus, cab or underground in khaki. By this means they were able to secure a hundred spies that were dressed in khaki!

Burgon, in a letter next day, when back in billets after more trench digging for the infantry, airs some disillusionment for the first time over his belonging to the as yet unused cavalry arm of the British Expeditionary Force:

Somehow I feel when I get back here that it would have been better had I gone into something which would have brought me more closely in touch with the war. We are really doing nothing except what we should do in peace.

*　　*　　*

Rupert Brooke died in Greece that month (July 1915), and the diarist was staying at Rugby with the poet's (and her sons') old housemaster, Mr Steel, who showed her this 'moving account'[1] of the death and burial of his brilliant pupil, a contemporary of Julian in Steel's House:

Rupert Brooke died at 4.46 with the sun shining all round his cabin, and the cool sea breeze blowing through the door and the shaded windows. No one could have wished a quieter or a calmer end than in that lovely bay, shielded by the mountains and fragrant with sage and thyme.

All our ships were under orders to sail for Turkey the next morning at 6 a.m. So – we decided to bury him the same night on the island. We felt sure he would not have wished to be buried at sea, and if we had left his coffin on the French ship until we could reclaim it, we might never have seen it again; for they were bound for Asia, we for Europe. Under the circumstances then we decided to bury him on Skyros that evening, and found a most lovely olive grove about a mile up the valley from the sea.

We buried him there by cloudy moonlight. He wore his uniform and on the coffin were his helmet, belt and pistol (he had no sword). We lined the grave with flowers and olive, and laid an olive wreath on the coffin. The chaplain, who saw him in the afternoon, read the service, very simply; the firing party fired three volleys and the bugles sounded the Last Post.

And so we laid him to rest. He once said in chance talk that he would like to be buried in a Greek Island. He could have no lovelier one than Skyros, and no quieter resting-place.

On the grave, we (his brother officers) heaped blocks of white marble; the men of his company made a great wooden cross for his head with his name on it, and his platoon put a smaller one at his feet. On the back of the large cross our Greek interpreter wrote a Greek inscription in pencil, which means

> *Here lies*
> *the servant of God*
> *Sub-Lieutenant in the*
> *English Navy*
> *Who died for the*
> *deliverance of Constantinople from*
> *the Turks*

The next morning we sailed and had no chance of re-visiting his grave.

But no words of mine can tell you the sorrow of those whom he has left behind him here. None of us knew him without loving him, but those who knew him chiefly as a poet of the rarest gifts, the brightest genius, know that the loss is not only ours, but the world's. He was just coming into his own; what he had written had reached a zenith of perfection that marked him as belonging to the very finest.

It was so hard that he should die the day before we opened battle – cut off by disease, when he had given himself to England, of which his last poems have shown him to be the truest singer.

The diarist adds:

The still further sad ending to this tragedy is that W Denis Browne who wrote the account, was killed a fortnight after.

*   *   *

Burgon was digging again, with sixty men in the large grounds of a château two or three miles behind the lines, and close to Ypres. After the day's work he got a lift into town and describes what he saw:

The only thing I can at all compare it to is Pompeii – a real city of the dead. But at Pompeii the houses are never more than one storey high, and one knows it to be a ruin of many centuries back. Ypres bears every sign of having been recently inhabited by a rich and prosperous people. The houses are large, and often two or three storeys high. But they are mere skeletons, and generally both the inside and the front have been blown out – not one single street that has not every single house in it so hopelessly damaged that total rebuilding will be necessary.

I entered the town by myself, and made straight for the large Scole and the Cloth Hall. All civil inhabitants are long ago departed. Only a few English troops – for the most part R.E.s[2] – are billeted there. They are engaged in pulling down dangerous houses and clearing the streets. I reached the Square – and there in front of me was the Cathedral and the famous Cloth Hall. You have often seen photographs of them. One pinnacle stands at each end of the Cloth Hall, but the floor is shot away the whole length of it, so that one can stand – as I did – below, and look up into what was the great hall itself.

What was so curious was the solitude. It becomes very oppressive and uncanny, not a soul to be seen, not a sound of any kind to be heard, except the quiet drip of the rain from a leaden sky. I stood for fully five minutes at one corner of the Square under the shelter of an arch – I felt like the only living person in a city of the dead. A motor-cyclist tore across the far end, going south. Then there came the sound of distant rifle-fire and a couple of shells whistled through the air – I should say 500–600 yards to my right. Silence again. Then a clatter of horses, and a staff officer with red tabs, followed by his orderly, trotted across the square. Hardly had the sound of the horses died away, when I caught sound of the dull, even thud of marching feet, and three minutes afterwards, three companies of infantry swung round the corner and crossed right between me and the Cloth Hall. They seemed rather overcome by the oppressive silence of the place and the awful signs of devastation, and there was little talking.

I pottered about the town; passing down one street I heard a piano. Looking in at the window I saw a Tommy playing – his choice was, 'Her sunny smile'. The room was well-furnished – pictures a little askew, but good carpet and lace curtains. Except for the Tommy and me, no sign of anyone.

It was beginning to get dark, and the rain had turned to a downpour. I really was not sorry to go. I got a lift back part of the way on a limber, and part on a motor machine-gun.

Every day we dig. This morning they put half a dozen high explosive shells into a field about 300 yards away from us. The scream they make going through the air is a little disconcerting, but one makes so absolutely sure it will not hit one that it is more amusing than anything else. Of course being bombarded in a trench where all movement is precluded would be a very different thing.

Another night:

I had the most interesting, and in a way, the most exciting evening I have ever had in my life.

. . . I had always meant to get up to the front line of trenches (while I had the opportunity by being up here) if I could. Accordingly a North Somerset officer and I started off last night at 9.00 pm with the object of getting as far as we could. He had been out here since November and is an old hand. I jumped whenever a bullet whistled overhead, or, what is really more trying, whenever a bullet hit a tree, say 300 or 400 yards off with a terrific smack, and one made certain one was not hit.

Our idea was to go up in the rear of some French troops. It is only after dark of course that the real activity begins between the trenches and civilisation. On the roads long transport convoys rumble along, troops march silently from or to the front line, and the country at large is clear of the vigilant eye of the aeroplane observer. We were soon stopped by two friendly Frenchmen who informed us that further up the road there were some French sentinels with orders to let no one past. Undeterred, we went off across country to the left. The night was light with a round yellow moon, and the continuous flares and intermittent rifle fire, at each step growing clearer, showed we were not far off our destination. A cross country walk of about a mile brought us to a road where there was an advanced dressing station in a ruined farm. A motor ambulance, round which were standing some black French troops, was before the door. I walked into the farm and entered a small room lit by a flickering candle, in the corner of which sat a French doctor, a coloured man with a long black beard. He was most polite, asked no awkward questions, and told us we were at this point some 900 yards from the advance line, '*la première ligne*'. We started off again along a sort of road, but keeping well in the shadow of the hedge which grew on one side. We rustled through a cornfield in which were most enormous shell-holes, and then as the road ended in nothing, and the bullets to my inexperienced ears did not seem very far off, I suggested going up to another farm a couple of hundred yards away, and seeing if there was anybody there who could help us. Here we found some French transports drawn up in the central yard, standing in perfect silence. Under the shelter of a sandbag wall, two French N.C.O.s and I had a talk about how we were to proceed. This particular Zouave regiment was coming up to dig just behind the first line – another Zouave regiment was in the first French line – our lines were to the right. We decided to follow the digging party and then make further plans.

The '*boyau*' [communication trench] from this point became so filthy and wet that most of us walked at the side of it, bending low to get the shelter of the parapet on our left. After 15 minutes of slow walking, accompanied by much joking in a quiet undertone on the part of the French, we reached the spot just south of the château and park where they were to dig; here we were about 400 yards from the German lines. We found the Adjutant of the French regiment (a sort of sergeant-major) and asked him if we could get on. Of course from here it would have been really dangerous to go on without a proper guide. As luck would have it, he told us he had a Zouave who could talk English and could take us up to the French first line. We were delighted, and stumbled along to the head of the party to find him. He proved an extremely nice fellow. He had been a waiter or something of that kind in London and talked quite good English. Telling us to follow him in single file, we crossed a field which took us to the edge of the château park. We climbed into the park. I have never seen a place in such a state – it was not a large property, but must have been full of timber. There was hardly a large tree left standing, and we clambered laboriously over fallen trunks and roots and under branches which spread in every direction.

After about ten minutes it became obvious our guide was a little mystified as to where we had got to – and no wonder, as there was not a vestige of a drive or path of any kind. However, we pushed slowly on, barking our shins and tearing our putties till we got out the farther end and clambered into another '*boyau*'. This led us through a kitchen garden, past some glasshouses and finally into the main street of the village which was a scene of absolute desolation – not a house which was not severely battered, and fallen masonry heaped in the road. It was a curious sight – the moon made deep shadows, and one had to be careful not to stumble into the French soldiers who seemed to occupy every corner, talking in low voices. Finally this second line brought us right up to the bank of the canal on which was the French *'première ligne'*. There was a certain amount of rifle fire going on, the bullets either whistling overhead (which sounds exactly like being in the butts at Strensall,[3] and is certainly no more frightening) or striking the sandbag parapet with a dull thud. As we turned into the front line trench, we caught sight of a number of Zouaves, six or seven of them, grouped just under the edge of the parapet on a sort of specially-constructed platform. One of them was working a searchlight. I remarked that surely it would not be long before the searchlight (which of course appeared over the parapet) was knocked to pieces. As I spoke there was a loud report and a sound of broken glass – the searchlight had that second been smashed to atoms by a bullet!

At this point, only the canal separated the German and French lines. They were built one on the eastern and the other on the western bank, and at the very edge of our bank about 20 yards separated us from our friend the Boche. I popped my head over and had a look. Exactly opposite was a house occupied by the Germans – the distance was just about that of a fair-sized street.

The French trenches are first-class – far better than ours. The ground helped them at this point. It sloped upwards to the canal (as so often happens out here) – so that their first line was dug well into the earth, and also had such a high sandbag parapet that it was a good 12 or 15 feet high, and to shoot or look over, one had to clamber up on to a ledge. Immediately behind the firing trench were dug-outs, and immediately behind the dug-outs was a good broad path, almost a road, along which one could walk unmolested unless a shell happened actually to drop on one. The whole slope of the bank was not more than 30 yards in breadth – but it was a regular rabbit warren.

Here we parted with our Zouave – but had not proceeded far on our quest for *'les tranchées anglaises'*, before another fellow took us in hand and showed us everything of interest. At one point, round the corner of a dug-out, we came upon a little sunburnt, baggy-trousered Zouave on his hands and knees, just fixing the fuse of a bomb – he had rather a primitive-looking trench-mortar. We stayed (at a safe distance) to watch the operation. The fuse lit, the little fellow dashed towards us as if for his very life – and then we all waited to see the result of the explosion.

A loud report, and off went the bomb, sailing beautifully through the air towards the German line – I should say probably their second line, of which the French seemed to know the position. The little Zouave sat on his haunches in the light of the moon anxiously counting. At last came the sound of the exploding bomb. 'Ha! Ha!' said he; *'c'est juste dans les tranchées de reserve. Je le sais. J'ai compté les secondes!'* And he burst into uncontrollable laughter, rocking himself up and down.

We left him, and continued our way south down the line. Suddenly a man appeared, breathless and running. Were we the English doctors? One of our men had been severely wounded 100 yards or so further down the line. We told him, No, but the French doctor was coming along just behind us. When we reached the place, we found a very jumpy RE officer – young and quite unnerved. He had been mending some barbed wire fencing put across the canal to prevent the Huns from coming down in boats. (The Huns, by the by, have been running the canal dry – there is not much in it but a few feet of water and dead bodies) and while on this work one of his best men had been shot through the throat about a foot from him. The man in question was lying there on a stretcher. I looked at him, and there was no doubt he was dead already.

We talked to the engineer officer for a bit, and then he suggested showing us the work he was trying to do. The moon had gone in and it was quite dark, so we crept out round the end of the trench and into a little gully which led down into the canal. We clambered carefully along this and found ourselves on some flat muddy soil, which a few weeks ago had evidently been covered with water and was part of the canal bed. In the dim light we could distinctly see a sort of elaborate barbed-wire fencing which crossed the canal. We did not stay there very long – it was not very safe, for one thing, and for another there was a most horrible stench which I remarked upon. 'Oh, that is a dead cow', said the engineer; 'it's been there for weeks.'

We tried to cheer up the engineer and his men – all rather un-nerved – and then thought we had better begin to move homewards. The engineers put us on the right communication trench and we started off, paddling through mud and water. We managed all right, and soon afterwards struck a party of REs coming up with material for dug-outs. They again directed us and we finally turned into bed, tired, but well-satisfied with our evening.

The continued inactivity was demoralizing not only to Burgon but to the regiment as a whole – even 'new billets in a delightful farm' did not improve matters, in fact rather the reverse:

Since we arrived in these new billets there has been a large number of cases of drunkenness – due, I think, partly to the fact of coming to a new place, when the men try all the 'estaminets', and partly to the fact that they are heartily sick of this peace soldiering – inspections, schemes etc. I wish to goodness we could do something. The trenches would be greatly preferable to this. We shall undoubtedly lose a great many good men who wish to transfer to the infantry if we remain inactive much longer.

In a village near where they had been exercising, *Burgon continues*, there was the headquarters of a Spahi (Algerian cavalry) regiment. The central square was full of their transport wagons, and every yard and outhouse used for their Arab ponies. The streets were crowded with huge dark-faced fellows with yellow turbans, blue jackets, bright red waistbands, corduroy breeches and high boots. They rode their lively Arab ponies with ease, seated on an extraordinarily odd sort of saddle, which looked more like a small wooden chair fastened to the horse's back than anything else.

*   *   *

Here the diarist has an excerpt from a recent letter from Morris who is in the Aldershot area:

Balfour's[3] speech last night makes one realise that dying for one's country is a magnificent thing. And then Gilbert Talbot. Of course, as you know, he and I were on the same staircase for two years at Oxford – and I can remember now ragging him many a time about his future life, saying he would be Prime Minister. What a rotten war this is and how I long for the whole thing to be over – but I want just to go out first. I should be awfully sick if I missed that now.

Julian writes from across the world:

Recruiting here is moderate, not up to 2000 a week in all Australia, and we have already published 10,000 Australian casualties. There is certainly plenty of patriotic feeling. Melbourne Grammar School had just had its O.M.G.S. dinner. The Big School was specially decorated for the occasion with all the flags of the Allies. The Governor[4], Sir Arthur Stanley, came and stayed the whole evening from 8 to 11 p.m. All the national songs of the Allied Nations were sung, in each case by a native of the nation concerned. A Frenchman sang the Marseillaise magnificently, putting so much feeling and venom into it that he might well have been in the act of bayonetting a German at the moment. He was loudly cheered. A Russian sang the Russian National Anthem splendidly. A Belgian, who had been wounded at Antwerp and fought in half a dozen battles previously and who is touring Australia now as a pianist, played some Belgian national airs. An Italian played on the mandolin some martial Italian songs. All the consuls of the Allied Nations were present and over 400 Old Boys. No drinks of any kind were indulged in – only lemonade and coffee. There were really fine speeches, especially Sir Arthur Stanley's, and all struck a high note.

Altogether the evening was a great success. A good number of Old Boys were present in khaki, having been given 'leave' from the Camp to come in for the occasion. Melbourne Grammar has sent more Old Boys than any other school in Australia to the Front, not of course nearly enough, but the number is steadily increasing as people out here begin to realize more and more the appalling nature of the struggle in which we are engaged.

The break-through for Julian, long itching to get to the scene of action, had almost come (5 July):

I lunched yesterday with the Archbishop who was most cordial and pleasant. I told him I wanted to go as a chaplain to the Dardanelles, and after some discussion he accepted my name and said he would write at once to the Chaplain General of the Forces for Australia (Church of England), who is the Archbishop of Perth, and give him my name. I do not expect to be gazetted for five or six months at least.

Meanwhile Burgon remained inactive:

Yesterday we had to march up to regimental HQ (some two miles from our squadron) to hear the promulgation of a court martial on a prisoner from this regiment. He had struck a superior officer, i.e. his Squadron Sergeant-major. The man was condemned to death. There was a dreadful silence while the Adjutant paused a few seconds after reading this out. The poor prisoner must have had an awkward few moments until the Adjutant continued that the General had seen fit to commute the sentence to imprisonment.

. . . The digging party left this morning. It makes us very short-handed. There is nothing to do except exercise the horses and ride about, and I don't think I have ever been so thoroughly bored and depressed.

He comments on the polo they are playing (on untrained horses, of course):

Doesn't it seem ridiculous – in time of a fearful war like this, with Ypres practically in sight from the polo ground? I am really not quite certain how long I shall be able to stand this life.

He reflects the following week on their unknown padre:

He has never been to see us here or at our former billets. He is, I believe, liked in the Brigade, but it seems so strange that the man does not come round. He has celebrations of the Holy Communion, but he never speaks of them at Church Parade, and one is left to find out through Brigade HQ. As far as I know, there has not been one within reach of us since I have been out here. At any rate I have not been to the Holy Communion since I came out, and I have never heard the service mentioned by the chaplain or by anybody else.

Meanwhile Julian's attempts to become a chaplain are not being very successful:

So few Anglicans are being appointed. . . . I can't bear being out of it all, and I am beginning to understand how keen the brothers have been to get to the Front however difficult, dangerous and unpleasant is the work that has to be done there.

Burgon has time for reflection:

The whole question of the advisability of Conscription is extraordinarily interesting. If we have it (and I think all those actually serving hope that we shall), what a difference it will make to the future history

45

of the nation. Already the war has left a mark on our people for generations to come, and I suppose on none will the mark be more enduring than on the class of society from which has been drawn that vast number of educated civilians needed to officer the new armies, and fill up gaps in the regular forces. Hundreds and hundreds of young men, who a little over a year ago never dreamed of even the mildest form of military service, have now been commissioned officers for many months. It is interesting to hear from one's friends and to look round and see for oneself what these new officers – amateur officers – think of the life. For after all, if we do have Conscription, it will only be the present situation intensified a thousandfold. There is no doubt that some find their new life remarkably congenial, but that others – and I think they are the majority – find it both irksome and interesting – narrow and cramping in many respects and yet wide in its possibilities.

Perhaps it is partly a question of age, and partly of temperament. There are many subalterns of thirty years and over in the new armies. It is naturally hard for them to submit again to a discipline which is strangely reminiscent of school days. In civilian life they had probably been their own masters, acquainted with various out-of-the-way corners of the world and accustomed to think and act for themselves. The last vestiges of discipline vanished with the close of their 'varsity days. And now once again they find themselves '*in statu pupillari*', members of a vast machine where personal liberty must necessarily be largely curtailed, and unquestioning obedience is expected.

It is curious to me to note how some of the older men (e.g. subalterns at 40 – I could give you several examples at first hand) seem quite content to be once again under rigid discipline. One cannot help feeling that they belong to a number of those (there are many such in questions of religion) who like to have things settled for them. To some natures it is always trying to come to a decision; now that they are in the Army, all necessity to do so, and all responsibility except about most trivial matters, is suddenly removed, and they appear to be invaded by a feeling of peace and utter contentment.

But to do these men justice, I think there is still a stronger reason for their cheerful subjection to discipline. Most Englishmen, whatever their age, never lose that sporting instinct which is part of the national temperament, and they are perfectly ready to be 'dressed down' by an officer superior in rank but much inferior in years, if by doing so they are contributing, however indirectly, to the efficiency of an army whose only object is to crush the hated Hun.

. . . .Did you see a small drawing which appeared in '*Punch*' some months ago now? An elderly bald-headed recruit was being initiated into the mysteries of drill. He happened to be the greatest authority on Greek particles! In his excitement, he turned to the right instead of the left. 'Didn't you hear the order, or don't you know your right from your left?' yelled the irate sergeant-major: 'Haven't you any brains?'

One thing is certain. The dominant feeling is one of satisfaction. In spite of burrowing and trench warfare, there is romance. Our part may be a small one, but it is being played as a member of a great company and on a great stage.

At the end of this tirade I say most heartily '*Gott strafe Deutschland*', and may the war end soon.

Burgon's comments on Conscription had obviously evoked a contrary view from his brother Geoffrey at home, for Burgon writes to him:

With regard to Conscription, I cannot agree with you. I think the country should have it tomorrow for the duration of the War. The very strongest evidence is not lacking that it would hearten the men actually at the Front and would proportionately dishearten our enemies.

* * *

The long-hoped-for move out of billets happens at last:

21st Sept., 1915
Bois des Dames. Nr. Bruay *(This place name was added years later in Burgon's writing)*

I write to you from a large forest, in a corner of which the regiment is bivouacked. We left billets last night just as it got dark. The moon was up as the head of the Brigade left the billeting area and moved off. The Royals headed the Brigade.

Nothing could have been more romantic. The endless column of mounted men moving snake-like over the countryside, which was bathed in a still silvery moonlight. The men were in good heart, singing and cracking jokes with the troops in the villages which we passed. One village was full of The Black Watch. They turned out their pipers and played us through amid great enthusiasm. A few hundred yards, and we were out in the open country again – and on a green slope to our right stood an old shepherd leaning on his staff. At his feet lay his wise old sheep dog, and behind browsed the flock, their fleeces gleaming white in the moonlight. The old fellow stood silently contemplating the column – the personification of peace and war.

And so we marched on. The people crowded to see us pass and their open doors threw a cheery gleam over the road. Sometimes we passed scores of lorries parked in the square of some little town under the shadow of the church – sometimes we pulled to the side of the road to let some large Staff limousine fly by with glaring headlights, or country carts laden high with hay, lumbering home late from the fields.

Somewhere about 11.00 pm we left the main road and followed a lane which led us up into the outskirts of a large forest. Soon we were under the trees and stumbling along over boughs. Then came the order to form column of troop – no easy matter among the trees – each troop was in line behind the other. We dismounted and soon had the lines down, and the horses fixed up. In half an hour's time the fires had been lit, and the men stood round eating a hunk of bread or smoking a last pipe before turning in. The horses were comfortably munching their hay – the transport had come up. Our blankets were laid out under the trees. Below us were the lights of a mining town – all around the bivouac fires among the trees, and above, a clear sky and glorious moon. A hot cup of coffee, a cigarette, and we rolled comfortably into our 'flea-bags' to sleep snug and warm till morning, when we awoke to find the sun streaming through the trees, and the blue smoke of the fires, (over which frizzled the breakfast bacon), curling lazily skywards through the still frosty air.

He was clearly in great heart at the prospect of action:

My troop is in good fettle – horses and men very cheery and ready for anything that may come. My two servants are splendid on a show like this, both old soldiers with 17 and 16 years' service behind them respectively. They are up to every dodge and trick, and neither I nor my three horses go short!

But he remains intensely interested in home:

We got yesterday's '*Times*' here in the forest just the same as in billets. The budget is interesting. No more halfpenny post-cards will make a difference to parsons I'm afraid. Did I tell you I have grown a

JULY 1915 – FEBRUARY 1916

moustache?, and am always called 'Bishop' as at Oxford? I am altogether in favour of Julian's returning to England at Christmas time – *as
he was clearly going to do, judging by a cablegram on 30 September:*

Coming home seeking chaplaincy Flanders leaving P & O *Morea* Christmas
week.

'*This*', *writes his mother, 'is very joyful news'.*
    *For Burgon's regiment the Battle of Loos was a non-event. There was
very heavy infantry fighting around Hill 70, in which the Scots Guards
lost all its officers and 800 men. To his great disappointment Burgon
himself had been left with the horses, while a dismounted force of 500
men from two cavalry regiments had been sent up to hold Loos; there
were*

about 3,000 horses to look after, and this within easy and regular
shelling range of the German guns.

In a long letter he says:

From all this you will see that I did not take a very glorious or heroic
part in the famous Battle of Loos, but I was right on the spot, saw a
great deal of the actual proceedings, and had a wonderfully interesting
time.

*Then in early October came the orders to Burgon which were to deter-
mine the emphasis in much of the rest of his army service:*

I go again to Whisque near St Omer for a fortnight's machine-gun
course. . . . In some ways I am very keen to go. No horses allowed.

*That very week he heard the strongest rumours that all the cavalry
would be turned into infantry:*

We would certainly make a magnificent infantry division, as we still
have a far greater percentage of regular soldiers than any other branch
of the service. But it would surely be short-sighted to transfer all the
cavalry in this way. Still, many people – and I am one of them – think
that the cavalry will now do nothing more as the cavalry, at any rate on
the Western Front during the present War.

Within a few days he was writing from the disused monastery at Whisque where:

instead of a company of robed and girdled monks sitting down to supper in the refectory, a hundred or more young British officers are tucking into roast mutton and pudding. . . . Just near here in a château live all the journalists, John Buchan, Philip Gibbs etc. . . . Much of John Buchan's article on the Battle of Loos was censored. The whole thing was actually a big muddle and a wash-out. Flaring headlines like 'Two Real Victories: German Line pierced' were all nonsense.

He goes on:

One feels more and more, when one talks to fellows who are drawn from every part of our expeditionary force, that we are absolute amateurs at war. How vast our Staff is! How many of them are regular Staff officers who have been properly trained? Take even our cavalry officers – how many of them join the army to make a serious profession of soldiering? Very, very few. The majority join to have a good time – and they certainly have it. Moreover if our regular soldiers do not take soldiering seriously, certainly the nation has never made war a business. The brains of the nation have not gone into military channels, but into civil. It is only now that we are beginning to count the able business-men of England among the active contributors to the organizing departments of our military machine.

The diarist is nothing if not game:

This morning the papers tell us of another Zeppelin raid in London at 11.30 last night when the House of Commons was sitting. Could anything more annoying be imagined? We were in London for a week, hoping every night for a Zeppelin raid, and then it goes and takes place a couple of nights after we were there.

Hearing from his brother Geoffrey of a 'thundering good sermon' preached in Leeds by their Father, Burgon comments:

I went to a service in the Chapel here – the Chapel for once was used for the purpose for which it was built. On the platform at the east end they had rigged an altar. On it were two lighted candles, and a green curtain hung behind. Next to the green curtain were pictures of German machine-gun emplacements, and sketches of the Lewis machine-rifle, and so on all round the building. The padre was one of the machine-gun sergeant-instructors. Before the war he had been chaplain to the Enfield works. At the outbreak of the war he enlisted in the Artists' Rifles – and on Sundays he leaves his khaki behind and dons cassock and surplice, and instead of instructing us how to kill Germans in the most sure and scientific way, he exhorts us to remember that God will set our deeds before us. It is indeed a confusing set of principles through which the average human being is asked to steer his way in this curious old world of ours.

By the end of October 1915 he is back with his regiment, and moving into billets 'for the winter':

We are scattered over two villages and several hamlets, and using 37 farms! All the horses are under cover and the men too. I myself have an excellent room at the 'Mairie' – quite the most comfortable one I have ever had. The war correspondents Macartney of the 'Times' (John Buchan went home in disgust after his Loos article had been censored) and Gibbs dined with two of us on Friday night – both extremely nice, especially Philip Gibbs who is perfectly charming and extremely able. He writes for the Daily Telegraph, Daily Chronicle and a number of American papers. It was pleasant to talk about the Sorbonne, Western Canada, and a hundred and one things and people interesting to no one out here.

In early November he writes home for his football things:

The Colonel is very keen on football being played by the regiment during the winter, if trench-digging and other duties allow. He has ordered a hundred pairs of shorts from England, and different coloured jerseys. An Inter-Squadron league is to be started, and I shall be on the Committee of Management.

After a long interval in the diary, Julian appears in it again. In a letter written on 29 September, he does not refer to the fact that he is leaving to join the British rather than the Australian army:

The Headmaster announced my coming departure to the whole school on a memorable Friday, and said some kind things about me, which were greeted by ringing cheers from the boys.

Meanwhile, in early November, Burgon had a happy four days' leave in England, his first since arriving in France six months before; he saw most of the family in London, all going to the theatre one night after dining at Hatchettes. He went by train to Wiltshire to spend a night in camp with Morris at Fovant, and was finally seen off at Victoria Station.

It is a wonderful sight (writes his mother) to see 1,500 men and officers returning to the Front after leave. The same thing goes on daily. What struck me most was the cheerful bravery of the women who sent their men off almost invariably with smiles.

To get back to his regiment from as far as the train would take him – Hazebrouck – Burgon tried everywhere in the town for a car, but to no avail:

I went to the Medical Ambulance convoy – a string of motor-ambulances were standing idle down a side street. The sergeant-major was rightly obdurate – 'You must ask at the officers' mess'. I penetrated to the officers' mess – all subalterns: 'Ask the colonel'. The colonel lived half a mile away. Off I went to where the colonel lived. The sergeant in the ante-room held out little hope – 'So many applications, sir, for our ambulances – very strict orders have just been issued'. I waited until the colonel was free and then was shown in. At first a complete refusal. Then he gradually began to melt. I pressed my case – he was fast yielding – when the door opened, and in walked the General – i.e. the director of all the Medical work of the Second Army. Of course it is contrary to all military regulations to use a car for any but official duties – but I saw he must be tackled, so in answer to his curt, 'What do you want?' I launched forth and got my case started before he had a chance to edge in a word of discouragement. 'This is the sixth application today', he said. 'I'm sick of it. People think I'm a professional jobber of cars. Padres are the worst. They're always asking to be taken about the country. The Medical Corps is not a general motor company, and the sooner you realise that, the better'. His moustache bristled, and the rows of ribbons on his breast twinkled at me as he heaved with annoyance.

I agreed cheerfully that it was clear he must be pestered to death, but Aire was such an extraordinarily short distance – a good main road all the way – the ambulance car would be back almost before it had gone. I was already very late back from leave – without a car, short though the distance was, I should be another twenty-four hours behind my time. He hummed and hawed. 'Your name?' I told him. 'Your regiment?' I told him – a distinct change. Some more talk, and then finally he turned to the Colonel, who had been listening all this time. 'Well, Colonel, I shall make an exception this time – write out an order for a motor-ambulance, and Mr Bickersteth, perhaps you will come round now and have some tea with me while you are waiting for the car to arrive'. I accepted with alacrity, and so off we went and had tea together, and a good chat. When the Colonel arrived for tea, he was sent several times to the window to see if the car had arrived, which annoyed him but amused me. Finally the car came. I picked up my hamper etc. at the station and came speeding off down to Aire through the glorious moon-lit frosty air. At Lambres I left my kit in the care of the transport officer, borrowed a push-bike and arrived here just in time for dinner.

He does not forget to tell his mother:

The food I brought back has been most successful. The ham and tongue are first-rate. The pheasants we have tonight.

Fresh billets in villages several miles away were ordered

because the infantry want ours – a great nuisance as we thought we were settled for the winter.

They trekked off in pouring rain and a bitter cold wind along roads inches deep in mud, and had a lot of difficulty in fixing up men and horses in passable accommodation – lean-to sheds for the horses

after we had chucked out all the farm implements; and hay barns for the men.

There was consternation among the local inhabitants:

when one of our sergeants put seven horses in what he thought was a nice dry shed. It proved to be the village hall, often used as a mission room.

This morning (he ends the same letter) was the first occasion as far as I know since leaving England when hour and place allowed me to go to Holy Communion.

His depression at the Royals' inactive war continued (4 Dec):

I feel the part we are playing in the War is very disappointing. I do not mean the cavalry have not done their part, as in critical situations they have been called on and have not failed. But to be utterly inactive and useless, and likely to remain so, is fearfully trying . . .

He writes on Christmas Day:

How I wish the war was over! I loathe every minute of it. The life seems to me every day more and more utterly stupid in every way. The regiment of course is splendid, all good fellows, every one of them, and the officers too are good. But as for the life, it is utter stagnation . . .

We saw the men at their dinners – pork, which above all things they like.

In the afternoon there was a hockey match between the Royals and the Third Dragoon Guards:

The General, who is 47, played for us, a tremendous sportsman and always fit as a fiddle. As a young man he had won the Grand National! We had a comparatively quiet dinner. I must say I have an extremely comfortable billet, with my stable, my bedroom, my sitting-room and a kitchen for my two servants.

But he is bound at last for the trenches – as an infantryman:

We bid fair to be in the thick of it in a very few days. We were to have started tomorrow morning early – but now I believe we go on Sunday, 2 Jan. (Ninny's[5] birthday, is it not? Give her my love). We have passed two days of 'Sturm und Drang' getting everything ready. I have seldom spent two fuller days in my life. The truth is, the infantry are prepared for this kind of thing, but we are not. Our kit is cavalry, not infantry kit, and shorn of our horses we have poor means of carrying everything we should carry. We have had to decide what is the best method of carrying a pack. The pack itself is merely a mackintosh ground sheet wrapped round a coat, underclothing, towel etc. We have nothing provided in the way of a proper square infantry pack. Every item of the men's kit had to be complete. The whole organization of the regiment on infantry lines was novel too. I expect Ralph would have laughed to see our first 'Company' parade. We all got rather mixed up with platoons, companies, squadrons, troops. The men enjoyed it thoroughly.

We are going to a pretty hot part of the line – an average of thirty yards between us and the Huns all along it. The censor would not allow me to give you any further particulars than this – and until it is officially announced that we have gone up, which no doubt before long it will be, I think you must treat this letter as confidential. My second servant stays to look after my four horses; my first servant comes with me.

I do not think all this will affect leave particularly. After all the infantry come straight to England from the trenches. Either 24 or 31 Jan. will be my date. Personally, I prefer the latter, because of old Julian, whom I set my heart on seeing.

May 1916 be happy for all of us, and may it end as satisfactorily for us (as a family) as has 1915.

Ten days later his platoon (his troop had become No. 5 Platoon) is moving up a communication trench:

It is at least a mile and a half long, the whole of it floored with wood. Down this we tramped. Progress was very slow. The stuff we were carrying was heavy – frequent rests were necessary. We met various parties returning. The trench was narrow, and we were a large party, so we let them pass. It was a beautiful starlit night – with a young moon. Star shells followed each other incessantly, making the night day. In the burst of artificial greenish light the figures of the men and the heaped-up earth of the trench stood out clear cut against the sky. Every now and again the Huns swept the flat country on each side of us with machine-gun fire. One could hear them traversing from one side to the other. Machine-gun fire when high and at some distance sounds tremendously loud. Then there would come the occasional whistle of isolated rifle bullets – all of which is quite entertaining when one knows one is safe in the friendly earth. Finally our trench debouched into the quarry – like enough to any quarry except that the sides are not very high. All round the sides dug-outs had been dug right into the banks, and in each one was a little fire. As we crossed the quarry pretty quickly for fear of stray bullets, and dumped our stuff in the middle, the whole effect was most picturesque. The quarry itself shrouded in the dim silvery light of the moon – the fires all round at the mouth of each dug-out, throwing into relief the figures of the soldiers as they stood in the doorway – the frequent bursts of light due to the star-shells – the deafening fire of our guns some few yards behind us, and the sound of trench-mortar fire in front of us, added to the impression of a little corner of this huge battle line, which I shall never forget.

We take over the line tomorrow. . . . We will be about 40 yards from the Boches, and I gather that mines are the worst trouble. I am enjoying myself immensely.

Years later Burgon was obviously re-reading the diary, and added after the last sentence, 'This was literally true'.
He was soon to have his first narrow escape in the trenches:

We were about thirty yards from the Germans . . . It is an eerie experience one's first night in the trenches. Fortunately it was a glorious still moonlight night . . . Flares were continually sent over . . . About 1.00 am my time for relief came and I went for a rest in a small dug-out 50 yards behind the line. The cold and the rats made sleep impossible; I think I've mentioned that the trenches are alive with enormous rats, grown fat on the debris of war. . . . At 5.00 I and another officer walked further back down the communication trench to our Mess, simply rather a bigger dug-out where I got the servants to make us some tea – and then returned at 6.00 am, which is the morning time for 'stand to'. Directly this was over, rifles were inspected – and then every man took off his boots and socks, rubbed his feet with grease and then put on clean socks and his boots. This is supposed to be done several times a day, and has (with the floor boards and improved draining of the trenches), done much to prevent 'trench feet'.

On this particular morning, I was to stay on duty till about 9.00 am when I was to be relieved for breakfast. I was the only officer in the front line. As I was standing there, up came Waterhouse cheerfully to relieve me. We stood talking a few moments. Then he said, 'Have you a sentry posted round this corner?' I said 'Yes'. 'All right', he answered, 'go off and get something to eat and I'll carry on till you come back'. He turned the corner. I walked about six paces away, which took me three or four seconds. I had hardly gone the six paces before there was a tremendous explosion in the trench just round the corner. The parapet just in front of where I had been standing had most of the sandbags carried away. I rushed round the corner almost to stumble over the bodies of Waterhouse, my troop sergeant (Sergt Futcher) and the sentry. I saw at once the man was killed, and Sergeant Futcher though just breathing, was practically dead. Waterhouse was terribly wounded and by the look on his face I knew he could not live – I had seen that look before. I immediately sent one man for the stretcher bearers and the doctor, another to report at once to Irwin, our 'Company' Commander. Sergeant Elliot (the bombing sergeant) and I put a field dressing round Waterhouse's head, and directly the stretcher bearers came we lifted him on to the trench stretcher, in which it is more or less necessary to keep in a sitting position, and he was carried off down the communication trench. He lived till he reached the dressing station, but half an hour later word came up to me that he was dead.

Waterhouse's death is a terrible loss to the regiment. He was an Old Carthusian – we played in the same school XI in 1905. He was a good soldier – an exceptionally fine horseman and a very nice fellow. He was wounded at Hooge on 13 May and had only just rejoined the regiment.

My troop sergeant, Sergeant Futcher, is also a great loss. By common consent he was the most promising young sergeant in the regiment and was marked out to become a squadron sergeant-major. He was just my age, and a month ago I got him leave to go home and get married. I have written to his young wife. At the moment he was killed he had a mug of tea in his hand and a piece of bread and bacon.

Well, 'carry on' was the word. I got the trench cleaned up, posted another sentry and then at 10.00 am went down to get some breakfast, which I rather needed. The rest of the day was quiet and I was glad of it. To be so very near death is no slight shock.

A few days later was his birthday, 14 January:

It was our last night in the trenches, but a very satisfactory one, i.e. strafing the Hun. We decided we would give them a bit of warming up in retaliation to the continual nuisance they had been with their trench-mortars and bombs (the latter thrown by catapults). The 3rd DG bombing officer, our trench mortar expert, and the artillery liaison officer, all put their heads together and decided that at 8.00 pm that night they would begin a '*straf*' [sic], first with our own trench mortars (heavier than the German's!), with our bombs, and then if they retaliated, the guns were to come in. At 8.00 pm Irwin, Cubitt and I took up position in the front line to observe the trench mortar fire. The front line was as safe as any other place. First came a few shots from our trench mortars, then a number of bombs from the sap-heads, and all the time a continual stream of rifle grenades from my sector. Then our guns began before the Huns had an opportunity of retaliating. It was a magnificent sight – a storm of shrapnel bursting in the air with red balls of fire over the German trenches. This storm would last three or four minutes, and then one would once again hear the under-current of trench mortars (which seemed to be falling with a thud into the German lines), rifle grenades and bombs. After a quarter of an hour of this, the Huns got thoroughly annoyed and replied with a tempest of shells – all of which went straight over our first line and were aimed at the batteries themselves and our support line and communication trenches. It seemed as if we had stirred up a hornet's nest, and what was worse, our guns seemed rather weak in keeping up the contest, but after a time they began again – and guns of bigger calibre than 15 pounders. The air was literally alive with shells shrieking over our heads. We three sat in a fire-bay, smoking and talking quietly. It was a curious birthday evening occupation.

Meanwhile Julian was deep in his Australian good-byes (4 December 1915):

Farewell dinners and tea-parties, writing of reports, correcting exami-nation papers, sorting out old files, packing and moving from my lodgings – all have poured upon me in an overwhelming jumble of events. People have been awfully good to me, and I have received many tokens of their respect and I think genuine sorrow at my departure. The boys gave me a cheque to buy a Communion Set to use as an Army Chaplain; the masters also gave me a cheque, and fountain pens and socks have descended in streams upon me.

Burgon, after a few days in his billets at Béthune, was back again in the thick of things:

Last night I had to take a large fatigue party up to dig. We were a hundred yards behind the front line in the open, a nasty place – and we hadn't been there ten minutes when I had a man killed. He was badly wounded in the face, and by the aid of flickering matches at the bottom of the trench I stopped the bleeding with a field dressing. But he died a quarter of an hour later, and then I had to get the body away.

He reflects from billets:

One of the worst parts of this war is the smells. Directly one gets near the firing line, the same old smells assail one's nostrils. How to describe them I don't know. There is the sour smell of billets occupied for months past by troops French and English – it is the smell of decayed bully beef, sweaty clothes, latrines and disinfectants. Then there is the awful smell of the trenches after an engagement, the smell of gunpowder, and dead bodies and blood. It is a stench I shall never forget. One talks of not being able to get scenes and sounds out of one's mind. The same is true of smells.

Not for the last time Burgon's activities find their way into the National Press. He is 'the officer' quoted verbatim in this dispatch by Philip Gibbs to the 'Daily Telegraph' *on 4 February, 1916:*

'A HOT TIME'

They had a hot time in the trenches. The enemy's artillery was active, and the list of casualties began to tot up. A good officer and a fine fellow was killed almost at the outset and men were horribly wounded. But all these troopers showed a cool courage, and it was only now and then when a parapet was blown in and when the bombardment was most intense that any of them showed a little worry. The officers went up to chat with them then, as British officers do at such a time, but they were surprised by the steady nerves of the men. They showed a kind of disdain of all this 'strafing', and the men in the dug-outs did not let it interfere with their sleep.

Things looked bad for a few minutes, when a section of trenches was blown in, isolating one platoon from another. A sergeant-major made his way back from the damaged section and a young officer who was going forward to find out the extent of the damage met him on the way.

'Can I get through?' asked the officer. 'I've got through,' was the answer, 'but it's chancing one's luck.' The officer 'chanced his luck,' but did not expect to come back alive. Afterwards he tried to analyse his feelings for my benefit. 'I had no sense of fear,' he said, 'but a sort of sub-conscious knowledge that the odds were against me if I went on, and yet a conscious determination to go on at all costs and find out what had happened.'

He came back, covered in blood, but unwounded.

So the cavalry did its bit again, though not as cavalry, and I saw some of them when they came back, and they were glad to have gone through this awful business so that no man may fling a scornful word as they pass with their horses.

The trenches are not the place for cavalry, but when they get there they show the spirit of their famous regiments and 'stick it' well.

*　*　*

59

Meanwhile in Egypt the almost impossible had happened. Morris, guarding the Suez Canal, had connected with Julian homeward bound from Melbourne on the P&O liner 'Maloya' (which it finally was, not the 'Morea'), and they wired home on 27 January to tell their mother:

Spent a day together both flourishing Julian Morris Bickersteth.

'This is joyful news indeed', says the diarist, for the second time in this volume.

Later Julian told them the remarkable way in which he had met Morris on the Suez Canal, and the diarist recounts it:

As the '*Maloya*' steamed up from Suez, the banks of the canal were lined with troops. The passengers made a collection and bought all the tobacco on board and threw it to the soldiers as they passed. A Bradford man on the ship kept asking the names of the various regiments – most of them seemed to be West Yorkshires. At last, near a pontoon bridge at Kantara, the '*Maloya*' had to tie up in a siding to let another steamer pass. Now comes the remarkable fact – the ship was tied up exactly opposite Morris's regiment, the 15th West Yorks; and so Julian had travelled 9,000 miles to meet Morris in this way. If they had arranged it beforehand, it could not have been more wonderful. Julian caught sight of a smart young officer looking up at the steamer, and it turned out to be Morris. They shouted to one another, and the people on board said to Julian, 'You are really a wonderful family to be able to arrange your matters in this manner!'.

Two of the companies of Morris's battalion had gone seven miles out to the trenches, and it seemed a mere chance that Morris's company had been chosen to stay behind. He had previously obtained leave from his colonel to go to Port Said with Julian. He therefore asked if he might come on board. The Captain said it was against the rules, but if the Pilot was agreeable he would for once give way. The Pilot said 'Yes', the gangway was let down, and Morris walked up it. This was about 8.00 am. He remained on board and went up the Canal on the steamer as far as Port Said, having breakfast and lunch with Julian. They were therefore twelve hours together and Julian saw Morris off by the Cairo Express about 8.00 pm. It was 26 January, 1916.

At home there was more excitement to come; Burgon arrived in London on 30 January. His parents met him at the Strand Palace Hotel to which they had come down from Leeds the night before.

He looked remarkably well, and does not seem upset by the terrific experiences through which he had just passed in those terrible trenches at Hulloch.

He went off almost at once with his father to see the Archbishop of Canterbury and Mrs Davidson:

The Archbishop said he did not think the War would be over this year, and he would be surprised to learn that Mr Asquith[6] expected it either. He said that Lord Kitchener had told him he agreed with his commendation of the chaplains at the Front, and would have said so in the House of Lords, only he got so bored with the discussion that he left, and so his praises were unspoken. This is a pity as it would have cheered the chaplains.

There has been a great deal of discussion as to the wisdom of the Archbishops and Bishops in not allowing the clergy to serve as combatants. I think it would have been better if they had placed the clergy entirely at the disposal of the Government to take posts as orderlies and Red Cross Workers, and set other men free.

Then came the exciting day they had all been waiting for, 3 February:

Father, Kitty[7], Ella and I reached Victoria again at 3.20 to find that the train had come in ten minutes earlier than it was announced, and the officers were beginning to pour away from the platform. In a minute 'Ninny' came excitedly racing down the platform saying, 'He is here, he is here, and I was the only one who met him'. Sure enough in the distance we could see Julian's tall figure, and we soon gathered round him. Monier came a few minutes later, but Burgon had not yet arrived. Julian's first question was, 'How is Burgon?' and he was very astonished to find he was actually in London on leave. Julian looked exactly the same, but very well in health. We did not leave the station until Burgon came. The first thing he said to Julian was, 'Tell us what you did in India' – a very old family joke, referring to Julian's tour with the present Duke of Sutherland some years ago in India.

They soon drove off ('in two taxis') to the Strand Palace Hotel for tea, and the large party later went 'to hear "Faust" at the Shaftesbury, the theatre very empty owing to fear of Zeppelin raids'.

Next morning, 4 February, they left London by train for Yorkshire, and had a few days at Heaning Hall[8]. They had lovely walks in good weather and simply enjoyed being together again. Burgon's leave ended on 8 February. Four of the brothers dined together in London the night before. Back with his unit he speculates as to whether to follow up a suggestion that he should join the Intelligence Corps:

I doubt whether my German would be good enough, and anyhow the advice from senior men in the regiment is that it would be unwise to leave the cavalry.

Julian had brought with him a fascinating diary of the five weeks' voyage from Melbourne, covering twenty-one pages of typescript. At Adelaide, Fremantle, Colombo, Bombay and Aden they had gone ashore. They were six hours in Adelaide, and a former member of the Melbourne Grammar School took him

to see the sights, the Cathedral, St Peter's College, the most richly endowed school in Australia[9], the Art Gallery etc., and something of the city. Although the hills round Adelaide are quite brown, it struck me the city was quite one of the prettiest in Australia, and the circle of parks and trees most effective.

At Colombo they had thirty-six hours to spend. He was up before dawn and was rewarded by

a magnificent sunrise behind the mountains of Ceylon. Last night we had come under the lee of the island, and the air was laden with the rich scents of Ceylon, wafted across the water to us by a light breeze. We made the harbour by 8.00 am, and getting ashore soon after, caught the 9.15 train into the mountains on our way to Kandy. Perhaps one of the most beautiful train journeys in the world, it fulfilled all our expectations and renewed my memories of eight years ago. The colouring, the richness of the vegetation, the native life, combine to make a picture not easy to forget. We got out after three and a half hours in the train at Peradeniya and after lunching at a bungalow drove through the wonderful gardens. An old guide, who had seen 28 years service there, took us round and showed us many of the trees, shrubs and flowers. Nutmeg, cinnamon, clove and many spice trees filled the air with sweet scents, and every now and then a boy would rise silently from beneath some tree and offer fruit or nuts. Three sides of the gardens are surrounded by a swift-flowing river, shaded by giant bamboos.

We drove out to Kandy, four miles, and went to the Queen's Hotel, one of these colossal globe-trotter's hotels, ruined now by the war, but still kept open for the few who pass this way. The rest of the afternoon was occupied mostly by a delightful visit to Principal A.G. Fraser of Trinity College, Kandy, who literally rose from a bed of sickness – having a temperature of 104 that morning from malaria – to take us round the school. So great is his fame that he has boys from all over India, and even two boys from Africa, sons of the Prime Minister of Uganda. The school is run on public school lines and is amazingly successful. A drive round the lake after dark, with a giant moon flooding all the scene, and fireflies, bright specks of light, chasing each other in the dark bends in the road, made an unforgettable picture.

The ship's captain made Julian the ship's padre with responsibility for organizing regular services on board, and also invited him to arrange

the military lectures, which have been an unqualified success. At all of them I have to take the chair and have to introduce the speaker.

He also

did a good deal of secretarial work in connection with the men on board going home to get commissions. General Cockburn said he would do his best to help any whom he felt were suitable to get commissions, and he asked me to get particulars.

. . . . So I had a stream of passengers coming over to see me, and I presented the General with a list of 30 names from the 1st and 2nd class men who were hoping for commissions. The list contained all kinds of details about them, such as school, university, profession, nationality, military service and so on. All this information took a long time to collect, but it was worth while worrying about it, and both the General and the men have been grateful to me. The Captain was kind enough to thank me the other day for what I was doing – or rather I should say trying to do, to keep things going on the ship. Everyone calls me the Padre.

Only the next Viceroy of India, Lord Chelmsford[10], declined Julian's invitation to lecture, begging to be let off speaking, as he had a huge pile of books on India to read before he got home. Julian later discovered that

the new Viceroy had been offered a naval cruiser to take him to England from Port Said. He refused, preferring to take his chances with the ordinary passengers. It's extraordinary to reflect that he had been a Territorial Captain of an English regiment on the plains of India since the war began, and now when he goes back there he will be the most important and protected person in all the Indian Empire.

At Bombay and Aden Julian had also gone ashore; and then in the Suez Canal there had been the classic meeting between the two brothers at Kantara.
*   The diarist concludes:*

Julian was able to tell us a great deal of his life and difficulties in Australia, and he certainly seems to have been very happy and successful in his work there.

She went down to help him shop in London for his outfit, and they came home via Oxford:

The place was lovely – bathed in sunshine, and Julian was delighted to be in Christ Church again. But the desolation of the place could hardly be described. You would not have known it was term time. During the whole day I only saw one undergraduate in cap and gown, and one don. In Christ Church there are only 26 men, five of these being American and some of the others foreigners. The dining hall is closed. Even the soldiers who were training there have all gone, and I only saw one college announced as being the headquarters of a regiment. The Town Hall and other public buildings are used as hospitals, so there are a good many wounded about, and as you walk down the High you see the figures of Red Cross nurses in the windows of the Masonic buildings. Each College Chapel has a Roll of Honour hanging outside.

Three days later Julian wired from London:

Accepted for foreign service leaving London for France 22nd.

The diarist writes:

I feared that he might be sent off quickly after seeing the Chaplain General, but I had hoped that he might have kept him with us in England a little longer. However this cannot be helped.

Burgon, as one would have expected, was

glad to hear Julian has been so quickly accepted, though I had little doubt he would be. We shall give him a welcome out here, and I think he will find much useful work to be done. How I wish Father could come as well. All the men like him so much, and he is cut out for a chaplain but, however keen, I suppose he can't choose. Certainly if I had the chance, I should close my military career tomorrow with the greatest pleasure. I have been moved from C Squadron to the machine-guns, which I very much dislike. I have forgotten all I knew about the machine-gun, and take very little interest in it. I rather wish now I had gone definitely for the Intelligence. However, one must take it philosophically I suppose.

VOLUME IV
FEBRUARY – JULY 1916

Julian reaches France and starts chaplaincy duties with The Rangers and
London Rifle Brigade – diarist's husband awarded TD and made a Chaplain
to the King – Morris's battalion in Flanders – Julian's full Easter Day and
attendance at a chaplains' conference – he goes twice to see Morris on the
eve of the Somme offensive – the three brothers meet – Morris is killed on
1 July – Julian's exhausting battle – Ralph is married – Burgon,
still inactive, has his first flight in an aeroplane.

*By 22 February, 1916, Julian was in France. He had had only three
weeks in England after nearly four years in Australia. His mother saw
him off at Victoria Station:*

We secured a seat in the Pullman and put his valise and sack [sic] close
by; he was very uneasy for fear he had too much luggage!

*But all was well, she heard three days later; he had gone to General
Headquarters (GHQ) at St Omer – but only for a day or two, he
thought:*

before going to wherever I am sent . . . I hated leaving, but it is good to
be in the middle of the big show.

*His first night in France was in a 'third-rate little hotel', with three other
padres, all beginning, as he was:*

Our bedrooms were small, but very comfortable and absolutely clean.
I suggested Evensong, and we all four had Evensong together. I took it.
It was very cold, but my British warm kept me cosy, and I had an excellent night . . . I was awakened by the lumbering of many huge motor
lorries passing along the narrow street. I got up and looked out on a
fairy scene. Quaint old gables surrounded me, all covered with white,

the snow having fallen quite heavily during the night. But it was bright and frosty, and the air smelled good.

At 10.00 am we presented ourselves at the Headquarters of the Chaplains' Department. I was the first called in, and the Deputy Chaplain General, Bishop Gwynne[1], asked only a few questions about myself, and then said he was going to send me up to the 56th Division in 3rd Army. He explained various things, saying I was to report to the Senior Chaplain of the Division. Please, therefore until further notice, send all letters c/o Senior Chaplain, 56th Division, France. I will give you a more explicit address later.

The Bishop could not have been pleasanter. He explained a good deal about the work to be done and how he thought it best to attempt it, and obviously wished to be considered not just a superior officer, but a real Father-in-God; it will not be difficult to feel that he is indeed the latter. We had three or four minutes prayer together. We reported to the Camp Commandant again to relinquish our billets and then walked round to the mess. At lunch who should come up to me but an Old Rugbeian padre? He was at Rugby with me and afterwards at Trinity, Oxford, and has been out here two months only, attached to GHQ. I didn't recognise him for the moment, but he recognised me; and having lunched together, he proposed taking me out in his car; HQ chaplains are apparently the only ones out here who have one at their disposal.

They had a 'most capital afternoon'. Okell, the Old Rugbeian, took him all round

the various soldiers' clubs and churches, all beautifully arranged. I saw all kinds of people. I met men who know me or the family at every turn.

The diarist, sacrificially, comments:

Julian, as usual, has fallen on his feet, and is most fortunate to be sent at once to the firing line, and not to a base hospital as is usually the case on a chaplain's first going out.

Four days later, the ship in which Julian had just come safely the whole way from Australia struck a mine in the English Channel, and sank in half an hour, 'a great many lives being lost'.

Burgon writes on 16 February:

Still another move for me in prospect: the guns of all cavalry regiments are to be brigaded. That means that the Machine-Gun Section of the Royals (which consists of about 70 men, 90 horses and four guns) will be united with the same units of the 3rd DG and the N. Somerset Yeomanry as a Machine-Gun Squadron. We shall be seconded from the regiment. We are not part of the Machine-Gun Corps, which is, I think, wholly or almost wholly, an infantry concern. But we belong to our Brigade and are commanded by the Brigade Machine-Gun Officer. Of course, to a large extent it means good-bye to the regiment – I will be commanding about forty men and two guns.

As a command, of course, it is better than a troop, and one is more on one's own – but I am not really keen enough about the gun, nor do I know my men well enough to make this counterbalance the unpleasant fact that it will be necessary to be seconded. I would rather have been seconded to the Intelligence Corps. Actually I do not think the war will last beyond the end of the year. I have ceased to worry about anything, and regard all possible eventualities quite philosophically.

Fighting seems incessant, and the whole business a hopeless nightmare. From all this it is a great comfort to turn to the book I'm reading at present, Bridge's anthology '*The Spirit of Man*', and see that man has been through bad times before, and has been able to rise above them and create in himself a philosophic calm based on the certitude of better things to come.

But the full-blooded Englishman is never very far away:

Yet in spite of all this, one has an extremely healthy feeling that will welcome the next opportunity of sending as many Boches as possible hurtling to eternity.

Meanwhile his parents are visiting Norwich:

'A city of darkness that can be felt; the black-out is for fear of more Zeppelin raids. It is impossible for even the old inhabitants of the city who know the streets really well to avoid running into one another in the darkness, and they have therefore taken to wearing illuminous [sic] buttons as some sort of protection against collision.'

Julian is beginning to pen screeds home from the Rangers, the London battalion to which he has been attached. They are still in training behind the line, marching many miles a day in the snow and slush.

But I can't tell you how much I am enjoying it all. It seems to me the fulfilment of all my dreams for so many months past, and I am as happy as the day is long. . . . I am sorely tempted sometimes to leave the 'padre' work to others and take a commission as a combatant; but on second thoughts I feel that the 'padre' work is great work – more difficult in many ways than that of an ordinary officer, and well worth all the effort and energy I can put into it.

His cousin, Clare Monier-Williams, by good fortune already in that very battalion, writes home to the diarist:

Julian has made a great hit with everyone, and also in no small degree with the French curé of our village here, with whom he is arranging services in the church. Julian lives with the Division, and messes and does everything with us, and is most sporting in walking on all the marches we do.

Here there is an enclosure in Burgon's latest letter, a note to him from Philip Gibbs, the Daily Telegraph *war correspondent mentioned earlier. Obviously Burgon had told him that his mother was putting together this diary of wartime happenings as they affected the family, and Gibbs comments that he is sure this is immensely worth doing:*

especially if you are not afraid of putting in little details of every day experience. The big things belong to history and will be familiar enough, but afterwards the next generation will search for the intimate records and the psychology of the men who served.

Burgon adds notes both in the margin and on the volume's fly-leaf; in the former he comments:

True enough, and perhaps justification for this family diary.

And on the latter, obviously much later:

The diary contains many trivialities, and yet taken as a whole will, I hope, give succeeding generations an idea of what we lived through

during the First World War – though thank God we did not know there
was a second one coming in 1939.

*Geoffrey (who by now was serving in War Office Intelligence in
London) comments on Winston Churchill's speech about mismanage-
ment at the Admiralty, for which he received a public reproof in
Parliament from the Prime Minister himself. Geoffrey wrote:*

I thought that Churchill's speech was a contemptible performance, and
he deserved the dressing down he got from Balfour. One doesn't want
him to be killed, but I can't help feeling that a well-directed German
bullet might save our Empire much future trouble from his clever but
unscrupulous brain.

*How well the diary was helping to hold the family together comes out
in a comment from Burgon asking for a copy of Julian's last letter:*

I'm afraid this will be a trouble, but it is worth it as it keeps us all in
touch, which I often notice other families do not do, and suffer
accordingly. When Julian came back from Australia after four years,
one hardly realized he had been away for so long – he knew everything and we knew all about him. This is entirely due to your good
management of letters, and Father's self-denying permission to his
secretaries to spend time copying – which I know he never grouses
about!

*The sense of willing and idealistic sacrifice for the cause which ordinary
families were showing comes out in this story, says the diarist:*

When in Norwich, Canon Meyrick told us of a boy whom he knew well,
who was wounded in France, his left hand being entirely shot away. He
was very much annoyed when people commiserated with him for this,
and when someone said to him, 'I am so sorry you have lost your hand',
he replied indignantly, 'You talk as if I had lost five pounds. If I had
done that, you might have condoled with me, but I have not lost my
hand – I gave it.' In a newspaper about the same time it was reported
that a French *poilu* whose leg had been amputated, when commiserated
with, replied, 'I think I have got off very well. I gave my country my life,
and she has only taken my leg'.

Julian, laid low in early March by inoculations, writes about his first (and last) ecumenical venture in France:

I was anxious to avoid inconveniencing the men by using their billets (which would have meant their putting kit away etc), so I approached the Sacristan of the church and asked him if it would be possible to use the nave of the church only. To my surprise he agreed readily, saying that M. le Curé, who lives in the next village, had even offered the church as a hospital if necessary, and he was quite sure we might use it for a service. I only thought of asking to use the church half an hour before the time of the service, so I just had time to telephone round to the headquarters of the various company billets and inform the officer-in-command of the change, and post a couple of men on to the road to turn men into the church. I hadn't even time to get my cassock and surplice out, so I took the service in my military clothes. I got a rifleman to ring the great deep-toned bell, and in a few minutes we had the church crammed with men. All the seats were filled and a good number were standing at the back. A Corporal, (who has incidentally just been made director of the Drury Lane Orchestra with a retaining fee of one thousand pounds a year!) was to have played the harmonium but he was kept by regimental duties. But I soon found another musician, the battalion being very rich in musical talent. I had no hymn books for the men, but I chose one or two familiar hymns, and you should have heard them sing! We began with 'Fight the good fight'. I then took a very shortened form of Evensong and we sang part of 'Onward Christian soldiers' instead of a psalm, and had 'Jesus, lover of my soul' before a short address, which I gave standing in the lofty pulpit. It was the first time I had ever stood in an RC pulpit, and I wonder how many Anglican priests can say they have ever stood in such a place. I spoke for less than five minutes on the psalm for the day – a splendid text – the 139th 'God sees and knows all we do. We cannot escape Him even if we would'. Then we had 'Nearer my God to Thee' and finished up after the Blessing with 'God save the King' sung at the top of the men's voices. Some seven or eight of the officers came, and more would have come but they were busy. I can tell you it was an inspiring sight and did much to encourage me.

Next day was the Fête Day of the local patron saint, and M. le Curé invited us all to the 11 o'clock Mass. The Colonel was anxious to send some men for 'international reasons'; so some forty or fifty men who were not otherwise occupied, including nearly all the RCs of the battalion, who do not number more than twelve or fourteen as far as I can make out at present, went to the service. I accompanied them with Clare and the other officer who is an RC. Most of the villagers were there. The Curé had got two of the riflemen in the battalion to act as servers, and it was curious to see these two in their service uniforms and muddy boots kneeling on either side of the priest during the Mass. At least they were not ashamed of witnessing to their faith.

At the end of the Mass and after the devout RCs had all come up to kiss the medal blessed by the Pope, the Curé came down to the chancel steps and gave a delightful little address to the soldiers. It was interpreted for him by one of the riflemen who speaks three or four languages perfectly, his father being a well-known Savile Row tailor who has a large house in Paris. Put shortly, the Curé welcomed us all to the village, thanked us for what we were doing for *'la belle France'* and hoped that we should all return safely to those who in the home-land were praying so earnestly for our safety, and finally committed us to the care and protection of the *'Bon Dieu'*. He then asked us to sing the creed in English so that we might feel we had joined in the service. This we did – singing the Apostle's Creed, and he complimented us upon this. Then we sang the English National Anthem while the good little Curé rubbed his hands in glee. I feel I was hopelessly at sea during the Mass, but keeping my eye on the RC officer I made no mistakes – not that there are many you can make if you are merely present at the service.

All this interchange of religious courtesies was extremely gratifying. The Senior Chaplain of the Division to whom I wrote an account of our service wrote back and said he was amazed, and that it was the first ser-vice of its kind that he had heard of. Alas! for my faith in the dawn of a possible re-union – a long way off of course, but still at least I thought I had detected a coming greyness. But yesterday I discovered that those set over the Curé have refused to allow other joint services to be held there. This is sad.

The diarist has a proud moment on 14 March:

Yesterday when Father got down to church, (i.e. Leeds Parish Church) everyone began to congratulate him on his honour. He was much mys-tified till they told him that it was announced in the Honours List yesterday that the King had given him the Territorial Decoration. I am very pleased, as this has not been won by length of service, but by merit, and if anyone deserves it, Father does for all the work he has done for soldiers since the war began.

Back on duty with the Rangers after ten days in hospital, Julian writes from his billet in a hotel:

All kinds of spiritual possibilities are opening out before me, and I foresee wonderful God-given opportunities which I shall hope to be able to seize. I slept well in a bed occupied eighteen months ago by the hateful Boche, everything spotlessly clean though I don't suppose the Hun left it so.

A few days later they moved nearer the line into an area not before occupied by a British battalion:

The village was chiefly notable for its dirt and smell. One day, however, has already worked wonders and our men have swept and cleaned up to a great extent so that the French will hardly know themselves here. They will probably relapse into their piggishness on our departure.

He is obviously loving the personal contacts, comments his mother on reading this:

I met two ASC[3] men on a path and stopped and spoke to them. I make it a practice always to stop and speak to men when occasion offers. One man came from Peckham Rye, and his mother was at school at the St Mary's Lewisham Church School[4]. I only mention this to show how easy it is to hit upon some mutual acquaintance or place known to both parties.

Morris, now in France with his battalion after three and a half months in Egypt, is not far from Burgon, who writes rather testily on 15 March:

I heard from Morris today. His letter seems to have taken eight days to reach us. The foolish boy does not tell me his whereabouts. It is quite allowable for one brother to write to another when both are out here and tell him where he is, so that they can arrange a meeting. I shall write to him about this. All I may tell you now is that if there is any push this summer, Morris is not likely to be in it. I say this not to allay anxiety, but because I am pretty certain I am correct from certain pieces of information which have come into my possession.

*Against the comment that his brother is unlikely to be in 'the push',
Burgon has written years later, sadly, in the margin 'completely wrong'.*
*Julian's battalion is nearly in action; he comments from his strong
position as padre to a fighting unit:*

You have no conception of the contempt which the men out here have for the non-combatant corps. They are, many of them, very sore at thinking of how many men at home sit tight in comfort and safety and earn huge salaries and wages munition-making, while they face the guns and daily death, and endure separation from their families and endless discomfort for 1/- a day. There doesn't seem to them to be any justice in the scheme and I can't see myself how there is. If any firm, after the war is over, ever takes a civilian in preference to an old soldier, even if the latter is less skilled in the job he is wanted for, I would like to see that firm fined £1,000. The returned armies won't stand being ousted for jobs by the 'bomb-proof' crowd, as they naturally call those who stay in safety when they might come and lend a hand out here.

*Burgon meanwhile had ridden thirty-five miles to try to find him, but
they missed by about three hours. Julian wrote:*

Could anything be more aggravating? We shall probably be back in Amiens next week and it is sickening that I should have just missed him. Family meetings under these weird war conditions are not often easy to bring about, and so delightful when they are effected that the disappointment is all the keener when they fail to come off.

*He was much moved by a service in a 'large town' a mile from his billet.
(It was actually Arras, says a later note.) The service was held in a room
beautifully-fitted as the chapel of a Christian Brothers' Boys School:*

There were some startling contrasts. The celebrant's voice was occasionally drowned by the roar of guns, and the words 'In earth peace, good will towards men' in the Gloria in Excelsis seemed falsified by the noise of the anti-aircraft guns which went off incessantly at apparently no great distance from the house where we were. But nothing could destroy the beauty of the service or its meaning for us.

Afterwards, Julian went with another chaplain to see the ruined Cathedral:

The roof was almost entirely gone and lies a heap of masonry, bricks, mortar and dust in ugly heaps. The windows are all destroyed – the stalls broken down – in fact, the whole place is a scene of absolute desolation. The High Altar is cracked in two – the cavity for the relics laid bare. The chandeliers are smashed to atoms and the tombs and side chapels hardly recognisable. The central tower has fallen through the nave and has left a heap of masonry thirty feet high. I picked up two or three small pieces of mosaic as mementos.

Then we went to see the Soldiers' Club which is a marvel of organization and the work of a chaplain attached to this Division. He has only been a fortnight in the town, but he has already turned the large underground vaults, cellars and chambers of the Archbishop's Palace into a first-rate canteen, writing-room [and] concert hall. Goodness knows where he got all the materials from. But the chief feature is a perfectly beautiful little chapel, which with its arched roof and simple furnishings must be just like where the Early Roman Christians worshipped in the catacombs. Here 20 or more could gather, and here the chaplains of the Division hold a daily Eucharist. There is a little Priest's Chamber for robing. A beautiful Crucifix of ebony, with the figure of Our Lord in white, was above the Altar. Here they reserve the Sacrament and have found it most valuable to do so for the sake of wounded soldiers. Men have only to ask for a Celebration and one of the chaplains is always ready to celebrate day or night. You can imagine how gratifying it was to find all going so well, and so much being done.

Just before Easter, and fresh from a chance to talk to some of his battalion about preparations for Easter Communion, he reverts to an earlier theme:

Had I been in England at the beginning of the war, I should have been sorely tempted to join the ranks, in spite of all the discomforts and dirt and undoubted hardships from which I should have turned with loathing – but which would have brought me in close touch with the ordinary men and opened one's eyes to their point of view. The War has given parsons this opportunity which nothing else in their lifetime would have given them.

But he is energetically getting on with his priestly duties; every Sunday is full with five or six services, all at his instigation and held in different venues to suit the officers and men, mostly the latter, as the officers tend to say, 'Yes, padre, it would do the men good', but not turn up themselves:

The Public Schools (Julian reflects) have not produced a type of man who feels any need for religion.

During the week he is busy caring for the battalion's leisure hours, and in no time has hired rooms in an estaminet and fitted them up as a recreation centre which is rapidly patronised by up to two hundred men a day.

His Easter Sunday 1916 was 'wonderful'. He writes about it at great length; in the diary it covers seven pages of closely-packed typescript, 'showing' says his mother proudly and truly, 'what wonderful work a chaplain can do at the Front'. He is still the only Church of England padre in the Brigade, so he attempted more than he would normally do. The day began with a call from his servant at 5.30 am, 'a glorious morning with the sun already bright and the birds singing'. His first service was in the local school room, for twenty-eight communicants; then by bicycle to a barn for fifty-six Anglicans of the London Scottish ('in their kilts and bare knees').

Meanwhile, the Presbyterian padre was holding a parade for the rest of the battalion. (Julian met him for a chat on the edge of the village). Then he pedalled back furiously to his own mess for a quick breakfast, with The Rangers church parade to follow in an orchard nearby:

The singing went splendidly, with for the first time YMCA hymn books for every man on parade. The village bell began to ring not 80 yards away for High Mass as I started my address, but it stopped half way through, so I was able to finish without shouting.

Immediately the half hour service was over, it was into the schoolroom for a second Communion service, this time eleven officers and sixty-two men crammed in somehow or other.

By 11.15 he was on his bicycle again, the server bicycling along beside him, for the next church parade, the whole battalion of Royal Fusiliers drawn up three villages away in a hollow square against a long belt of trees:

which formed a noble background. I strode on to the parade ground two minutes late. A band led the singing which helped my voice.

Again there was a Communion. Among the seven officers and twenty-five men was the Brigade Major,

a very nice fellow wearing the ribbons of the VC and DSO, both of which he had won in this present war.

Lunch was in that mess, and soon after he was back on the bike for five kilometres to a village occupied by the Army Service Corps.

Here he had only a handful of men, because almost everyone was unexpectedly out on their wagons moving the brigade's rations:

We had a delightful little Communion service and one of the men present who did not receive the Sacrament told me afterwards he would like to be confirmed, so I must give him his first confirmation class as soon as possible.

After a cup of tea, he went on three more kilometres to the Divisional Training School for a shortened Evensong and address;

Quite a large congregation in a big room on the top floor of the beautiful old château.

And again, after the service he went to a smaller room to give thirty officers and men communion:

From my improvised altar I could see right down the two mile avenue of trees, the trunks of which now cast long shadows over the green corn fields. The lights of the evening were exquisitely lovely – what a setting for my last Communion of the day – during which I had nine services in all, six of them celebrations of the Holy Communion with two hundred communicants, all men. After a good dinner with pleasant mess companions, I left at a quarter to ten and bicycled back in the dark, beneath a sky which was a myriad mass of endless twinkling stars. There was a profound silence except for the distant rumble of guns. . . . So back to my Curé's house and bed. I ask you, could you want a happier Easter Sunday?

A week later, he reflects sadly on the godlessness around him:

Never has the failure of the Church of England been more apparent than it has been to the chaplains at the front: man after man with no knowledge of the Faith of his Fathers, man after man to whom religion is simply a name and has never touched either his heart or mind; man after man who has never been brought into contact with any sacramental teaching of any kind.

I wonder how many teaching sermons are preached in England today. The endless exhortations to good works or expounding of scriptural texts seem to teach those who have to listen nothing. I cannot see how we are to win the men of England without a fervent Evangelical Catholicism – that is, a clear exposition and insistence upon the importance of Sacraments – shot through with a burning love for the Master.

We had a most interesting meeting on Tuesday at Divisional Headquarters with the Senior Chaplain. It was the first time I had met the other chaplains of the Division and they seemed to be a most excellent crowd – thoroughly keen and as far as I could see very efficient. We started with some short prayers. Next week, at my suggestion, we are to start with a celebration of Holy Communion – the meeting now having been fixed as a weekly event.

The Senior Chaplain went through our areas with us, and we settled up everything so that there was no overlapping and that every unit however small in the Division got the opportunity of ministrations of some chaplain or other.

Then we had some points about burials and crosses made clear, in view of an early move to where such things, I fear, will be needed.

We have no fewer than four clergy in the Division who are not doing chaplains' work – two RAMC orderlies who are privates, and two officers. All four take celebrations sometimes but not much else as their COs don't encourage them to do any work outside their own regular duties, but two of them were very useful on Easter Day.

Mellish's VC[5] will do the chaplains good. His heroism and decoration have been very popular out here, and all agree he thoroughly deserved to win the coveted distinction.

Julian writes that on 7 May that he had just had a church parade for the whole battalion in commemoration of those who had fallen in the fighting round Ypres exactly a year ago:

The battalion came out of that 52 strong, so you can imagine how terribly they were cut up.

Two days later, he sends home a long screed describing the Brigade sports – in which

our battalion divided the honours with the London Scottish – this pleased me as I am chaplain to them both. . . . There were of course no prizes or awards, but there was a great deal of inter-regimental rivalry and I never saw a healthier set of men. . . . I don't believe there is a finer fighting division in the British Army than the London Territorials. True, the men represent a high standard of education when compared to other divisions – as there are still many men in the ranks who have had public school education and practically all the officers are public school or 'varsity men.

That letter of 9 May ends:

Thank goodness conscription at last – the whole British Army out here gave a sigh of relief when the news came. Every man will now have to do his bit.

* * *

By now Morris had arrived with his regiment (15 Battalion The West Yorks) almost next door, and they soon bicycled to see each other, connecting once again with much delight only two months after their Suez Canal encounter:

I can see how fond of Julian both officers and men are – he seemed to me absolutely the right man in the right place

was Morris's comment.

    Burgon (16 May) is still training with his machine-guns in the sand dunes near Le Touquet:

We have had a really splendid week here, made all the pleasanter because our CO has been laid up in hospital with a sprained leg! On top of the delights of no colonel, there is tennis and golf and a perfect polo ground at our disposal, and two boats on the shore. This I admit sounds dreadful for a soldier's life during The Great War.

Julian had been issued with a steel helmet:

I wish you could see me in it. I am told they have already saved thousands of lives since they were adopted. All front line troops have them, and the supply seems to be coming along splendidly.

He and the other chaplains had been discussing the letter sent by the Bishop of Kensington to each chaplain in the Army and Navy, asking for answers to various questions in connection with the National Mission, such as:

In the course of your ministry in the Navy or Army what have you found to be the chief difficulties and deficiencies in the religion and religious life of the men? In what direction does the Church seem to you to have been responsible for these deficiencies? Can you suggest any remedies? What have you found to be the main causes of indifference, criticisms or opposition? Can you suggest any ways in which these could be met? In view of the National Mission, what special effort would you wish to see the Church make in preparation for the men's return home?'

Some of these questions are to be discussed on Friday when we meet the Archbishop at Army Headquarters.

He is obviously excited by a visit

to a twenty-eight foot deep cellar which for six months has been used as a place of worship by RCs, C of E and Wesleyans[6]. The Wesleyans' padre had discovered its existence under a house in one of the villages where his men were billeted; apparently it could date from the times of religious persecutions in France, and was used for worship after the Revocation of the Edict of Nantes[7].

Cavalry training in the dunes near Le Touquet continues for the Royals' machine-gunners – Burgon giving his mother a graphic description of the manoeuvres they get up to:

Under real conditions there must be great satisfaction in hearing the rattle of one's guns and seeing Boches falling, even though in cold blood it could hardly be called an edifying occupation for a respectable Christian.

Julian, meanwhile, has got to the Chaplain General's Conference well behind the lines. Some 120 chaplains were present, and to his obvious disappointment

it soon became apparent, all the more so when speeches were made at the conference later, that the majority present were much after the Chaplain General's own heart. There were not more than a dozen moderate High Churchmen present. I had not realised before how successful the CG had been in appointing men of his own way of thinking. There were quite a few padres there with moustaches[8], and as they wore khaki collars they looked very much like combatant officers. The proceedings started with a short intercession service taken by Bishop Gwynne. Then the Archbishop spoke somewhat haltingly, his theme being the importance of our work and the amazing opportunity we had of influencing not only the coming generation, but the course of the world's history for the next hundred years. The service was followed by a short conference, the object of which was apparently to obtain from the chaplains useful hints in connection with the coming National Mission.

Nothing much was suggested, and I thought the Archbishop seemed disappointed, and well he might be. Someone volunteered the information that the men of our armies had learnt corporate life in the Army and had acquired a taste for it which would have to be gratified. Where was it going to be gratified? In the public house. How was the National Mission going to check this? The Archbishop pointed out that the corporate spirit was no new spirit to the Britisher, that in his friendly societies and trades unions it was already well-developed. Another suggested fewer sermons and shorter services; men who had become used to a half-hour service would never be happy at one lasting an hour and a half like our parochial matins. The Archbishop said a committee was already discussing this point, but the great difficulty here was to satisfy the liturgical scholars who objected to first this and then some other part of the service being omitted.

A short discussion followed on the best way to present the Gospel to the country, the experience of the chaplains being thought to be valuable in this connection, but here the discussion was most disappointing. Several chaplains spoke, in a rather fervid way, of the importance of assuring men that Christ was their Saviour and their Friend, ignoring the fact that what the Archbishop wanted were practical methods. One High Churchman, one of the very few such present, spoke strongly and feelingly of making the Sacraments the channel by which men were taught to approach God and by which God can approach them, and urged the importance of restoring to its right position the Lord's Own Service; and he added a point, which I heartily endorse, that in the understanding of the men there is no doubt whatever of the divine nature of that service. There is something unmistakable about it . . . we have fed the hungry with Matins and Evensong for generations, when all the time they were hungering, without knowing it fully, for the Bread of Life.

I would personally lay aside all demands for a fasting Communion and would even permit evening Communions, if only we could restore the Lord's Service to its proper position and surround it with the reverence due to it.

Studdert-Kennedy[9], who has, I believe, had some considerable success as a Base chaplain, having filled a large theatre with men every Sunday either at Rouen or Havre, spoke somewhat emotionally for a few moments, saying that what he thought the men wanted was not fewer sermons but more and more sermons, and what they did not want was weak and superficial talks, but rather deep thinking.

Julian was not much impressed with the day:

We found it, with its three and a half hours ride (in a green London bus!) over very uneven roads each way, not a little tiring; I think most of the chaplains agreed that the day was rather wasted, and the Archbishop's address quite lacking in fire or inspiration. Could we have spent longer in our conference or been given some other opportunity to meet the other chaplains for talk, we should have found the day both more profitable and enjoyed it more. I do not think the Archbishop went away with very many new ideas for the Mission.

But soon he was deep in practical work:

I was sent for to take a funeral, that of a Captain Christmas of the 3rd London Regiment, who had died twelve hours after being severely wounded in single combat with a German officer. The German officer was wounded also, and both were brought to the same Field Ambulance and died almost at the same time, and both were to be buried in the same cemetery. Two lads in the escort found the whole thing too much for them. I think they belonged to the Captain's company, but they collapsed before the end of the service.

82

We buried the nameless German officer with equal honours, and the escort marched to the graveside behind his body as they had done for the British officer.

. . . We are training very hard, so hard that Sunday is no longer a day of rest. No Church parades were possible yesterday at all. I had two early celebrations of the Holy Communion. I shall try to have one on Ascension Day. None of the senior officers in this battalion are communicants or care about such services at all, and never come to voluntary ones. They are quite oblivious to the fact that their example in this respect would mean so much to the men.

In fact, it is true to say that the average old public school officer disregards entirely, with one or two exceptions, his responsibility to his men from a spiritual point of view. He makes it his business to see that the men under his charge have enough to eat, and are warm and dry as far as possible, but he doesn't seem to imagine they also have souls.

The old public schoolboy officer is as nice and pleasant a man as you could wish to meet, has a fine sense of duty, and faces the future danger – 'going over the old sandbag' as he calls it – in a half jocular, half serious way. He secretly in his heart hopes he will be the one to get a 'Blighty' wound or if that bit of 'luck' – 'luck', mind you, it's always 'luck' – doesn't come his way, that the best thing will be that he gets through without a scratch – and if, well, if he 'stops one' in a vital place and it's all up, he's done his duty and there's bad luck to it. He feeds himself on hope, not on the mercy and grace of God. Anyhow he intends, if he can, to die like a gentleman with his face to the foe, splendid in his cheery optimism and disregard of danger. Yet how one's heart yearns that their eyes could be opened – that they could see the chariots and horses of fire, and could be more aware of the spiritual realities which surround them, and more cognisant of their own spiritual needs.

Just a few do seem to understand, and there is something about their whole bearing which in my mind places them head and shoulders above their fellow officers. It is difficult to explain, but their manner seems to be one of quietly and humbly waiting on the will of God, content to do their duty, however it comes, and leaving the future in perfect faith and trust in God's hands. This kind of character always has its effect upon the men. They are so quick to read their officer's character and understand his every whim and wish; and naturally so, seeing that his every command they must instantly obey, and for their slightest mistake it is his duty to reprove them; however young he may be, he has to act as their father and guide in everything.

There can be no doubt that things were different in the early days of the war, and that chaplains got a far better response to their appeals than they do now, just as intercession services at home were better attended in 1914 than they are now. The truth lies in the fact that just as we had become used to a state of peace, we now are rapidly becoming used to a state of war, and war with all its brutalising powers is having its effect upon all of us, lowering our spiritual capacity and weakening our spiritual sensitiveness rather than the reverse. I don't believe 90 per cent of the men out here think twice a day about what or who they will meet on the other side, if death comes their way. If the thought does occur to them, they banish it instantly, with the hope of getting through all right.

As chaplains it is not wise to dwell on this particular point at any great length – Commanding Officers often object to such a discourse as likely to undermine the morale or at least the cheerfulness of the men, and as being liable to turn their thoughts in a morbid direction – and yet our duty is to warn our men of the 'Wrath to Come' as well as of the Everlasting Love of the Father.

These are difficult problems which we have to face and our chances of saying much are limited – and the time is so short. Never have I had to tackle such difficult work. So much seems to be against you. Any padre can go about and be pleasant among officers and men. That presents no difficulty to me – and I chat up and down the lines daily with the men and in the huts and billets.

My recreation room is really successful and very popular. We take forty or fifty francs a day by selling 1d cups of tea and 1d pieces of cake. The library is made use of to the full. We have nearly 300 volumes, and over 150 are always 'out' – and yet to get down underneath to the spiritual needs of the men, to get them to awake to the great truths of Christianity, this is a work which only very few can achieve – and mind you, that is our real work. It makes me see how we chaplains – as you know with your far longer experience as a chaplain to the troops – feel the need of a living faith ourselves, the longer we work at the job – for we cannot give what we haven't got.

He had another afternoon with Morris:

I bicycled over and soon ran him to earth . . . acting in command of a company now; he has a horse, so I rode beside him on my bike as he brought some men out of working on repair to the trenches, and I then had tea with him and stayed to dinner.

A few days later they did the reverse, Morris going for a ride with a fellow subaltern to find Julian, and writing home:

We eventually spotted a smart young padre bicycling at a tremendous pace, and he turned out to be Julian. We went off together for lunch at a jolly good restaurant. Then he came back to our billets and we had tea in the company mess.

Later in the letter, Morris mentions that

whenever I am in the trenches I either send you a letter or a field service postcard.

Clare Monier-Williams writes again to the diarist about the

superb job Julian is doing: he is such a thorough sportsman in every way, and absolutely untiring in looking after the wants of officers and men.

All the brothers make proud and affectionate reference in June to their father's appointment as one of the King's Honorary Chaplains[10]:

It is an honour right enough (says Burgon), though just one hundredth of the honour you ought to have.

Burgon muses again (4 June)

on the unsatisfactoriness of my position in the cavalry. . . . When I read Morris's and Julian's letters it only makes me feel worse. There comes a time, I begin to think, when to stay in the cavalry with a temporary commission, however seriously and diligently one may work, is wrong.

Certainly his continued peace-time conditions at Le Touquet are unnatural:

parades and schemes last from 5 am to 1 o'clock. After that we are free for tennis, golf, polo or whatever is on, and in the evening there is a dinner party, concert or some other diversion. It is a strange way to be living during the greatest war the world has ever seen.

But he continues to use his mind:

I am reading your book on prayer. I think it is the best book on prayer I have read, though I think all such books have certain disadvantages – still this one is very good. I have also been reading Sorley's[11] poems this week – they are wonderful. I think the first of the two sonnets and *'Expectans Expectavi'* are really marvellous from a boy of his age. They express some of one's deepest feelings in the simplest and therefore the most moving way – I have read the book from cover to cover – and I am going to give my copy to Beach Thomas, the cultured correspondent of the Daily Mail out here – but I shall get another copy for myself.

'At last', writes the diarist, Julian's hopes have been realised (4 June):

I have just had such a splendid Sunday – I am very well and have at last gone up to the Line. Since yesterday morning, I have been at the place where we have our chapel underground – you know the name. Of houses there are scarcely any left; nearly everyone lives in cellars or dug-outs. The whole place is under shell fire pretty constantly, and the trenches run right into the village. The Huns were putting quite a lot of shrapnel over us yesterday afternoon, but no damage was done. Today I have had three packed services in our crypt.

At least I feel in touch with the real thing, and everything is differ-ent. I had over sixty communicants at one Celebration this morning. The chapel, which is cruciform in shape, can with great crowding hold 110 men; we have a beautiful little altar – lights and a Crucifix. I have got servers for every day this week, and I am celebrating the Holy Communion every morning. The same chapel was used today (1) for Roman Mass; (2) an ordinary Church of England service, shortened Matins; (3) Holy Eucharist; (4) Presbyterian Service; (5) this evening a Wesleyan Service; (6) Church of England Evensong. I took (2), (3) and (6) and had the little chapel packed with men for each service that I took. A harmonium helped the singing, and as the chapel is twenty feet under the ground, we all felt quite safe.

. . . I am sleeping in a half-cellar, i.e. half above ground and half under. It is however fairly well protected by sandbags, and its chief drawback is its dampness and the rats. I assure you I am taking and shall continue to take all due precautions myself. I am being allowed to go into the trenches whenever I please. I am the only Church of England padre up here and have a good deal to do, I am sorry to say, in the taking of funerals – the cemetery is beautifully situated. I shall be up here for ten or eleven more days from today, then we go back to rest. I am supremely happy to be actually in the real thing at last. The men are wonderfully responsive. I wouldn't have missed this experience for the world. It is a privilege to be allowed to share their dangers.

A few days later, things are quieter; his crypt chapel services continue to be well attended; he has his first case of shell-shock to cope with, helping 'one poor fellow into the dressing station as he cried like a baby and quite unable to stop'; the mud is terrible, but

I am really enjoying life under somewhat difficult conditions.

Julian and Morris write a joint letter on 16 June

in a little mud-daubed out-house where we are presently going to dine together. . . . We try to see all we can of each other while we happen to be close. There is so much in his mind that is interesting and important but we may not speak about. You must not worry, dear ones, if there are no letters from us for several days at a time. It does not mean that we are in any way in distress or wounded. . . . I don't think I have ever seen Morris look better; he has responsible work and seems to be both efficient and capable; I hope his captaincy comes through quickly. . . . Later. . . . We have had dinner – an excellent dinner – soup, Yorkshire pudding as a separate course, meat and vegetables, plum pudding, egg savoury, all cooked on a brazier or a rotten little French stove, and excellently served by Morris's mess servants.

Julian finishes:

I do not know if we shall be able to meet again for some time. These short meetings have been very delightful and will be worth recalling in after years.

Burgon had not yet got over to see them. Writing the same day as Julian and Morris (16 June) he tells the diarist all about their continued calm existence in billets near the coast:

The other day a private soldier in the 3rd Dragoon Guards was formally married to a French girl at Offra – she lived in his billet, or rather in the

87

farm to which belonged the barn where he slept. I wonder how many of these genuine marriages there have been since the British soldiery has been in this country – not very many I should think . . .

A day or two ago I went into an estaminet to get a cup of coffee and asked the *propriétaire* what he thought of Lord Kitchener's death. 'Who is Lord Kitchener?', he said, 'and when and how did he die[12]?'.

June 16, Friday, I continue this today, and what a peaceful scene is before me as I sit writing to you both. This old house dating from the 17th century stands on a slope and commands the greater part of the village. My room, which is upstairs, has two large dormer windows. I have placed my table before one of these, and as I write there come floating up all the noises of a village which has recently been invaded by a squadron of 220 men and 300 horses! Below me is the curé's garden – an impression of roses, pear trees, white carnations, cabbages and peas – and there is the curé himself, in old cap and cassock, working among his flowers and vegetables. Beyond that a wooden bridge crosses the stream where some of our men are washing their limbers amid much laughter and singing – (what eternal washing and cleaning there is in the Army, and tomorrow morning everything will be dirty once more and the same round will begin in the afternoon). On the further side of the bridge is a forge where a string of our horses are being shod by the farriers.

How many war tragedies do the roofs of this village cover? Well, here we are living peacefully enough and my thoughts often wander to Julian and Morris. 'Oo are them, Bill?' said one Tommy to another as a squadron of cavalry came clattering down the cobbled tortuous streets of a French country town. 'Them?' said Bill. 'Why them be the cavalry'. 'Cavalry?' was the answer. 'Why I didn't know as 'ow they knew there was a war on'.

In a long diary letter, Julian comments on a baptism which clearly meant much to him, in the crypt chapel twenty-eight feet deep:

When we are out of the trenches this lad will come to me again for further instruction on Baptism and preparation for Confirmation. He is a nineteen-year old London Scottish boy. . . . I heard confessions this morning, and had the usual daily celebration later; in the afternoon I paid my first visit to the front-line trenches. . . . I make a point of wearing my white collar (celluloid) all the time I am up in the line, except when actually in the front line trench, so that wounded and others would recognise me at once . . .

Your letters make an accurate surmise and Burgon has, I understand, tumbled to what is in the wind. More I may not say. We cannot help feeling it is now or never. You will go, will you not, to the early celebration next Sunday? I shall like to think of you being there.

The diarist makes a poignant entry:

I heard yesterday of the considerate way in which the French announce to the relatives the death of a soldier:

> 'Etant d'avis de décès envoyé
> par le Ministère de la Guerre Orleans
> le 1 Avril, 1916
> Les membres du Conseil d'Administration centrale . . . à
> Monsieur le Maire de . . .
> Nous avons l'honneur de vous prier de vouloir bien avec tous
> les ménagements nécessaires en la circonstance, prévenir . . .
> que le sergent . . . né a . . . fils de . . .
> EST TOMBÉ GLORIEUSEMENT
> POUR LA PATRIE
> Tué à l'ennemi le . . . au
> Mort pour la France
> Inhumé . . .
> Nous vous serions tres obligés de presenter à la famille
> les condoléances de Monsieur le Ministre de la Guerre
> ainsi que les notres.
> (Signé) (Le President du Conseil d'Administration)
> (Le Chef du Bureau Special du Comptabilité)

But humour is never far from the surface in this redoubtable mother of five servicemen. The following letter to the War Office from a soldier's dependant clearly tickled her:

Respected Sir, Dear Sir,
Though I take this libetty as it leaves me at present I beg to ask if you will kindly be kind enough to let me know where is my husbin though he is not my legible husbin has he has a wife though he says she is ded but I dont thing he nos for sure but we are not marryd though I am getting my allotment reglr which is no fault of Mr Loy George who would stop it if he could and Mr Mrkenna but if you know wre he is as he is belong to the Naval Fling Corp for ever since hev joined in the January when he was sacked for talking back at his bos which was a woman at the Laundry where he worked. I have not had any money from him since he joined though he told Mr Harris what lives on the ground floor

89

that he is a pretty ossifer for six shillings a week and lots of under closin for the cold wether and I have Three children whats is bein the father of them though he says it was my fault. Hoping you will write to me soon and you are quite well as it leaves me at present I must now close hoping you are well.

The diarist here puts in a paragraph from her daughter-in-law Kitty. Lady Bradford[13], then a Lady-in-Waiting to the Queen, had just written to her with:

an interesting picture of the Court just now: 'You ask about Windsor. 'Tis so difficult to write of it – it was very quiet and nice, except for visits to Hospitals etc. and a wonderful Anzac Service in Westminster Abbey -. . . the poor king was still very lame and very sad at heart! It was their first holiday for seven months and they made the most of it. We spent some charming afternoons on Virginia Water, HM at the tiller and picknicked in the boat house. All the Princes were there at one time or another. Princess Mary is a charming girl. The Prince of Wales greatly enjoyed a few days there between Italy and back to France. He told me he wished he had died before this war – he had lost most of his great friends and 'seen such horrors', but he is winning golden opinions 'out there' and doing so well. My Queen was more charming than ever – always the joy and life of the Court and not allowing anyone to be 'too sad'.

Preparations for Haig's[14] great offensive on the Somme, which would cost tens of thousands of British, French and German lives, were now well advanced. As the diary shows, the brothers were all keenly aware that something momentous was about to happen. The diarist's entry for Sunday, 25 June reflects this all too clearly:

Sunday, 25 June. Our great bombardment began yesterday. We hear from a staff officer that 144 batteries (not single pieces but batteries) of the newest guns have just been shipped in a few days to our troops in France from England. There is no doubt that such a bombardment has never been seen before, and our artillery must be awe-inspiring.

As if to corroborate that things are moving, Burgon writes a final letter from his 'peace-time' billets:

This is the last letter I shall write to you from here. I hope to be not far off, below if anything, J. and M. soon. I am awfully bucked to hear that the date of Ralph's wedding is fixed for 18 July. I wish to goodness I could get back for it, but I fear it is quite out of the question just now.

Julian bears out the rising tension (23 June):

I may not speak of future plans, but if Ralph is married on 17 July, I hope it would be possible by then to get leave, if all is well, but it is difficult to foresee where we shall be. You will understand.

Their mother does indeed:

Ralph's wedding is now definitely fixed for 18 July. We greatly fear that the present offensive will prevent either of his brothers at the Front getting to it.

The chaplains had been told to 'be ready for anything'. The services on 25 June in barns or the open air were non-stop from 7 am. The old French woman, who owned the barn they used, said to Julian after the day was over:

What men! What splendid men; what a religion yours is, and how they do sing. I see that you too love the Mass. It has done my heart good to see such devotion, such reverence, such hearty worship!

One short but heartfelt service

was somewhat interrupted during my address by five enemy aeroplanes which came over and dropped bombs in a neighbouring field. I wanted the men to sit on the grass for the address but the colonel, who was standing ten yards in front, whispered to me that he could have no movement of any kind made by the men, so I proceeded with my address, the men remaining standing. It is always hard to talk to a standing congregation; and when the air is rent with the sound of exploding bombs at no very great distance, it is not easy to keep the men's attention. But I caught them for a moment at the end, and more so perhaps during the Blessing, having previously explained that I as God's minister was about to bless them in His Name and ask for His protection for them in 'the great endeavour'.

The German planes had moved off by the time that we had sung 'God save the King', and so the battalion was able to march off the quite open space where the parade was held without the fear of being detected. An aeroplane can never see troops if the latter remain absolutely stationary. If they move, they can be spotted at once. Every man there knew that it might well be his last service on this earth, and although the note struck was one of 'Joy', joy in self-sacrifice, joy in showing forth love which Christ Himself showed on the Cross, a joy in which we are called upon to join with Him, that 'Love casting out fear' might be ours, yet there was no mistaking the solemnity of the occasion.

From the distance, the sound of guns is now insistent and becoming stronger, and is becoming louder as the hours go on. Our next service was Evensong at 7 pm. This was attended by the Brigadier who came over specially from some little distance. I had had three-quarters of an hour's talk with him the day before, having been asked into tea at HQ. He took me out into the garden after tea, and up and down an avenue of apple trees in the great kitchen garden of the old château we strolled discussing many problems – not excluding the religious question of what it meant to face death and of what we could know of the 'Hereafter', and of what should be our attitude of mind and soul when going into battle. Selflessness was his idea and that if one could put self entirely on one side, nothing else matters. Obviously his ideal was to do all he could for the men and officers under his command and not worry about himself. Anyhow he is indefatigable, and when the Brigade has been in the line he has constantly visited the trenches.

The little church was again overflowing with men for Evensong, and we had a good number of officers as well. After the last service two of us were busy for some time hearing confessions, and so ended a Sunday which will always be memorable. From the four battalions there were over four hundred communicants during the day, and a reverence and heartiness in the services of which there could be absolutely no mistake. At least these men have tried to prepare themselves to meet their God. I would indeed that we could touch that many others who as yet are quite indifferent. Probably nearly every one of them is baptized – they also belong to the Fold, but the Church means nothing to them. If only they could gain some faint conception of the joy of such services as we had yesterday, how they would throng to them. Each battalion should have of course its own C of E chaplain. He would find plenty to do.

So many of these men, or rather I should say the vast majority of these men, who come to these voluntary services and to whom the Eucharist means so much come from well-worked London parishes where the full Catholic Faith is taught and practised. There is nothing priggish or weak or sentimental in these lads coming up to make their communion or making their confession on the eve of battle, enabling us priests to see how hard it is for a Christian boy to keep himself undefiled in the rough and tumble of active service conditions. How often it drives us to our own knees to discover what a struggle so many of them are having to say their prayers openly in the huts and billets. Many of them have won finer victories in this way than the whole British Army can ever hope to win against the Huns. Thank God we priests can give them, through the mercy of God, some help and encouragement when they come to us for confession. The fine teaching of so many London parishes always tells, and it would be good if many a hard-worked London priest could hear of the splendid fight the lads are putting up for their Master. So we go on. What next Sunday will be like or where we shall be, God alone knows, but we have lived. God is with us, and as our epistle taught us, 'Perfect love casteth out fear'.

On 1 July, the offensive on the Somme opened, with 19 British divisions committed. By nightfall, no less than 57,000 British troops had become casualties − a figure that was to rise to 80,000 by 17 July. The impact upon the Nation was devastating, yet that battle was to prove the turning point of the war.

On 2 July, after going to the 9 am celebration with their youngest son Ralph, the diarist says: 'We know that our three sons in France are all in this attack.'

But Burgon's regiment had in fact moved on the First of July itself. He writes on 4 July, three days after the battle:

At present, as you can imagine, I cannot get over to see either Julian or Morris, but I am thinking a very great deal of them, as I know you are. One day you shall have a long letter of all our experiences during this time. At any rate, you can be perfectly happy long before the date of Ralph's wedding. . . . I have had a very strenuous three days, getting to bed each night about 3.30 am. This must go now. Au revoir, my dear father, and believe, as I somehow think you know, that I am your very loving son.

Julian had written on 26 June:

I write just a few words to tell you how happy I am in being able to be in this Great Effort. It will of course be a difficult time for all of us. The heavy shelling has brought continuous rain, and we can expect a good deal of physical discomfort, but this I do not mind in the least. I only hope and pray that I may be able to be of some use and be able to 'play the man'. My position will be with the Advanced Dressing Station, and

I am to be allowed to move forward at my own discretion to the regimental aid post.

My hope is to be able to help with the wounded and dying. I shall never forget the happiness of this week's stay in rest billets. Our little barn church has been a centre of Christian worship for those who have cared to come. We have had really wonderful services. I do indeed wish I could do more for these men. I feel I might have done so much more to aid them spiritually but for my own lack of faith.

I am looking forward to a happy week of 'leave' in July when we may, please God, have the opportunity of talking over my varied experiences in this campaign. I won't however lose this opportunity of telling you what I know you already know but which delights me to write, of how much I feel I owe you for the past – for example, precept, care, education and a thousand other things which I cannot enumerate here. I don't believe a fellow ever had such parents, and I'm not much of a hand at showing gratitude, but I feel it from the depths of my heart. Au revoir.

'The days drag heavily', writes the diarist, *'as we are so full of anxiety. This morning we had the great cheer of the following joint letter from all three brothers, who had their long-hoped-for meeting on St Peter's Day, 29 June. Julian writes:*

My dear Father and Mother,

I begin the letter because I'm the eldest. I am also a Captain although temporary and honorary, while Burgon and Morris at present can only manage three stars between them. From this you will see the really amazing fact that the long-promised meeting between us three brothers has actually taken place. Burgon came over from a place about 18 K. away, and Morris sent an orderly who found me and I bicycled over and we have just spent the afternoon together. I need hardly say we have had a delightful time – a full account will follow tomorrow, but today there is only time for this short line of love from us three. We are all splendidly well, in fact we have just commented on this and agreed we never felt better in our lives. We have agreed to try to meet again in a fortnight's time as Burgon has come down into this area.

Much love from all. At last we have pulled off a meeting. You shall have a long letter one day about the interesting times we are living through.

Julian

Burgon is just off – and I am going to ride part of the way back with him. It has been a splendid day. Best love

Morris

But on 5 July (Julian's birthday) the diarist briefly records:

Last night at 8.30 we received the following telegram from the War Office:

'Regret to inform you your son Lieut SM Bickersteth was killed in action on Saturday, July 1st. War Council expresses its regret'.

I cannot say much about this in the Diary, but we were in a way prepared for it. It is a joy to think that the three brothers had that happy meeting two days before Morris went into action.

Morris's letter describing the meeting, his last letter ever, was dated 29 June, and reached his parents on 5 July, the morning after they had heard of his death four days earlier:

Today there has taken place here the most historic meeting the family has ever had. I was sitting in my Coy. Headquarters about 9.45 am when who should walk in but Burgon.

It was an absolute surprise – and the most delightful one I have had for many a long day. I had nothing to do until 11 o'clock when I had to attend an officers' pow-wow which lasted an hour. So I gave him some breakfast and we talked hard – he telling me lots of news I particularly wanted to hear – and of course I giving him all my information. All this in after-days will be related to you – but unfortunately it is not possible now. We first decided to ride over in the afternoon to see Julian, but we had an order about half past ten saying the GOC of the Division would inspect the Battalion at 3 o'clock, and that meant of course that I had to stop here. So I sent an orderly on a bicycle over to where I thought Julian was. He is a capable fellow and brought Julian straight back here, about 2 o'clock.

The first thing we did was to laugh for about five minutes as it was so extraordinary all of us meeting together. We all three looked very well and were in good spirits. Well, I had to go off for this parade and so they followed at a distance and saw the whole thing. Of course, the entire battalion was on parade, and so they could not have had a better opportunity of seeing us. The GOC addressed us, and I think the turnout was quite smart. When the parade was over Julian and Burgon caught the CO as he was marching off, and he asked them in to tea in the HQ mess where I joined them a few minutes later. We left there about 4.15 and had twenty minutes' quiet talk together, when we wrote that short note to you. Then about half past four we all three rode out together. Julian on his bicycle, Burgon and I on our horses, followed by his groom on a horse behind. Julian came about half a mile with us and then turned back, and I rode on with Burgon for about seven or eight kilometres.

June 30th, Friday. I finish this today as I had not time last night, and I fear I must not add much more now. Yesterday was a great success. I never have enjoyed a meeting more, and it has bucked me up tremendously. It is extraordinary to think that if Ralph had been with his regiment we all four should have met. You will have seen from the papers, so there is no harm my mentioning it, that there has been a heavy bombardment all along our front for the last few days, and the Hun now knows what our fellows had to suffer at the beginning of the war.

I went to the Early Service last Sunday at the YMCA and I thought of you all, you are just the most perfect parents in the world and I knew you would be thinking of me too. Please thank Ninny for her letter; it is awfully good of her always to write. I wrote to Ralph a day or two ago, to tell him how awfully glad I am about his wedding and to congratulate him from the bottom of my heart. Whatever happens and wherever I am, I know I shall be thinking of him on 18 July, and shall be rejoicing in his joy.

The diarist adds: We also received the following from Julian dated 30 June:

Our meeting yesterday of the three brothers was really historical, and although we had only an hour or two altogether it was splendid, and put us all three into excellent humour.

The diarist carries bravely on:

6 July, Leeds. To our great joy we had telegrams saying that Geoffrey, Monier, Kitty and Ralph were all coming home to us, and it has been a great comfort having them. Monier also brought us a letter which Morris had given him in case he was killed. Geoffrey tells us that so far we have had 50,000 casualties in our Army – ten per cent of the total due to our own Artillery – not the latter's fault, but the men's, who will not advance according to programme. They go ahead where they can, instead of by their watches. However, there is an enormous number only slightly wounded. It is said that Haig expects to have half a million casualties when he has carried out his plan.

Things have started very well; the Germans are horribly nervous.

The 15th West Yorks bore their full share of the huge losses; another Leeds mother, whose boy got a 'blighty' wound that day (i.e. came quickly back to England), told the diarist that when the roll call was sounded after the battle, only one officer and fifty-two men answered it. Burgon's first comment on the battle, came on 7 July:

The papers have now told you about the offensive between Hébuterne and Fricourt, so there can be no harm in mentioning it. Morris attacked at Serre, Julian at Gommecourt – I have had absolutely no news of them, nor do I expect to have for some days. We are further south – I will not say exactly where – so far we have taken no active part, though yesterday afternoon I had one of the most wonderful experiences of my life. From some commanding ground I watched the attack on La Boisselle, and the bombardment of Thiepval. The whole thing was an open panorama in front of one, as clear as an old-fashioned battle picture. We watched the waves of infantry advancing. Never have I seen such a sight – villages a mere heap of bricks surmounted by a sheet of smoke and flames.

I am very fit, and only hope Julian and Morris are too.

'All yesterday', *writes the diarist,* 'we were so wondering how our darling son was killed and hoping he had not suffered long hours before he died, so that this morning we were very thankful to God for the following letter from Major Hartley in temporary command of the 15th West Yorks. It is dated 3 July, 1916:

I am deeply sorry to have to inform you of the death of your son who was killed (instantly) yesterday whilst gallantly leading 'B' Coy. to the attack. Though I have only recently joined the battalion, I quickly realised how he had endeared himself to everyone.

By the same post Father heard from Mr Chappell, the chaplain to the battalion:

July 1st. I have tried to find some good news of your son but I can only find the worst. He is missing. I am making all enquiries but I have not much hope. God help you. You must prepare Leeds for splendid and heroic news, but oh so terribly sad. There is no time to write more.

July 2nd. I thought I had better send you another line as you will be in suspense, but it is only to say that still no news is forthcoming of Morris. More men have come in, and say they saw him fall. His servant looked at him after he had fallen and felt sure he was killed.

July 3rd. Now there is no doubt whatever, Morris is killed. I saw his brother this afternoon and gave him all particulars. He will write these. May God strengthen and comfort you. I must confess to a feeling of despair. I feel broken-hearted. The brave men I knew and loved. It is a supreme test to our faith. I will write you a summary of the fight some day, but now I am too tired to think. It seems hard, terribly hard, and I pray to God to give me light.

Tell Mrs Bickersteth I am praying for her.

Leeds people must know that every man was a hero.

The diarist writes: We have at last received the following letter from our dear Julian who, although absolutely worn out himself, went all the way down to Serre to get news of Morris:

The news will have reached you of our darling Morris and of his splendid death. I have secured full and complete particulars from a lad who was by his side at the last, and these I will write here and now. I have much to record of these last three terrible days, but I want to tell you first all I could find out about our darling Morris. From Friday night till Monday afternoon, with only a break of an hour or two's sleep, I was hard at it. Of that I will tell you later, but I had no opportunity of getting down to the 31st Divisional area till yesterday afternoon, Monday, July 3rd. Of the three Church of England padres in Hébuterne, where I was all the time of the battle for Gommecourt, one was wounded, so Palmer and myself were not sorry to be relieved on Monday afternoon, and after a meal I went over to a neighbouring village to see all that was left of our own battalion, The Rangers. They came out of the battle only sixty or seventy strong and four officers. You know what that means, and they got only twenty hours rest and were put into the line again – those that were left.

Having seen them and discovered who was still alive, I got a pass and rode on my bicycle straight south to the village where the 15th WY have been all the time, with my heart full of apprehension, news of the terrible loss of life further south having reached us. I entered the village and seeing a military policeman at the cross-roads, stopped and asked him about the 15th, but his information was vague, except that they had terrible casualties. I went on and passed two more 15th WY men and they told me that only about fifty men and no officers got out of the attack.

About Morris they were not certain, but they [had] both heard he was dead. With my heart sick within me, I pushed on to the Quartermaster's store and there I found the Transport Officer and the Quartermaster of Morris's battalion; they both looked haggard and tired, and on my question I read in their eyes the news before they spoke. They handed me the list of officers killed and wounded. Besides our dear Morris, Capt. Neil Whittaker, Maude, Booth, Lintott, Saunders and Everett were known to be dead, whereas Vouse, Willey, James and Humphreys were missing – every other officer was wounded, heroes every one!

Neither officer could give me any details, but they sent me to find a Sgt who they thought was near Morris when he fell – meanwhile they kindly took me round to their mess and gave me some food. There I met Chappell, the chaplain, almost broken-hearted over the terrible losses of the battalions. After dinner, an orderly came in and said that a private was there who could tell me of how dear Morris died. I went out at once and found a handsome boy of eighteen, who immediately gave me all the details I so badly wanted to know. He nearly broke down several times, poor boy. He was slightly wounded and had been buried alive, but he had got out and he was the last man Morris spoke to. His name is Private Bateson, No. 1218 and his home address North Street, Fryston, Castleford, Yorks. He told me that he knew Morris from the first, having been in his original platoon in 'B' Company before Morris was made Company Commander. After a terrible bombardment when the 15th lost many men, the moment came for the attack, 7.30 a.m. Saturday morning, 1 July. It was a lovely day and the sun was brilliant. Morris had been walking up and down his front line encouraging his men, and sent the first wave over punctually to the second. He himself as Officer Commanding the Company was to go with the 8th wave. The first wave reached a slight rise ten to fifteen yards from our front line trench and disappeared at that little rise. The next wave followed and the next and so on, but alas! the German lines were full of Germans with machine-guns, and the German artillery was plastering no man's land, which lay between the two lines, with shrapnel. Far then from taking the first three German trenches which had been the objective of the 15th, the brave lads never reached, or only very, very few of them, the 1st German trench; and all the time Morris was walking up and down the trench, sending off each wave with a cheery word and a look of encouragement.

The lads knew well enough what they were going out to, but no one wavered, no one faltered and at last the time came for Morris to go out himself with the eighth and last wave.

'Come on, lads,' he cried, 'Here's to a short life and a gay one', and responding to his heroic cheerfulness and splendid example, that last wave of heroes leapt out of the trench to face the worst. After going ten yards, they found the remainder of 7 and 6 platoons – only a few of whom were left alive – lying just behind the rising ground, and the three platoons were mixed up together for a few minutes. Morris apparently gave the order to lie down for a moment to try and disentangle the living from the dead, although there were very few of the former and here it was that the lad Bateson crawled to his side to obtain permission to go back as he was wounded. Morris, in spite of the turmoil and terrible fire, coolly wrote him out a chit, signed it and told him to get back as best he could. (A 'chit' is necessary in the case of a very slightly wounded man; otherwise he has to stay with his unit.)

Directly after Morris handed the piece of paper to the boy, he looked round to see if there was any support from the trenches behind and at that moment a shrapnel bullet struck him in the back of the head; a second later another bullet passed right through his head, coming out through his forehead. He just rolled over without a word or a sound and Bateson was able to see that he was quite dead, killed instantly. Bateson was on his left, and as dear Morris rolled over, he rolled to within two feet of him, so he was able to verify the fact that the end had come. Bateson did not leave his side until five minutes after he was struck, and he never moved or breathed again.

This excellent lad who had told me his story so simply and bravely, went on to say that seeing he couldn't do any more for his officer, he let the sergeant know that Morris had been knocked out, and so the sergeant took command and then, how he doesn't know, he managed to get back into our trench.

Immediately afterwards, a shell fell on the parapet and blew it in and he was buried, but fortunately he was dug out in time and though terribly shaken and un-nerved, he managed to get back to the Dressing Station. What was left of the battalion got back to Monk trench, a hundred yards behind our first line trench from which the attack was started, finding it absolutely impossible to hold our old front line, and that is how the situation is at present. You will see then, dear ones, that it is quite impossible to get the body back. It may be possible after the battle has quieted down to recover bodies under an armistice. I shall go over again and see what can be done, but I don't worry about that so much and you mustn't either, dearest ones, for 'He shall change our vile body that we may be like unto His glorious body'; and I never felt so strong in my faith that the dear lad isn't dead but lives. I can't write much about his wonderful courage and splendid character, the tears blind me, but I never felt so sure in all my life that God has taken to Himself one of the very best men that ever walked this earth, and we must not sorrow for his sake. It must be so wonderful to pass on into the Presence of the Son of God, and our darling was such a 'white' man, one of the purest and best that ever lived, he must be happy near to the All-Pure One.

How his men of the 15th loved him! There was no mistaking that. They loved him because they respected his noble characteristics; they loved him for himself.

We may indeed be proud of him, and we know, don't we, darling ones, that he is happy now; and it is such a cause for thankfulness to God that he didn't suffer at all and that he passed away at once. His grave is all the world, and his memory is ours to cherish for all time, and he isn't far from us. You will have, I know, a Requiem Holy Communion. I wish I could be there, but I shall be taking several here, and will thank God at one of these for his sacrifice.

I must try to get home as soon as possible. I hardly care to write about my own experiences during the battle, my heart and mind is too full of our dear one, but you will want to know, and I came through without a scratch although constantly under fire for 72 hours.

My dear, dear love to you both. May God bless you.[15]

Julian writes at length to his eldest brother Monier, and vouchsafes a brief paragraph about his own experiences:

I have seen sights and heard sounds the last few days which will live with me to my dying day, and filled me with an agony of sympathy for those suffering indescribable things. I have identified over seventy bodies, some of them scarcely identifiable and have seen men wounded beyond recovery; I have been surrounded for three days with nothing but blood, blood, blood. Yet rising out of this sea of misery and pain, human nature, the spirit of man, has won the day. His is an immortal soul. The courage, self-sacrifice and endurance of countless numbers of these men will be an inspiration to me for all time, though I may never blot out from my eyes the hideous realities of these dreadful days. I seemed to have packed into them the experiences of a whole life-time.

I never realised war could be half so devilish as it is in its worst stages, and yet men do rise superior to the worst agony. To have lived among such heroes is worth everything.

It is good that I was able to see so much of dear Morris during the last few weeks – our visits to each other have always been short but full of happiness to each of us, and our last meeting was just splendid. I came away feeling quite happy about the dear boy. If there ever was a man ready to go into the Presence of his Maker, it was he. He knew he had to face death, and spoke with me quite quietly and simply about it. His only fear was, 'would he lead his men straight?' That he did so in moments of intense anxiety and positive panic, I have definite evidence from several who saw him until he himself was killed. We may well be proud of his splendid courage. I know he felt he might never get out of it alive, and he was very anxious to see me before he went into battle. Fortunately I was able to see him twice after his note, sent by a trusty runner, asking me to go over, and we discussed things together quietly. He had absolute faith in God, and he told me that life after death must be very wonderful and happy for those who tried to do their duty. Nothing struck me more than the obvious influence he had over his own men. They spoke of him as if they loved him and respected him, and they would do just anything for him. He was utterly without all self-satisfaction, and yet none of us brothers ever touched his success.

The diarist next enters this:

Yorkshire Post 11 July, 1916

THE 'LEEDS PALS' LOSSES
Letter from Col. Taylor[16]

To the Editor of The Yorkshire Post
Sir, As I am still in hospital, and consequently some time must elapse before I am able to obtain all the addresses of the relatives of the officers and soldiers of the 15th Battalion West Yorkshire Regiment who have recently fallen in action in France, I would ask you to grant me a little space to make known personally to all those relatives the deep sympathy I feel for them in the irreparable losses they have sustained.

For myself, I mourn the loss of tried comrades and dear friends, men with whom I have been closely associated, day and night, in sunshine and storm, for the past fourteen months. But with my sorrow is mingled an immense pride, a great gladness, as I hear from all sources of the magnificent bearing and heroic conduct of our dear lads, who have cheerfully given their lives for their King and Country. The tidings of their gallant conduct and courageous deeds causes me no surprise, as I well knew how splendidly they would stand the test when the supreme call was made upon them.

To those who are left behind to mourn their losses, may God grant consolation in the sure knowledge of their dear ones' valiant death. For the wounded I pray earnestly for a speedy return to health and strength. For myself my only wish is that I had been able to be with the Battalion in their great and glorious attack.

Until I return to France my postal address will be 94, Piccadilly, London W., and I shall be glad to hear from all members of the 15th West Yorkshire Regiment, or their relatives, to whom I can be of comfort or assistance in any way. Yours, etc.,

> STUART C. TAYLOR, Lieut. Colonel
> 15th Battalion West Yorkshire Regiment.
> H.M. Queen Alexandra's Hospital for Officers
> Millbank, July 9, 1916

Five days after the battle Julian writes again to his parents:

My own darling parents, My heart and mind are still full of dear Morris and his splendid end, and I can hardly care to write about myself at all, but I must give you a brief account of how I got through those terrible days of the battle. You now know that the attack was delayed for 48 hours unexpectedly. This enabled us three brothers to meet, a meeting we had long planned. We all three knew of course it might be our last meeting on this earth, as we knew full well the difficulty and dangers of the tasks that lay ahead. But we did not talk of this much. We had only two and a half hours together, most of which time was taken up by an inspection of the famous 15th WY, now alas so terribly shattered. The General of the division spoke encouraging words to them, and as it turned out afterwards was far too optimistic as regards the difficulties of the task allotted to these heroes. It was a great sight to see this battalion on parade; they were so steady and so smart. No wonder they were known as the smartest battalion in the division. No wonder their General was proud of them. Morris, dear boy, stood at the head of his company, and Burgon and I crept up close behind to see where he stood and what the General had to say. We heard Morris give the sharp words of command to his company, and then when the little ceremony was over, having been concluded by the presentation of a Military Cross Ribbon by the General to an officer, since killed, Burgon and I stood and watched the battalion march away with Morris leading them all. Major Neill kindly asked us all three to tea, and then we had half an hour together before Burgon had to go. Morris ordered his horse and he rode some distance with Burgon. I went too on my bicycle about half a mile to rising ground above the village, where we could see the German lines clearly and counted no fewer than fourteen observation balloons. Here we stopped for a moment and looked at the scene of the coming battle. The two brothers on horseback looked so upright, so manifestly at ease on their horses and so smart. We planned to meet again in a fortnight's time and I shook each brother by the hand, and with a cheery 'good luck, old boy' each to each, they two went on and I returned to my village on my bicycle. The parting was hard, but I remember feeling so absolutely happy about them both.

I really can't believe that darling Morris has gone. You know how reticent he always was about himself – he was one of the most unselfish of people. He was always thinking of others. His men loved him. He didn't speak much to me of his feelings and forebodings, I don't think he had any of the latter, except the fear that he wasn't sufficiently competent to lead his men. You have heard in a previous letter how magnificently he did this. He spoke quite calmly about the possibility of death, and he knew as we all three did that it had to be faced. Not one of us could pretend that we did so without fear, but I am sure in Morris's case he was thinking more of you than of himself. He said to me, 'I have purposely put little about what we are expecting to do or rather to face into my letters. I don't want to add to their anxieties at home'. But I know he was glad to have the opportunity of talking with and seeing us both. We didn't discuss very much – there wasn't time. We all three were so happy about Ralph's happiness, and we discussed the military situation and where each of us was expecting to be in the attack. We did agree, Morris and I, on a previous occasion that death must be very wonderful and not a thing to be feared in itself at all.

The next day, 30 June, we were all busy making final preparations during the morning. It was a difficult day. Cheerfulness was forced, but never absent. The village we were in was not shelled, though the noise of bombardment was terrific. At 8 pm we started, that is my battalion and the London Scottish, platoon by platoon across the fields towards the famous village where we had been so often before, the home of the underground chapel, and already the spot where many a brave lad had laid down his life. There was something heroic even in this quiet preparation and starting off.

I wandered around the platoons and tried to raise a laugh among the men, who always responded and to all appearances were very cheerful. Every now and then a man would come up to me and hand me a letter or some valuables with instructions for them to be sent to relatives in case of their death.

Then we started out. I joined Major Lindsay, who has been such a help to me in my Church of England work in the London Scottish. The Major and I talked of many things, of the coming battle mostly and how it would go. He spoke of his wife and child and told me of the joy he had in his little boy's faith and of the wonder of his childish prayers. He lay bare to me something of the intense happiness of his home life, and went on to say how confident he felt he would come through safely. 'The faith of my little boy is so real. He prays every night for my safety. God could not disappoint a faith like that'. We parted at the entrance to the famous village. I never saw him again. He was shot dead in the advance the next morning.

Fortunately we got our two battalions into the next village without casualties. They both passed up into the trenches to their special assembly posts to wait until the time came the next morning to attack. I found Crisford[17], and he and I deposited our few belongings in a damp little cellar, which we were expecting to retain for our use for the night at least, intending to get some sleep if the incessant roar of the guns would allow it. Darkness had now come and we were just preparing to get a 'primus' stove going when the village itself began to be heavily shelled. Suddenly down the steps of our cellar came 10 or 20 men seeking shelter from the shells.

There was very little room and most of us had to stand up. The men brought with them bags of bombs, already detonated and ready for use. These with characteristic coolness they dumped anywhere on the ground. They proved to be all London boys from one of our Fusilier Battalions and were such a cheery crowd, especially one typical East End lad, who stood next to me and with whom I had quite a long talk. I saw him next day as he was being carried into an advanced dressing station grievously wounded in three places, and he called out to me cheerily, 'Is that you, padre? Do you remember me? I was talking to you last night in the cellar'. And I had time just to press his hand and say a few words before he was hurried off into a waiting motor ambulance. 'Ships that pass in the night' indeed, and yet a word here and a word there, who can doubt their value?

After a time, the severe local shelling decreased somewhat, and none having fallen on our cellar, I left my kit in charge of my servant and, in company with Crisford, sallied out to the advanced dressing station. Here in the officers' quarters we found three doctors playing 'poker', who greeted us warmly and offered us drinks and smokes. From them we got further details of plans of how the medical authorities intended to deal with the large number of wounded expected, and we studied carefully the final plan of the trenches and the whereabouts of the trench medical aid-posts where the various battalion doctors were to be accommodated in dug-outs to deal with cases on the spot. These aid-posts we were to be allowed to visit at our own discretion; the wounded were coming in to the advanced dressing station pretty steadily now, but Crisford and I decided to snatch a few hours' sleep, if possible, before the great rush came.

Another chaplain was there, Palmer, and we three were the three chaplains, all Church of England, specially selected to be there. There was a kind of wire bedstead, simply hen-coop wire stretched over wooden uprights. We had about two hours' sleep and at 4 am got up. The noise of the guns had increased rather than decreased; it was already light; Crisford and I found the wounded already coming in quickly. The stretcher bearers of the RAMC[18] had their hands full, and were bringing in 'lying cases' every few minutes.

These lads were laid outside the ADS[19] on their stretchers and had to wait their turn. Downstairs in the two dug-outs, the doctors were working hard, but could not keep pace with the numbers. They began to arrive in ever increasing numbers, staggering along the main village street or being carried on stretchers by faithful stretcher bearers. Never was nobler work done that day than by those who went up to the trenches to bring down wounded. It soon became quite impossible for the doctors to dress the wounds at all. All we could do was to see that the bleeding had ceased. We managed to bring cars up to outside the ADS itself. Each car would take four lying cases and four sitting down, or eleven sitting cases. We put on all the lying or stretcher cases first of course. I was being given different jobs to do by the doctor in charge, first to get away the walking cases, then to superintend the loading of cars, then to see that the worst cases had 'Oxo' or hot tea to prevent collapse, then to clear out a couple of dug-outs which in the rush had been filled with wounded and being rather out of the way ran the risk of being neglected, being out of sight. There were of course some terrible cases of wounded, and not a few died before or as they reached us, but all through I was struck by the fact that those worst wounded seemed often to feel less pain than those who had slighter wounds. The shock of a shattered limb seemed to destroy the nerves in that part of the body. One lad said to me, 'Oh my leg is so stiff, sir', and the boy's leg was smashed up altogether. And yet of course the suffering was very great. But I heard no word of complaint and scarcely a groan. Perhaps the most terrible thing of all was the laughter and tears of the shell-shock cases. I found that hard to stand; every effort to quiet them failed.

We soon had about fifteen wounded Germans, stretcher cases, brought in, mostly fine big sturdy fellows. These we did what we could for, and laid them to wait under the shade of an out-house while the British wounded were evacuated first. I felt no animosity towards them, and I think it gave me great pleasure to be able to give morphia to one or two suffering badly and a cup of water to several of them. They were very grateful. We did all we could for them, short of sending them off before our lads to the ambulance.

It was now getting near midday and the sun was hot, the only hot day we have had this summer and I prayed to God to help the wounded lying in the open. Our mortuary was now full up, and we began to lay the dead in a small open space next to the ADS. At present we were too occupied with the wounded to think about trying to identify the dead. It was close to mid-day. From now onwards, the village street was very unhealthy, shrapnel and heavy explosives falling continually all round us. The bringing in of wounded became more and more difficult. Quite a few of the motor-ambulances were hit by shrapnel bullets, but none actually put out of action.

The news from the battle was alternately good and bad. First we heard that the three German trenches had been taken, then we heard that Gaurement had fallen, and then that we had to retire. German prisoners had stopped coming along since 10.00 am – they are always a sign of progress. All that we could gather was that things were going fairly well. About 5 or 6 pm the news came through that we were retiring. It was then that our sorely tried lads suffered most. They had won, in spite of terrible casualties, their way to the third German line and, being unable to hold it without bombs, had to retire. Party after party were sent up to them with bombs, but never got to them. It was an impossibility to cross the open land between the two lines, and the German trenches we had taken were so much destroyed by our own guns in the bombardment previous to the battle that they afforded but little protection to our lads when they reached them. Back then through the hell of fire our brave fellows came, and only a few reached our own trenches again. Scarcely an officer in the whole division was untouched, and most battalions came out about 100 strong or less. It was hard to keep back one's tears when one thought of the brave show our fellows had made when marching out of our rest billets a day or two before.

I had time now, or rather I was sent off, to get a little food and managed to get a cup of tea and to eat some biscuits, with hands stained with blood of the dead and dying. There was no time or opportunity to wash, and then after a few minutes back again to the work of lifting, cheering, soothing, encouraging, bandaging. 'Off to Blighty, old man', brought a smile to any face. Many a lad asked for a cigarette although from the nature of his injuries there was no possibility of his being able to smoke it. When told to make their own way to the 'Elephant' dug-outs at the entrance to the village, one lad limped off with a pal and said, 'Come on Jack, this way to the Elephant and Castle'. So the ghastly day wore on. Still the sun shone, and if ever there was a lull for a moment in the noise, there always seemed to be some birds singing. Perhaps they were glad to see the sunshine after so many weeks of rain. Fortunately the breeze was from the west, so we did not have to fear a gas attack.

Towards dark, reports came of numerous wounded lying out of and in the trenches who could not be brought down. Would we send up more stretcher-bearers? Our own stretcher-bearers and those attached to each battalion were absolutely fagged out. Carrying wounded men down narrow trenches is a colossal task, and they had been doing it all day. But we made up three parties of the least tired stretcher-bearers, and put each party under charge of one chaplain. Crisford took one party, Palmer another and I another and we went into three different sections of the trenches. We all three knew the trenches, and so we made our way first to the regimental aid-posts. I stayed up in the trenches until 3.00 am doing what I could, sending parties or stretcher-bearers to the ADS. I visited our Battalion Headquarters and found only four officers who had come out of the battle unhurt, two of whom had not been able to leave their dug-out, namely the Colonel and the Adjutant.

The Colonel was lying on the floor fagged out, and it was difficult to find out news of anyone. It was quite impossible to go over the top of the trenches to get wounded in from no-man's-land, but under cover of darkness a large number of our lads were coming in, crawling over the top and dropping into our trenches. A few hours later our Brigade, all that was left of it, was relieved by a reserve regiment who in numbers outnumbered all the men whom the four battalions of our Brigade were able to muster.

I got back to the village just after dawn and helped to bring down the trenches a heavy German who was wounded through the lung and who'd been lying in our battalion aid-post all day. He was the last wounded man to be 'cleared' from our aid-post. The evacuation of wounded by motor-ambulances was still going on when I reached the village, and I helped again at this until about 5.00 am when I went down to the doctors' cellar and snatched a couple of hours' sleep. I discovered that Crisford had been wounded in his sector and had already been evacuated by motor-car. Palmer and I carried on alone, though badly in need of the help of a third chaplain.

Sunday, 2 July. We scarcely knew it was Sunday – in fact we had lost all count of time, and the same work went on to-day, though the main rush of wounded was over – but we got a lot of bad cases, men crawling in during the night and making their way down our trenches during the day.

Then began the saddest task of identifying the dead. There were now some seventy or eighty lying side by side in a little field next to the ADS. There seemed nobody to do it except Palmer and myself, so we got to work. We removed all personal property and placed it in a sack, and identified the body by the identification disc or the pay book, and then marked it carefully by writing details on a label and tying the label to the coat or tunic and then passed on to the next. All the time the words beat in on my brain, 'The living, the living shall praise Thee'. I can't tell you why these words came, but I couldn't get them out of my head and I was not anxious to, as they comforted me with the thought that these whose bodies are here are not dead – they are alive – 'the living shall praise Thee'. These are the living.

Great difficulties arose as to getting the bodies buried. There was nobody to dig graves. Single graves were quite impossible. A big trench would have to be dug out, but how?, and by whom? Every man available was needed to man the trenches. Eventually however, the APM[20] of the Division arrived and promised to get some men. Later in the day these men turned up, and I got them started on a huge trench in our little cemetery. About 1.00 pm I was getting pretty tired, and went for an hour's rest in a little dug-out not far from the ADS. When I got back I found everyone in a state of great excitement, as there was an armistice going on to clear no man's land of wounded.

The Germans had apparently started it by coming out holding up white flags and getting to work on their wounded lying out, and one or two of their doctors waved to us to come. News having been sent down to the ADS of what was happening, our divisional guns stopped firing and every available man went out with stretchers right over the top of the trenches into the open, and began feverishly collecting our wounded. There was no time to even look at the dead – the living were all we had time to deal with. Unfortunately I came back to the ADS just too late to take part in this splendid effort – I was just going up when the guns started again and any chance of getting out was over. Palmer, however, managed to get as far as the German wire in his search for wounded. I believe he got in about a hundred in this way and made pretty certain of leaving no wounded man in no-man's-land. How thankful we were for this.

After the armistice was over, the Germans shelled the village again heavily. On one occasion we had just got three stretcher cases into a car when the road was plastered with shrapnel. Everybody scattered for some shelter but we rallied at once, as the poor men in the car had no protection. I fished out the driver and told him to get the car out of the village as soon as he could. I never saw a car started more quickly. I think he got out all right, but it was a narrow shave.

The new wounded were suffering terribly from exhaustion now but were splendidly cheerful. I had no time to think much during these terrible hours, but there was forced on my mind this thought, again and again, namely the invincibility or immortality of human nature. Everything was against it. Death, wounds, terror, weariness, but everywhere human nature triumphed; the wounded were gay, the weary were cheerful, and men put their terror behind them. Man has an immortal soul. He cannot die. 'Man cannot die', that's what I have got firmly fixed in my mind from this battle, and the thought now comforts not a little when I think of our own sad loss and the loss of so many another brave fellow. To see these shattered battalions coming out of the battle is almost more than one can bear. We have, I fear, in my battalion over 400 missing. Of these we do not know whether they are wounded or dead or prisoners. I have traced 300 wounded who got back to our ambulances. About 150 got out untouched. The task of writing to their people is quite beyond me, and I do not know how to write to those whose dear ones are missing. Thank God our dear Morris is not amongst the missing – or rather at least we know he did not lie out wounded to die in the open untended and uncared for, with time to think of the end coming.

By 7.30 pm I had thirty men sent by the APM digging a huge trench, and meanwhile smaller parties were digging other graves, and Palmer and I were already conducting funerals. From 9 to 11 pm he carried on in the cemetery, and at 11 pm I came out to do what I could. I found that my thirty men had made good progress with the trench, having dug down four feet already and made a trench twenty-six feet long by 6ft 6ins. broad. Just as I was giving directions for it to be dug a little deeper, the Germans started bombarding the cemetery heavily with shrapnel. Things began to look a little serious. We all, however, lay absolutely flat at the bottom of the big grave, and hoped and prayed that no shell would burst just over our heads. After a very uncomfortable half-hour, the shelling of this particular spot ceased and we were able to resume work, but the men were a bit shaken and as they had worked very well and were tired out anyhow before they started, I told their NCO they could go away and get some sleep.

Five minutes after they were clear and had got back to wherever they were finding shelter for the night, mostly cellars I think, the Germans started a heavy bombardment of the whole village. I fortunately had just got back to the ADS and was able to find some cover, but this bombardment lasted two or three hours. In a lull I managed to get down to a dug-out near the entrance to the village, because there was no room for anyone to sleep in the doctors' cellar at the ADS. These doctors were absolutely fagged out and those off duty were sleeping, most of them for the first time since the battle started. I had no sooner got to their dug-out than the shelling began and went on all night. Being near the cross-roads at the entrance to the village, the Germans plastered the corner with shells. It is rather a curious feeling lying in a dug-out hearing those huge 'crumps', as they are called, falling all round and wondering where the next one was going to. However I got a little sleep, though I had nothing to cover me and was cold.

Next morning, Monday, 3 July. Both Palmer and I went on with the burying and identifying of dead, but we were both pretty tired, so I took the opportunity of running down in a motor-ambulance to the Field Ambulance to ask if we might have a relief. The worst of the work was over. The wounded had been reduced to a normal flow, and both Germans and British were fagged out.

That afternoon we were relieved I went over to see my own battalion and directly I had a cup of tea I went off, as you know, south to get news of the 31st Division. All that is left of our battalion are in the trenches again. Poor lads, they are hard hit and had hoped for a rest, but are sticking it, though it has never ceased to rain since the battle. Everything is flooded. I didn't know there could be so much rain in the world! The trenches are waist deep in water and the mud indescribable. Wounded are still coming in from the battlefield – the longest time out is five days. Four men, three of our battalion and one of the London Scottish, actually were out wounded five days sheltering in shell holes or disused trenches, and living on iron rations taken from dead comrades.

I see Beach Thomas has got a little bit about our glorious failure in the Daily Mail on Tuesday or Wednesday – the battle for Gommecourt. Do read it – he does not say a word too much. I can't write more now – I have so much to do in trying to trace wounded and missing and writing to their people. My birthday was a sad one indeed though I liked so much getting your letters. May God help you, dear ones, in these dreadful days. Thank God we have our faith in Him and to help us. Let us pray for those who have no faith in Him and his eternal promises, and yet have lost their own dear ones.

* * *

On 10 July Burgon had still not heard of his brother's death on the first day of the battle:

We are kept posted with all the news and as far as one can tell we seem to be doing very satisfactorily.

And then a little note relating to the end of horsed cavalry ever being seriously used again in war:

Today all our men have put up Machine Gun Corps badges. I hate it, but I suppose it is inevitable. Of course officers have not had to change.

And for the third time in ten days:

I have not heard a word from Julian or Morris.

He was only seventeen kilometres away from them. By 12 July he had obviously heard that Morris had fallen, but there is no record in the diary of his immediate reactions, in the way there is of Julian's. Instead comes a very long letter describing their 'historic meeting'[21]:

'Well', said Julian in his cheerful way, 'we've met once and we'd better arrange to meet again. Of course', he added, 'we can't arrange anything for certain, can we?' This last remark, considering we were on the eve of a great battle, sounded so naive that Morris and I roared with laughter. I turned to Morris and said, 'Well I heard there was a bit of a war on somewhere, didn't you Morris?' 'I did hear something about it', answered Morris very solemnly with a twinkle in his eye. Then we wrote our joint letter to you and Julian said he would see it went. By this time the horses had arrived. Morris was mounted on a good-looking little pony and Julian came on his bike. We wished all the others good-bye and good luck, and then rode out to the south in the direction I was going. About 500 or 600 yards from the village we reached some rather higher ground and here we stopped to look at the line, over which a black pall of smoke lay. Julian pointed out Gommecourt and other land-marks, and Morris showed me just where he was going, though I could not see Serre from where we were. Then Julian, who found it impossible to come further, shook us both by the hand, wished us au revoir and good luck, turned quickly, mounted his bike and rode away fast down the hill.

Morris said he would come on to Acheux with me, so on we rode commenting on the interesting things we saw. 'Doesn't it all seem a hopeless muddle?', said Morris. 'All the troops and transport and stores, and yet someone knows I suppose where he can lay his hand on every unit at this particular moment'. We rode on together to the cross-roads where we grasped each other by the hand, and Morris gave me one of the most radiant smiles I ever remember having the good fortune to have seen. It struck me very forcibly at the time. 'Good-bye, old fellow', he said, 'and good luck'. 'Good-bye Morris, and the very best of luck to you and your regiment'. And he turned his horse and rode back the way we had come, and I rode on feeling very forlorn and wishing the next few days were over. Old Hunt jogged along behind me, the very soul of unmoved stolidity.

*   *   *

Ralph's wedding took place as arranged on 18 July despite Morris's death. 'We knew that was what he would have wished,' writes the diarist. Neither Julian nor Burgon could get home. After it their father and mother went for a little holiday at Wells in Somerset:

Thursday 20 July, The Deanery, Wells
Father and I came to this perfect spot yesterday, and are thankful for the rest and quiet. The Dean (Armitage Robinson) and Amy (née

Faithfull) lay themselves out to be a comfort after the strain we have been through. It is our first visit to Wells, though both Monier and Julian were at the Theological College. From the Dean's garden we could see nothing but buildings of the 13th century. The Palace with its moat is wonderful. Bishop Kennion[22] was much struck with Julian's letter of 6th July. He says:

> I have read this wonderful letter with the keenest interest. It was very good of you to lend it to me. Anything more graphic – and more terrible in its way – I do not think I have seen in connection with the war. It is absolutely free from exaggeration or thought of self on the part of the writer, and just tells its own story in the most natural, simple and forcible manner. Two or three things I can never forget about it. The faith of the three brothers – and particularly that of the writer – the cheeriness of the wounded and the touching allusions to particular cases, as when the writer speaks of the Major talking so happily of the joy he had in his little son's faith.
>
> How wounded men could live through 'five days' of it before they were brought in seems almost incomprehensible. I have heard much of the immense physical strain upon the chaplains. We have never seen so vivid a picture of it as your son unconsciously gives.
>
> GW BATH & WELLS

Julian's next letter of 16 July 'describes', writes Burgon in a marginal note many years later, 'what a first-class chaplain, (as Julian undoubtedly was) can accomplish':

In spite of the fact that we are in a village near the line with working parties in the trenches continually, I have had some fine services today. As usual I got a cellar, capable of holding up to 30 and, with the enthusiastic help of several men, we have made it into a beautiful little chapel. It was difficult to find much with which to fit it up. But I sent out parties to 'look around', and we found enough wood for benches and an altar. I found two three-branch candlesticks without pedestals and very dirty, also a picture of the Saviour bearing the Cross, and an old very interesting Crucifix with a hand-wrought lead figure of Christ and the Virgin – a real find this, as it must be of some value, but was thrown away by the out-going inhabitants under a heap of rubbish.

The altar we draped with an army blanket, the six candle-sticks brightened by willing helpers and furnished with candles, were set upon special wooden bases cut out for the purpose, the picture of the Saviour cleaned and hung on the wall above, with the Crucifix in the centre. Two glasses full of roses taken from deserted gardens placed on either side of the Crucifix, a fair linen cloth spread over the Altar, and a Prie-Dieu set on one side for the minister, completed our church furniture. Two old lanterns were also found, cleaned, fitted with candles and hung from hooks to the centre of the arched roof. The whole place immediately took on the look of a chapel, and the atmosphere was there before we ever began our services. A little trouble is always rewarded, and there is no comparison between services taken in such surroundings and those in an ordinary barn without any previous preparation. This chapel was even more effective in its decorations than the famous one, twenty-five feet below ground, which we used in Hébuterne, before the battle, for a daily Eucharist.

Three times today I have celebrated in our new chapel and had wonderfully reverent congregations. To give you a contrast – I went over to a neighbouring village to take Morning Service and Holy Communion for another battalion of this brigade. The services were both held in a large barn-like erection capable of holding 400 men and used for concerts and cinema shows. There was no atmosphere at all. To the men it was simply a concert hall; they live so much in tumbledown barns and broken up places that a solid-looking cellar, whitewashed, cleaned and fitted up like a church brings them back again into the atmosphere of home, and is worth anything to the chaplain in his ministrations.

I have got together another six servers, all my previous servers being killed, wounded or missing, and I am gradually putting a choir together again. Among recent new drafts I have found several keen men, one was an organist and choirmaster from Bristol and various others members of church choirs. I have made a point of seeing personally each member of the new drafts which have now brought us up to more than full strength again, in spite of our great losses. I am getting to know every man as fast as possible. The sad thing is that they are from all over England – farmers and farmhands from Somerset, Devon, Cornwall and Dorset, miners from the Midlands, boot-trade assistants from Kettering and Nottingham districts, and many others. The London element is beginning to be a minority. You can imagine there is some heart-burning over this, and I don't find it easy to get on with the yokel as I don't really understand him; but they are all souls to be saved or helped, and I am finding solace for the sadness of the loss of so many splendid men in working hard for the new battalion. So you see I am full of work, and really do feel that I am getting a grip of the chaplain's task out here as never before. Having been with the lads in danger and lived close to them through these difficult and heart-breaking days has given me a bond of sympathy with them that nothing can destroy. The battalion authorities allow me to do as I please about services. I am becoming less and less enamoured of the compulsory Church Parade – I think we shall do far better work as chaplains by insisting on the voluntary service. Sunday evening services with hearty singing will always attract men who are not usually church-goers, and we must not try to win all the battalion to church by one fell swoop – nothing could be more impossible.

I have quite a large number of names now, I am glad to say, of Confirmation candidates, and I am hopeful of starting classes tomorrow week. Tomorrow we go into the line after six days' rest. Things are much quieter now in the area to which we return. I will try to write at least three times a week, but I have an enormous number of letters to tackle and making-up of lists to do. The 'Push' seems to be going well, but I cannot make out whether Burgon has been in it or not as yet. Indian cavalry seem to have been used, but is he the same division as they are?

Did I tell you that one man belonging to this division came in wounded after lying fifteen days between the Boche and the British lines? He crawled a little every night and lived on rations taken from dead men and water which had collected after the recent rains. We had two of our lads who did a similar thing after eight days and nights out and that was thought remarkable enough, but to rescue a man after fifteen days is amazing. How he ever escaped being seen by our patrols and Red Cross parties is astonishing, unless he was lying dazed most of the time. This man will recover, it is hoped.

*　　*　　*

Burgon is indeed still kicking his heels (16 July):

Once again I write to you from the same place . . . I am in a very different position to when I had a troop in the regiment. Now I am completely on my own. Nobody comes near me or bothers me, I am my own master. My men and horses are camped in the rear of the regiment and I run everything myself just as and when I like. The men no longer belong to the Royals as a matter of fact. They all have the crossed machine guns of the Machine Gun Corps on their caps and MGC on their shoulder straps – and so we are only attached to the regiment for duty. I only hope there will be some 'duty'. It does not look like it at present. The padre this morning preached rather a fatuous sermon on patience. But the idea was good enough – we need every ounce we have at the present moment, both officers and men. I hear Father's sermon was most extraordinarily beautiful and eloquent. I do wish I had been there.

A squadron of the 7th DG, as you will see in the papers, made a small charge the other day and killed a few Boches with the lance – but the cavalry have not had a chance as yet and will not have one in my personal opinion at all.

The diarist adds:

In this letter Burgon alludes to a wonderful sermon preached by Father on 9 July at the Parish Church, Leeds the Sunday evening after we heard of Morris's death. Father had been laid up for some days, but was inspired to preach and show the people something of the Faith that was in him. His text was, 'More precious than gold'. The church was packed, every gallery seat taken; and the great majority of those in the congregation had lost loved ones in the battle, as the preacher had himself.

By now Burgon had received from home a copy of Morris's last letter before the battle:

It is a magnificent example of an Englishman's faith. . . . It is encouraging to think that many subalterns out here would be prepared to submit to the same confession, though outwardly there is much to lead one to expect otherwise. With many, indifference is a pose.

Burgon had been (24 July) with Philip Gibbs again:

He had been north to see Julian's Division. I had asked him to do so. Gibbs did not find Julian – he was back at some rest billets. But he told me everybody said Julian had done magnificently. The Divisional General was loud in his praises, and so was everybody whom Gibbs asked about him. This does not surprise us who know Julian, but all the same it was nice hearing for me, and will be for you too.

There is mention again of the National Mission. Burgon writes:

At church parade this morning the padre preached well on it. The General and his staff were all there.

And the diarist goes on:

The National Mission to which Burgon alludes is being prepared all over England by the Church of England. We have started prayer circles in Leeds, and many of our women and girls have been to retreats and quiet days. The Mission itself is to be only a few days in each parish, when the Bishop of each Diocese sends his messenger, but the preparation for it is the real matter of importance. To secure this, itinerant clergy are being sent out two by two through the country districts, and women are going from place to place on a pilgrimage of prayer. Julian and other chaplains are working hard among the troops, and we are trying to prepare for a better Britain when the men return.

Julian had found time to search for Morris's burial place, but the area was still extremely dangerous, and he was advised by an RE Captain to go back:

The Huns were putting over 5.9 shells, raising enormous clouds of black smoke. The cemetery I was making for was very close to where the shells were falling. It is, of course, quite possible *(he is writing three and a half weeks after Morris fell)* that his body is not yet brought in.

He continues to be very busy, and had begun daily Evensong and a daily Eucharist:

I wear a cassock of course, and I am less of an officer and more of a priest. The men see me socially and in military kit often enough in the Recreation Room and in the trenches, but when I am in the Barn-church I am their priest and minister first and foremost. Thank God they do come and talk, and I have had some intensely difficult but wonderful times with them in this way. We had a little voluntary choir tonight – all keen men, members of church choirs. I am thus getting to work quite differently from what I did when I first came out. Then I was the military chaplain first and foremost and really had to be, till I found my feet and got to know what I could and couldn't do in the Army. Then as it dawned on me that the men I was dealing with were not the old type of army man at all, but just the men of a citizen army, it became necessary to change one's methods.

Then I found how much I had gained by not rushing things, but by getting to know officers and men first and establishing myself on a thoroughly friendly footing. I become more and more in favour of voluntary services, and of establishing a church or place of worship in each centre or village we come to.

Julian is glad to give the diarist credit:

The Regimental Sergeant Major of our battalion – an important person on whose right side it is wise to keep – was wounded and in the Leeds Infirmary last April or May and was visited by you. He has never forgotten it, and was delighted when he discovered I was your son. Although he is an RC, there is nothing he won't do for me to help me in my work, out of gratitude for the kind words you spoke.

. . . . The great battle slowly goes on. Progress must be slow and I doubt if Burgon will get much of a chance. I hope not in one sense, but would awfully like him to distinguish himself, as he might very well do. He wants me to go over and see him, but he is 30 kilometres away and I should not be allowed to be away for more than a day. Sixty kilometres in one day is a bit far, especially as he might not be there when I arrive, but I shall try it, if it is at all possible.

Burgon's 'wonderful long letter' (the diarist's phrase), begun on 6 July (before he knew about Morris) and ended on 25 July, takes up 25 closely-typed pages of the diary. It mostly describes the action his regiment never had in battle! But it also includes another more extended account of the three brothers' meeting two days before Morris was killed, and of his view of the second day of the battle (2 July) actually going on:

Sheets of flame, and smoke, lines of running men, an orderly racing across open ground.

All this seen through the field glasses of Burgon and three fellow sub-alterns from their vantage point on rising ground just above the town of Albert:

It was one of the most amazing panoramas it has ever been my fortune or perhaps my misfortune to see. . . . It was hard to tear ourselves away, but we had to get back; so we rolled up our maps, put away our field glasses and walked to where our horses were waiting and rode home, passing a detachment of twenty German prisoners guarded by two mounted Tommies with drawn swords, and behind a sergeant and a lieutenant each also carrying a drawn sword. Imagine my surprise when I recognised the officer as a friend from Christ Church days. So we rode along together to the Corps 'cage' where already over a hundred Boches had already been collected. I chose a good tempered fair-haired giant of a fellow (I had got my friend's permission to talk to one of the prisoners) who was ready to tell me where he came from and what unit he belonged to and how glad he was to be a prisoner. . . .

He finished his monumental screed with a description of

the most marvellous experience of my life. I flew over our own front line and over the German front line, penetrating two miles into German territory.

He went up in a Morane monoplane behind the Royal Flying Corps captain he had known some months before when the pilot was in the cavalry; he had not intended to ask for a flight . . . 'but when he offered, of course I said "yes".'

So at half-past four you might have seen me duly habited in fur cap, goggles and long leather coat and gauntlets climbing in behind Miller. I had never before been in an aeroplane. 'Where are we going?', I said. 'Oh well', said Miller, 'I think we might go to Pozières. We took it last night, you know'. 'How long will it take?' Miller looked at the wind. 'About twelve minutes to get there', he said, 'and five minutes to get back. Then we'll make a little tour of the line. I'll show you everything'. 'And what about the Boches?' 'We shan't meet any Boches', he said with so much quiet certainty that I felt he knew. 'We shan't need a Lewis gun. I shall merely take a revolver'.

So talking, we climbed in. He turned a switch. The men on the ground pushed us, one gave the propeller a turn. 'Contact', said Miller – a rush of the propeller wings, a terrific whirr of engines – air flying back in one's face as if (as indeed it was) from a gigantic fan (the propeller) – all the engines in these Morane machines are in front of the driver – a lever between his legs moved laterally actuates the ailerons which are hinged pieces at the extremity of the wings. The same lever moved forward from front to rear actuates the rudder. We began to run along the grass – then the men turned us. We ran past the aerodrome at a terrific pace, and suddenly I was conscious that we had left the earth.

It is a wonderful sensation – up – up – up – the land flew away below,

a vast green map below one. I say green because green was the predominant colour – red patches showed villages and long ribands of
white crossing and intercrossing – the roads. At last I was actually looking at 'the map' which I had so often studied on the printed folded piece
of paper one calls a map. We were flying along the valley towards Albert
– Heilly – Mericourt – and now nearing Fricourt. Once I felt bad – we
climbed – the machine turned (as it seemed to me the novice) almost
half over – our nose stuck up in the air and a great white pall of cloud
seemed to engulf us. But we were soon through this – and below us again
the beautiful real 'map', only this time in detail smaller. We were about
3,500 feet up, and fast approaching the Line. The predominant green
vanished, and predominant yellow took its place. The land was seamed
with endless tracks crossing and recrossing; Fricourt seemed a rather
yellowing patch in a yellow land; what green there was seemed dull and
blasted. From that height woods appeared like small patches of gorse,
and even here the yellow peeped through. This of course was where endless shelling had at last eradicated all signs of trees, and left only yellow
shell holes in their place.

Although my head was exactly eight inches behind Miller's, all talking was totally impossible. The noise of the engines and the fearful rush
of wind, so great that at times I was forced to put my head between my
legs and so get advantage of Miller's back, prevented any spoken word.
Sometimes there is a telephone (to telephone eight inches); there wasn't
one on this machine, but a small writing block was let in the side, and
on this Miller wrote. First he wrote FRICOURT, and pointed to it over
the side. Then he wrote DELVILLE WOOD, then LONGUEVAL, then we
turned a little and on the paper I saw him write CONTALMAISON, then
BAZENTIN LE GRAND, then BAZENTIN LE PETIT – each time he pointed
first to the paper, and then we looked over the edge (3,500 feet) and he
pointed to the place.

Below I could see batteries in action – flashes and puffs of smoke,
mostly white, sometimes green smoke, but no sign of movement at all.
Trenches to the untrained eye are hard to detect. They look as dark
lines. Miller told me that even he could detect no life, though no doubt
there were thousands of English and German eyes on us. We were not
shelled, and apparently we seldom are until we get to the neighbourhood of Bapaume. Bapaume is patrolled by aeroplanes, and is also
well-supplied with 'Archies' (anti-aircraft guns). But they practically
never come over into our territory. Miller, as I said, was perfectly
decisive on this point. 'We shall see no Boches', he said, and we didn't.

On we went – below us were several of our standard biplanes circling about – and then on the paper appeared FLERS, and then MARTINPUICH. I can hardly describe to you how odd it was to me to see those two places, so often studied on the map, so often discussed, names as familiar to me as London and Leeds. Flers seemed to have a good deal standing still. The church was clear, and houses and roads leading to the Place; we went right beyond Flers, and then I got one of those views which will be for ever imprinted in my mind's eye – a view of a vast country beyond, Hun territory, roads and avenues leading right into it, villages and woods untouched, our promised land – and even as I looked I could see tiny streaks along some of the roads – Hun transport! – puffing trains and a dim hazy horizon. We turned back, and I suppose it was wise – we were two miles into Hun territory. We circled over Pozières and La Boiselle, and then once again over High Wood and Delville Wood. On the paper appeared CAVALRY. This showed me the exact spot where the cavalry had charged.

And now we were vol-planing down pretty fast. We had to land between Caterpillar Wood and Montauban owing to the magneto going wrong – and I came back in a motor-ambulance. . . . Well, this was wonderful. Everybody is green with envy. I have seen the whole battle-field, every detail of it set out below me like a coloured model of wax.

In the middle of this long diary letter is the single sentence he permits himself at this stage on his brother's death:

having written thus far before knowing of the fearful break that has come to our family circle.

From Burgon there is not the emotional outpouring as in Julian's letter to their parents. But that none of them ever forgot their loss is evidenced by the memorial they kept putting annually in The Times. *The three surviving brothers, then aged 93, 88 and 82, only made the decision to stop doing so sixty years on:*

The Times 1 July 1976

IN MEMORIAM

Bickersteth, S.M. In memory of our brother Lt. (acting Captain) Stanley Morris Bickersteth, 15th Bn. West Yorkshire Regiment, killed on 1st July, 1916, on the Somme. E.M.B., J.B.B., R.M.B.

VOLUME V
AUGUST 1916 – FEBRUARY 1917

Burgon's machine-guns in action – Julian's prolonged battle and field
ministry – the brothers meet in the mud – diarist's husband invited to be
Canon of Canterbury – Burgon's doubts about the war – Julian's
Confirmation Service.

29 July, 1916, Julian writes:

We shall finish this afternoon our six days' rest, and very pleasant it has
been living above ground in the full light of the sun, instead of by candle-
light. This village has not been shelled at all while we have been here,
so we have had a peaceful time, although we have never ceased to have
in our ears the roar of the guns, now closer, now further away, telling
us of the proximity of the greatest battle in all history, which still rages
fiercely and will still rage for many days to come.

My little church is really splendid. Made out of a barn, we had to cut
down some of the cross beams which intercepted the view and cut the
barn into three partitions. This was a difficult task as the beams were
all oak which resisted the effort of all but our best saws. A couple of
sappers, a sergeant carpenter and a number of volunteer parties accomplished the work, and we have had daily services there since Wednesday
evening. I have borrowed the harmonium from the village church,
which has been badly knocked about, more by our own guns and the
colossal reverberation made by them when placed close to it, than by
the effect of the enemy's shelling. We have been able therefore to establish Choral Evensong, and we sing the whole service including the
psalms – no mean effort – but we are largely supported by old members
of church choirs. I have given a short address each evening, and then
taken Confirmation classes. Here my schoolmastering is proving useful, as these men know but little more about the Church and their Faith

than the Australian boys I had to teach at Melbourne. At present I have twenty-five men attending the classes, and four or five more who will, I think, come. I shall try to get the Deputy Chaplain-General down into this area to take a Confirmation Service in the near future. It will be the first this Division has had. I am gradually collecting a little band of enthusiastic churchmen – several of them CEMS[1] members, and they are doing noble work among the men, bringing them along to services, acting as witnesses in the case of Baptisms, and serving for me at the altar.

A few days later he managed to see Burgon. It was the first time they had been able to get together since Morris had been killed a month before:

Burgon, I thought, looked remarkably well, though annoyed at being taken out of the proximity of the battle. He had an exciting experience in an aeroplane, and saw all the battle front from a great height above it.

Just before they met, Burgon had had a dangerous three days in the line. He was sent up with a party to improve a strong point, and came in for heavy shelling there:

We were forced to cower like rabbits in our little lairs – I wish they had been half as good as a rabbit's home! We were near our ammunition dump. One of the Hun shells hit a pile of bombs, and a sheet of solid flame seemed to tower for one moment towards the sky, and then came a deafening explosion. It was pretty well dark, and I was eating a potato and a cold paté in the dug-out I had constructed that afternoon from a Lewis gun emplacement. Once or twice when things slackened I put my head above the corrugated iron roof covered with sand bags – and it was a wonderful sight. Star-shells and various coloured rockets made bright the front line. The flash of shrapnel exploding in the air to our flanks (and sometimes over us, though I didn't wait to see that!), our own guns answering with flashes that for one brief moment lit up everything, the outline of the men, either stretcher-bearers or carrying parties, against the flare of the battle – immediately to my right a great wood, inky black in the darkness though lit from time to time by a tearing crashing 'crump', made a remarkable scene very typical of modern warfare. I had another man hit about this time.

By midnight, things had quietened down a good deal, but I got no sleep as I had to visit my guards constantly – and about 2.15 am was woken up by one of the guards with the words 'Gas, sir'.

I wasn't long in turning out, I can tell you. It was a barrage of gas and tear shells. My eyes watered so that I could hardly see out of them, and the men had to 'stand to' with respirators.

But all things have an end, and yesterday morning we got back here for a rest. The bright spot in our return journey was Julian's sudden appearance. He found me after a bicycle ride of 70 kilometres.

I thought he was looking extraordinary well. He was cheerful and fit and not in the least nervy. We naturally talked much of Morris and of that great meeting on 29 June, but I do not think Morris would have reproached us with being sad had he been able to speak to us. I think we both understood quite clearly what Morris had done – and when you have really understood that, there is not much more to be said.

I got Julian to tell me everything he was doing. What we thought would happen is happening. He is doing great things. Of course he has difficulties, but I honestly do not think they are many. We had tea together. We went out and talked in the beautiful summer evening. Then we dined and then we went out and talked again under the stars, and he sat on my flea-bag as I got in it and rolled myself up for the night 'à la belle étoile'.

In a long letter on 9 August Julian describes in detail how he connected with Burgon to their mutual joy. He expands on their discussion about Morris's death:

It was so good to be able to talk about Morris. You see I had had no one to talk to about him before, any more than Burgon had. Neither of us could help thinking of our last meeting when we were three, and so we could find no occasion for happy laughter which had characterized the previous occasion. But we had a quiet sensible talk about it all, and we both agreed that dear Morris in spite of many disappointments had had much happiness, and had been singularly favoured in many ways. First, the home life, then St David's, Rugby and Christ Church, Oxford, with visits to Germany. Then that wonderful tour of Australia and South Africa and interspersed with many happy holidays to France, Switzerland and Norway. As a family we have indeed wonderful happiness to look back upon, given us through the care and love and self-sacrifice of you two dear parents.

For his parents' sake, Julian continues to make strenuous efforts to find Morris's body, but as the place where he fell was still in no man's land, he knew it would be foolhardy to risk more lives searching for it. He writes to his mother:

I come to the view that it is now unlikely that Morris's body will ever be recovered – in fact, it is more probable that it has been blown to pieces by now. . . . We have so much to be thankful for. The dear lad was quite dead before he was left, and his death was as instantaneous as possible. . . . I fear we must accept the fact that we shall not find his body now.

He is writing on 19 August, Morris having been killed on 1 July. By the end of the month, Julian is in a rest area:

Here in the château we all have extremely comfortable bedrooms, Madame having shown us all over the house herself. On Sunday we are to have a Church Parade and the men are to have a day off, so I shall have the chance of some good services. I don't think I have ever felt so fit as I do now. The open air life and hard work agree with me, and I can work many hours a day. Of course I haven't so much brain work as I had in Melbourne and that always is fatiguing. Madame la Comtesse is '*bien aimable*' and arranges flowers for our dining-room and shows us other little attentions which men like, especially after having been so long without seeing a petticoat.

As usual he is not idle:

Here I have spent my time so far in establishing a Recreation Room – no mean labour in a country village which possesses nothing which is required for the purpose. Everything has to be fetched from a town six miles away, which has entailed much riding about on a bicycle for me. We had battalion sports in a field on the outskirts of the village on Saturday, including many amusing items. The Comtesse gave away the prizes, and we entertained her to tea. The headquarters officers are invited to tea in return next Wednesday, which for us simply entails leaving the dining-room and walking along the paved gallery to the drawing-room, which she has made her living-room.

It is pleasant to hear the sound of children's feet on the stairs and in the garden, after our life for the last four months. The Comtesse has one little boy, the young count, and two little girls, and they have two cousins, a bigger boy and a girl, staying for the summer holidays.

'After a long time of waiting', writes the diarist, 'we have received the following from Burgon, who was in all the heavy fighting on Sunday, 3 September.' He writes, dated 5 September:

Such a splendid mail awaited me here when we returned last night after five days in the front line where we had a pretty hot time. Our party consisted of seven officers and about 100 men. But I am thankful to say we got out without any bad casualties. I was lucky myself, as one night as I was standing looking over the parapet with my No. 2 Gun number, there was a terrific swish – and a 'dud' landed twelve feet in front of us, covering us with earth and giving us a good fright. 'Gum! I was nearly stoking the fires or blowing the trumpet that time!', exclaimed my companion, making I suppose a reference to his destination in the next world.

On Friday we got news that the attack was put off till Sunday morning, 3 Sept. These postponements are very hard for the infantry. Early next morning, on the right of the South Lancs Company, the Germans had stood up on their parapet, crying 'Don't shoot! We are sending back two Englishmen', and our, at first suspicious, troops suddenly saw two English privates in tattered uniforms spring over the parapet and run towards them. These two men had been the prisoners of the Boches for six days. Why they were now released neither they nor anyone else quite knew. At this point the Germans were in a very tight corner and it may be that they had no means to get rid of them – but the men say there was a sergeant also prisoner, and they kept him.

Saturday wore on – and at dusk preparation began. It is perhaps difficult for you to realize all the preparations there are. At 5 pm we went down to Brigade Headquarters and synchronized our watches. During the day the trench presented a very normal appearance. With the failing light, working parties arrived to deepen the trench – to improve communication lines – to put up boards 'To Battalion Headquarters', 'To Aid-Post', 'To Clearing Station', etc. A party of RE's arrived to make steps etc. over the parapet. The trench mortar-ites put in an appearance and began to get their guns into position. 'The Devils' followed them with ammonal cylinders thrown by a trench gun, each cylinder having the explosive power of a 15-inch shell. The doctor of the South Lancs. came to take over my dug-out for a dressing station – extra telephone wires were laid – and over all these preparations a beautiful crescent moon and a starlit sky kept watch.

About midnight an RE officer and two men went out in front to lay the tape, along which our men were to file. They were on our right, and we had not been warned they were out. About 1.00 am I was looking over the parapet when one of my men touched my arm and whispered 'There are some men over there, Sir'. I looked and saw several shadowy figures out in the open, thrown into relief by a particularly bright flare. At the same moment three shots rang out and a working party on our right in the sunk road came running down the trench shouting 'They're coming over, Sir, they're coming over – Stand to'. I shouted 'Nonsense' and told them to stop where they were. I suspected they were our own men, though of course one could not be certain, so rapidly ordered my fellows to dismount the gun and put it on the parapet, and then with a loaded revolver rushed off to see what was happening. I could find no officer of the working party who, to put it bluntly, were badly struck with an attack of 'wind' – so to make sure it was all right, I got hold of a good stout-hearted corporal, and together we jumped over the parapet and ran out along the sunken road until we reached a large and convenient shell-hole. There we lay still and waited. A flare went up and a momentary glance all round was sufficient to show there was not a living soul within a hundred yards of us. This was enough for me. I knew they must be our own fellows, who had now passed to the right laying the tape – and so we crawled back – and when we got near to our own parapet, I stood up and shouted, 'Don't shoot me for Heaven's sake. I'm not the bl——dy Boches'. Pardon the language, but it was a ticklish moment. Everyone's nerves are a little stretched on such occasions.

At 4.30 am the infantry filed out – with rifles, picks and shovels. They seemed to stand about quite a time – while the officers marshalled each company and saw everyone knew his place. Just as they were lying down and all seemed ready, some shots rang out from the German trench. I feared they were discovered – as indeed they partially were. The Hun had seen the movement and, being windy, he began letting off rifles at random and sent up rockets, which broke into three red flares. The shrapnel was some time in coming – 5 or 6 minutes – and then it burst right along our parapet, and not in the open. We had to keep our heads down, but the infantry in the open suffered not one casualty.

Behind the gaunt trees of Thiepval a faint light began to appear – every moment it grew stronger. It was approaching 5 am. A very faint red appeared in the East – it was 5.05. We were all looking at our watches now. 5.06.; 5.07.; 5.08.; 5.09.; and at 5.10 to the second (zero time) such a hell on earth began that I have never seen the like. There had been no preliminary bombardment – only an intense one beginning at zero (5.10 am) lasting four minutes on our front line, then lifting for three minutes to the second line, and then switching on to further supports and communication trenches. Imagine a hundred Maxims, all letting loose at the same moment, but instead of bullets, shells – one constant roar. The enemy front line, 150 yards from me, was one solid sheet of red flame – and all around the horizon ran the flickering red stream. I looked for a short minute in spite of shrapnel – I couldn't help myself – then dived to my gun. Our trench was full of smoke. Trench mortars were letting off at full blast, and within a few minutes shells were beginning to fall on our front and support lines. But by now everything was forgotten in the excitement of pressing that little double button of my gun. Through the smoke and above all the noise I could see the flame spurting from the barrel and hear the deafening rattle, as the bullets flew over to the German parapet, traversing a couple of hundred yards of their front. I had hardly fired 50 rounds before a shell burst on the parados behind, and a huge chunk of earth fell into the bottom of the trench. I thought my corporal must have been killed. He was only a yard away and I could hardly see him for smoke. Inside the little shelter (only shrapnel-proof) were the number one of the gun and myself.

Suddenly the gun stopped – cross feed – a bad one. Out came the feed block – out came the bolt – the offending cartridge was removed – reloaded and off she rattled again. Through the loop-hole I could see the reddening sky; and stark and gaunt against the warmth, stood out the black trees of Thiepval like so many gibbets. The bombardment was still intense – though the barrage had lifted. My gun was still going strong, though the water was steaming and a breathless gunner No. 2 kept pouring cold water into the barrel casing. What was happening? Had we got in? Were we consolidating? Were our fellows working up to the north? Was it safe to go on firing? I had fired five or six belts straight off and decided I must get information somehow or other before going on. So I made my way along a very battered trench till I reached the dugout which had been taken over for Battalion Headquarters.

I went down the steps and at the bottom a curious scene met my eyes. The Adjutant sat at a little table, his features lit by the light of a flickering candle. On the ground, his ear to the telephone, sat the Colonel, as white as a sheet, and every part of him bearing witness to the awful strain he was going through. 'Is there any information, Sir?' I asked, 'Information?' he said, 'I don't know! I can't make out what's happening. I believe they got in twice and come back twice. God only knows why. Something must have happened. At any rate I'm going out to see. Yes – go on firing like hell'.

He pushed past me and by the time I reached the top of the steps I saw him walking rapidly down the trench to the right, accompanied by two men he had collected from somewhere – and that was the last I saw of him. He was missing when things at last quieted down about midday, and though they sent a patrol out next night, they never found him. He got his men to take the line a third time – and was reported wounded in the head and to be lying near the enemy's wire – but he was never found and the men came back a third time to take their own original front line. Why? Nobody knows.

All along the line, the attack failed. The 6th and 8th Battalions of the West Yorks. were the attackers in the 146th Brigade. Some got held up and some pushed right on. Part of the 147th Brigade got to the third line. But all came back. North of the Ancre the 39th Division attacked – two battalions in this Division had actually consolidated in the 2nd line – and a battalion on their right started to go back. This battalion had not got in – and they were almost certainly ordered to retire by a German. The other two consolidated battalions, seeing a retirement as they thought all along the line, retired themselves. The fact remains that from one end of this huge attack – probably the largest that has ever been made on Thiepval except 1 July – to the other, every division which took part in it was back in their front line by 9.00 am, some of our men crawling in laboriously all day. One man, evidently badly wounded, reached our parapet towards evening and was just crawling over when a Hun shot him, having probably watched his efforts all day. On another occasion we saw two bombing parties (who had been cut off and were trying to regain our lines) entirely blotted out by a couple of shells. Such things make war very horrible and yet they affect one extraordinarily little. It is only when someone near and dear to one, like Morris, makes the great sacrifice, that one understands that war is essentially wicked, but in this case right, and that what our dear old Morris has done for us is really too big a thing for us to attempt to express in words – for it is more than doubtful whether we really understand its significance.

We were relieved on the Monday night – and glad I was to get my fellows out of it. As we got down to the valley it began to pour and we got soaked to the skin before we got back to Bouzincourt. It was pitch dark – we floundered through mud, whistling and singing as if we were going to a bean feast – reaction I suppose.

We are now resting, and when we go up again, as we shall soon, we shall be in reserve, so you can be quite happy. I am very fit and very happy. How preferable all this is to billets.

*   *   *

Julian's battalion was close by. He writes:

I must be quite close to where Burgon is. From a ridge yesterday I watched mile upon mile of flashing guns and bursting shells and great clouds of smoke amid a wilderness of utter desolation.

Real active service conditions test the weaklings, but missing one or two meals and trying to sleep in the open, with a fleece lining to keep me warm, have not impaired my fitness. We do not know exactly into which part of the battle we shall be flung. This morning I took the most wonderful service I have ever taken. On the side of the hill I set up my portable altar on four packing cases, and no fewer than 400 men turned up from the Brigade. It was wonderful to see them kneeling in a great semi-circle round the improvised altar, officers in large numbers, including two colonels, kneeling beside their men. I got some shelter from the wind by placing the altar behind a hut, on the lee-side, but unfortunately the wind changed, and it required considerable attention and infinite care to conduct the service without mishap. My surplice blew over my head on one occasion, and the hastily-improvised screen of stretchers crashed down during the administration, narrowly missing the altar. But nothing could take away from the deep impressiveness of the service or the devotion and reverence of the men. I administered the Blessed Sacrament straight into the mouth. It would have been quite unsafe to place the 'Wafer' in the hands of the recipients, the wind was so strong. I think a lasting impression has been made on the whole Brigade by seeing so public a manifestation of Christian worship. I had to speak loudly against the wind and the roaring guns, but I think all heard. We closed by singing the 'Nunc Dimittis' to an old Gregorian chant, and the sound of that volume of voices rising above the wind will linger in my ears all my life. What better preparation could men have in the hour of danger than meeting their Lord publicly, open, unafraid? May God have them in His keeping.

The contrast is ineffably sad and was presented to me yesterday with an ugliness which is hard to efface from the mind. One of the men in this battalion, newly arrived from home, took his own life just before moving up here. It was my sad task to arrange for and carry out the burial, so I waited until after the battalion had moved off. The inhabitants of the little village were very shocked, and our sad little procession to the cemetery beside the river was along a street where heads appeared dubiously, gazing on the corpse with curious eyes but with many a whispered *'mal fait'* as we passed. An old door served as a hearse; two Frenchmen, for francs, dug the grave. One old woman came, in pity perhaps for so sad an ending to a human life, and wept silently while I read a few prayers.

It is not for us to judge the man; he had been with us only twelve hours, and so I had never spoken to him. Perhaps a nameless terror of the future, or some sadness in his past history, lost affection or thwarted will, prompted his action. The road to death is not hard to find out here, and it would not have been difficult to find a 'way out' in honourable fashion. But the ways of the world are strange, and the workings of the mind of man hard to unravel.

So we go on, day to day, each day providing some new experience and crammed full of incidents which I may not relate here.

. . . . PS. I carry round my neck in a silver pyx the Blessed Sacrament in one kind[2], to administer to the wounded or dying.

Both French and British troops 'are advancing on a Front of six miles', writes the diarist, who is 'encouraged' [sic] by a letter from Julian (9 September):

The battlefield with debris and other terrible sights is too appalling for words. I should never wish to give you a description of it. It is quite impossible to imagine anything worse. I saw one trench yesterday simply filled with German dead. There must have been hundreds of them. They had all been bayoneted or shot in one of our advances. There is no time or opportunity for burying the enemy dead.

Burgon too is on the move 'almost daily . . . things seem to be going very well'. But the diarist realizes something of the cost to the individuals: . . . 'These battles are a terrible strain to the chaplains; Julian has been out seven months now without any leave, and I feel sure is getting very done'.

Julian himself wrote a long letter on 12 September:

Incident after incident has followed with such rapidity that I find it hard to recollect the order of events. . . . I cannot describe the battlefield which lay just ahead of this dug-out in which I found shelter for four nights. Anything more terrible can never be imagined. The enormous quantity of unburied dead of both sides makes passing up and down to the Front Line a very sad business.

Our Brigade attacked on Saturday, Father's birthday. The noise of the guns was terrific, and the German barrage very severe. I went up to our aid-post to help wounded down, and to take up a fresh supply of shell-wound dressings. The wounded were coming down in a continuous stream, and not a few were being hit again on the way. Our doctor was hit in his aid-post a few minutes after I had left to take one of our sergeants down, who had been badly wounded in the stomach. The aid-post was merely a small hole in the ground. Indeed, in this part of the war area any fixed trench system is unknown, as compared to the fixed parts of the Line.

Our lads did awfully well and, though casualties were heavy, they were nothing like the earlier battle. But the conditions under which the battle was fought, and the appalling state of the country behind the battle line made things far more dreadful and unnerving. I had several narrow escapes, but all went well. On these three or four days I have had more shell-fire to worry me than on that other occasion. But the little dug-out was a safe refuge. A shell fell just on the further side of the parapet one night, and the hot blast came down the stairs and blew my candle out in a second. But I had built, with the aid of my servant and of another padre, who for the last two days shared the dug-out, an overhead cover crossing the trench outside the door of the dug-out, and this was a great safeguard.

Palmer, the other padre, did splendid work and got further up than I did – quite close behind the battle line. He seems to have no nerve at all. I must admit I find it increasingly difficult to face enemy fire, but our task is absolutely nothing compared to what the brave lads in the trenches have to endure when they take part in an attack.

I have seen now many dead men, many dying men and many men terribly wounded, but not until the last few days have I seen men in the process of being killed. It is a terrible sight. A shell which burst 200 yards from me killed a General and his Staff Captain who was up near the Front. There is so much I should like to tell you, which would never be passed by the censor and it would not be right for me to write. It is not then possible to make a letter descriptive enough for you to picture the scene more nearly. Perhaps it is just as well. I pray God I may forget some of the sights of the last few days.

I had this morning, 13 Sept, a wonderful Communion Service, held, owing to the rain, in a marquee which our Brigadier kindly lent me, although it was used partly as his office. It was absolutely crowded with our lads, although so many of my communicants have fallen. I had gathered together ten servers who helped me at Celebrations since July 1st, and of these only one remains who went into the battle. The others are killed, missing or wounded. My organist – such a nice lad who is organist of a church in Bristol – is wounded and missing – I'm afraid dead.

Under such circumstances as this, it is not easy to be bright and cheerful, and yet we must brace ourselves, as best we can, and 'carry on'. This only will win the war. And the broken friendships must be taken up again later on – as I do believe they will be. Opportunities for spiritual work here are quite wonderful – officers and men come and talk on all kinds of subjects. . . . I long to hear if Burgon is safe. . . . Two only of our officers of those who took part in the attack came back. Of my Confirmation candidates 18 are killed, wounded or missing.

So Burgon, resting with his horses among the stubble-fields, rightly surmised that Julian's division was in the thick of the battle:

We hear the bombardments – we see the star-shells and we wait. It took us five days to get down here, and now we have waited 36 hours and I fear may have to wait still longer. . . . I saw Philip Gibbs[3] on my way through Amiens – as usual he was full of interest – though what he said I cannot repeat here. I wonder how much you are hearing in the papers about this offensive. It is certainly good news. Julian's division, I take it, has been in this show, I rather gather round Givenchy, but really I don't know, and quite likely if it was there, it is relieved by now. I do hope the dear fellow is all right.

I long to get home and see you. But never mind, this war in spite of its terror, its boredom and its passions both good and bad, brings home to me more and more the comparative utter unimportance of this present material existence which we call life.

Julian somehow or other still finds time to write (13 September)

from the shelter of a tarpaulin bivouac – what the Australians would call a 'humpy'. It is open at one end and I can see a perfect little picture in the triangle so made. Twenty men are seated round a brightly burning camp-fire. The fire lights up their faces, and the sound of their voices singing well-known songs comes clearly across to us. 'Keep the home-fires burning' is one of them, and I wonder how many of them will ever gather round a homefire again. A full moon fills the top of the triangle and completes the picture.

For the moment nothing but the incessant roar of the insatiate guns suggests war. Living as I have been in the middle of this amazing 'push', my whole mind is steeped in experiences of a novel kind, and charged with incidents never to be forgotten. To detail of them wouldn't be allowed. I must store them in the memory for your future benefit. Never have men in the history of the world been called upon to live in such fierce and terrible days. One day becomes glutted with incidents which would give one enough to think about and talk over for generations.

There is one thing that I want you to thank God for specially, and that is that our darling Morris did not lie out wounded. Nothing in the whole war has so broken my heart as the news brought again and again of wounded men left out to die. There have, of course, been thousands of cases. Men crawl into shell-holes for temporary protection after being wounded, and then get too stiff to move again. The battle moves away from them and no one knows where they are. Parties searching for wounded often miss them and more often get killed themselves. It is frequently too dangerous to get near them at all. No one comes and gradually they get weaker and weaker till they sink. The cries for water from wounded men left out in inaccessible spots are absolutely heart-rending. May God help them! Our dear Morris had none of this. The RAMC do quite wonderful work, but can't always find the wounded even if they can get near them.

Tomorrow we move up, probably to take part in the next great battle – perhaps the greatest battle in the history of the world. I can't help feeling victory awaits us. Perhaps it will be the beginning of the end. But no one wants to leave off until victory is achieved. I am very fit and well. It is really very wonderful being in this greatest of battles, perhaps in the history of the world. I wonder how the progress of the war will be viewed this day week.

In amongst all the stress and strain was the thrill of another meeting between the two brothers. Julian writes about it on 18 September:

Wonders will never cease! Today, in the middle of torrential rain, in the chaotic wilderness of the battlefield which stretches for miles and is scored with innumerable temporary tracks and constantly changing paths, where to find your way among the millions of shell holes, disused trenches and destroyed villages, baffles most people, I met Burgon.

Such a meeting would be absolutely remarkable on any part of our Front, but here amid indescribable chaos, where one brigade doesn't know where the next one is, where the divisions are constantly shifting, where all the ordinary roads have long ceased to be roads, and the whole landscape is totally changed and changing from day to day, and where no one ever knows where anybody is, to meet as we did was amazing. What happened was that I had set off to see my battalion which for twenty-four hours, was in reserve trenches, or what are called trenches, one mile back over 'utterly-strafed' country. Not an inch of the ground is free from shell-holes, many of them twelve feet deep. Going was very heavy, and not knowing exactly where they were, I stopped and asked two men who happened to be Rangers and they pointed in a direction over the rise to my right. Not ten yards away I saw an officer approaching by himself. He smiled and waved his hand and to my amazement it turned out to be Burgon, in a 'tin-hat', as we call our steel-helmets. I was wet through and he looked pretty wet, but I sat down in the mud and laughed with astonishment and the joy of seeing him. He had come twenty kilometres at least and after being entertained by my Divisional Headquarters Staff, had come on, borrowing fresh horses and taking them as far as it was safe to take horses and had struggled on in the hope of finding me. I might have turned aside anywhere and we should have missed each other. We might have passed each other within sixty or eighty yards and failed to recognise one another in the driving rain. We first found my battalion, had a word or two with the Adjutant and then came back to where he had left his horses, which the Divisional Headquarters had lent him. We decided this was the best thing to do, as it would have taken us nearly an hour to get from where I had met him to my little shelter, and I could have given him no sort of entertainment there.

We reached the horses, each mounted one and left the groom to walk back, and rode back to the Divisional HQ. Burgon, with the readier pen, will describe to you the interesting sights on our ride, not the least of which was a splendid Brigade of picked French troops moving up to the attack. They looked magnificent, gaily marching through the rain, neat and tidy in their light blue great-coats, and magnificent specimens of humanity. It was impossible not to wonder in one's mind how they would return.

After passing these troops and endless motor lorries we reached Divisional HQ where they very kindly gave us a splendid tea, which was most welcome. After a long talk, Burgon then had to go on. He picked up his own horses, and the Divisional HQ very kindly offered me accommodation for the night. The Senior Chaplain took me under his wing and has provided me with dry clothes and a bed, or rather a stretcher, on which I shall have a most comfortable night and return tomorrow morning to my little shelter behind the firing line.

Burgon, I thought, looked very well, but is not hopeful that he will be wanted after all in this show. . . . How thankful we should be if an honourable peace were possible soon. . . . God bless you both. Not all the rain in the world could rob this day of its unexpected happiness.

I think Morris arranged it – who can say he didn't?

Later that month (it is September 1916), Julian permits himself a rare soliloquy:

This War may bring out some of the good qualities in man, but the evil it does is incalculably greater. The whole thing is utterly devilish and the work of all the demons of hell. It will take generations to eradicate the evils done to civilization by it. I feel that our whole moral outlook is being systematically lowered, and it is a terrible thought to me to think of our fair-fingered gentle English women toiling day and night to make shells to destroy the homes of other women. My opinion, which I think I discussed with you in the little drawing-room at Heaning Hall last February, has not altered. It is all devil's work.

Now don't read between the lines and say I am depressed and 'what he writes shows that he needs a rest', and so on. On the contrary, I should have long since collapsed but for the bright side of it all – self-sacrifice, heroism and unselfishness manifested in so many cases.

He continues to have plenty of demanding work to do:

Yesterday we had more casualties just round about here. One poor fellow, a gunner, died in my arms in the aid-post, whither he had been hurriedly brought by his comrades, hoping that it might be possible to save his life. The doctor looked at him, shook his head and passed to another patient. It wasn't even worthwhile dressing his wounds. Three morphia tablets helped him to bear the pain, but he was conscious up to the end. The doctor kindly left me alone with him, so we were able to have prayers together and a little talk, and I administered to him the last Sacrament. The roof of the little dug-out was low and the place was dark and he tried to raise himself to look out of the narrow doorway as if to have a last look outside. Grey and pitiful enough was that scene. Rain and mud and all that remained of what once was a pretty wood, the ground churned up like waves of the sea with shell-holes – and so, my arms supporting him, he died. I buried him today in the little graveyard I am trying to make on the crest of the hill. Most of the dead, alas, round about here are buried where they fall or where they are found.

He goes on:

I wish you could see my little 'humpy'. It is so comfortable. In size 8 feet by 4½ feet and in height nearly 5 feet. It is not tall enough for anyone to stand up, but it provides me with protection against the cold night and is weather – if not shell-proof.

This morning I found Alban, a Birkenhead Vicar, who is a private in the RAMC, and Lance-corporal Barnes of St Mary's, Lewisham, and we three had a Celebration of the Holy Communion in my tiny dug-out. We could just three of us kneel in comfort. Every few seconds, the blast of one of our guns would shake the whole air, but nothing disturbed us. I never felt so close to you in all my life.

The battle was going well but, as Julian shows, at a terrible price. This second phase of the Somme, which he describes so vividly, cost the British another 100,000 casualties. Haig had refused to be deterred by the events of 1 July and the series of battles fought with great intensity throughout August and September, with such a tragic loss of life, inflicted a massive defeat upon the enemy, as Julian's jubilation reflects. It was a defeat from which they never really recovered, but a long hard struggle was yet to be fought and the price of final victory would continue to be high to the very end:

Tuesday, 26 September Victory! This sweet word is now a word we can use as a crown of achievements during yesterday and today.

It is not easy to be quiet and unemotional when for the first time in the history of this great war, it can be truly said that we have the Huns on the run. How long they will continue to run I can't say, but it is splendid that our division has such a large share in this victory.

Burgon remains in some comfort behind the lines, writing to the diarist from

a room in the Curé's house where there are books in the shelves around me. I have no idea how long we shall be here. I want to come on leave, I want to go into action during the winter, I want peace. There are three wishes . . . I think after the war I shall write a book, and in it I shall put everything that is filthy and disgusting and revolting and degrading and terrifying about modern warfare – and hope thereby to do my bit towards preventing another.

At last Julian can leave his 'hole-in-the-ground' which has been his home during the battle for a fortnight. The enemy were at least two miles away and retreating every day. Walking over the old battlefield and reflecting on so many of his brigade being now dead, he found the body of a British soldier:

Everything he had on him, even his regimental badges and buttons, had been taken by the enemy and he had been dead nearly a fortnight I should think. I buried him with the help of two officers, marked the spot as best I could and reported the burial to the Graves Registration Commission. His will be but one of the thousands of graves of unknown British soldiers which are to be found all over these battlefields.

As to the Battalion, I simply don't know it. There is scarcely one familiar face left. Only one officer, except the Headquarters ones, is still with us from when we had those few days behind the line four weeks ago. All my altar servers are gone, and my Confirmation class has ceased to exist. Still we must 'plug' on, as you are doing so nobly and splendidly in grimy old Leeds; and never have we been so close to the Master as when we were permitted to taste something of the sorrow of the world even as He tasted it to the full.

At long last comes news of his first leave:

'At last! At last!' – *he writes on 18 October* . . . I hope to reach London on 22 October.

139

Till then:

I cannot tell you how thankful I am that we are absolutely out of the line and resting, and well do our splendid lads deserve it. God alone knows what they have been through and how many we leave behind. Burgon is still, or rather again, in the battle area, but I doubt if he will see much fighting. I do indeed hope not. After the fighting I have seen, I am quite convinced that no subaltern stands a chance of avoiding becoming a casualty out here. He simply must be killed or wounded sooner or later. Thank God our dear Morris was saved all great physical suffering.

I have seen many terrible sights, and sights which bring tears to the eyes, but nothing more sad than a young officer straight from the battle, who reached our aid-post only a few hundred yards behind the firing line from where the attack was made last Sunday. He was in terrible agony. One arm was blown off completely and the other seriously injured, and our efforts to sooth him were quite unavailing. He could not live, but we hastened the weary stretcher-bearers on their perilous and terribly arduous way, in the faint hopes that something might be done for him at the Dressing-Station, if he got there alive. I shall never forget his piteous moan, 'If only I could sleep, if only I could sleep', and then in an eager voice, 'Padre, is that you? Is there a God?' My quick answer and assurance of the never-failing love of the All-Merciful brought out the words, 'Yes, yes. You must be right, but it's hard, isn't it, to understand'. And then an awful paroxysm of pain seized him, he cried out aloud in his anguish while I prayed aloud, holding his head with both my hands and the doctor did what he could for his terrible injuries. Poor lad! Such a handsome, blue-eyed public school boy, nineteen years old perhaps. 'Will he live?', I said to the Medical Officer as they carried him away on the long and painful journey of four miles to the Dressing-Station. 'Perhaps, but it is not likely', was the answer. That night, as I knelt in our dug-out, I thanked God that if our dear Morris was to go that it should have been instantaneous.

Julian adds in his own hand years afterwards:

The boy died four hours later.

Burgon wonders where Julian is:

I do wish I could hear something of him, if only a field post card.

Mention of his chaplain brother leads him to muse about the Church:

What is essential in our creeds, her organization, her procedure, and what is not? That is the question which one shrinks from answering, though I am convinced that there is something very wrong with the Church. . . . I should like to see Father deal with this from his great experience – during this coming time at Canterbury. He will have leisure to think about these things, and I believe that when he looks back on his crowded years of service as a vicar he will see pretty clearly what is the true proportion of all these varying problems – and there can be no doubt that his opinion would be extremely valuable.

'It was rather a bombshell', *writes the diarist about the invitation to Canterbury,* 'and not quite what we expected to do when we left here. It seemed such a tremendous contrast to our active life, but we felt that the very offering of the post – a Residentiary Canonry – meant that we must give it our most active consideration, and also made us conscious that we really did require rest after a strenuous twenty-five years of work. . . . So we went to see the Archbishop, who could not have been more cordial and assured Father that it was not in any way shelving him, but Canterbury was a quiet resting place where he could do as much or as little work as he liked, and did not at all preclude his having more active work later on'4.

Sam accepted the Prime Minister's invitation, and on 23 Oct. 1916, when Julian arrived on his first leave from the Front ('We were delighted to see how well he looked'), his parents took him straight down to Canterbury to show him what was to become their new home:

Julian was delighted with everything he saw, and we had an opportunity for much quiet talk with him in the train going to and fro. The horrors that he has been through in this Somme fighting are past description. The chaplain Palmer who worked with him has the Military Cross. There is no doubt that Julian equally deserved it, but everyone cannot be decorated for the self-sacrifice and magnificent work they have done.

That evening Monier, Kitty and Geoffrey dined with us at the hotel. After dinner Father and Julian went out to see some of his Australian friends and also the parents of two boys who had been killed. Julian takes infinite pains in communicating with the parents, and has a most remarkable number of letters appreciating what he has done.

Geoffrey, when we were in London, told us that Sir Douglas Haig is delighted with the 'tanks'. He expected during the advance on Martinpuich, Flers, Combles and Thiepval to lose 70,000 men, instead he lost only 30,000. The tanks therefore saved him an Army Corps. The tanks themselves weigh forty tons each.

Monday, 2 October. Ted Talbot (The Rev E Talbot of Mirfield) was here on Saturday and told Miss Baines that Sir Douglas Haig had made a speech to the generals and other members of his staff in which he told them that he had great belief in the power of prayer, adding that he believed much of their success should be attributed to the chaplains, who by their magnificent work had kept up the morale of the troops.

*   *   *

Burgon is still away from action:

Of fighting, *(he writes on 20 October)* there seems little prospect at present. . . . This evening when I had finished working on billeting plans for the winter, I rode down to the sands about three miles away, and had a gallop – it was glorious down there. . . . The old curé was upset at losing me at the last place. He wanted to know whether my successor could talk French. I said I doubted it (he is a captain in the Horse Gunners and a great friend of mine). 'Very well', said the curé rather deliberately, 'he will know Latin, having been to school and being well-educated. I shall talk Latin to him – he will know enough to answer me'. The picture of the Gunner Captain, a typical young, short-moustached Regular officer, being addressed in the Latin tongue on his arrival by the benign old curé is an amusing one.

He goes on to echo his mother's pride in Julian:

Well, I hope you have a good time with old Julian. I am glad Palmer has got the Military Cross. Of course there can be no shadow of doubt that Julian ought to have got it as well. They were always mentioned together. 'Palmer and Bickersteth doing simply grand work, both of them' was the verdict of the Divisional Staff. But like all these things, decorations are governed by so many considerations outside the personal merits of the possible recipients. In some ways it makes all decorations somewhat of a farce. And then of course the great fact remains that dear old Morris, and Gordon Jelf[5] – indeed all those hundreds who have made the really supreme sacrifice – get no earthly recognition for their parents. But there is truth in the lines quoted in the *Times Literary Supplement* article on Trench Journals (12 October): 'More honourable far than all the orders is the cross of wood'.

All the same, Julian should have got the MC and I jolly well hope he will before long.

But frustration at his own inactivity continues:

I ask myself which is preferable? The short, sharp life of the infantry-men – (I do not suppose there are many regimental officers who have been out here more than a year – scores and scores not nearly so long) – or the long drawn-out existence of the cavalrymen, a large percentage of whom, both officers and men, have been out since 1914, a consider-able number (like myself) eighteen months, and a very, very few less than a year. No doubt when we look back we shall thank God to have got through it at all, but the process is trying, and in my book on the bloodiness of the war – I use the word 'bloodiness' I am afraid in its purely vulgar sense – boredom will be the head of one big chapter. Let after generations realize how utterly and hopelessly boring the whole proceeding is. If only I could give to our grandchildren and great-grand-children some picture – a true picture – of what this war is like – its wonderful sacrifice, but its equally wonderful brutality – its grandeur and nobility, but its equally great selfishness and self-seeking; its intense excitement, but its long boredom and monotony; the extraordinary efficiency and the marvellous inefficiency of the Army; the contrasts of this kind could be numbered by the score.

He goes through the motions of being cross with Julian for telling his parents during his leave all about the final moments of that first-ever flight in an aeroplane back in the summer:

It was very naughty of Julian to tell you all about the end of my flight over German lines. Taking into consideration the fact that I had never been in any sort of aircraft before, I doubt whether there are many who have had a more amazing experience in the short space of three-quarters of an hour. The bare truth is this. We hit the ground at the rate of eighty miles an hour (the flying rate of the machine); the small wheels hit the far edge of a shell-hole, the machine turned completely over, and all that could be smashed was smashed to atoms, the frame alone remaining and under this I was pinned fast, so fast that I could not move hand or foot. The pilot was in like position; men came out and pulled him from the debris and he came round to me and helped to cut me out. They cut my helmet off and my goggles, and then pulled me bodily from under the machine. Except for a feeling of great weariness, a headache and a cut on my cheek (my goggles had practically been smashed in my eyes) I was none the worse. We were surrounded by a crowd of officers and men, who could hardly believe their eyes when they saw us standing there, both ghastly white but neither of us any the worse.

When we came down there was one officer in sight – no other human being – but the smash had been watched by hundreds of eyes, and directly we lay helpless on the ground, men by the score scrambled from the second-line trenches and lent a willing hand to get us out, proffering tea, food, stretchers – anything that their sympathy prompted. My pilot put me into a motor ambulance which was fortu- nately nearby and was kindly offered by a doctor – and so I went back to the aerodrome. There I picked up my horses and was back in billets three hours after starting from them, and five minutes later I was pay- ing out the men who little dreamt I had been to Flers and Martinpuich that afternoon and had been tipped out of a machine travelling at eighty miles an hour!

Well, that is all very old history now. It happened months ago.

Of all the experiences of my life, this one that sunny afternoon in July is undoubtedly the most amazing.

In November, Burgon writes that he may well come on a six weeks' machine-gun course in Sussex,

which would mean I shall get Christmas leave in our new home. . . . But for the moment I am riding and jumping every day. I have four jolly horses, two beautiful chargers, my little African mare, and an excellent pack horse.

Julian is back with his battalion which is behind the Line. They had a man accidentally wounded at the Brigade Bombing School:

We did all we could for him, but he never recovered consciousness and died a day later. He died at the Casualty Clearing Station. I took six men over to form a guard of honour. We arrived to find the RC padre about to take the funeral. I was certain that the man was a C of E man, so asked the RC priest if he would mind delaying the service for a few minutes while I sent to have the man's papers looked at again. With charming courtesy he not only agreed to wait, but when word was brought from the CCS that I was right and the man was C of E, he retired most gracefully and brushed aside my apologies by saying it was a pleasure to meet me.

I am living now in the Chaplain's House, a house set apart in this town for the use of chaplains. Palmer and I will live here when our battalions are out of the Line, though one or other of us will always be here. Probably also the Presbyterian Padre will join us and even perhaps the RC. In this Brigade we all four are great friends.

No doubt Julian was not the only padre to press higher authority for spiritual needs to be met:

I went yesterday to see the Brigadier to demand, or rather to ask politely, for at least one day in eighteen to be treated as Sunday. Under the present system of reliefs and working parties, the men do not get one single day to themselves ever – consequently I get no chance at all of a Church Parade. I said that to ask for one day in eighteen seemed hardly excessive, and that the men would undoubtedly work harder and better for the rest, so that in the long run we should not lose from a military point of view.

This morning an order came through that one day out of the six we are out of the trenches, every other time we are out, was to be given to the men to do as they pleased. Thereat there is much rejoicing among officers and men, and I feel thoroughly satisfied that I bearded the General in his den and pressed my point successfully.

I now have a horse for my own use, such a nice beast, lent to me by the battalion. So with a horse and a bicycle I am doing well.

18 November. He continues to be busy:

I have had all the Brigade, and a good many divisional troops to look after – a battalion concert to organize and run, Confirmation classes to keep going, fresh candidates to see, and various other duties.

I went out with a wiring party into no-man's-land last Friday, got back at 4.00 am – a most interesting experience. I was glad of it because I do so dislike the men to have to listen to someone who has not been with them under all conditions.

In a 20 November letter home, Julian encloses one he had from a 2nd Lt A Glover of the 7th KOYLI⁷ giving the first indication that his brother Morris's body had fairly certainly been recovered. It came nearly five months after his death, and follows apparently another (lost) letter which this young officer had written to the diarist's husband

with all that I could ascertain from my Sergeant-Major regarding her son's burial.

The second letter, to Julian, reads:

The Sergeant-Major's name is Gough and he is at present acting RSM of this battalion. He says our battalion reached that part of the line where the Pals 'went over' about a week or so after July 1st, and whilst they were unable to clear no-man's-land they were able to send out burial parties about twenty yards in front of our original front line. It was in that area that the Sergeant-Major came across a body, from which he took the pocket-handkerchief, clearly marked in one corner with the word 'Bickersteth'. He tells me there was absolutely nothing else in the pockets, and therefore no further means of identification. He also says that very little effort was made to identify the bodies for a reason which I hope you will appreciate.

When I wrote to Dr. Bickersteth, I believed it possible that he might have received the other more precious belongings of the dead officer. I cannot imagine who got them, unless it be that the Boches had been searching previously.

The Sergeant-Major's statement is the only evidence I have that Mr Bickersteth was buried, but I think it is pretty conclusive.

There is no comment by the diarist.

*   *   *

At this point in the volume no fewer than forty-four pages of typescript are taken up with two letters from Burgon dated 8 and 26 September respectively. No reason is given for their inclusion here, covering as they do a period two months before, which Burgon had already described in the letters he wrote at the time. But among the many paragraphs repeating and expanding on the earlier incidents is a remarkable soliloquy on the war and its aims, on its ultimate futility and the need therefore to end it as soon as possible. Burgon comments in his own hand, perhaps fifty years later: 'These pages are interesting as describing the views of war-weary soldiers – NOT defeatism – but what was in the thoughts of ordinary Englishmen at this stage of the Somme fighting.'

I admit my views about the war have somewhat changed and the question constantly presents itself – 'Is the thing we are fighting worse than the methods we are forced to use in trying to fight it?' In other words, war has now come to be such a horrible fearful thing, that one wonders whether for sheer wickedness it is not worse than the domination of the world by German ideas. After all, what are German ideas? Chiefly at the moment to get world power, an aspiration which I am bound to confess I am pretty certain we too should have, were we in German shoes. Her methods to attain this end have been ruthless, involving the violation of small countries, but this is merely part of a carefully thought-out and very thorough plan. In our own past, though we have no such black blots on our history, we have not been over-careful of how we came by additional territory, (though here please do not mistake me and say I am one of those who say graft is the foundation of the British Empire). Were Germany to get what she wants, or rather were she to get what she now would be ready to accept, a place in the sun, I do not think we should have to fear the over-running of the world by German autocratic ideas – Hohenzollern tyranny, Prussian oppression, could never exist in the 20th century. Quite apart from the rest of Germany never allowing it, socialism and other international forces are far too strong to brook any such nonsense.

We cannot and we shall not crush Germany; to prolong this idea is to prolong the war to no purpose. Personally, I believe that were Germany to accept peace now on the basis of the *'status ante bellum'* (except for the rehabilitation of Belgium and parts of *'France envahie'* which she would have to undertake), we should not have fought in vain. I do not believe that this 20th century which is going to see the triumph of labour, of socialist tendencies, of democratic ideals, will ever again be troubled by sheer undiluted militarism, which since 1870 has been Germany's role.

This being the case, what exactly are we fighting for? People at home fondly believe that having gained crushing military and moral victories, we shall be able to limit the size of the German Fleet, limit too (like Napoleon tried to do and failed) the size of her army, dethrone Junkerism, dictate to the Hohenzollerns, and so forth. I repeat, we shall never do that. So I believe the only way (and perhaps the most Christian way?) of bringing the German nation to a proper understanding of its crimes is to make peace. The Germans would then lose the great solidifying effect which the waging of a gigantic war gives, especially when ninety-nine per cent of the population genuinely believe they are fighting for their existence; endless disintegrating forces would begin to work – and the intelligent German would see that we were not trying to destroy him off the face of the earth, that all we would not brook was any continuance of a bullying, domineering militarism (though the danger of this, as I have said, in my opinion, would in any case fade with greater social problems at the coming of peace). He would see further that he had been misled, the glory of a fight with one's back to the wall would depart, and criticism and blame would fall on those to whom it was due.

These few ideas (badly expressed here) I was able to put rather more intelligently to Neville (Talbot) as we weltered through the mud and filth. Neville did not altogether agree. He thought that a nation which could violate Belgian neutrality must be beaten to the ground. 'Well', I said, 'You have lost your Gilbert and we have lost our Morris, and perhaps both our parents would say "Fight on – to make peace is to mock their heroic deaths".'

And yet I wonder what Gilbert and Morris themselves would say. For do you realize what's happening out here? Some day, as Philip Gibbs said to me the other day in Amiens, somebody will have to tell the truth. For what in truth is gained? You see huge headlines in the papers and read stories of wonderful victories. You never hear the other side – perhaps you guess it – but it is lost in the splendour and romance of war. 'Capture of Gueudecourt and Morval. Combles in British hands – huge booty'. What does it mean? It means perhaps a total advance of a mile or so on a 4000 yard Front. The gain of three villages. What are the villages? A heap of ruins, a mass of shell-holes, shattered dug-outs, trenches blown in, stinking bodies. Bapaume itself is in ruins. Peronne is in flames. We carry a line of trenches; the enemy fly in confusion, as they did (the morning of the day Julian and I met) from the quadrilateral between Bouleaux Wood and Morval. It is hailed as a great victory. Our men, tired out, press on with set teeth, with no wish whatever to kill Boches, with no glint of battle in their eyes (as Beach Thomas[8] has it), only asking, 'When shall we be relieved? When shall we get out?' They feel they will not be withdrawn until they have lost a certain percentage – fifty per cent is the common report. But many battalions have lost more than that and are still in the Line.

Our trenches are a succession of shell-holes, our supports and reserves get in where they can in any sheltered trench or disused dug-out. The Front Line troops exist on bully beef and biscuits – impossible to get them a hot meal. After a day or two it is almost more than the

148

human frame can stand. They see only one small sector of dark, desolate shell-pitted country in front of them covered with the foul debris of war, their officers and their comrades are being killed right and left, two days of rain have soaked them to the skin. They are exposed to continuous shell-fire, machine-guns play along the lip of their shell-holes, the wounded lie out and cannot be reached. They are ordered to attack in the driving rain of the chill dawn. They flounder forward at the given moment, and those who are not struck down in the passage across the open scramble into a new line of shell-holes rather worse than those they have just left and are full of German dead and a few still living, who hold up their hands in sheer exhaustion. We too are exhausted. But it has been a great 'victory', and the men in the suburban train at home on their way to the office comment on the progress we are making.

Do not misunderstand me. There is no poor morale, no bad discipline, no unwillingness to obey orders, no hanging back when an attack is ordered. No. Our troops are magnificent. Fifty per cent of many of the divisions now engaged in the 'push' joined up this spring, were trained in England for a few short months and are now shot straight into the midst of this chaotic battlefield of mud and blood – and they are behaving heroically. But, for the most part, they are not wildly enthusiastic about shoving a bayonet into the stomach of a fair-haired German boy about their same age and imbued with much the same ideas on war as themselves. Why would they be? They know little and care less about the great Prussian Evil (with a capital E) which we are fighting. The supply of rations and the getting out alive are far more important things to them.

I lunched with Gibbs the other day in Amiens and said to him, 'Why does the *Daily Mail* talk such rot about our great victories? No one denies the ground gained is nothing, and that the number of Boches killed is the great thing. But even so, why do we not hear a little more about the darker side of the picture?' And Gibbs answered, 'Ever since I have been a journalist, I can honestly tell you, Bickersteth, I have tried to tell the truth and nothing but the truth. But things have now come to such a pass that I think I ought to chuck the whole thing. I am not allowed to tell the truth or what is worse, I am made to tell lies. Beach Thomas, who feels things tremendously, puts into his articles not only the light, but the shadow and very deep shadow too. I do the same. What happens? Before it leaves this office, the shadow is cut out, and only the light remains. So, though what remains is true, thus isolated it amounts to a lie. We are not allowed to tell how companies come out only a few men strong, how men leave the trenches almost mad with nervous excitement, how often the best glint we see in a man's eye is not the glint of battle but the glint caused by the knowledge of a safe 'Blighty' one.'

And without the shadow as well as the light how can people at home form any idea as to what is really happening? The report that Thiepval has almost fallen fills everybody with delight, and people at home picture our cheering men and the great ludicrous tanks lumbering ahead and the surrendering Boches and so on. They don't realize, or rather the nation as a whole does not realize, the horrors which have accompanied that gain of a few thousand yards. Gibbs told me that G K Chesterton[9] wrote to him the other day complimenting him on his articles, praising the great spirit of the Briton, and using the same old phrases about carrying on to the finish. Gibbs wrote back and told him what he thought (though his letter only passed the censor with difficulty and after great argument) – Chesterton wrote back totally unconvinced and spoke of the necessity for sacrifice, but the point is, are we justified in making more sacrifices? It is an unpopular argument, I know, but there are many of us out here who are beginning to ask these questions. And the fact that we do so is not a proof of weakening morale. Such thoughts are forced on one. And even so, there are very few who would agree with Gibbs and me; it would be a pity to give up now, they would say. Another six months will put us in such an advantageous position, and then we shall be able to dictate. Well! If you could prove to me that another six months – another year even – would give us this great superiority, then I would say, go on at all costs. But I frankly do not believe it. I do not believe the Germans are really short of men yet. They say another 1,500,000 can easily be procured – they can and will undoubtedly raise more money – and their food restrictions, though irksome, are not in the least fatal. They may retire to a second and shorter line on the Western Front and leave us a few more thousand square miles of devastated French territory, and that is all.

Great questions have to be settled, Poland, Belgium, Austro-Hungarian nationalities and a thousand other problems. They have got to be settled during a cessation of hostilities. Let us stop the war and settle them. I cannot see that in a year's time Germany will be any more chastened, nor that we shall be nearer chastening her. I believe that if peace were declared on the condition of her evacuating Belgium and France, and recompensing these two countries for their monetary losses, Germany would soon find that she was chastened – a lesson we shall never teach her. Germany is now crippled for a generation. Shall we have crippled her more after another year's fighting? And if we could succeed in doing so, would it necessarily be wise? I rather think history says, No. Certainly we were against there being a weak France in 1815, and again in 1871. And Germany today is weak. We are only keeping her strong by continuing the war.

* * *

Early in December, when Burgon has arrived from France for his machine-gun course at Uckfield in Sussex, his parents left Leeds for the Canterbury canonry, to which the Dean inducted Dr Bickersteth on Wednesday, 9 December, 1916. His arrival coincided with Asquith's resignation and the start of Lloyd George's premiership[10]. The latter, writes the diarist:

has formed his new Government, and a very good one it is. Balfour goes to the Foreign Office, Lord Derby to the War Office, Curzon to the Admiralty, Lord Robert Cecil Blockade Minister, and the Vice-Chancellor of Sheffield University to the Education Office (H A L Fisher). Jellicoe is now First Lord, and Beatty commands the Grand Fleet.

The German Reichstag have met and voted in favour of peace. The Kaiser is willing to open peace negotiations!

But the diary makes no further reference.

Burgon who has begun his 'boring', very hard-working course in Sussex, seizes the chance of a week-end off:

15 December, Linton Park, Maidstone.

Cornwallis (who is on the same show as I am, was at the House with me and is in the 17th Lancers) was coming here (his home) for a day's hunting. He knew my week-end was off and asked me if I could come. In the leave book I have put down for absence of one day for local hunting. So did he – and this was granted – so here we are.

Meanwhile Julian's long-prepared-for Confirmation has taken place (13 December):

The service itself was really splendidly impressive, with over a hundred candidates from the Division assembled in the church by 2.45 pm last

Tuesday. Some had come in a motor-bus, others in a field-ambulance, others straight from the trenches. I arranged to get my London Scottish lads out of the trenches early in the morning, and directly they came out, weary, hungry and covered in mud, I sent them off to the baths, fed them, and provided warm fires at my billet for them to get dry. The consequence was that they were rested and clean and quite smart by 2.45 pm and I was very proud of them, 10 in all, a splendid lot. Several more were prevented by sickness from coming, one having gone sick only that morning. I had then twelve Cheshires, who belong to the pioneer battalion of our division, and having been stationed in the town where I am, came under my care. Besides these, I had one or two of other regiments and twenty-two of my own battalion. One of our officers played the piano, I had two violins. Nine chaplains were present, robed, besides the Bishop of Khartoum[11] and two others in the congregation who had not brought robes with them. The Bishop's talk was really good and the men listened well. The reverence and earnestness of all were quite noticeable. It was my first experience of a soldiers' Confirmation – almost within rifle-range of the Germans and in a church constructed out of a broken tumble-down room. All the time the Bishop spoke we could hear from time to time the bang of one or other of our own guns firing, and occasionally the sound of an 'arrival' from the German side.

Tea was provided afterwards in a neighbouring canteen. The chaplains moved about freely, chatting to their own candidates, the Bishop having stood at the door and shaken hands with each candidate as he came in.

Just as the Bishop was preparing to go, one of my candidates who had not been at the service, although I had made arrangements for him to come from the Divisional School where he was undergoing a course of military training seven or eight miles away, arrived after I had given up all hope of seeing him. He had missed the motor bus, and had walked all the way in the rain and mud. I immediately informed the Bishop, who agreed really very kindly to confirm him before he left. So without putting his robes on again, he went into the church and went right through the service again just for this one man. I think this fellow deserved this act of consideration on the part of the Bishop. This little episode is typical of the keenness of the candidates. Is not all this very encouraging for the future of the Church after the War? Many a man told me that it was only the coming out here which had turned him to God once again – more than one man confirmed had not been a church-goer since boyhood. If only we can put the truth before them, they seize upon it and feel the need of these things as never before.

Julian adds that he is signing on for another twelve months[12], and comments on the peace overtures:

No one here imagined for a moment the peace terms as offered by Germany could come to anything. There is only one thing that everyone here agrees on altogether without qualification, reservation or argument, and that is the desire for peace. Oh! to get this wretched business over. There is only one question that no Tommy is ever tired of asking, 'When do you think it will end, Sir?' Yet I do think it is true to say that no one wants to see the business only half done. Peace must be restored to Europe not only for a year, but if possible for all time. Our children and our grandchildren must enter into the heritage we are seeking to win for them, and there is no short cut to the achievement of that end. It must be fought out to the bitter finish. The failure even to open negotiations, however, will herald in, I fear, a fiercer and more bitter period. The summer campaign of 1917 will outdo the 'Somme', even as the 'Somme' outdid Loos and Neuve Chapelle a thousand times.

Gas, tanks, and heavy guns will play an even larger part in this struggle. Who can stick it longest? That is the question.

In mid-January 1917 Burgon's Brigadier in France replied to an account Burgon had evidently sent to him of the Uckfield machine-gun course. It was probably pretty critical! The reply gives an indication of how highly his Brigadier Harman thought of him:

Very many thanks for your letter.
I am passing it on to various people, it will interest them. I am sure it certainly does me; you see it is you learned people's job to write intelligent letters, and not for us poor ignorant soldiers.
    Hope there is no chance of your being kept at home. I want you back here with me.
    Best of luck,

Harman addresses him as 'Bishop'. As we have seen, it was the name by which he always went while in the regiment. Burgon adds much later at the foot of the letter:

This characteristic letter from Jakes was the first intimation I had that he might at some future date offer me some job on his staff, which he did in January 1918 by asking me to be Brigade Intelligence Officer.

But for the moment, back in France, he is well behind the lines in charge of 300 horses and 150 men.
Julian is also out of the line. He writes on 29 January, 1917:

The regiment is getting together splendidly, and the old spirit is still alive and gradually permeating the newcomers. It is interesting to see how the spirit of a regiment lives on, in spite of the colossal casualties of this war.

Both brothers comment on the intense cold (27 degrees of frost); at home in Canterbury the diarist is in bed with pleurisy:

I find it the best place to be in this bitter cold.

Julian is in the trenches by 4 February, where

we are having 30 degrees of frost. My dug-out is not exactly warm, but a 'bed' (rabbit wire) keeps me off the ground at night – two rats regard themselves as the proper inhabitants, obviously resenting a newcomer.

But he goes on:

In the utterly strafed village, close by here is a remarkable sight. In the churchyard, alone, in solitary grandeur, stands a lofty Crucifix. The figure of the Saviour is untouched. Only low pieces of the walls of the church remain standing. What stumps of trees remain are charred and bereft of every branch. Alone stands the Crucifix. Today I went all round the Line. Again and again, one's turns and twistings brought us to face this remarkable sight. Many men pointed it out to me, 'Have you seen the Crucifix, Sir?' One Company Commander into whose dug-out I stooped low to enter: 'That's what helps me, Padre', he said. 'Chance? Not it. It's a miracle, if you like to call it that, but I know this – the sight of that Crucifix helps me carry on. It makes me feel it's worth while persevering'. This too from an officer whose company had been heavily bombarded by the enemy not many hours before.

And truly it is a remarkable sight. The glistening white Body on a dark Cross facing the Germans. I am glad it faces the Germans. I feel that that, and all that Crucifix stands for, is what we are fighting for. I wonder what the Huns think as they look across at it from their trenches.

Snow still covers the ground and sparkles like fairy land under the rays of the sun by day and the moon by night. Nature seems to have done her best to conceal the ravages of War. Even shell-holes have a beauty of their own, covered over with ice and a sprinkling of sparkling snow. The only ugly spots are where a shell has recently fallen and churned up all the ground into a black ugly mess. Really we all prefer this weather to the damp. Certainly it is easier to keep well, and sickness among the troops is practically non-existent.

You would be surprised if you saw how well we live in the trenches. We have always four courses at dinner. At breakfast we have porridge, eggs and bacon, tea and coffee; at lunch, roast meat and a pudding; at tea, jam, bread and butter, and a cake from some home parcel; and at dinner, soup, meat, sweet and savoury. For drinks we have red and white wine and whisky. Whisky has been very difficult to obtain lately. We always finish up at night with hot rum punch, a really excellent beverage I assure you for these bitter nights.

He spent an afternoon in a Gunner officer's observation post, and describes in detail how the officer ordered his guns to shoot. There was some retaliatory German fire, some of the shells landing quite close:

After a few minutes the strafe stopped on both sides and peace once more reigned over the frozen land – and what was the good of all this display of hate? Perhaps we have killed a few Boches, anyhow we put the wind up them! But what result has it had upon our side? We did not find out till we got back to our aid-post, and heard that as a result of the afternoon's shelling which we had witnessed, three of our lads had come down wounded. I was distressed to find the most severely wounded was one of our nicest lads – a good communicant and as straight and clean-living a boy as you could wish to find. 'It is no good, Padre,' the doctor at the Dressing Station said to me, as I watched him removing the bandages from his head, 'he can't last very long. He won't recover consciousness'. I put my hand on the poor broken head and prayed for a moment in silence for him. The doctor tied up an artery and did all he could for him and sent him in a swift car to the Field Ambulance.

The two other cases were not so bad. This morning we got news that the badly-wounded fellow had died at the Casualty Clearing Station. His only brother was killed on 1 July.

That was the result of that afternoon's shoot. I must now write to the lad's people. I have written many such letters now, but always with a heavy heart. This fellow never missed an opportunity of making his communion, and his home meant everything to him.

Here then is the record of only one afternoon on a tiny portion of the Line, and this is going on along its whole length. This is called peace-time warfare.

*   *   *

Burgon writing on 9 February, 1917, reports keenly:

The Chief of all the Intelligence out here says the war cannot go on beyond August. 'Not only Germany but the whole world will be unable to bear the strain'.

But there are two sad exclamation marks in the margin, obviously dating from much later.
Julian writes about the weekly chaplains' meeting:

The Divisional General came and gave us a talk. A typical 'regular', his whole outlook was influenced by his training. The pooling of Religion, and the importance of making our fellows 'hate' the Hun sufficiently to induce them to kill him with greater readiness, were his two chief themes. He most courteously asked us our opinions, and did not seem surprised to hear that we did not quite agree with him. He thanked us for the work we had done, reminded us of how much we could do to keep up the spirits of the men, and told us that he did not mind where we went in the trenches – which is good.

On 19 February Julian describes a hard-working Sunday with three morning services; the burial after lunch of six men killed the previous day; visits to some Royal Engineers and then to a Trench Mortar Battery 'a few miles to the south'; then Evensong and a Holy Communion,

dining afterwards at their HQ Mess, the pipers playing merry pipe tunes outside meanwhile.

So I had quite a strenuous Sunday from the amount of cycling I did, though my services, except the first, were not very well attended. This is inevitable when one's brigade is in the Line – in fact it is extremely difficult to arrange services at all. It often takes hours of work fixing up one service, to which one may get only half a dozen men, but however small my congregation is, I never feel as if it had not been worth while.

Burgon's machine-guns have been supporting a Canadian unit with 'indirect fire':

The barrels of my guns are all worn out through continuous firing.

I am full of admiration for these Canadians. It is refreshing for me to be with them again. Full of 'buck' they are, and extraordinarily efficient. These few weeks *(he is writing on 20 February)* have rather whetted my appetite for Canada again. They are great people.

The diarist completes the fifth volume and the two thousandth page of her monumental work:

26 February, 1917. Today's paper tells that the Germans have been forced to retreat about three miles, and we have occupied Serre. So at length after eight months the place in which our darling Morris was killed on 1 July has fallen into our hands.

VOLUME VI
MARCH – JULY 1917

The Russian Revolution – unsuccessful gas attack (Burgon) – Easter battles
(Julian): he uses German prisoners to help with the wounded – Burgon in
action with his machine-gun section – Zeppelin raids at Home – Julian
mentioned in dispatches: shares in sports day and attends a chaplains' retreat
– Burgon's costly trench raid – Julian's night with a condemned man –
the brothers meet again – Julian promoted Senior Chaplain
56th (London) Division.

Volume 6 opens with a copy of a letter Burgon wrote on 17 February,
1917 to his eldest brother's small girl, not quite five years old, who had
sent him a food parcel:

18th Feb., 1917

My dearest Ella,

Where do you think your little parcel of cocoa and milk found me?
In a dug-out – not very far from the Germans. A dug-out is like a house
in the ground. You go down some steps and at the bottom you find
yourself in a little room lit by candles stuck in bottles – in one corner a
wooden bunk, in another a small brazier in which there is a coke fire,
the smoke escaping up the steps through the door, a packing case forms
a table, some wooden boxes seats. From outside comes the dull report
of the guns, and one can hear the shells moaning through the air as they
go towards the German lines. Occasionally a few German shells burst
on the road a few hundred yards behind us. My soldier servant has just
said, 'I don't know what we can have for tea, Sir! Rations won't be up
till 6.00 tonight and there's no tea or cocoa left'. 'We shall have to wait
then, that's all', I said, and just at that moment a man came slipping
down the muddy steps of the dug-out and said, 'Parcel for you, Sir', and
handed me your little parcel, Ella. I opened it and there was a tin of
cocoa and some milk tablets. Wasn't that lucky? I told my man to make
some hot cocoa at once, and then the Canadian Officer with me, my

sergeant-major and our two servants all had a hot mug of cocoa – and all felt very grateful to you, my dearest Ella. It was a good idea of yours, and if only I was with you I should like to give you a kiss and say thank you. But you must take this letter as saying thank you instead, and next time I am home I will tell you more about everything out here.

You know what we are fighting against the Germans for, don't you Ella? The Germans say 'We are strong and therefore we shall make everybody do what we want', (just as if you said to Edward[1], 'I am stronger than you and therefore you will be my servant and do whatever I tell you'). We answer the Germans and say, 'We also are strong and for that very reason we are going to protect the people who are weak, and see that they are just as free and happy as the strong'. Germany would not listen to us and therefore we had to fight against them and make them listen. You will understand what a great thing Uncle Gordon[2] and Uncle Morris have done in dying for England. All Englishmen and English women and girls and boys say to the Germans, 'We do not mind what we suffer as long as we can make you clearly understand that because you happen to be strong you cannot do just what you like in the world'.

Well, good-bye Ella, for the present, and thank you again for the cocoa and milk. Give Daddy and Mummy a kiss from me, and one on each cheek for Edward and a big one to you from just here X.

Your loving Uncle Burgon.

He writes to his mother on 25 February:

I get *'The Times'* regularly and follow everything pretty carefully. But of course the dominant topic here is what quarter is the wind in – was the raid a success last night? And are there any tinned milk and rations tonight? These interests dwarf such things as the Imperial Conference, which in a hundred years' time school children will be taught to consider the great event of this year.

He adds:

I agree with all you say about the good things coming from the war, but they are out-balanced by the bad.

159

Early in the following month, Burgon had a night in the trenches:

As usual, we had the most extraordinary good luck – not a single casualty in the 80 odd men we had up there. West of us the heavy stuff fell in the valley about a couple of hundred yards in front of us – but we had a great deal of rifle and machine gun fire over us, which by the grace of God hit nobody, though we were on the side of the hill in the open with practically no trenches, just open emplacements for the guns, and the bullets were throwing up earth in every direction. At about 6 o'clock when it was beginning to dawn, it was a very wonderful sight; from our position we could see a good deal of the operation – our men going over – our barrage and their answer to it. Well, you shall have a full description of it one day.

He got back to billets to find his horses looking splendid:

and I am going out this afternoon. . . . It will be the first time I shall have been out mounted with my section for three months. . . . The cavalry, if it survives, will really be a valuable national asset after this war I think.

At home the diarist records her displeasure at a decision by the (evangelical) Chaplain-General:

It can hardly be believed possible, but the Chaplain-General is trying to stop the 9.30 Holy Communion for soldiers in the Cathedral (Canterbury) on Sunday morning. There were over 100 men present last Sunday morning and several officers, but the Chaplain-General prefers all to be on Church Parade. Fortunately, General Young is indignant, and says it has nothing to do with the Chaplain-General. The Church Parade is his affair, but the General has power to excuse men from that if he chooses, and if they have sufficient reason. The Dean has been splendid. He opposed the change at first, but on Sunday congratulated Father on the numbers and the success of the service, saying that evidently there was a great need for it. The General said, 'It is perhaps the first time I have ever tried to do something to help on the spiritual welfare of my men, and now I am stopped by a Bishop.'[3]

The diarist comments:

It remains to be seen what the Dean will do. The General is going to see the Archbishop about it.

Julian had short leave in early March; he writes on return to France after a calm crossing in the welcome company of several Australians,

men not officers. One splendid fellow I had a delightful conversation with. He came from Dubbo in NSW and had that wonderful look in his eyes which comes to those who spend all their lives in the bush. He told me how he hated Sydney and other coast towns, and loved best of all to be far from the haunts of men in his native bush. 'I shall hope to see the Western sheep plains again', he said, 'if I don't get plugged'. It was his first sight of France, and he was very interested. He was certainly a fine type and, though I didn't ask him, I have no doubt he was a church-man and a communicant, as he had been the constant companion of the Bush Brothers.

At his home in Canterbury Julian's parents were getting a taste of war – their first experience of a Zeppelin raid on Friday, 16 March:

At 11 pm we heard bombs dropping near and so did not go to bed, but simply lay down dressed till 1.30 am. The searchlights were very brilliant, but we could see no 'Zepps' though a neighbour heard the engine. One bomb was dropped at Nackington, about 1½ miles off, but did no harm. The General tells me we have no anti-aircraft guns here at all. What struck me as almost comic was that the old watchman who goes round the Precincts every night and all through the Cathedral, went past my window at 11.20 pm and although bombs were dropping in the neighbourhood at the moment, called out, as no doubt he and his predecessors had done for centuries, 'Past eleven o'clock. Fine night. All's well!!'

At the Chapter held this morning, a letter from the Chaplain-General was read, ordering the Holy Communion for soldiers not to be celebrated at the same hour as Church Parade. He actually said in conversation with the Dean: 'When I preach to the men I like to be heard by them all, and I don't like the best men in the congregation to drift off to another service' – a terrible thing to have said when it is taken into consideration what the other service is. They are to try a

Celebration after Church Parade, and we shall see what happens. Father is much depressed about it, especially as at the Celebration this morning (the last to be held at that hour) an officer came up to him and said, 'This is the best thing the Church of England has done yet.'

On his way back to his two beloved battalions Julian ran into the Deputy Chaplain-General in an Abbeville shop:

Bishop Gwynne happened to come in while I was there, having left his car for the moment. I made myself known to him, and he was full of the success of the Chaplains' School which has just been started, over which Cunningham⁵ of Farnham is to preside, to which each chaplain in the army is to go in turn for a week's course.

Julian's old school Rugby comes in for a mention again:

In Abbeville there is an excellent officers' club where four of us sat down to tea – all ORs.

Back at last with his unit (it took him forty-eight hours travelling from Canterbury to 'the bosom of my battalion'), his charm soon got him a good billet:

Everything is very congested and billets were very scarce. I was preparing to sleep the night on the mess room floor, but during the afternoon poked about and found a house which up till then had resisted all efforts on the part of harassed billeting officers. A smile and a few pleasant observations on my part in my rapidly-improving French melted Madame's heart, and I found myself asked in and actually given the best room in the house, large enough for me to hold Confirmation classes, well-furnished and with a fireplace where a fire now merrily burns as I write. A wire bed from our pioneer officer promises a good night's rest, and I don't suppose there is another officer in the village better housed. In some places there are three or four officers sleeping on the floor in one room.

But hard work went with his winning ways, as is evident in a letter the diarist must have extracted from Julian for her record. It is from the Assistant Chaplain-General, First Army, The Rev. Harry Blackburne.

My dear Bickersteth,

I just want to write you a line to thank you for the pledges you put in for your regiment; it clearly reveals one really important fact, that you know your men extraordinarily well. I am exceedingly sorry that your division is leaving this Army, and I hope we shall meet again soon. It must be a great joy to you, as it is to us all who really care, to feel that the Church and its teachings hold such a right and proper place in your regiments. May God bless your work for Him abundantly in the future as He has done in the past. Yours very sincerely, Harry W. Blackburne.

*　　*　　*

The diarist has scores of pages and hundreds of newspaper cuttings on the contemporary scene during 4½ years of war; here there can only be a handful of them, for example on 17 March, 1917:

The Russian Revolution goes on quietly [sic]. The Czar and Czarina are prisoners in their palace. The Czar has refused to let his son be Czar and has abdicated in favour of his brother, the Grand Duke Michael, who in his turn will only be Czar by the united will of the people, in other words by a General Election.

Burgon, in a letter on 18 March, comments on the Revolution, saying that he can think and talk of nothing else:

The one question the soldier asks is 'Will it make any difference to the length of the war?', and I think it is now fairly clear it will not. Well, we are living in wonderful times. Here is a revolution which will probably have as far-reaching effects as the doings of 1789-1792. Does it mean civilization has progressed in that bloodshed has been negligible in Petrograd, or does it mean that in Paris the reactionary forces were stronger and the abuses worse? I should have been inclined to say that in Russia the abuses were almost as great as before 1789 in France – and that although the immediate adhesion of the troops to the cause of the Duma prevented any serious civil war, yet we have progressed since the 18th century – and the moral sense of the people would in any case have made the excesses of Sept. 1790 of the Gironde and of Robespierre impossible. I like to think so, at any rate. I want to know Geoff's opinion about the whole business. Will you please tell him he could not give me greater pleasure than by sitting down and writing me his views about it all? I remember his prognostications of January, i.e. a revolution must come, either before the end of or directly after the war.

He goes on to describe a very civilized evening:

Last night we dined with the people who own this château. We occupy one wing of it only. They invited four of us; and their party consisted of the old man, the old woman, a niece and their son, nineteen years old, in training, and going into the trenches in a month or two. As you know, it is difficult in France to fix the class of a person. They are more than the yeoman farmer, yet not gentlepeople. They are far more intelligent and refined than the suburban type, and yet would be uncomfortable in a house in the Champs Elysées. They gave us a very good dinner, and the conversation in French was brisk all the time. After dinner, a French soldier came in and played the violin and piano. He is one of the French battalion billeted here and engaged on building the railway. In peace time he is a musician, playing in the orchestra at the Paris Opera House and even giving small concerts of his own. War made him put on his blue uniform, and here he is – and acting as trumpeter and opener of gates at the level crossing – his profession saves him from *'pelle et pioche'*. Imagine the scene. A square room, uncertain whether it belongs to a glorified farm house (which it did) or to a château fallen on evil days, a large wood fire in an open grate, a round table in the centre under the lamp hanging from the ceiling, glasses of Madeira and cigarettes going the rounds, and in a corner by the piano the French soldier in his blue uniform contrasting with our khaki, fiddling away now Bach, now Chopin, now some lighter romance.

A very long letter (23 pages) from Burgon reached the diarist on 27 March. It must have been written when he had some time to himself, as there is a mass of detail on every page describing his visit earlier with the Canadians on Vimy Ridge. He had taken some of the 6th Machine Gun Squadron to work in support:

The Maple Leaf reigned supreme. Wherever one looked it was predominant – on men's caps, on notice boards attached to various HQ billets, on motor bicycles, on limbers, on ambulances. Tall clean-shaven men stood about talking in their dry snappy accent, the old familiar expressions, the old abrupt ways, the old racy oaths, the old atmosphere of reserve and detachment, the old feeling of bustle and 'Guess I'm right there'.

It was a tonic, as I love Canada and the Canadians. Canada to me is Western Canada and this was a bit of Winnipeg or Edmonton with their straight streets, skyscrapers, and business blocks, and hustling baggy-trousered population translated into a khaki army and splashing through the mud of the tortuous streets of a filthy French village, wretched in its shattered daub barns and broken houses.

'Good limousine, that', said the CO jokingly as we stood surveying our Daimler lorry which had brought us many miles without a stop. 'Guess it's some baby-carriage all right', said the Town Major, who immediately took us in hand and allotted us one of the broken windowless cottages as our headquarters, and a wooden hut for the men. We talked of the war and particularly of this sector of the Line. 'Got 'em beat', said the Canadian. 'Guess they realize they are up against something when they are opposite us'.

His new companions for their part soon realized with astonishment that this particular 'Imperial' (as they called all British soldiers) knew their home country:

For instance, the cook was of a type I know well. Eight years ago he left England for Canada and had worked in every camp from Edmonton to the coast. Wolf Creek, Edson, Mile 53, Tete Jaune Cache, Mile 134, Fort George – he knew them all, and what a talk we had, while his master looked on and stared at me. 'Fancy an Imperial knowing T Jaune Cache and Mile 134', he exclaimed. 'Guess you know a bit more than I thought you did'.

They have brought all their self-assurance and independence and resourcefulness from Canada with them; and the very qualities which pioneer life, or for that matter, the whole spirit of Canada from East to West, calls out in a man, are carrying them through the war with flying colours. As in the West, a man's position does not stand for much, but his work does. The men salute, but they are equally ready with a perfectly free, 'Good morning' or 'How are yer?'.

Burgon goes on:

For the last few days we were in the trenches as we were forever waiting for favourable conditions for the gas attack. It is an important affair since the gas was of a new and particularly deadly kind, guaranteed after a few minutes to penetrate the German respirators. The first discharge was to be let off at Zero hour, then there was to be a wait of about two hours, then another discharge of the ordinary poisonous gas followed by an attack by two battalions. It was therefore almost more than a raid, it was a small attack, though the features of the operations were really those of a raid, as no ground was to be held. The two battalions were to be 'over' for an hour and a half, do as much damage as possible and then return.

Everything depended on the wind; and Eaton and I, who were living at Villers-au-Bois in reserve, daily examined it; indeed a score of times daily we went out into the open fields with compass and handkerchief or cigarette smoke or wetted finger and tried to gauge the wind's exact quarter. We were to go up directly it was certain whether it would come off, but from the nature of the case we could not be certain till about two hours before. Zero was at 3 am. Every night we sat up till 12.30 waiting for a message from the Brigade. DOG was the code word meaning the show was off, and CAT meant it was on. The evening of Feb. 28, or more accurately, at 12.30 am on Thursday morning March 1st, we were waiting for our message as usual. For three nights DOG had come regularly. But today the wind had seemed favourable. At about a quarter to one the orderly came. I glanced at the message and saw CAT. In twenty minutes we were off.

From the first I think some of us had harboured a few doubts about the success of the scheme. The gas had been in the front line a whole week. It was there blocking the narrow trench when I went up to view 'the Pimple', and considering how information gets about, this fact could hardly have been unknown to the Germans. Add to this two things:

(1) a raid had been made by the 1st Canadian Division on our left on the night before, and they had found the Germans 'standing to' in their gas helmets. though no gas had been used;

(2) an officer and a sergeant of the Gas Company had been going round our line the night before, had mistaken their way (a very easy thing to do, though of course they should have had guides), had walked into the German trench, had met six Huns, and had put up a good 'scrap', the officer getting away but the sergeant being captured. Members of the Gas Company are not allowed in the front line unless gas is about. However, we hoped for the best and waited.

At 3 am the first discharge of gas took place. We saw it rolling in a thick bilious-looking cloud towards the German line. Almost at once a fusillade of rifle fire began. Owing to the nature of the ground you will understand how this came straight across the valley at us. A good deal of it passed overhead, but a good deal also spattered up the ground all round and 'pinged' against our very low parapet. At 3.15 am we began a moderate bombardment for twenty-five minutes, the artillery and ourselves. At 3.25 every one shut off, and we went to our dug-outs.

You must understand that this whole affair was an experiment of our new gas – it was a bigger raid than had ever taken place before, and that interest in the business was widespread. Had it been a success there would have been much writing up in the papers by war correspondents and so forth. The English official statement said, 'We discharged gas this morning east of Souchez. Our men subsequently raided the enemy trenches and took some prisoners'. The German official statement ran thus: 'East of Souchez a strong attack was repulsed'. Of the two the German gives far the truer statement.

The whole thing was unfortunate, and in my humble opinion (and it is shared by many) gas as an effective fighting ally is played out. The average private soldier hates gas. He would far rather 'go over' without it. The Canadians had never failed to make good in a raid before, and their failure on this occasion was entirely due to the gas being totally ineffective.

But how Burgon had loved being with Canadians again:

Good-natured, obliging, independent yet disciplined, full of initiative and resource, yet obedient, thoroughly efficient. I never met one, officer or soldier, whom I disliked, and with whom I would not have been proud to serve.

*　*　*

On 27 March Julian writes about a visit to the Somme battlefield of nine months before; the area had obviously hardly been touched since. The Colonel had asked him and the doctor to see if they could find any of their dead from 1 July of the previous year:

We were amazed to find a great number who had been lying exactly as they had fallen ever since July 1st, in what was until three weeks ago no man's land. All bodies fallen in or near the trenches themselves had been buried. I found just behind the German front line a simple cross with the words, '13 *tapfere Engländer*'[6] written on it. I wasn't quite sure of the second word, but anyhow it showed that the Germans had respected our dead and given them as decent a burial as possible. In the middle of no man's land and near the German wire were a large number of our dead. The Germans had taken everything from their pockets. There was nothing at first sight to make identification possible beyond their shoulder badges. We found four officers' bodies, one of which I was able to identify. I am making every effort at present to be allowed to take a party down there and to bury the bodies in the Hébuterne cemetery.

* * *

It was now Holy Week 1917, which perhaps moved Burgon to send his father some thoughts on religion at the front:

There is no subject on which it would be easier to generalize or more dangerous. If, for instance, you chose (as I did last time I was in the Line) any two reasonably intelligent officers and asked them whether in their opinion life in the trenches has led to a revival in Christianity, you would probably receive two different replies. One would (and did) say, 'I can assure you there are no atheists in the trenches'. The other would say, 'I have seen little or no sign of any such religious revival'. Both to a certain extent would be right, for it is a commonplace that the brutalizing effects of war demoralize a man, and stifle many higher spiritual faculties; and equally certain that the very horror of it all and the uncertainties bring to the top beliefs and aspirations which would otherwise probably never have seen the light.

There is a marvellous increase of personal philanthropy, if it can be so called – charity and kindness to one's neighbour, willingness to share the last crust, to choose the dangerous post, to help in whatever way possible the lame dog over the stile. It is the so-called practical religion professed by many in peace time.

The statement that there are no atheists in the trenches does not argue the immediate conversion of all who have experienced shell-fire, though I think it does mean men are beginning to realise they are potential Christians. The constant *'tête-à-tête'* with death, or the loss of a friend at one's very side, are naturally sweeping away mere conventional faith. The question is forced on one: What do I believe? And why? I do not say this leads very far. Men who have been through great adventures are at the time too much occupied to analyse their feelings very closely. Even the practical uncertainty of 'going west for keeps' often appears to leave a man entirely innocent of any romantic spiritual awakening.

Others, however, there are who do possess the basis of sound teaching, learnt at their mother's knee, though long hidden and forgotten. Half shyly, they suddenly realize its value, and it needs but a spark to produce a white heat of Christian endeavour. Padres have had wonderful experiences in seeking and preparing Confirmation candidates of this type. These are they who will be the focus of religious energy after the war, and within limits they should be our teachers.

The average British soldier is very fatalistic. 'Well, sir, yer'll be 'it when yer'll be 'it and not afore'. He hates to talk about his soul and resents the highly patriotic tone, except when presented in a sentimental song at a 'smoker'[7]. He grouses interminably, especially when life flows easily. Real discomfort or hardship spurs him to the greatest hilarity. He uses filthy and abominable language, treats church parade as a parade, and does not stay to the Communion as much through moral cowardice as anything else. The padre is appreciated by the men in so far as he busies himself with their recreational and physical comfort, and respected if he visits the front line and shares their dangers. When he does both, he is loved. His uniform is probably more of a disadvantage than advantage, though as usual it is personal attraction rather than religious sentiment which draws.

Another fact is equally certain. Religion which suddenly bubbles to the surface at the moment of danger is very healthily considered to smack too much of the death-bed confession and to be about as valuable (which does not mean to imply it is valueless). Many of us have had that determined, half-sporting feeling that we will be especially careful not to be extra-religious because we are in an extra-dangerous spot.

I must stop this long letter with the very best of love from one who has more to thank his father and mother for than he can ever hope to express or repay.

On that same day, Julian had found himself drawn again to the battlefield where Morris had died:

I placed a cross within a few yards of where Morris must have been when he was struck, and took careful note of the place. In the midst of the desolation and the endless circles of shell holes, I read the Burial Service aloud and scattered earth to the N E S & W when I came to the words of the committal. I felt that I was standing on holy ground, sanctified forever by the blood of heroes. It was a privilege to be allowed to do even this, exactly nine months after the day.

Burgon is having a busy Holy Week:

Good Friday – and not one per cent of the Brigade aware of the fact, certainly not of the significance of the day. One finds it extremely difficult oneself to realize that the events of nearly two thousand years ago are so stupendous that to be occupied by our own affairs, to such an extent that they absorb every thought and energy, is simply silly. The present is so very present, just now especially. There can be no services today, and I much doubt whether it will be possible for the padre to arrange any on Easter Sunday.

Julian's battalion was in action by Easter Monday (9 April 1917):

The great attack began at 5.30 am on Easter Monday. Our turn came at 7.45 am when our fellows went 'over the top' splendidly, and achieved all their objectives, in spite of a lot of opposition. Considering what we achieved, our casualties were not heavy. I have just today concluded the burial of 62 Rangers, including two officers, and I suppose we had 150 wounded. But we took 300 prisoners ourselves – our one battalion. It is the first battle in which we have been engaged that it has been possible to follow up behind, and pick up wounded and dead in the old authorized fashion.

He also wrote about the battle to the Bishop of Exeter's widow, his grandmother:

I was able to live with my battalion all the time and saw quite a lot of fighting and had one or two narrow escapes, the nearest being a shell, which fell three yards from me, but which did not explode.

On the opening day of the battle I took charge of 200 German prisoners and used them all day as stretcher-bearers for our wounded. They worked very well, and were very happy to be captured.

To his mother he says at the same time:

The Senior Chaplain tells me I was recommended for mention in dispatches last year by the Division for work on 1 July and on the Somme generally, but that it did not get beyond the Corps. Still I am glad the Division was satisfied with my work.

* * *

April was the month that America came into the war. 'The Battle Hymn of the Republic' was sung at a great service in St Paul's Cathedral. But both the brothers were busy with the 'Great Push':

Tired and worn, but still sticking it (Julian writes), our chief enemy has been the weather: bitter, blinding storms of sleet and snow – mud feet deep and clinging closely to every part of us – never really warm and never dry – often without any hot food for days together, sleep almost as unknown as dry socks. The hardships of this spring campaign have probably never been equalled, and yet our men carry on. They are wonderful. . . . At the back of our minds is the growing conviction that the Germans are gradually being beaten and cannot win.

The cavalry have

been moved about a lot (during all this activity) but we are a nuisance to everybody, and then they add insult to injury (Burgon comments) by telling us we have done useful work.

By 2 May Julian can write – out of the Line:

The sun still shines with clearness, and the warmth is truly delightful. Splendid campaigning weather. Opportunities for work among the men are multitudinous, but there isn't time to seize them. The pace is too hot. It cannot last. Our Somme offensive lasted for months. How long can this one? It has started much earlier than last year. We have all the summer before us. I think the Germans must break first.

I shall apply shortly to go to the Chaplains' School, a house at old GHQ where chaplains have a rest and some mental refreshment, but somehow, even in the most trying moments, I shall not be happy away from this amazing turmoil and rush of events.

He finds time to write to Geoffrey:

Did I ever thank you for that very delightful [sic!] book 'The Adventure of Death'? I think it is about time I gave you a book or rather about time you bought one for yourself, so I enclose a cheque for a guinea.

Meanwhile Burgon reckons the war has gone on long enough (5 May):

Personally, as I have felt for months, and feel even more strongly now, we have to a large extent gained the objects for which we went to war, and in spite of all the foul inhuman behaviour of our enemy, we should be doing the right thing (and also the most advantageous thing) if we at any rate opened negotiations with a view to peace. I do not think going on fighting is a responsibility which any human shoulders should try to bear.

These are not thoughts that have occurred to his busier chaplain brother:

I live so much in the midst of death that much of the horror and even the sadness is lessened. So many of the very best fellows in the world have passed on. Only yesterday a brilliant handsome young artist, an officer attached to the regiment, was buried by an enemy shell only a few minutes after I had been talking to him; and no effort of ours, after he had been dug out, could revive him. And this goes on all the time. It must be amazingly interesting on the other side.

He goes on a few days later:

My work is the same most days – with the wounded in the Aid-posts and Dressing Stations, burying the dead, visiting the living, writing to the bereaved, eating, sleeping, reading a little, praying a little. Only very seldom do I get the chance of holding services. Last Sunday passed, for instance, without any possible service.

Burying the dead is not always easy. It often has to be done after dark because it is not advisable to employ any men in the open digging in the daytime, as the Hun can see a lot just here, and has the nasty habit of firing on small parties.

Burgon continues on his post-war theme:

The world seems to be in such a hopeless muddle now, and we have every prospect of getting into a far worse one directly peace comes.

Ella Williams, 1865. Taken by Lewis Carroll at Christ Church, Oxford

The Rev. Canon Samuel Bickersteth

Mrs Samuel Bickersteth (the diarist)

Morris Bickersteth. The West Yorkshire Regiment.
Killed in Action, 1 July 1916.
Portrait by C. Jameson

The Rev. K.J.F. Bickersteth MC.
Senior Chaplain, 56th (London) Division

Lieutant J.B. Bickersteth MC.
The Royal Dragoons

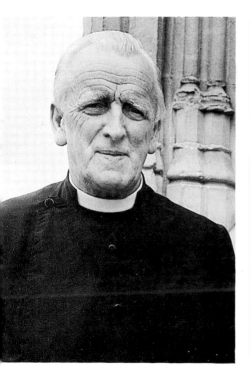

Julian at Canterbury, 1962

Burgon at Canterbury, in the late 1960s

A Dirty Day in Flanders, by David Baxter *(Imperial War Museum)*

A chaplain conducting a burial service on the battlefield of the Somme,
September, 1916 *(IWM)*

A cavalry machine-gun team on training, near Querrien, July 1916 *(IWM)*

London Scottish of 56th (London) Division. March 1916 *(IWM)*

Church parade before going into the line. The King's Liverpool Regiment *(IWM)*

A chaplain writing a Field Postcard home for a wounded man. July 1916 *(IWM)*

Arras, June 1917, by Geoffrey Rose *(IWM)*

A 'humpy' dug-out, by J. Nash *(IWM)*

Montauban Wood with graves, by Sir William Orpen *(IWM)*

Meister Omers. The 13th Century home of the family from 1916–1936.
From a watercolour by M. Mallorie, June 1931

Burgon and Julian on holiday in the late 1950s

By 21 May, Julian is away from the Front Line and less pressed:

Although the guns thunder away day and night, we do not pay much attention.

Yesterday, a glorious day, we had a real Sunday. The Brigadier ordered a Church Parade for the whole brigade together, with the exception of the Scottish who hold a Presbyterian service. This is the first time we have ever had such a service since I have been with the Division. Battalion parades have been the biggest I have ever addressed. I am not in favour of such large parades, for there are always a lot of men who cannot hear, and the musical side of the service is always a difficulty. However, the General had ordered it, so being in the Army we obey.

On very high ground the Brigade was drawn up in a hollow square. The machine gun company, the trench mortar battery, and the whole Field Ambulance also attended. There must have been well over 2,000 men on parade. Green, the other C of E chaplain and myself were accommodated on a military GS wagon with a table covered with a Union Jack separating us. He took the service and I preached. The drum and fife band of the RAMC led the singing. I preached on the 'Home-coming of Jesus Christ'. Afterwards I was told that everyone in front heard me and as far as I can gather, nearly everyone at the flanks. The distant roar of the guns reminded us incessantly of what we had just left behind. Aeroplanes circled overhead continually. From where I stood I could see over the heads of the troops, a glorious view of rolling country, shining with the fresh green of spring, dotted here and there with un-strafed villages.

The service, in spite of its difficulties, went quite well, but I cannot feel satisfied that this is really the right way to teach men to worship God.

Julian goes on to record

the best story of Huns being captured long after a battle. One of our large shells blew in the entrance to a long German dug-out rather north of us. This dug-out at that moment contained twenty-seven Germans and a quartermaster, and was also a Quartermaster's Store. On the plentiful rations that were on the spot they had lived for twelve days and then thought it was time to dig themselves out, which they proceeded to do, much to the astonishment of some British troops in the vicinity. There suddenly appeared from the bowels of the earth, twelve days after the battle had moved far ahead, twenty-seven stalwart Huns, led by an equally stalwart quartermaster. They surrendered gladly.

Burgon describes an unsatisfactory and expensive engagement (not far from Arras and therefore from Julian) on which 'the simplest soldier', as he describes himself, comments after the action:

It looks to us as though the authorities had said, 'We are going to use men on horses at all costs', and they did. The 'cost' to the Cavalry Division was 500 men and 1200 horses. 'By these casualties', the Army Commander said to the Divisional Commander, 'you have saved the lives of 5000 infantry'.

Burgon says:

That is all very well, but we could have saved the same amount of infantry with one tenth of the cost to ourselves, had the operation been carried out in a different way.

The way it was in fact carried out is described in detail by Burgon. After a terrible night in shell-holes filled with water, and a day of uncommonly accurate German shelling,

I and one or two subalterns in the Royals were getting what shelter we could in an old Boche gun emplacement (in fact we were actually sitting on the Boche field gun which was pointing in the direction of Arras) when the first heavy crump fell about 250 yards behind us. Then another, rather nearer, then another a little further off, but to the side – then another nearer still and to the other side. It looked bad – right in front of us were the whole of the Royal Dragoons, all the N Somerset Yeomanry except the men who had gone up dismounted, and besides them the led horses of the 8th Brigade and various other oddments which always seem to join themselves on to a body of troops on such occasions. Two or three heavy crumps in that mass of horses would spell real disaster. We half started to our feet, expecting the order to move either backwards or forwards, no matter where, so long as we could get the horses out of that valley which the Germans were searching with diabolical accuracy. Even as we discussed the best thing to do if orders did not come, a crump came singing over our heads and burst right in the middle of Miles' squadron about thirty yards from where we were.

Miles rushed forward, shouting 'By God, there'll be nothing left of my squadron if we don't get out of here'. When the black smoke cleared away it left a horrible picture of writhing horses and men. Some lay still. Crumps now began falling everywhere. It was a hard test for the men standing there inactive – many of them holding three, four or even five horses.

There was nothing for it but to move another 300 to 400 yards back, which we did in fairly good order – considering the difficulties, in very good order. I rushed to my section, steadied them up with a few words, numbered them off to see they were all there and sent them on behind 'C' squadron of the regiment. Infantry were coming through us at the time – and they one and all took to the old trenches and shell-holes – but we had to stay in the open with our horses – and simply pray that a high explosive did not fall on our heads.

Again I am glad to say I did not have a single casualty in my section, either horse or man. Mine is the only section in the whole squadron which came through without a scratch – and among the men I believe I have got quite a reputation for luck. On various occasions the same good fortune does seem to have attended me[8].

The shelling continued for about a quarter of an hour, leaving dead and wounded men and horses all over that valley; then it stopped. We stayed where we were in driving snow and sleet till nearly dark – then received orders to proceed back to Arras by the cavalry track. Owing to the fearful weather, the cavalry track had been churned into a sea of mud, so deep and treacherous that it rivalled anything that the Canadian West could produce. It was almost dark, and so you can judge what a really terrible experience this was, after three days and nights continual privation, horses and men tired out; the men had had nothing to eat but bully and biscuit for two and a half days, and nothing but cold water to drink, and the same applied to the officers; the horses had not drunk for two days; many were lost on that track from sheer exhaustion.

. . . the whole thing seemed to me to be of political rather than of military value. At any rate we have now been withdrawn again. . . .

On 30 May, Julian's name appeared in the London Gazette among no fewer than ninety chaplains who were mentioned in dispatches. His mother writes proudly in the diary:

the most delightful thing that has happened during the last ten days is that Julian has got a Mention for conspicuous bravery. As Ralph says, 'This must have given Morris in Paradise a very happy birthday in June'.

The diarist here permits herself a rare single sentence of self-pity:

It seems no longer do we breathe more freely with Julian out of the Line than Burgon goes in.

They were rightly worried about Burgon who had just been having (and was going to have again) a very dangerous time near a village called Epehy, in an outpost which had become known as 'The Birdcage':

It is an isolated T-junction of a trench system, pushed out 1000 yards ahead of our main line, and only able to be approached by night, as one has to come down over a bare hillside in full sight of the Germans.

Burgon was to take two machine-guns into it, with an NCO and eighteen men. The Boche Line was only 150-200 yards away and German raids were commonplace:

it was a jumpy experience to be out on a pitch black night. The wires rattle in the wind, the grass rustles, there are a thousand disquieting sounds and shadows. Trees which in reality just appear above the horizon assume the proportions of a man creeping towards one about thirty yards off. One can imagine anything. As a matter of fact, there were Boches messing about round our wire. We had patrols out, but they were not as strong as the enemy's ones. Before one working party went out, I swept the long grass with fire from my gun, just to touch up anybody who might by lying there. Then I took the wiring party out myself, and posted the covering points. They had, in my opinion, a very efficient young officer with them.

About midnight, the Germans began to shrapnel us, their patrols having reported we were working. The shrapnel burst with thunder-claps right over our heads, which was rather terrifying, but fortunately only two men were wounded. The coming of the day that morning was trying, and our eyes were tired. Never was there a longer dawn, nor one peopled with more curious shapes and shadows. As I lay in the long grass hour after hour, with straining eyes on the look-out for the least sound or suspicious movement, I fear my thoughts for a soldier were rather heretical. There passed through my mind the memory of days at Oberammergau, of wonderful afternoons in the woods of Saxon Switzerland, of my kind old German landlady and of her good-looking peasant son (now perhaps creeping towards me through the grass, a bomb ready to throw in his hand), of Dresden and Fräulein Gottschaldt, of perfect nights on the Bruhlische Terrasse, sipping beer to the strains of the first class orchestra (after hearing the Valkyries at the opera), with fairy-lighted steamers passing up and down the Elbe, and the bridges picked out with lamps. When shall we see that Germany again? As someone wrote the other day, '. . . most of us, even up to the actual outbreak of war, used to think of Germany as the home of small and inoffensive people'. . . .

However, going back to the business in hand, everything passed off quietly, and by 11 o'clock it was a hot and cloudless day. Many were the aeroplane fights we witnessed, till one became quite callous. A few days earlier, a sausage balloon had been brought down, one of ours, just behind our sector. It had been brought down by the great Baron[9], the German airman who was responsible for the downfall of our well-known Ball. The method of procedure was this – two Boches fighting machines approached the sausage at a moderate altitude; they were at once engaged by two of our machines, and in the melée no one noticed a single German machine flying by itself at a tremendous height. In the middle of the scrap, this machine, driven by the Baron, swooped down on our sausage balloon, bombed it, and got away unscathed.

Snipers on both sides had a field day:

We knew for certain where one sniper was – in a particular tree – and the brigade sniping officer was determined to have him. He and the 3rd DG sniping officer started at 8 pm while it was still quite light, to walk to the Birdcage; the bare hill was a dangerous place leading down to the valley behind it. Our officer was ten minutes in front, and had already reached the communication trench in the Birdcage from where he could see the German sniper's tree, before the 3rd DG officer began to cross the dangerous area. As the latter crossed the hill, the sniper shot at him. The officer did not notice and continued walking. Our man, seeing the danger, himself put a couple of bullets six feet in front of the 3rd DG which made him fall like a log. After a few moment he became tired of lying down and decided to bolt for it. He did so; the German sniper became so excited at this that he leant right out of the tree to shoot at the running figure. Whereupon our own officer with his telescopic sight shot him dead, and he came crashing head foremost from the tree. So that ended him.

The following night I was relieved and was not sorry.

The morning after he was out of it, Burgon had lunch with the Brigadier:

I showed him my sketch maps of the place and told what my ideas were with regard to the position of MGs in the Birdcage.

He finishes:

There is something highly exhilarating about 'handing over'. One feels superior in knowledge and experience, anxious not to 'put the wind up' the newcomer unduly, yet not averse to impressing him with the 'bloodiness' of the place. 'Here they snipe during the day'. 'By that big coil of wire over there the Boches creep out at night' – and so on. The doings of the last few days, terrifying at the time, assume quite rosy colours. 'But it's all right', one hastens to add, 'it's quite cushy really, there is nothing to worry about'. 'Oh no,' says the newcomer, rather uncertainly, 'I see there isn't. Where's the bulk ammunition and where's the bomb store?'. And so the game of question and answer goes on till all the accumulated experience of the past days is imparted on the one hand and imbibed on the other. And the sergeant-major comes up and salutes, 'Relief complete, Sir'. Then off the relieved ones troop, and it doesn't matter if it snows ink. We've had a rather trying time and it is over – for the present.

Well enough of myself. How splendid about Julian's being mentioned in dispatches. I am writing him a line today. He will get something more one day – and deserves it now. But even this recognition will give him and his brigade much satisfaction.

PS. The Divisional General has now taken to calling me 'Bishop' – unwarranted familiarity!

Julian's brigade is resting; he writes happily:

In this delightful camp amid the apple blossom and the hawthorn I have not been idle. Never have I had such a good opportunity for doing true chaplain's work. Two services each day, Holy Communion at 8 am and Evensong at 6.30 pm followed most evenings by a Confirmation Class, are truly delightful.

I am finding time to visit our prisoners. Every battalion has a few men in its guard room undergoing field punishment. We have one man under close arrest who I fear is likely to be shot. He has deserted four or five times and he never really belonged to us. He was sent to us under the Conscription Act and deserted before he ever reached us. I don't think he has any hope of being let off. He has already been sentenced to death once and let off with fifteen years penal servitude, which was suspended to give him the opportunity of regaining his character by bravery in the field. After rejoining his company in the trenches he promptly deserted again, so I fear it is all up with him. I had a long talk with him today.

Add to all this the organizing of a concert and the Recreation Room, seeing men privately on all kinds of matters, and the 101 small things that crop up to do, and you have a pretty full day.

He adds modestly:

PS. I have had a good number of congratulations on my 'Mention', but I haven't any idea what it was for.

The sports behind the Lines

were a great success from every point of view. All the Divisional Staff came over, and the Divisional Band came and played as well as our own massed bands. There were races of every description, including one on bicycles for chaplains and doctors, in which I managed to pass the post first. Some of the doctors were not very proficient in the art of bicycle riding, and the race caused much amusement and enthusiasm. Three-legged races, sack races, relay races and all the usual types were run. Our battalion came out first with most firsts and seconds. But the best part of the afternoon for me was a visit to the sports by Philip Gibbs, and I had a delightful time with him. He is optimistic about Russia, but doubtful as to their 'pushing' capacity for this year. We got on to the question which I can see interests him more than anything else, and that is, the moral issues of the war, and he was anxious to know all I could tell him as to what our men thought about the necessity of 'carrying on' and if they discussed the moral side at all, and how far they felt upheld by the need of carrying on from the highest ideals. We were so absorbed in our talk that we paced up and down behind the lines of spectators, regardless of the races or the cheering for quite a long time.

Philip Gibbs, described that same sports day and Julian's part in it in a dispatch which appeared in the Telegraph *on 4 June and was clearly a result of their talk together. Gibbs wrote:*

This was the sports day of the London men, and they were making the most of the peace and sunshine and laughter, every glorious minute of it. Laughter and cheers swept continuously along all sides of that hollow square about the playing field. They laughed and cheered mightily at a bicycle race between padres and doctors riding on French boneshakers over rough ground. It was won by a long-legged Church of England padre who has been with them on many a field of battle and comforted them in body and soul in many hours of horror with a fine devotion and utter truthfulness of spirit, which will have nothing to do with the falsity which slurs over the frightful conflict between Christian ideals and the devilries of war, so that his men go to him with their doubts and despairs, and find a human, honest, understanding heart.

Julian adds a PS to his letter:

Once the *Telegraph* article had been read by the battalion, I am now known as 'the long-legged padre'.

Burgon is still resting too (13 June):

Pity the poor cavalry-man – we were out all yesterday in great heat practising counter-attacks etc. Half the day he is on his horse and is supposed to have everything correct, and the other half he's on his flat feet, and is expected to know and execute everything the infantryman carries out every day of his life.

Burgon adds:

With the great success of our advance beyond Messines, somehow I feel a little hopeful about the war's being over this year.

In a final letter (10 June) before his battalions come to the end of a rest which they have had for a full fortnight, Julian waxes ecstatic:

We find it hard to believe a war exists at all. The men are all wonderfully rested and in excellent spirits. Here I have been able to establish my ideals for what a chaplain should be able to do. Both battalions for which I am responsible are practically in the same camp, the huts being adjoining except for a shady lane which separates them. I have myself had a hut big enough to use as an office as well as a bedroom, between the two camps and at the edge of the officers' lines, so that men as well as officers of both units have been able to visit me without attracting special attention. Here I have had many interesting interviews, and got through a great deal of letter writing.

So much for myself. This barn church, with its exquisite lights and shades as the sunlight pierces the holes and crannies, became hallowed ground for us. For here in our daily Eucharists and daily Evensong we draw near The Presence; here we have had daily Confirmation classes; and a notice put outside that chaplains would make appointments at any time to hear confessions brought not a few to unburden their souls, and thus to gain fresh strength and hope in 'carrying-on'. I do not think I have ever got into such close touch with officers or men.

It is very sad to see how short we are now of chaplains. Vacancies take ages to fill up and, as far as I can make out, many divisions are short. Why this should be, goodness only knows. It makes me despair of the Church of England. Rome makes no mistakes. We have no fewer than five Roman priests in our division for barely 400 RCs, and at the present moment only six C of E chaplains. Frantic appeals for more make no difference.

I do not suppose a single department in the whole government has escaped revision or drastic alteration since the war began, except the one which administers the chaplains' 'show'. No one seems strong enough to protest against the incompetence. True pastoral instinct is really dead, if it ever lived, in the hearts of those who think one chaplain can look after a constantly changing flock of 30,000 to 40,000 men.

His first chaplains' retreat (June 15) gave him a week's opportunity to think and pray and look to the future:

Chaplains' School of Instruction, BEF
June 15, 1917

I reached this place (St Omer), old GHQ., yesterday, and the Retreat began last night. Canon Cunningham is the conductor, and already I can see that he will be admirable. We had a wonderfully interesting discussion last night before the Retreat began; starting on Preaching, it developed into what was the general duty of a chaplain at the Front, what the ideal he should put before himself, how far divide his time to lifting the general 'morale' of the whole number of men under his care; what we were to make of the religion prompted solely, as far as we could see, by fear – each point led on really from the last.

What I am becoming more and more convinced of is this, that there is growing up quite distinctly a new band of the younger clergy in the Church of England who have been out here as chaplains and have faced not only the shells and bullets with their men, but also have now the great facts of the deadness of religion permeating our whole national life. These are the clergy who, by God's grace, are going to find some means of waking up the Church at home, not in any spirit of self-satisfaction, nor with any illusions as to the difficulty of the task before them.

Starting with themselves as penitents and seekers for the Truth, they will endeavour, by God's grace, to stir up the Church and rekindle old enthusiasms, cut away the dross and clear the channels for the Holy Spirit of God. This party, if you must call it a party, is neither spikily High Church nor Protestant in the accepted meaning of those terms; the great majority seem to come from the Catholic school, or to have been much influenced by it, but not one is deaf to the claim of non-conformity to recognition, and all see that the truly catholic man is he who is sympathetic to the position adopted by other Christians. I think you will find the chaplains of the BEF will be a pretty forceful, and yet humble, body of men on their return to England. We shall return in a practical prayerful spirit, seeking with wide-open eyes the guidance of the Spirit of God, and determined above all to build upon our own mistakes and failures.

On his way back to his unit

I met such an excellent fellow at GHQ who asked at once if I was any relation to the Oxford 'Blue'[10] and I was glad to be able to claim a near relationship, and he told me how much he admired the way he managed the team when he was captain, and how much everybody admired him; this too from a man who had tried for a place and did not get in. He said how well everybody felt that the team had been led, and how glad everybody was that the captain played the game of his life and won the match through his own play and the way he handled his side.

Then in the evening, after an excellent dinner in the Officers' Club, Julian went for a stroll:

I found a tent full of Yorkshire lads who invited me in, and I sat down and we had a yarn for over an hour. All except two wore the gold [wound] stripes and two had been wounded on July 1st, the others at various dates, but to my joy I found all belonged to the 31st Division and of course had known Serre and the fighting round it. One fine-looking fellow started talking about the trench fighting previous to 1 July, and when I told him I came from Leeds, said he had many friends in the Leeds Pals battalion and had had a talk once to one of their officers, a splendid chap, the most popular officer in the battalion – he was always talking to his fellows in a friendly way and looking after their interests. 'Mr Bickersteth was his name, Sir. There was many a lad in the Brigade who was sorry to hear about him going under, outside his own battalion. So many of us knew him. He was a "pal" to his men, he was'.

'I happen', I said, 'to be his brother'. You should have seen his surprise. It was good, wasn't it, to hear the absolutely unsought testimony of how our dear Morris was loved by his men. What a lot of good he must have done.

Is there anything to equal the happiness of the 'camaraderie' and friendship of the life out here?

The diarist expatiates on honours and awards:

There is a new Order instituted by the King, being an Order for both women and men who have done war service, but not in the fighting line. It is the Order of the British Empire and is to have classes. The women of the two upper classes are to be entitled 'Dames'.

The whole question of Orders and Medals in this war is a thorny one. For this new Order, for instance, the Minister of Munitions has sent in 25,000 names!! It is disgraceful the way the Staff and others who have never been in the firing line get the DSO and the MC. A bundle of Orders comes to the War Office and first goes to the highest Staff, who take their pick, and then the next in order, and so down to the Divisional Staffs and Brigades until these last who who have been in the firing line have very few orders left to receive. The same is done with foreign orders such as the *Légion d'Honneur* and the *Croix de Guerre* and those of other nations. They come to the War Office and are distributed in the same way. The other day twenty-one Orders were given by mistake to twenty-one men who had refused to be vaccinated. The lists got mixed up. At last it has been arranged that the GOC can give an MC at the Front within twenty-four hours after the brave act has been committed, and a Divisional General a DSO within forty-eight hours; only for the latter there must have been two witnesses.

Burgon is in the Line again, a part of it he describes as 'cushy':

To spend day after day of this peerless June weather in hot, dusty, sweaty, fly-covered trenches is to say the least of it very trying. The Germans are pretty quiet. They shelled just on my left this morning about 10 o'clock, and if most of them had not been 'duds' they would have done considerable damage. But only one burst.

He adds:

I do not in the least feel thrilled at being faced with 'the enemies of all that is fair and beautiful and of good report in Europe', as Father suggests. Merely excitement at being so close, and a determination to stop them. I feel no rancour against the German rank and file whatsoever. Of course, my views might be different if I were taken prisoner. That I can't say.

But his ideals remain:

This I think will reach you on or about the day of the unveiling of Morris's memorial[11]. The longer the world exists the more clearly will posterity see the greatness of the cause for which he and thousands of other Englishmen have died.

Trench raids, many of them successful, all of them brave endeavours, were of course a great feature of the First World War. This one eventually, many months later, brought Burgon a Military Cross:

Now that it's all over, I suppose there is no harm in telling you about it. The raid had been planned for nearly a fortnight, but for various reasons had been put off. Finally it was settled for Sunday night last, i.e. the small hours of Monday morning. Those who were taking part in it were taken out of the trenches to a ruined village a couple of kilometres or so behind, and had a good sleep at night and trained during the day. Of course we are novices in raids and we had everything to learn, but we decided on the rough formations we were to move forward in, practised the deployment as soon as we got inside the enemy wire, detailed the covering party, the men to mark the gap in the wire, the stretcher-bearers, the prisoners' escort and a host of other details. All Thursday, Friday and Saturday we practised and on Friday and Saturday nights also practised by night. The Divisional General and all kinds of people came to these practices. It was all rather a new toy for them.

The raiders were divided into two parties, each with a German post to raid. I was with 'A' party, and Johnnie Dunville was our scouts officer. We had to leave our outpost line, find our way across about 800 yards of no-man's-land and strike (by compass bearing) the wire exactly in front of the particular trenches we were to raid. The place was so far off it had never been properly reconnoitred, and the gunners had never registered on it. Aeroplane photographs alone showed us more or less the kind of thing we had to tackle. I took the covering party for 'A'; there was a sunken road on our right, a trench which our gunners could not barrage, and a wood, all of which we knew were full of Boches. My job was to stop any of the enemy coming out of these places while our fellows were dealing with the Boches in the actual trench we were raiding. The gap in the enemy wire was to be made with a torpedo, a wonderful and fearsome weapon; when it goes off with a terrific explosion, it blows a gap wide enough to drive a coach and four through, curling the wire up neatly each side.

Owing to the long distance, it was necessary to lay a tape out the whole way from our wire to theirs, so that we could come back quickly and without losing our way.

All these things we practised, by day and by night, until everybody knew his job.

At last the night came. We were to be supported by an artillery barrage for which various heavy batteries had been roped in and also some guns on our flanks, so that with our own horse batteries (which of course are regular batteries) we had plenty of support. Besides the actual and heavy horse batteries, we had all the machine-guns shooting from behind us and over our heads. The artillery and the MG barrage was to be not only on our immediate front but a good many thousands of yards on each flank, so as to thoroughly mystify the Boches. Zero hour was at 1.10 am. At 8 o'clock that night we gathered in a little hut outside a ruined house in an utterly ruined village and dined. It was a very cheery meal and everyone was in good form. At 10.30 pm we went straight from our post out on to parade where we found our 100 raiders (each party consisted roughly of 50 men, and there were six Sappers per party to work the torpedoes). On our arms we had white bands so that in the darkness we should not be killing our own people. And so at 10.30 pm you might have seen 100 men or more marching silently off down the village street, the gaunt walls of the ruined houses showing ghostly in the light of an early moon which would be sunk before we got to grips with the Hun. I carried a revolver, two bombs and a big stick, and thought what a delightful occupation this was for a Christian in the 20th century AD.

By 12.30 we were at our posts and sat down at a gap made in our own wire, through which we were to pass. At 10 minutes to 01.00 Dunville and the scouts moved forward, holding the tape, while two men at our end held the reel. 'B' party were about 400 yards to our left, but we were to converge on the German outpost line and hoped to meet after each settling our own German trench. At five minutes to 01.00 we moved forward, following the tape; we went 450 yards through thistles almost as high as our heads, and came up again with Dunville and the scouts. In absolute silence we waited again for a few moments. At about seven minutes past one we moved forward again about 150 yards. This brought us within about fifteen yards of where shells would be dropping at Zero hour.

At 1.10 to the tick all our guns started. The shells seemed to whistle literally a few feet over our heads and fall with a blinding flash and a concussion just in front of us. We lay cowering in the thistles. It was a wonderful sight. The whole countryside was lit up, and of course the Hun put up Verey lights by the dozen, and as soon as they saw something was up, green lights went up for SOS and red lights for retaliation. The barrage began 100 yards this side of the Boche wire. It stayed there thirty seconds and then went on to their wire and trenches, taking thirty seconds to travel the distance – a creeping barrage. It remained on their trenches for three and a half minutes. Therefore at Zero plus 4½ (in other words, at fourteen and a half minutes past one) the barrage lifted off the bit of trench we were to raid (though in all other parts of the Line of course it remained on the enemy front line system), and the Sappers ran in to put the torpedo in the wire. We had meanwhile been creeping up behind the barrage nearer and nearer, and at Zero plus 7½ (i.e. at seven and a half minutes past one) we were to go through the wire and make for the trenches.

My job was to get into action with the guns just outside the wire and engage any target, especially hostile MGs or advancing Boches that I might see. So far everything had gone well, except that we had met with a certain amount of rifle fire from the moment the artillery opened; and as a matter of fact, directly I heard the barrage I knew we were in trouble. It was extraordinarily accurate (only two shells fell short, one immediately behind us), but it was not nearly strong enough. There were not enough guns, indeed there aren't enough behind us, even with outside help, to produce a real drum fire such as I have seen on various occasions, notably on the Somme and at Arras. The Boches were never really stupefied or overwhelmed. Some were killed; but the rest, when the barrage lifted, popped their heads over the parapet and began to shoot. So that when 100 yards from the wire, we were already coming under a very stiff rifle fire. Then we bumped up against some wire which we did not know was there. It was hidden in the thistles, so the aeroplane photographs did not show it. This delayed us, and you must remember that the things are worked out so much to the second that the least delay means a serious dislocation of the plans. We were only allowed ten minutes for our work (which to put it bluntly was to kill Boches and take a few prisoners).

We crept forward, the rifle fire becoming still more troublesome, and men began to get hit. A sergeant crept back shot through the chest. Trench mortars began to fall – a man got a bit in his back and lay there groaning – a third hit in the leg, and so on. The scouts with Dunville had now reached the proper wire. We were about twenty yards behind them. Then followed further delays with the torpedo. The first wire was not thick and we had cut it. This had to be blown up. The torpedo did not fit together, or else the sappers were a bit fuddled at being shot at. A shout for the other torpedo (each party carried a reserve one), and while the second was being brought up, the first went off. The sappers and scouts ran back immediately before the explosion for safety's sake. The men behind them thought they were retiring and began to retire too.

Meanwhile I was in action with my two guns, shooting right-handed, and then when I saw the men were a bit 'sticky' I veered round and shot straight at the flash of the rifles in the German trench, which was about fifty yards off. At this moment poor Johnnie Dunville came back with his arm shattered and a wound in his chest, and I feel pretty certain that about the same time the Boches began to come out of their trench and throw bombs. They certainly had a small trench in front, probably a series of listening posts joined up, in which they had bombers. So much time had now been wasted that there only remained a few minutes to go before the signal for withdrawal would come. The noise was deafening – our own barrage still at full blast – the German mortar bombs and grenades on all sides, and a stiff rifle fire. Some of the raiding party now ran forward, but they could do little in the face of such opposition and had not Henderson's hunting horn sounded the withdrawal, I doubt whether many of them would have been left.

My position was somewhat unpleasant. The rest of the party withdrew, expecting that I should follow up pretty steadily behind them, with my face to the foe, so to speak, shooting if necessary. Unfortunately, we had a badly wounded corporal lying on the grass by our side, and we had to get him back, so that about 1.30 am, I found myself fifty yards from the Boche trench (less from his wire) with four sound men, and this wounded fellow, who was so bad he could do nothing to help himself and kept on falling off whichever back we hoisted him on to. I brought up the rear, with my revolver drawn. It took us ages. I thought we should never get back – over 800 yards remember – half a mile at a snail's pace. The danger I knew was the German barrage, which might begin at any moment, and sure enough, when we were just getting near our outposts, heavy stuff began falling around. By the grace of God there was a small trench just inside our outpost wire, and into that we scrambled; it was not more than three feet deep, but we lay at the bottom in the mud with the wounded man, and hoped for the best. It was now 2.00 am and we had been out in no-man's-land for an hour – one of the worst hours I have ever spent. When the barrage lifted, stretcher-bearers came up and we then went on to outpost headquarters where I reported my return.

Outside the dug-out where the Colonel was, I found one officer lying dead, Dunville fearfully wounded and practically unconscious, another badly wounded, two dead sergeants and a number of wounded men. The scheme had been too ambitious. Many German dead were found by both parties, but we got no prisoners and the operation had to be written off as a failure (which, as I have already said, did not surprise me). It was certainly a useless sacrifice of life. Dunville died this morning. Yesterday I went to the other officer's funeral, and today I went to his. Both were delightful boys, but Johnnie Dunville I felt most. He joined at York the same day as I did, and we hunted together. He motored me about everywhere, and many are the cheery times we have had. The whole thing was a kind of nightmare and I am thankful it is over. I knew it would be a pretty stiff job and I therefore had to face the possibility of being knocked out, a thing I had never had to do quite so squarely before. It brings you to bedrock rather.

I promise you I shall be in no more danger whatever for the present. We are '*à cheval*' in a few days.

He adds in a letter of 30 June (1 July was the anniversary of Morris's death):

He has not been out of my thoughts these few days. Yesterday a year ago I said good-bye to him at Acheux. Tomorrow he started on the greatest and most interesting journey man is called to take. My good-ness, Mother, when you really face this life, it does seem a foolish temporary thing in many ways.

Julian comments to his mother on the same day:

The memories of yesterday a year ago, the last time I saw darling Morris, are very vivid and tonight I think of that march up to the trenches with a glorious sunset, and the strange forebodings about the morrow. I think July 1st will for ever stand in the history of the world as one of the epoch-making dates in all history. It denotes the beginning of the turning of the tide – the turning point in the Great War. If it was necessary and right, as I believe it was, of God's all-seeing Providence, for our dear Morris to pass on so soon and so young to the Larger Life, I cannot help feeling glad that the day was July 1st and not sooner or later. He found himself among that splendid crowd of glorious men who 'passed over' at the time – a noble company.

I mustn't write more to-night though my heart is full, but I have a long day tomorrow and may not be able to crawl into my little shelter until some time after midnight tonight.

On 5 July, 1917, he writes a long letter describing his ministry to the deserter mentioned above whom he had visited in detention. 'This intensely moving account of it all', wrote Burgon in the margin, years afterwards, 'would make a wonderful one-act play'12.
It begins with no hint of the high drama to come:

I was distressed to hear from our Colonel that the man I have written about who came to us under close arrest as a deserter six months ago and who has deserted again four times since, had been condemned to death. The previous sentence of death passed on him had been commuted and then suspended to give him another chance, but he deserted again during the Battle of Arras and so lost his only chance.

Monday, July 2nd. I left our HQ in the Line fairly early and went straight down to see the Senior Chaplain, who himself intended to take on this sad business, but as I have been seeing the man practically every day for three or four months I asked him to let me see it through. I felt it was my duty. So after some lunch with him I went to our Transport Lines and saw the firing party, picked by military requirements from our own men. These men had been sent down specially from the trenches. I made several arrangements about the digging of the grave, and then went on to the spot where the promulgation was to take place. This consisted of the prisoner being marched under escort to a spot just outside the village. Here he was placed in the centre of a hollow square formed by representatives drawn from each battalion in the Brigade. At a given signal the prisoner is ordered to take two paces to the front, which he does, and his cap is taken off, and then the officer in charge of the parade reads the sentence, which concludes with a recital of the crime for which the prisoner has been found guilty. I stood close behind the prisoner to support him by my presence all I could. There was a terrible silence when the promulgation concluded with the sentence of death. The man seemed a bit dazed, but stepped back to between his guards fairly smartly. I walked off the ground with him. He was taken to a little back room on the second storey of a semi-detached villa in the village.

Let me try to describe to you the man, before I tell you more. Heavily built, rather vacant-eyed, low forehead, very dirty in appearance in spite of all efforts of the military police to make him clean himself; his utterance was indistinct and his mastery of the English language somewhat limited. His previous history was typical, I suppose, of many others, but not without its sadness. Our modern civilisation had done little for him. His father, a 'cabby' in East London, had died when he was a boy of thirteen. His mother, reduced in her circumstances, lived afterwards in one room. The boy was sent out to 'do what he could for himself'. He lived from hand to mouth. He learnt enough to avoid the police, to get enough to eat, but his home ties soon began to mean less and less to him. Occasionally he brought his mother home a few pence to add to the limited family exchequer. On this effort he dwelt in his reminiscences to me with pride. Who knows it may stand before the Judgement

Seat for much; it meant at least a spark of filial duty. But with no one to help him much, he drifted into bad company and before he was twenty found himself in prison.

On coming out the first time, he still kept in touch with his mother, but a second conviction soon after meant a longer time in prison and when at last he was free again his mother had moved from the single room she occupied before he went to prison, and from that day to this he had never seen her again. He never found out, or troubled to find out, where she had gone. His two sisters had several years before gone into service and disappeared from the family circle. The Military Service Act caught him in its meshes and he became a soldier. During his training in the East End, he found one good woman who lived next door to the Military Depot or Guard Room, who used to give him meals on credit. The address of this woman he remembered, but not her name. Accustomed always to do as he pleased, he had deserted twice before he left England and was brought across under arrest. Escaping soon after, he was caught and sent up to the Line, only to escape on the way, and when apprehended, we had to send our battalion military police to fetch him – not a very propitious entry into the regiment.

This was six months ago, and from that day to this he has almost the whole time been in our Guard Room.

This was the man I had to tackle with only twelve hours more left to live. There were not a few who said he was mad, or at least that there was something wrong with his brain, but our doctor had been unable to certify that he was in any way not responsible for his actions, and certainly he was quite intelligent in a good many ways. He could read and write well.

He sat down heavily on a chair. The room was furnished with a small round table, three chairs, and a wire bed raised six inches from the ground. I took a chair and sat next to him. 'I am going to stay with you and do anything I can for you. If you'd like to talk, we will, but if you would rather not, we'll sit quiet'. Two fully-armed sentries with fixed bayonets stand one by the door and the other by the window. The room is only nine feet by ten feet. Anything in the nature of a private talk seems likely to be difficult. An appeal that the sentries might be removed is not accepted. There are no bars to the window and the prisoner might seek to make an end of himself. So I sit on silently. Suddenly I hear great heaving sobs, and the prisoner breaks down and cries. In a second I lean over close to him, as he hides his face in his hands, and in a low voice

I talk to him. He seems still a little doubtful about his fate, and I have to explain to him what is going to happen tomorrow morning. I tell him about Morris and of how many splendid men have 'passed on'; what fine company he will find on the other side.

After a time he quietens down and his tea comes up – two large pieces of bread and butter, a mess tin half-full of tea and some jam in a tin. One of the sentries lends me his clasp knife so that I may put jam on his bread, for the prisoner of course is not allowed to handle a knife. After his tea is over, I hand him a pipe and tobacco. These comforts, strictly forbidden to all prisoners, are not withheld now. He loved a pipe – and soon he is contentedly puffing away.

Times goes on. I know that he must sleep, if possible, during the hours of darkness, so my time is short. How can I reach his soul? I get out my Bible and read to him something from the Gospel. It leaves him unmoved. He is obviously uninterested and my attempt to talk a little about what I have read leaves him cold. Where is my point of contact? I make him move his chair as far away from the sentry as possible, and speaking in a very low voice close to him, I am not overheard; but of what to speak? There is no point of contact through his home, which means nothing to him. I get out an Army Prayer Book, which contains at the end about 130 hymns, and handing him the book, ask him to read through the part at the end so that if he can find a hymn he knows, I can read it to him. He hits on 'Rock of Ages', asking not if I will read it to him, but if we can sing it. The idea of our solemnly singing hymns together while the two sentries eye us coldly from the other side of the room seems to me so incongruous that I put him off with the promise of a hymn to be sung before he goes to sleep, but he is not satisfied and he returns to the suggestion again. This time I had enough sense, thank goodness, to seize on 'the straw'; and we sat there and sang hymns together – for three hours or more.

The curious thing about this extraordinary man is that he takes command of the proceedings. He chooses the hymns. He will not sing any one over twice. He starts the hymn on the right note, he knows the tunes and pitches them all perfectly. Music has evidently not been denied him. The words mean nothing to him, or else he is so little gifted with imagination that the pathos of such lines as 'Hold Thou Thy Cross before my closing eyes' and many similar lines, which in my view of the morrow should cut deep, leave the prisoner unmoved.

Oh how we sang! – hymn after hymn. He knew more tunes than I did. After half an hour away for some dinner, I returned to the little room and in the rapidly fading light went on with the hymn-singing. I brought him a YMCA hymn book which contained several hymns not in the other. He was delighted, and we sang 'Throw out the life-line', 'What a friend we have in Jesus' and others. When 10.30 pm came I was anxious to see the prisoner sleeping for his own sake, though I was willing to go on singing hymns if he wanted to. His stock, however, was nearly exhausted, as he would never sing the same hymn twice over. So we agreed to close the singing, but he would sing one of the hymns he had already sung, a second time as a last effort. So he chose 'God be with us till we meet again'. He sang it utterly unmoved. While I was ruminating over how to make use of the hymns for getting a little further on he said, 'We haven't finished yet; we must have "God save the King"', and then and there we rose to our feet, and the two Military Police, who had replaced the ordinary guards and had been accommodated with two chairs, had to get up and stand rigidly to attention while the prisoner and I sang lustily three verses of the National Anthem. A few seconds later the prisoner was asleep.

I felt that the hymns, even if the words had not meant much to him, had been a prayer, or rather many prayers, and seeing him inclined to sleep, I did not try to get his attention to pray with him more. I have never spent a stranger evening.

I think it was a distinct effort on his part to give religion full play. To him, hymn singing meant religion. Probably no other aspect or side of religion had ever touched him, and now that he was 'up against it' he found real consolation in singing hymns learnt in childhood – he had been to Sunday school up to twelve or thirteen. Anyhow, that was the point of contact I had been seeking for.

All night I sat by his side. One sentry played Patience, the other read a book. Once or twice the prisoner woke up, but he soon slept again. At 3.00 am I watched the first beginnings of dawn through the window. At 3.30 am I heard the tramp, tramp of the firing party marching down the road. A few minutes later, the Sergeant-Major brought me a cup of tea and I had a whispered consultation with him as to how long I could let the prisoner sleep. A minute or two later I was called down to the APM, and he gave me some rum to give the prisoner if he wanted it. It was a dark morning, so he did not want the prisoner awakened for another ten minutes. I went up again, and at the right time awakened him. While his breakfast was being brought up, we knelt together in prayer. I commended him to God and we said together the Lord's Prayer, which he knew quite well and was proud of knowing.

Then he sat down and ate a really good breakfast – bread and butter, ham and tea.

When he had finished, it was just four o'clock and I poured into his empty mug a tablespoon of rum, but when he had tasted it, he wouldn't drink any of it. 'Is it time to go?', he said. 'Yes, it is time. I will stay close to you'. Down the narrow stairs we went, and through the silent streets of the village our weird little procession tramped. First, a burly military policeman, then the prisoner, unbound, and myself, followed close on our heels by two more policemen, the APM, the doctor and one other officer. We had about 300 yards to go to a deserted and ruined house just outside the village. I held the prisoner's arm tight for sympathy's sake. Reaching the house, the police immediately hand-cuffed the man and the doctor blindfolded him. He was breathing heavily and his heart going very quickly, but outwardly he was unmoved. I said a short prayer and led him the ten or twelve paces out into the yard, where he was at once bound to a stake. I whispered in his ear, 'Safe in the arms of Jesus', and he repeated quite clearly, 'Safe in the arms of Jesus'. The APM motioned me away. In three or four seconds the Firing Party had done their work. Poor lads – I was sorry for them. They felt it a good deal, and I followed them out of the yard at once and spoke to them and handed them cigarettes.

Another chaplain arrived (I had arranged this earlier) and he and I took the body in a motor ambulance to the nearest cemetery where I had a burial party waiting, and we gave his body Christian Burial.

I went back to the Transport Lines and tried to get some sleep.

He goes on, matter-of-factly enough:

Think of me now in a perfect spot, and best of all, I believe Burgon's brigade is passing through the next village tomorrow. If so, you may be certain we shall manage to meet.

On 6 July the brothers did meet:

'Today', writes the diarist, 'we had the great happiness of receiving a combined letter from Burgon and Julian, dated 6 July, Burgon beginning it:

It will surprise you to learn that I am writing in Julian's tent. This morning I was riding along with my billeting party, and passing some troops asked what division they belonged to. On learning they belonged to Julian's, I immediately dismounted and went to the nearest Battalion HQ and found out from the adjutant how the division was placed. On reaching the village where my billeting had to be done, I got to work and was inspecting the provision for watering our horses, when Julian himself bicycled up. He had learnt from the brigade which occupied the billets before us that we were coming in today, and therefore came over. He accompanied me on my billeting work and we had a lively little lunch together in a farm, and then he sat with me by the side of the road, while we waited for my squadron. He watched the squadron pull into the field and get the lines down – and then I bicycled off with him 5 kms to his village, having got leave to be away till nightfall. On the way we stopped at his Divisional HQ where he attended for twenty minutes (I would not allow more!) a chaplains' meeting. Then we came on here. It is a delightful village buried in trees, and the weather is peerless. Julian has a tent by himself in a field with magnificent timber all round him.

Everybody adores Julian. He has a smile for every man; and every man from the General to the newest-joined recruit, has a smile for him. Julian looks, and is, extraordinarily fit. Two days out of the Line, he is naturally a little tired, but he is sunburnt, and as usual occupied with all kinds of plans for his battalion's physical and spiritual welfare. For the last hour and a half we have been sitting out in the shade discussing every problem under the sun. Julian is very alive to all the difficulties which face the Church at the present moment, and I must say I agree with him when he says he is bewildered by the universal shout for progress and change. The numbers of papers and pamphlets we receive asking for our views on what the men believe, why they believe it, and if they believe nothing, what is the reason; how the Church should act, what changes strike one as being most necessary in the Church's organisation, in the presentation of her teaching and so forth. What unity is there with this diversity of effort? Who is our leader? What do we want? I do not agree with Julian about several things – notably on the advisability of 'getting a move on' now. He says that nothing big (as, for instance, the somewhat vague, as it seems to me, Life and Liberty movement) should be attempted during the war. Personally I think preparation must be made now. But I do feel we are bewildered in matters religious, much as the wretched housewife is with regard to what she must or must not buy for her household in the way of food.

. . . Later. Well, we have just had a very jolly dinner – such a nice crowd of officers – the whole battalion dining together *'en plein air'* – and now on a glorious summer evening Julian and I are starting back to my village; he is coming half-way with me.

And Julian:

Just a line added to Burgon's to tell you that we have had a glorious day together. We seemed to have so much to say to each other, and were jealous of every second as it hurried past.

From all I can gather, Burgon and his little MG party were left behind in their raid, or rather stayed behind after all the others had withdrawn, in order to help a badly-wounded man, who succumbed later, but in consequence they were caught in the enemy 'barrage'. A small bit of unoccupied trench scarcely three feet deep afforded them some slight cover until the worst was over, and then they got back without further casualties. Certainly I think he deserves an MC but, as you say, the raid not having been successful, I rather fear he may get nothing. However, he came 'safe' out of it, which is the greatest blessing.

Burgon adds a footnote years later:

I was recommended for the MC by the Division, but it was not approved.[13]

Reflecting on his discussions that day with his brother, Burgon in his turn waxes eloquent on the religious scene:

There are a thousand voices and as many conflicting opinions. William Temple[14] writes to say he does not necessarily want Disestablishment (though his Life and Liberty movement seems to take it as inevitable). Why not concentrate on the Archbishops' Report on Church and State (which, I may say in passing, I have only read in extracts – please send me a copy). Where is all this energy for reform leading us? Where is the leader? Who is the prophet? Are the men for whom all these wonderful preparations are being made in the very least interested? Has the National Mission caused even a ripple of interest out here? I do not speak about England, as I know nothing about it, though even there you seem to be flogging into life an already evaporating keenness. There are vital internal questions like the Sacraments, and incidentally the Reservation of the Sacrament, being discussed with all the vehemence of a political question, and great burning problems like

Re-union, about which we are given no authoritative decision. If the soldier had learnt anything out here, he has learnt discipline, and I believe he wants and expects his spiritual leaders, while avoiding the narrow dogmatism of Rome, to speak in no uncertain voice. Frankly, I do not know where the Church stands on some of even the most fundamental questions of doctrine and government and policy.

But in the local 'church', namely the Royal Army Chaplain's Department, there is promotion talk for Julian:

The Deputy Assistant Chaplain General has strongly recommended me as permanent Senior Chaplain and hopes I shall be appointed. I do not myself think this is likely, as the DCG very rarely appoints as Senior Chaplain to a Division anyone who has been a Battalion Chaplain in the same Division. To become Senior Chaplain of any division would not be to my taste at all, as I am so happy among my men. It would just be tolerable in my own Division, where I should still be close to all whom I have got to know and like so much during the last year and a half. But anyhow it would mean living at Divisional Headquarters and although it would always be possible to see one's old friends, if in this division, or to visit men in the trenches and make new friends in another, yet I should not care to live far behind things.

With his night with the condemned deserter still fresh in his mind, Julian describes the General's visit to their chaplains' meeting most approvingly:

He gave us an hour and a half of his valuable time, during which he discussed quite openly the whole question of the carrying out of the death sentence for desertion and other military crimes. He was most sympathetic, especially when he realized that our opinions were by no means influenced by sentimental considerations, nor too one-sided. He said that he expected the carrying-out of the death sentence would be discontinued in due course in our Army, as to the best of his belief it had been already in both the French and German armies, largely because the fire which a modern soldier has to face in battle is of such an appalling nature, owing to the terrible force of modern explosives and modern methods employed in barrage fire. In previous wars a man who was shot was very much a coward. But now the nerve strain was so terrible that it was not always possible to say how far a man was responsible for his actions when subjected to these conditions[15].

197

We put before him various suggestions, discussed the question as to how far such executions acted as a deterrent or the reverse, and mentioned what we thought to be a real necessity to which he agreed, namely, that all cases should be investigated by at least one other medical man besides the battalion Medical Officer, and that that other should be a specialist for mental cases if possible. At present the responsibility of saying whether or not the man under arrest is or was 'non compos mentis' rests entirely with the battalion doctor.

Then again the General agreed on the question of the standardisation of punishment at home and abroad. A man will overstay his leave at home by a day or several days and will get only a few days CB[16] as a punishment. He comes out here and if absent from his unit for an hour without leave is liable to be shot. It is hardly fair on the man to be subjected to such a great disparity of discipline.

We found the General in all these points most sympathetic. He himself told us also how he had answered the questions which he had been asked to answer in connection with Church Reform. The Bishop of Winchester, and others I suppose, have put out ten questions to thoughtful laymen on this question; and I'm bound to say the General's answers were singularly apt, well thought-out and practical.

On 17 July the diarist records:

Today the King has issued a proclamation removing German titles, and proclaiming that his house and family will in future take the name of Windsor. His children will be known, for instance, as Princess Mary of Windsor, Prince Henry of Windsor and so on. It is a fine snub for the Kaiser.

VOLUME VII
JULY 1917 – FEBRUARY 1918

Julian in hospital with trench fever – four days' intense fighting (Julian) –
he visits Talbot House – Burgon, bored by inaction, philosophizes on
Church and Nation – he begins a history of the 6th Cavalry Brigade –
Julian witnesses another execution – Burgon appointed Brigade
Intelligence Officer – Julian awarded the MC.

*The third Battle of Ypres, later called Passchendaele, began at 3.50 am
on 31 July, 1917, and the diarist comments wearily next morning: 'The
fourth year of the war is beginning, and was heralded in yesterday by
the start of another gigantic battle.' But a letter the same day from the
Church of England chaplain at No. 7 General Hospital in France
reassures her that one son at least is not involved:*

I am asked (he writes) by one of your brave sons, the padre Julian, who
has just come in here, to tell you: 1. That he is suffering from trench
fever but is not too bad, and 2. That he has just been appointed Senior
Chaplain 56th Division, and hopes very soon to be back to his beloved
work. This morning I had the joy of giving him his Communion. I will
look after him for his own sake and for yours.

*Also on that day came word from Burgon that his name is to be put for-
ward for promotion:*

The Division has called for names of those suited to be second-in-
command of a Machine Gun Squadron, and the General personally sent
a note to say that I was to be recommended. It means a captaincy (if it
ever comes off). It would mean leaving the Royals and all my friends
and again plunging into an entirely new set of surroundings, and personally, considering that I am not going to soldier after the War, I
should much prefer to stay here as a Lieutenant where everybody knows
me and I know and like everybody.

I rode over yesterday morning to the Brigade, saw the General and the Brigade-Major, and had a long talk with the latter who is very level-headed and a very nice fellow, Howes by name, an old House[1] man and a 21st Lancer. Although the General had recommended me, I don't think he really wanted me to go, but Howes said he certainly thought I ought to allow my name to go forward. For one reason – things change so quickly – the Brigade might be split up, and then I should regret not being eligible for the step-up. A second reason: if the General thinks you 'capable' as he does, of doing second-in-command (which is an important job) you have no right to say you won't do it. For ever afterwards you would feel you were not pulling your weight in the boat. So I there and then said 'Yes' to the General, and in my presence he signed the paper and it has gone on.

So promotion news from both the brothers reached their mother on the same day; and she heard later in the week from Julian about his going to hospital – that the trouble had come on suddenly one afternoon:

Next morning, after a sleepless night, my temperature was over 103, so our Medical Officer packed me off in a motor-ambulance. My servant and most of my kit came too. I only called at our Field Ambulance and came straight on here. It is a convent or monastery, built recently, but used since the war started as a Stationary Hospital. It is a very large place.

There are over 200 cases of gas poisoning here alone at the present moment. I am in a half-medical, half-surgical ward of officers containing thirty beds.

Today, Monday, I am normal. Yesterday afternoon, the Chief of the Deputy Chaplain General's Staff came in. I was feeling better. 'You've just been appointed Senior Chaplain of the 56th Division', he said; 'I suppose you know that?' 'No', I replied, 'I hadn't heard it, but it makes me all the keener to get back again'.

So I am to leave my beloved Rangers. You know how that will hurt, don't you? Yet if I was to become a Senior Chaplain at all, there is no other division in the British Army of which I would rather be Senior Chaplain. You will have the satisfaction of knowing that I can never live in the trenches again. I cannot live further forward than the Advanced Dressing Station. Apparently the DCG asked the General of the Division whom he wanted as his Senior Chaplain, and he wrote back at once and asked for me.

... The work is not easy and in many ways will be almost distasteful compared to what I have been doing. Still, knowing nearly everybody of importance in the Division is an enormous help, and will ensure me a welcome from the start. The other chaplains of the Division were kind enough to say that they hoped I should be appointed.

While in hospital he talked with one of the Corps chaplains, who over a three-month period earlier in the year had been responsible for the exhumation and proper burial of over 400 bodies in the area where Morris had fallen on the first day of the Battle of the Somme. Identification of any kind was impossible, but Julian writes to his mother that he is convinced

that our dear one's body now lies somewhere in this consecrated cemetery set 100 yards from where he fell. The cemetery will be kept for all time. I know this will be a great cause of thankfulness for us all.

By 7 August Julian is feeling better, and writes home from a seat in the monastery garden, where 'the old brothers' work the fruit and vegetables:

Next to me on the garden seat sits an old brother, resting for a moment from his toil. He is 72 he tells me, and enjoys fairly good health except from his *'poitrine'* which troubles him sorely in the morning. 'Would I take some snuff? No? I would excuse him if he took some?' which he proceeded to do from a dirty little box which he produced from the folds of his cassock. With it he also brought a small packet wrapped round with an old newspaper, which he carefully undid, and showed me with great pride two medals won in the 1870 War when he was a youngster. These, he told me, he wears on state occasions and are probably the only treasures he possesses in the world except for his old snuff box. Then he was called off by another old brother to do some more work, and he left the bench quite reluctantly.

Presently he sought an opportunity to return. 'Ah', he said, 'I did not know that you were a minister of religion', and he doffed his cap in a courtly way and thanked me for our conversation. 'May I ask, are you a Protestant?'. 'No', I said, 'not altogether', and then followed an explanation, which I have made dozens of times all over the country to many people, of the Catholic position of the Church of England. 'Ah', he said, 'I see you are not in communion with those German Protestants'.

Presently a very old brother passed. I saluted him and he stopped for a moment. I asked him his age. 'Seventy-six', he said, though with his bent back and wrinkled face he looked older, 'and I haven't much more to look forward to in this world except a long box with a lid on it', he added with a chuckle.

Julian was away from the monastery two days later, and writes that he is depressed at not being with his beloved Rangers in the great battle now in progress; but there is no lack of work for him to do:

The day before yesterday I started at 4 am, and went with the DACG[2] for a tour of our Front Line. We first motored four miles to a spot where it is not safe to take cars beyond, and then walked over the most appalling country which it has ever been my experience to see. Swamp, shell-holes, stench, water, mud, broken-down tree stumps, destroyed dug-outs and gun-pits, unburied bodies of horses and alas in many cases of men, all over the place . . . We investigated all the dressing-stations and places where I wanted to post chaplains, and never had a single shell nearer than eighty yards away. We returned through the famous ruined city of Ypres, my very first visit to this historic city. It is strange to see grass growing in the streets and squares.

The Pope's proposal for peace in mid-August meets with derisory comments from both Burgon and his mother, clearly mirroring the views of the English press that the Pope was markedly pro-German. But Julian says:

We reject all peace proposals, but I wonder how the public at home really think the war will end, not by fighting surely. We have got to break the German spirit which is the most remarkable fact of the whole war, permeating and unifying the whole German people as in no other country . . . I wish I had the time to tell you more of my thoughts on the continuation of this strife.

The diarist continues to get occasional letters from German friends; in August there was one from a woman in Dresden sympathizing with her over Morris's death.

All the papers at home (writes Julian on 20 August) talk about great British victories last week, which is absolutely maddening to us who know the truth. Our splendid lads did all and more than was required of them, but were overwhelmed in the counter-attack. It was not quite a 'July' (1916), but about as near to it as anything we have been in. . . . You know how that fills us with sorrow, we, I mean, who see the wounded coming in. At least six men died in my arms at the Corps Main Dressing Station during the twenty-four hours following the opening of the battle, and many more were hurried away to the Casualty Clearing Stations, only to die there. The splendid courage of these grievously-wounded men moves me to tears . . . how grateful they are for the least attention, while waiting on the table to be dressed. I got all our chaplains at the Dressing Station to take postcards in their hands and write to the relatives of wounded men a few lines, either from dictation or in their own words. This small act was so much appreciated by the men themselves, and will do something to relieve aching hearts at home.

. . . One boy, who had been presented for Confirmation at Talbot House only two days before, was brought in with a shattered right arm. He had gone straight from his Confirmation into the battle line. He was suffering terribly, but he seemed most of all keen that I should write and tell his mother that he had been confirmed. 'You see, Sir, I hadn't time to write yesterday, and now I can't write'.

A fine young officer belonging to one of our machine-gun sections came in badly wounded in the leg. His father, a Colonel on the Staff of the next corps, was only ten miles away and I was able, by much telephoning, to get into touch with him and bring father and son together.

Between us, my chaplains and I wrote and dispatched 3,000 to 4,000 postcards and letters to relatives.

Julian concludes:

I think I worked twenty hours out of the twenty-four for the four days I was there . . . I wrote a report on the whole organization of the chaplains and suggested a complete scheme of reorganization; the DACG accepted my scheme and I am glad to say adopted it '*in toto*' after submitting it first of all to the ACG; and being a man of much energy he had the whole new scheme working two days after I had left. I am glad to say it received the unanimous support of all the Senior Chaplains in the Corps, and the Corps General himself expressed his approval.

But I just hated being so far behind the Line. Scarcely half a dozen shells near us all the time. I had a wonderful walk round the famous Salient, or rather round part of it, the first morning we came up into the Line, as I think I told you in a previous letter. The DACG who has the DSO, a bar to his MC and an Indian Frontier Medal, took us, but we penetrated further even than he had before to a spot within 500 to 600 yards of the enemy. There are, as you probably know, no communication trenches, and the Front Line is merely connected shell-holes or isolated machine-gun posts in shell-holes, so we walked about over the Top in the open, but no bullets came near us and as I say no shell nearer than eighty yards all the morning.

The country is beyond all words appalling – especially this little piece which is nothing but shell-holes nearly all filled with water and many – I was almost going to say the majority – with a dead body in them. In quite a few cases the wounded have been drowned in the shell-holes; unable to move, the water has risen higher and higher. However, of these and of worse horrors I will not speak in a letter. We want to draw a veil over these things, and commend the sufferers to the Mercy of God and pray that their last moments may not be without the comfort and consolation of His Presence. Perhaps this 'passing' is not so terrible as we sometimes imagine. But it is hard not to yearn with an almost uncontrollable yearning for an end to these things, and to reflect that if only those who have the power to make peace could see or feel something of the horror of modern warfare, they would speedily come to some conclusion of this business. Don't forget that the warfare of three years ago as compared with that of today is as obsolete and out of date as the Crimea was to methods of 1914. Those who only knew Mons or Le Cateau have had no experience of modern warfare. What do they know of a creeping barrage?

We reached a famous tunnel now used as a dressing station. It is more or less safe from shell fire but not really from direct hits. However, during the battle two days later, no fewer than 580 stretcher cases alone were attended to and evacuated from it by heroic stretcher-bearers along a path which is no path, but merely a 'winding' among shell holes through mud often feet deep. Our stretcher-bearer casualties were heavier than usual, but their work was beyond all praise.

. . . On Tuesday last week I took over a party of our lads to a town some miles behind the Line to be confirmed. The Confirmation service took place in a well-known church club, the only one of its kind at the Front, I believe, and called after the Talbots, Talbot House or Toc H.

It is a large house in the centre of the town and fitted up splendidly. There are reading rooms, writing rooms, a library, quiet rooms, card rooms, canteen, café, open-air lounge, garden, concert room, and every possible device for making the soldier comfortable. Delightful pictures cover the walls, and facetious remarks are pinned up at various places by the altogether admirable chaplain-in-charge[3], imploring those who use the club not to remove all the writing paper from the writing room or otherwise pillage the club.

But the great thing which gives character to the Club is its chapel. It is right at the top of the house under the old oak rafters. A beautiful altar decked with rich hangings and canopy at once catches the eye. A Sanctuary lamp burns before it. A fine carpet is laid on the steps leading to it. A beautiful Crucifix and other altar ornaments adorn it. Some really good pictures are on the walls. A small side altar is provided for daily Celebrations, all in perfect proportion and taste. The whole is a veritable 'House of God'. I have never been at a more impressive Confirmation Service. Perhaps 120 men from thirty or forty different units brought in by fifteen or twenty chaplains were confirmed. The Bishop (the DCG) spoke well. The singing was all in unison and most uplifting. The men who were confirmed were many of them mere lads, but here and there an older man was amongst them.

The whole service, with its beautiful setting and with the knowledge that many of those confirmed had come straight from the battle and were to return again that night, could not fail to move the least impressionable. One of our candidates had been killed that very morning and two others wounded. When I mentioned the death of this boy to Neville Talbot, he was most sympathetic . . . but full of Christian hope: 'He will be confirmed in Heaven. I do feel we must get a right view of the passing of our Christian lads. What a splendid Confirmation Day he will have, and yet I know how you feel, old chap'.

After the service, I waited with others to get an audience with the DCG, who was most kind and gave me ten minutes in which I explained to him various changes I wanted to make among the chaplains of this division, to all of which he gave his consent, saying, 'I want very much to give you a good start, Bickersteth, as Senior Chaplain'. So I am hopeful we may get rid of one or two chaplains who are not really fitted for their job, and in return get some men I have especially asked for.

In that long letter Julian had enclosed one from the second-in-command of one of his old battalions, 'an agnostic, almost a militant one'.

> Senior Officers' School,
> Lille Barracks,
> Aldershot.

14/8/17

Dear Bickersteth,

I have just heard from the Colonel that you have been promoted to Divisional Bishopric, and hasten to offer you my heartfelt congratulations on this well-earned honour, which is, I trust, but the forerunner of many more to come.

During the whole period you have been with us you have not spared yourself, and all ranks (including your tormentor) have derived much benefit from being privileged to live with you.

There is, however, a pang of sorrow at losing you; as it will be very difficult to find a chaplain as good as you have proved yourself to be.

The very best of good luck and health to carry on your work in the large parish is my earnest desire.

> Sincerely yours,
> A G Ernest Syms.

Meanwhile Burgon, whose unit was twenty-five miles away, having nothing to do, had got time off and rode over to see his brother. Julian, he writes, did not look well:

He ought to have had a change after that bout of trench fever instead of joining his division in the line direct. We had a talk, and later I dined with him in 'B' Mess . . . it is not so lively as a Regimental or a Company Mess, but they were a very nice set of fellows and made me most welcome. After dinner, we fixed up my two horses in one of the APM's stables, and as the weather was stormy, it was a good thing to have them under cover.

At 9.30 pm the usual nightly fun began. The air became full of the drone of aircraft, and the sky was alive with the darting rays of a dozen searchlights; we picked up the plane, and there she was like a brilliant golden butterfly; she turned and came straight over the street where Julian and I were watching from the doorway of our billet, dropping two bombs in quick succession just behind the group of huts where all the divisional mess and horse lines are housed. These bombs killed several horses and caused a good many people to run. She then dropped several more bombs further on and finally disappeared.

Julian's servant had procured me a bed, and had put it in Julian's room, so there we retired after the bombing episode, and lying on our beds talked till the small hours.

. . . In the morning we went to Poperinghe by car and had lunch with Clayton at Talbot House. Talbot House is a wonderful institution. I had never seen it before, as it was only founded in December 1915, and I had not been in Poperinghe since that June.

It is interesting to compare his account of Talbot House with Julian's:

It is a big rambling kind of house in the main street leading from the square towards Cassel. At its large open doors blackboards give the latest war news. On the left inside is a canteen, and rooms with pianos, and straight through a garden with tables and chairs and hammocks, where tired men can rest. The whole place is for men – no officers admitted.

But a later note by Burgon reads,

This is wrong. Of course officers were admitted.

He goes on to describe the beautiful loft chapel:

At the far end, facing each worshipper as he scrambles up the steep stairs, is a list of names of those who have been killed in action and were connected with the place before. Gilbert Talbot heads the list. Through odd-shaped windows at the far end of the loft there is a view of steep foreign-looking roofs, and immediately below, of the bend of the street, as noisy and busy as the Strand with its continuous stream of lorries and hurrying khaki figures. Truly the chapel is an oasis in a world gone crazy.

We had our meal with Clayton and three private soldiers – the first time I had ever sat down to eat out here in uniform with soldiers.

At 6.00 Julian took me to see 'The Bow Bells' of which he is treasurer; surely the best show of its kind in France. It is really a 'slap-up' affair. All the men are professionals; they never go into the trenches, but practise continually, and their job is to amuse the men. Their leave they use visiting the music halls, picking up tips.

Burgon was back in his billets later that night:

Julian will tell you (he writes) about the general situation. I entirely concur with his views on the war.

So duly in his next letter Julian muses on the failure of the recent British offensive, in which

despite the initial advance, our troops ended up pretty well where they started.

This was in the main the same experience of all the divisions who tried to take this piece of ground, so highly prized by the Germans, the last bit of really high ground left to them in front of Ypres.

The ground over which we attacked was nothing but shell-holes, and the number of dead lying about is incredible. In our retirement we had to leave a great number of our wounded, and a good many officers and men were cut off and captured.

The effect of a battle of this nature is most depressing upon the survivors, and perhaps takes from one the power of preserving an even judgement; but this appalling carnage and ever-increasing losses of splendid men, without material success to show for them, makes me think that to continue this war much longer will be more wicked than to stop it. To beat Germany on land seems well nigh impossible. We may perhaps bend back her line here and there, but at what cost!

Victory in the field will never stop the war. Nor will Germany starve. What then is to stop it? Frankly I don't know, unless people at home will learn that to crush German Militarism you must crush the German people too, that you can't separate the two, and to crush them at all will be impossible. Then why go on? Is not our honour vindicated? Would not a round table conference help to clear the air and remove mutual misjudgements and misapprehensions? What about Stockholm?[4]

Leave in the end did come for Julian on 1 September. 'He looks thin and worn, and is not cheerful about our advance'. (comments the diarist):

After a night at home in Canterbury, we all went to London for a show, and there were raids by enemy aircraft. Julian and Geoffrey had been walking back from the West End; we had gone to bed but dressed hurriedly, thinking it wise to go to the bottom of the house. Still in our night attire we went out into the street, where we met Julian and Geoffrey arriving at the hotel, both hurrying back to see if we were safe . . . Julian chuckling to think he had been bombarded every night at the Front and now. . . .

Typically, while they went back to bed, and Geoffrey retired too, Julian went off to find out what he could do to help. One bomb had fallen 300 yards away, exactly in front of Charing Cross Hospital.

*   *   *

Burgon writes from France:

after a barren few weeks of which there seems to be nothing to tell you except for a fascinating evening with Philip Gibbs, now freelancing. Gibbs and I, as you know, have much in common and so we had long talks. His views agree with Julian's with regard to the War.

. . . Yesterday was the Corps Horse Show; all the cavalry brigades and divisions had an eliminating competition, and so only the best of the cavalry divisions were to be seen there, and I do wish you and Father could have been with me. It really was a wonderful show. There was some beautiful jumping, won as usual by Geoffrey Brooke of the 16th Lancers, whom you may remember we saw jump at Olympia just before the War. He was on the same horses yesterday as then, 'Combined Training' and 'Alice'. There was a great display of horsemanship by the Indians, who did most extraordinary circus tricks. Most enjoyable of all, everybody was there. I saw people whom I had not seen for years; George Black, who arrived with Sir Douglas Haig, I had not set eyes on since I left Oxford in 1911. He has Haig's troop and I believe Haig is very fond of him. I had some difficulty in getting at him as he stood near Haig all the time, but I managed to whisper 'George' just behind his ear, and then we had a great talk.

(He was later killed when he went into the Tank Corps, Burgon has added.)

I also saw Cornwallis, another of my oldest friends; both he and George are in the 17th Lancers, Haig's regiment. Nearly everybody in the Greys was there, and dozens of others whom only such an occasion would bring together. I suppose that now it is the only gathering of its kind which could take place, i.e. where the large majority of officers present were regulars, and where the turn-out of the competitors from the military point of view was as good as in the old days. I only wish some of our new Army officers, magnificent as they are, could have been present.

PS. Is there any means by which I could get a German newspaper sent out to me once a week – not for the news but for the German?

The diarist's husband was sixty years old on 9 September, 'and it was a great pleasure having Julian at home still. He and Father are both firmly convinced that the war will be over for Christmas'. Burgon could have been home too, for all the military activity they had to do. Instead he contributes to the birthday fun by recounting meeting some Australians, ex-Melbourne Grammar School boys who had been there with Julian, and told Burgon they all loved the Chaplain and enjoyed trying to do their hair 'à la Bickersteth'.

Everyone here (he adds) is reading my book 'The Land of Open Doors', which is most amusing. They all thought I had been pulling their legs when I told them I had written one, so one of the officers wrote to the bookseller and got a copy!

In a role he has not previously mentioned:

Last night I fitted up the shed where all the shoeing is done for the service, and it looked quite clean and nice. The parade at 11.30 was compulsory, about thirty-five men being there, only a very small percentage of the squadron, but custom decides that. Holy Communion which followed was voluntary; not a single man stayed, the only communicants were myself and another subaltern. I cannot help feeling that the padre himself is largely responsible for this. He is a perfectly charming fellow, has fought in three campaigns and is welcome wherever he goes, and yet does not seem to understand the necessity of getting to know the men personally, as Julian does. Until he gets to know them and they him, moral cowardice successfully smothers all vestiges of a religion which perhaps was never strong.

Julian is busy organizing his divisional chaplains:

Yesterday (20 *September*) I paid various visits in the Line including looking in at the Rangers' mess. It was awfully jolly being back again, and I shan't easily forget the shout of welcome as I put my head through the window of the little shelter which the Battalion Headquarters are using as a mess, followed by half a dozen missiles flung directly they saw who it was. It was all a delightful contrast to office work, which I hate more and more. I doubt if I shall ever be reconciled to the position of Senior Chaplain.

German air-raids on London continued; most of the people killed (thirty-two one night in the Marylebone area) had been standing in the streets watching what was going on. The diarist writes:

They do not obey the 'Take Cover' order, preferring to see what they can see. Our Tommies have no such reluctance, knowing from similar experience that to stay star-gazing above ground is no act of courage if a dug-out like our Tubes is handy for shelter.

Burgon writes on 21 September:

There are all kinds of rumours as to what we are going to do during the winter, I should say each one less likely than the last. What is really important is that surely there is a very serious peace talk going on behind the scenes at the present time . . .

PS. I have reason to believe I have again definitely been put in for the Military Cross, this time for the New Year Honours, but that doesn't follow I shall get it.

Americans have begun to be around, reports Julian (24 September)

We have only seen doctors so far, and we have ten or eleven Americans now permanently attached to the medical staff of our ambulances; they seem a particularly pleasant set of fellows.

That was the week, records the diarist, in which 'the Intrepid Italian airman' (Daily Mail) 'Captain the Marquis Guilio Laureti flew non-stop from Turin to London in seven hours two minutes, flying at an average height of 7,000 feet. He had written:

At times we were doing nearly 120 mph. I might have met hostile air-craft on the way, so I came prepared. My Fiat machine-gun was ready for action. But as a matter of fact I met nothing at all till I reached London. The air is a lonely region.

The King received him the following morning.

Lunching with Lord and Lady Beauchamp at Walmer Castle on 27 September, the diarist and her husband picked up various tit-bits, two of them duly recorded in her daily work on the diary:

Lord Beauchamp told us that they have a naval aerodrome near Walmer Castle, and they are such splendid fellows. A navy airman named Kelly brought down a German plane, and it fell into the sea. He dived down to see if the pilot was alive, and finding he was, threw him his own safety belt . . . Lord Ronaldshay, Lady Beauchamp's cousin, is now a Governor in India. He has travelled a good deal and had a wonderful collection of books, many to do with India, and of great value. These he was taking out there. The ship was torpedoed, and his books collected with so much care and toil are now at the bottom of the sea. Truly the waste of war is terrible.

The lack of action was giving Burgon time to read:

Today I have finished a small paper volume entitled 'British Freedom 1914–1917', published anonymously under the National Council for Civil Liberties. It is a telling indictment against what we have had to submit to during three years of War with regard to the suppression of our liberty – freedom of the press, of meeting, of communication, of asylum, the right to trial by jury, Habeas Corpus all gone; and the total abdication of Parliament and the setting up of special courts such as the Munitions and Military Service Tribunals are now commonplace in everyday life. I suppose these things are not really great hardships, and except by the struggling minority, pacifists and the like, are not much remarked; probably some are necessary, though I think the book is useful as showing how far we have travelled since 1914, and how careful we must be to get back immediately after the war the main principles of liberty, which it took us centuries to get.

I am also reading German, and last night read a novel of Nat Gould. Do you read Nat Gould? His books literally sell by millions. I had difficulty in finding this particular volume, as my servant had pinched it and it was rapidly going the rounds of the section.

'An unofficial air shuttle for leave purposes seems to have developed,' *writes the diarist:*

Often an aeroplane arrives from France, sometimes bringing a lucky officer who has come home on leave, thus giving him a whole extra day at home by carrying him across in half an hour, when by train and boat would mean a whole day.

She goes on:

Tuesday, 2 October, 1917, Leigh Mount, Cobham.[5] We came to town this morning, but owing to the nightly air raids decided to sleep down here. We reached London about mid-day and Father had just left me to lunch at the Athenaeum, and Monier and I were going out to lunch when the warning of an air-raid was given. We therefore took cover and went into the basement of Church House, where we found many others. Father was near the Athenaeum, where he said many women passers-by took refuge. The 'All Clear' notice was given after about forty minutes, and it was evident the raiders had not got really near London, though it was disturbing to the people to have daylight as well as night raids. As we left Waterloo, the platforms were crowded with families, poor mothers and children, who were leaving London. There is hardly a house to be got on the outskirts of London, and in the same way the inland villages of Kent are crowded with refugees from the coast towns.

On Thursday last, the diarist continues, Hindenburg was seventy years old and received congratulations from the Kaiser. He replied saying, 'The Germans must hold on and gnash their teeth till this bloody war is ended'. The *Daily Telegraph* comments, 'Hindenburg seems to forget the place to which those who gnash their teeth go'.

Years later there is a pencil note by Julian:

This was a wrong translation. What he really said was 'grit or clench their teeth'.

Burgon had heard from his mother:

It is very pleasant what you say about my applying for a staff job, or rather to go and be trained for a staff job, but you do not realize that in the cavalry there are scores of fellows who are more qualified than myself to do so, and one cannot push oneself forward in that way. You need never be afraid of my not seeking opportunities, or taking them when they occur. The chief thing to realize is that I have been out here for two and a half years, have been in action at some time or other in most parts of the Front, and have survived.

You asked me how my book had been received in the Mess – very calmly. It caused a ripple of interest to start with; people picked it up, glanced at the photographs, some even read it from cover to cover. I was asked a few questions: Had I really been verminous? Did I ever find out that Russian's name who died? What exactly is the Head of Steel[6]? And then the matter dropped. We are not up to discussing religion, politics, or any other questions of particular interest.

Meanwhile we are having an orgy of Horse Shows, Sports etc, and much as I love the animal horse, these Shows almost drive me daft.

But Julian was in the Line again:

It was a real joy to get back again to the atmosphere of trench life, so different from anything we experience back here at Divisional HQ. A very useful tonic too to buck one up, and to prevent me falling into lethargic 'brass-hat' aloofness from the real thing. Oh how a soldier (i.e. the man doing the real job) hates the brass-hat or staff officer!

Next night, after touring round several other units, he landed up at a battalion headquarters where the Colonel had just got a bar to his DSO for his work at Ypres:

he took me up the Line to his battalion Front Line and then insisted on my coming back to dinner with him. There was not much room in the Mess of the little dug-out, but an excellent dinner was served of five or six courses, with coffee, liqueurs and cigars. But the CO is not a man to feed himself and neglect his men. He is always thinking of them and their comfort and he is trusted and liked in consequence.

The diarist meanwhile had been staying in Rugby,

a moving and inspiring place to us, and this morning Father and I went to the early celebration in the School Chapel, where four of our sons, darling Morris included, obtained so much of the strength which has enabled them to play the man in life and death.

Julian, in a letter that same week-end, says:

I have just written (9 *October*) to Burgon to suggest we try to go to Paris together for a four days' 'jaunt'. I don't know whether or not we can manage it. I hope so. Neither he nor I can expect a leave before Christmas to England, so it would be a nice little break if we could go during November.

Yesterday I drove through the Somme belt, that is, the broad tract of country over which we fought last year. A more dreary or terrible bit of country it has never been my lot to see. Nothing but fallen-in trenches and endless single graves, heaps of chalk and completely obliterated villages, stumps of trees and broken wire, derelict tanks, half a dozen of which are to be seen from the road, rusty and rotting. It is for miles one great graveyard, and the vast majority of the graves are nameless.

Burgon has time to philosophize:

In a recent letter you quote Hood, a chaplain out here, as saying that he grows 'more and more convinced that the case of the soldier who returns from the Front to England so plastic for good or ill, depends on the kind of welcome he receives from those who have stayed at home'.

I presume Hood refers to the atmosphere both religious and social which he will find in England on his return. No doubt the present controversy in the press about 'Matins' and 'Mass' is unduly prominent, and the fact that an unseemly wrangle about the morality or otherwise of certain psalms recently occupied much valuable time in Convocation is very misleading. Yet do you really in your heart believe that the Church owing to the war is a greater power in the land today than it was in 1914? And has the Church shown greater vitality since the war broke out? After all, the increased interest in Foreign Missions, the Student Movement, the Christian Socialists, the Anglican Fellowship, the CEMS, were all familiar features of church life long before War brought people to think more seriously on many subjects.

Since the War we have had the National Mission. Whether it has really touched the nation you are far more competent to say than I, though I should like to add that I think the tendency to take refuge in the comforting doctrine that there is much unseen result from such appeals as that made by the National Mission is perhaps sometimes rather exaggerated and therefore dangerous.

To me the problem has always appeared as this; to find some method of really bringing the Church into people's lives (to the extent it was in mediaeval times) without having to make some break in the great traditions handed down through centuries. The Archbishops' Report on Church and State is a step in the right direction. But who really takes any interest in Archbishops' Reports? Does the average working man take any notice? Perhaps the keen churchwarden type does. In some ways, the lower middle classes seem to be the respectable pillar of the spiritual life of England, whether Church or non-conformist. The reforms advocated by the Archbishops' Report if carried out, as I hope they will be, will have forged an instrument to be used by the layman only when he is interested. The Church will have to do something which will shake the nation into looking at her seriously and saying, 'Well, at any rate she is genuine'. And here again I ask what can it be which shall not break her continuity?

At heart I am a Tory in Church and State, and we are always beings told that the working man is in secret an admirer of tradition. What then can the Church do? Well, I think the first thing is to preach an understanding of the present demands of Labour. This may seem very trite, but it so happens that I have recently been reading a good deal on this subject, and on any attempt to discuss such questions one cannot help being struck by the staring indifference one meets. There are a million and a quarter Trades Unionists in the Army, it is said. Quite apart from religion, what interest will the Trades Union soldier on his return find his Church taking in these problems with which, immediately he sheds his khaki, he will be brought into contact? Here is the whole world of Labour in a volcanic state, with the signing of peace the signal for a general eruption; and the average man of my class, and of the churchwarden type, is entirely indifferent, neither knowing nor caring to know the most elementary facts of the situation. If you were to ask anyone here if in his opinion Labour should be treated as a commodity, and if not, how he proposed to stop it, he would look upon you as a dangerous disturber of his peaceful outlook, as politics-mad or a red-rag socialist.

The Trades Unionist soldier will find the rank and file of churchmen (when he returns) very conservative, engrossed in much that is of trivial interest, out of touch with the wider spiritual atmosphere he has breathed out here, indifferent to the great distance Labour has travelled during the last ten years (say since 1906) and unsympathetic with (chiefly because ignorant of) the demand the wager-earners are making for a change in their status.

I would like to see the Church lose the upper classes (that is, if she has ever won them) and gain the working classes, for in so doing, she will control what will shortly be the ruling classes.

Churches might be used far more frequently, as is St Martin-in-the-Fields, for the purpose of lectures and discussions. I would not invite propagandists of any party to come and address the people, so making a service into a political meeting, but I would attempt to get practical men, who would present the problem in a fair, impartial light after the manner of the 'Round Table'. Whatever social class any congregation might happen to belong to, this would be equally beneficial. It would not merely be a course of lectures, given and then forgotten. The speaker should seek to influence the whole atmosphere of the religious life of the congregation – he should be a Christian who is necessarily a firm and intelligent sympathizer in the problems of the people. Once get an interested public in the Church, and we should have gone a long way towards being in a position to take intelligent action.

I am quite certain that the majority of men of our class are ignorantly playing on the edge of a volcano, and I am equally certain that the Church of England as a whole has no settled or intelligent policy to put forward, if and when the social upheaval comes.

He adds a PS:

Do our young clergy take an interest in these things? Are they ably- (or were they before the War ably-) instructed on all these intricate questions? If they weren't, they ought to have been.

*   *   *

On the last day of their Rugby visit the diarist writes:

We drove to the neighbouring aerodrome and were shown over by a young officer. Most of the machines were of the Sopwith type, taking a pilot and an observer and mounted with a Lewis gun. It was a glorious sight to watch aeroplane after aeroplane mount gracefully into the air, side-planing, ascending or descending, and then circling round and coming down in graceful curves to earth again. One machine looped the loop over and over again for our benefit.

The steady work of a Divisional Chaplain goes on. After no fewer than six services already on one Sunday, Julian had to

walk all the way back to Divisional HQ to get there in time for Evensong, when for the first time I had a church full. The Divisional HQ people are gradually coming along. This improvement is most gratifying.

He refers again to his Somme battlefield visit:

It was a melancholy morning. All was silent and deserted. Walking through the deep grass and a strange red weed was exceedingly difficult and very tiring. We had to leave the car on one of the splendid roads made by large Chinese or Indian labour companies. Indeed at one stage we were very grateful to some who were actually engaged in road-making. Our car stuck hopelessly in the mud and they came to our rescue; thirty or forty men pushed vigorously behind, with many weird cries and so much excitement that I could almost imagine myself in the East for the moment.

The French Government, it is said, intend to plant forests over a large part of this country, as any agricultural work on a large scale will be quite impossible. Isolated graves will be gathered into cemeteries which will be left as clearings in the forest. But this is only hearsay.

He comments on the seven other chaplains he has in the Division:

We are a happy crowd and very keen . . . all but two of us are High Churchmen. We two would be thought of as advanced Anglo-Catholics, but none of us cares to emphasise party distinctions in the Church, since we all breathe a larger, broader, more truly Catholic spirit by reason of our work out here.

Burgon again:

The General sent for me yesterday and asked me to be the editor of a magazine which he wished to get up for the amusement of the Brigade. I suggested it would be extremely difficult to produce such a publication regularly, and he then proposed we should bring out one number only, and, as we all expect peace during the coming year if not earlier, make it a real good souvenir of the Brigade. This I promised to take in hand and see whether it is feasible.

On 20 October, 1917, Burgon writes to his mother:

I shall not mind if we go into the trenches, but I do dislike doing nothing. You say, 'Promise not to go to the infantry'. Whatever my wishes were, I should not be allowed to do so. No one is. No one can leave the cavalry to join any other branch of the service except the RFC[7] (and that I don't want to do), nor has there ever been any time when officers or men have been allowed to leave the cavalry, which still contains the greatest nucleus of regular troops in the British Army, and is I think being kept for political as much as for military reasons.

Julian has been on – and off – a horse again:

The day before yesterday I tried my new horse, a splendid little mare with really good points and very fast. Unfortunately we came home separately – though that was not exactly my fault. She was very fresh, not having been ridden for a long time, and when riding back towards this village across country she got her feet into some wire, and I had to dismount and with considerable difficulty extricated her. This excited her, so that in mounting, the girth slipped right round, depositing me unexpectedly on the ground even before I had got on to her back. In the fall I lost hold of her reins, being more interested in extricating my left foot from the stirrup. The result was, off she went like a flash home-wards, with the saddle upside-down. She was caught in the transport lines of another regiment and returned safely by them to our stables, but she is rather lame today and I was glad of the rest after being bumped on the ground. But I am perfectly all right and so is the mare, which is the great thing, and I think she is going to prove a very useful animal.

Burgon got fourteen days' leave in November, lunching in Boulogne on the way home with an old friend with whom he had played for the University at football:

whose work is to bring over Chinese to Flanders for labour battalions. There are 8,000 there now, and he is just off to China to fetch another 2,000. They will probably be left to clear up after the War.

During his leave he dined with John Buchan[8],

who very much wants to get me on loan from the War Office to do pro-paganda work for England in America. That might be interesting!

*   *   *

Julian's division has been in the thick of the Cambrai fighting for some weeks. He writes a long letter on 3 December, by which time they were resting some miles behind the Lines. He describes burying one of his Corps chaplains,

such an excellent man who had been with a heavy battery which had moved forward very quickly. A Presbyterian chaplain of the Ulster

Division brought his body back some 500 yards or more, and I went up and found it and buried him not very far from where he fell.

Fortunately we had no casualties among our divisional chaplains, who were all of them up in the fighting in the trenches all the time and did magnificent work.

For two nights we had a terrible rush of wounded, and none of us went to bed at all. Doctors, orderlies and all worked without even a breather. Dawn found us still at it, bandaging, dressing, putting cases away to the Casualty Clearing Station as soon as possible. My old battalion lost fifteen officers and 250 men in the course of the battle, and were much shaken by the incessant heavy shelling before the main counter attack. One of the best Company Commanders was almost recklessly brave and by his splendid courage and determination held on to our position, being quite regardless of his own safety, jumping on to the parapet and hurling bombs and firing rifle grenades and otherwise encouraging his men. He was shot through the head and died after passing through our Divisional Dressing Station a day later. I tried to get him to speak to me, but I don't think he was really conscious. He was a Cambridge graduate, cultured and extremely well-read. And so another fine fellow has joined the Great Majority.

When will this senseless murder end? Is there nobody sufficiently Christian to back up Lord Lansdowne's[9] Peace Initiative? I have at present only just had the chance of glancing at his letter, but from what I saw it seems to be a wonderfully clear and statesmanlike effort to bring us back again to the right judgement. Under the conditions at present existing and with Russia out of it, and even in spite of the coming help of the USA, I do not see why the war should ever end, unless someone is big enough to lead the nation into a clearer view of the situation. The country is hoodwinked. Facts are distorted or totally misrepresented by the press. Everyone seems to be on the make. My nostrils are filled with the smell of blood. My eyes are glutted with the sight of bleeding bodies and shattered limbs, my heart wrung with the agony of wounded and dying men. Splendid, finely-built lads come in an endless stream to our dressing-stations, many scarcely breathing, some mercifully unconscious, not a few to spend their last hours amid the stench of blood and noise of guns, too weak to reach the hospitals. It is pitiful to see the men suffering from gas. They lie, their eyes streaming, their bodies burnt and blistered, and vomiting out their very souls – and but little can be done to relieve them.

One splendid Scottish sergeant came in with both legs shattered and two or three other grievous wounds. 'He will die in the car if we send him on', said one doctor to me, 'We will try to save him here', and then every device was resorted to save him from collapse. Hot water bottles, saline and other injections, hot tea, everything we could think of, but it was all to no avail. He died with his head on my shoulder within three hours. He was conscious up to the last. Another handsome Queen's Westminster boy came in bound tightly to his stretcher as he had been struggling fiercely. He was apparently not mortally wounded, and all his wounds were carefully re-dressed while four men held him down. He gulped down a cup of tea gratefully and seemed better, but I noticed his breathing suddenly became irregular and in five minutes, in spite of every effort by the doctors, he was dead – killed not so much by his wounds as by shock. And so with case after case. I have buried two doctors in the last day or two and many other splendid officers and men.

Of course you will say that my view is distorted by the sights and scenes of the last few days, and yet there is no one who has passed through a severe engagement who can help confessing that this endless flinging of metal against each other is really very foolish, and that the energy of the world today is misdirected; and yet how are we to get back to a saner view of things? Profiteers want the war to last for ever; aeroplane workers strike for higher wages so as to live in more comfort, while the Tommy earns a shilling a day with every prospect of being killed sooner or later. If he deserts he is shot. If an artisan strikes, the Government go down on their knees to him. Have we no strong men?

The diarist notes what Philip Gibbs was writing in the Daily Telegraph *on 5 December:*

So at the end of the year we find ourselves in a battle more decisive in its issues than all the fighting of the previous months . . . German prisoners tell us that they have been promised peace if they win this battle. . . .

Julian comments on 17 December:

The less said about the Cambrai battle the better. I do not think anything can now redeem it from being a costly failure. There will be no more joy bells ringing in England until peace is declared. Lord Lansdowne's letter is meeting with a great deal of support and favourable comment from officers out here. He will be a leader of a new party soon if he isn't careful, a Peace Party with a growing following.

Hopes of Christmas in a back area were fading:

I find it considerably more expensive living as a Senior Chaplain than as a Brigade Chaplain, so I must conserve my resources.

. . . I took seven services yesterday. As SCF I have far heavier Sundays as I am never of course in the Line, but I am getting accustomed to living away from the trenches, though I shall never be content to be away from the real thing.

The taking of Jerusalem is wonderful – a far bigger event it will seem ten years hence than, for instance, the taking of Vimy Ridge, which from a military point of view is of course immeasurably more important[10].

The diarist describes (28 December) what was to be the last Christmas of the war as

the quietest I ever remember. One son only, Geoffrey, was with us. We missed the grandchildren (Monier's two) very much, but it would have been unwise to bring them into the danger zone from air-raids. Geoffrey's happiness at his engagement helped us through. He left at lunchtime on Christmas Day to spend the rest of it with Jean[11]. Everywhere there is anxiety. We must hold on for the next few months till America comes in.

Burgon writes on 23 December:

We moved to our old billet two days ago. In fact the order to do so came only half an hour after I sent off my last letter. I am now again with the De l'Etoiles and got such a delightful welcome when I arrived. All the people are very glad to see us again, and we have almost precisely the same billets in every particular.

We had the most dreadful march here. I did not have such a bad time personally as I came on in advance, but even I had to force my way through snow which had drifted two or three feet in places. The squadron had to march sixty kilometres, the men tramping along on their feet, leading their horses. The roads were far too bad for them to ride except in one or two places. A sixty kilometre march on foot is a pretty good performance for infantry I should think, but if you add the fact that each man had three slipping horses to get along somehow, you will consider it a pretty good exhibition of staying power, when I tell you that not a single man or horse fell out, though some of them were just about done. I was standing about the roads till midnight, when they arrived and finally got to bed at 2 am.

On the strength of his splendid quarters, Burgon asks for several books in connection with the history of the Brigade which he is writing. Julian's Christmas was very busy. The CRE[12] built him a church at very short notice:

It is of timber and large enough to hold a congregation of 200. It has a chancel and vestry, porch, bell (taken from an old German trench). Its windows have oiled silk canvas for glass. Although the walls inside are not yet lined with canvas as they will be, it was ready for Christmas Day; we worked far into the night to put in its ecclesiastical fittings and to make it in decent order for the Christmas Celebrations.

We had no stoves, so it was rather cold, but people who live perpetually in the open air are used to sitting in cold buildings. With the exception of this one drawback, the church fulfilled all our expectations. We had seven services, so we didn't do badly.

After the Carol Service he went up to Vimy Ridge

in a car and after walking a short distance to a trench, an old communication trench, but still in use by us because on the farther slope of the ridge, although we are still some way from the enemy, there is a good view of all that goes on in the open. Here then, close to the highest part of the ridge, is a fairly spacious dug-out marked outside 'Ridge Church' on a notice board. Here my faithful Cheshire battalion had rigged up the simplest accessories for worship. A table covered with a blanket, a couple of candle-sticks and some sand bags for kneelers. Apparently this dug-out has been used before as a church. I shall try to get it properly fitted up as a church with permanent altar and seats.

It was mighty cold. Down the steep stairs of the dug-out the icy wind blew snow-flakes, but I had the novel little church filled twice over with devout worshippers, and in the fitful light of guttering candles we sang two or three Christmas hymns with real zest. This is the first time I have taken a Christmas service in a dug-out in the Line.

I got back in time to visit one or two Christmas dinners in progress at or near Divisional HQ and then joined a very quiet little dinner at our 'B' Mess. We had one toast only, to that of absent friends, which we drank in silence. We were all early to bed. It was really too cold to stay up long.

We have some American Staff Officers attached to us again. They come over in rotation from the training camps in the USA, and do a short course of practical staff work in the field. They are a fine lot of fellows. I have the greatest hope for the future with such men from a country which must be good to produce such a type coming in on our side. These staff officers are all of them 'men', well set up, gentlemen in every respect and I should say, from all I hear, extraordinarily efficient. There is not an ounce of boastfulness about them. They have come here to learn; without running themselves down or expatiating on their ignorance of modern warfare, by their manner they show that they are anxious to grasp all they can, and haven't got anything themselves to teach us.

*   *   *

Before the year's end Julian had his second experience of seeing a condemned man executed:

December 29, 1917.
The last twenty-four hours have furnished me with some severe tests of physical and mental endurance. Once again it has been my duty to spend the last hours on earth with a condemned prisoner. I cannot disclose to you many of the details of those trying hours, but I have, I hope, learnt much from the simple heroism of this mere lad of nineteen, who has been out here at the Front since 1914 when he was only fifteen and a half, and in spite of two wound stripes on his arm and all that service behind him, has met his end. It was my privilege to comfort and help him all I could, to hear his first and last confession, to administer to him the Holy Communion and to stand by his side till the very end. We have no time here amid the stern realities of war for pathos. We could not live at all if we dwelt on the 'pathetic' side of this vast tragedy, but there are few deaths I have witnessed which so wrung my heart-strings as this one.

He gave me all his little treasures to give to this or that friend. He wrote a letter to his sweetheart and sent her his letter wallet with its photographs and trinkets, a lucky farthing which she had given him for a keepsake, his last 'leave' ticket and other small things. He sent a letter to his best chum in the regiment and said he was sorry he hadn't made good, and wished them all a happy New Year and hoped they would all get home safe after the war.

Of our more intimate time together I may not speak. He slept peacefully as a child for several hours. Just before the end I read to him very gently that hymn which will for ever now have a new meaning for me, and which was in every line and every word appropriate. 'Just as I am without one plea!' As they bound him, I held his arm tight to reassure him, – words are useless at such a moment – and then he turned his blindfolded face up to mine and said in a voice which wrung my heart, 'Kiss me, Sir, kiss me', and with my kiss on his lips and, 'God has you in his keeping', whispered in his ear, he passed on into the Great Unseen. God accept him; Christ receive him. I do not think he died in vain.

Julian goes on in the same letter:

Yesterday afternoon I took over to Corps HQ seven NCOs and men, all of whom have thought seriously of and have given their names in for ordination. Other divisions in the Corps sent others in like case, and we spent a delightful afternoon. These seven are only some of those who are like-minded and intentioned in this division, but they were all I could collect under the circumstances. We started with an excellent tea, when tongues were soon unloosed after introductions had been made. When I tell you that one of those present was a Major commanding a battalion, who came with a private in the same battalion, and there were several other officers besides, you will understand that to get a general conversation going was something. Prayers and devotional address followed tea, then a general talk on prospects of ordination, and suggestions as to how we could keep together out here. Some of those I brought had come from the firing line that morning. The contrast between the comfortable well-lighted room and eager keen company in which they found themselves, and the icy post on the fire step was enough to warm their hearts and to encourage them to make fresh efforts to uphold the name of Christ amid the difficulties of their lives. The success of the meeting was certain.

*   *   *

1918 began with great news for the family – the diarist writes:

In today's New Year Honours Julian is among those who have got the MC. We are indeed pleased, for he does so richly deserve it. It is for services as a 4th Class Chaplain, so I expect later he will get the DSO.[13]

He was been in four big battles, the Somme, Arras, Cambrai and Passchendaele, sharing all dangers night and day with his men, arranging services for them on every possible occasion and never sparing himself'

Sunday, 6 January 1918, the Feast of the Epiphany, was appointed by the King as 'a Day of Intercession on behalf of the Nation and the Empire in this time of War' (see opposite). On the actual day, the diarist and her husband were in their old parish of Lewisham (he had been vicar there ten years earlier).

The church was full for the eight o'clock service when Father celebrated; and at eleven am when he preached, there was not standing room. The Mayor and Aldermen attended in state, and it was very impressive and solemn. St Paul's, where the Bishop of London preached, and every church and chapel in the Kingdom seem to have had the same experience. Many attended the House of God who seldom if ever go, and it shows how deeply the nation is stirred by the length and seriousness of the war.

Most unusually – indeed he has not done so before – the diarist's husband contributes two paragraphs, after this one of her own:

Wednesday, 9 January, 1918, Canterbury. We returned late yesterday afternoon, Father having first attended George Bell's[14] marriage at 9.30 am in Christ Church, Chelsea, to Miss Livingstone, a beautiful service completed by the Holy Communion. It was the coldest day this winter.

Father writes:

On Tuesday, 8 January, I lunched at the Athenaeum with the Home Secretary (Sir George Cave[15]) and we renewed old days at School and Oxford, while we were both at St John's (1876–1880). I asked him if he felt the Labour Party had a grip of the world-politics involved by the war? He thinks the Labour Party may very likely come into power, but yet have not developed a really great man.

I asked him as to his personal opinion of Winston Churchill's recent advance of twelve and a half per cent on the wages for time (not piece-work) of munition workers, which has already brought about a like demand from all other trades in private firms and resulted in an extra charge to the country of 130 millions per annum; he said at once that

FORMS

OF

PRAYER and THANKSGIVING

TO

ALMIGHTY GOD

TO BE USED ON

THE FEAST OF THE EPIPHANY

SUNDAY, THE SIXTH OF JANUARY, 1918

Being the Day appointed for Intercession on Behalf of the
Nation and Empire in this Time of War.

Issued under the Authority of the Archbishops of Canterbury and York.

THE KING'S PROCLAMATION

¶ *In the Order of Holy Communion after the Creed at least once in the day, and at Morning or Evening Prayer, or before the Forms of Prayer hereinafter set forth, the Minister shall read the King's Proclamation, saying as follows:*

Brethren, I bid you hear the words of His Majesty the King appointing this day to be set aside as a Day of Prayer and Thanksgiving in all the Churches throughout his Dominions.

TO MY PEOPLE.—The world-wide struggle for the triumph of right and liberty is entering upon its last and most difficult phase. The enemy is striving by desperate assault and subtle intrigue to perpetuate the wrongs already committed and stem the tide of a free civilization. We have yet to complete the great task to which, more than three years ago, we dedicated ourselves.

At such a time I would call upon you to devote a special day to prayer that we may have the clear-sightedness and strength necessary to the victory of our cause. This victory will be gained only if we steadfastly remember the responsibility which rests upon us, and in a spirit of reverent obedience ask the blessing of Almighty God upon our endeavours. With hearts grateful for the Divine guidance which has led us so far towards our goal, let us seek to be enlightened in our understanding and fortified in our courage in facing the sacrifices we may yet have to make before our work is done.

I therefore hereby appoint January 6th—the first Sunday of the year—to be set aside as a special day of prayer and thanksgiving in all the Churches throughout my dominions, and require that this Proclamation be read at the services held on that day.

GEORGE R.I.

he personally disapproved, but that Winston Churchill had so acted in despite of the advice and judgement offered to him by heads much wiser than his own. This seems to be the way in which public money is thrown away, without bringing greater contentment to the workers and greater output and increased efficiency. The only remedy would be restoration of 'collective responsibility' for the Cabinet as before the War.

The diarist goes on:

We had a letter from Burgon this morning, dated *6 January, 1918*:

I am more delighted about Julian's Military Cross than I can say. It is an honour to him and his profession, and I can well picture the congratulations he will get from all who know and love him in his division. I am writing of course to him direct. I do hope he manages to get leave before long. It surely must be due now. I only hope this decoration, and the Mention he had, not long ago, will lead to still further honours – there's not another padre in the Army who has done more for his men and officers than Julian. I only wish we had men like him in the cavalry.

For the first time since the publication of his MC, Julian writes on 6 January, 1918:

You will have seen about my MC. I know how pleased you will be – but I am honestly sorry about it. I hold, and shall continue to hold, strong views about chaplains' decorations. They never have 'to go over the top'; they have a comparatively easy job from the military point of view. I could in fact name hundreds of officers in this division still undecorated who more than deserve a decoration. I feel you won't perhaps agree with me, but I would rather have been without it.

(Not long later from Burgon:

No, none of us agree with you. Whenever your men have been in a tight place, there have you invariably been with them).

A chaplain, if he is a worthy priest, must be prepared to offer his life for his flock and to go into really dangerous places to save others. 'He saved others, himself he could not save'. We don't want to be decorated for doing that.

I shall have to put the ribbon up. More than one officer has been kind enough to congratulate me; and I was really delighted to know how pleased you would be. Monier, Kitty, Geoff and Jean sent me a wire, which I was very glad to get.

The diarist writes:

Monday, 14 January, 1918. Our dear son Burgon is thirty years old today. What an interruption this war has been to his career, as it has been in so many others.

Julian, unlike his brother, is very busy indeed:

I have at present more to do in the hours than I can get through.

I am hoping for leave in four weeks' time from now. I have fixed the Confirmation for 10 or 11 February and intend to get away after that. If I hear from Burgon that he can possibly manage leave by the end of February, I want to put off mine ten days, so as to include at least one week with him. There is so much of real importance that I want to talk to him and you about. Remember I have seen my brothers now only for one or two days in the last six years.

He is concerned for Burgon's soldiering:

I am very anxious for him to get an Intelligence job. He is so removed from the big events in the Machine-gun Corps, and I want to press him to get into Intelligence, or go as a 'learner' on the Staff. I shall write and urge this again soon . . . He is fretting away his valuable energies and qualities where he is.

In fact, Burgon has been writing in a less frustrated frame of mind, largely because he has been able, in the relaxed environment of the château, to get a lot of work done on his history of the Brigade:

The Brigade Record goes well. I have finished up to the Hohenzollern Redoubt (January 1916), and it is 8000 words already. There is only a rigid recital of events, which to my mind is rather bare bones, but I went over to the Brigade HQ for lunch yesterday, and they were delighted with it. It is just a straightforward account, not picturesque, but in strictly military language, but it really does not make bad reading. It will be more like a small book of 20,000 words containing only the history, instead of a magazine consisting of several articles, and it may have board covers if they are obtainable, which I doubt. So this is an added interest, and I want to see it completed.

The diarist comments, 'We do very strongly agree with Julian that Burgon's powers are being wasted where he is. He has never had a chance of distinguishing himself'.

The moving account of the second time Julian had to see a condemned prisoner through his last hours raises Geoffrey's wrath:

The description of that boy of nineteen's execution in Julian's letter made my blood boil. I think it is the most pathetic thing I have ever read in my life. How can these things be? The irony of a man dying with such magnificent courage after being condemned for cowardice! And the shrieking injustice! How about those Generals who failed in their duty at Cambrai – a failure which cost the lives of thousands of brave men? Were they shot? No – given soft billets in England probably. That poor boy's sweetheart! And think of Jean and me. Let us remember these things when we talk of the value of war.

Julian has obviously been much congratulated on his decoration.

People have been very kind about my MC, but I do not budge from my opinion on the whole subject which I stated in my last letter.

He took twelve services on the second Sunday of the year. For three hours in the evening he went from ward to ward of the Corps Rest Station with a harmonium

and a boy from the Field Ambulance played it for me. The men really liked it and sang heartily.

The diarist's nephew (Lieutenant Colonel Crauford Monier-Williams) wrote to her:

Julian's MC is one of the best-deserved and most tardy recognitions of the war. He is some name out here.

At least there is fresh stimulation for Burgon, reported a letter on 21 January:

Two days ago names of officers who spoke German were asked for, and my name was sent in, but I don't suppose anything will come of it.

He adds:

I am doing a certain amount of lecturing to the men now. Three nights ago I spoke for an hour on German Ideals and War-aims, bringing in *Mittel Europa*, and contrasted the genius of France and Britain with them. The men came voluntarily in large numbers and listened so that you could hear a pin drop, which with an audience of soldiers means something. I worked up to quite a peroration at the end, and told them that in a hundred years' time all the armies and guns and Victoria Crosses and generals would be forgotten, and Sir Douglas Haig's name would merely appear on the page of a history book. What would endure would be liberty. In all I say I try to put the matter of *Welt Politik*, i.e. Turkey and the Near East especially, her aims for Belgium as shown in Von Bissing's Testament which I have just read, Alsace Lorraine, the Herreros, and contrast our ideas by giving a short sketch of the rise of the Empire – rather a big subject, but of course one can deal very simply with a few facts.

Bishop Gwynne wrote to Julian on 16 January to congratulate him:

I was very pleased to hear that your work in the 56th Division has been recognized by the award of the Military Cross. This will be very gratifying to your relations and to your friends, both at home and out here. Besides being a great encouragement, you will find it a help in your work. I am proud of you and warmly congratulate you. God bless you in all that lies before you in this New Year.

*   *   *

In a letter dated 24 January, 1918, Burgon wrote:

The General asked me yesterday whether I should care to go on his Staff as Intelligence Officer with a view either to continuing in the Intelligence Department or being trained eventually for Staff Captain. I told him I should like to go on his Staff, but that if I came, I should like to do the thing properly and go away for a proper Intelligence Course. He agreed to this.

So he is going to put in a very strong application for me at once, and was kind enough to say he thought I should be more useful to the country on Intelligence or Staff work than as a section leader in machine-guns.

I am not frightfully enthusiastic about going to live with the Brigade Staff; they are awfully good fellows, but I do not think there is anything to do as Intelligence Officer, though I dare say I could make something of it. But the point is, it might lead to other things. Supposing the General, whom I like immensely and who is the ablest of the Brigadiers in the Cavalry Corps, gets a division, he might easily get me on.

However, as you know, I am not enthusiastic about anything except peace.

The job does not mean any promotion or any increase of pay, but it does mean getting out of a rut – all on the supposition that I can get out of the Machine Gun Corps, which, I assure you, is a very big supposition.

But it happened:

'*Saturday, 2 February, 1918*. Today we received the two following letters from Burgon. The change of work and the character of the work must prove interesting, and give Burgon a good chance of using his powers to advantage:

Epagne near Abbeville 25 January, 1918.
    In my little world things have moved rather fast in the last two days. I am to join the Brigade Staff almost at once, in fact in a couple of days from now. Brig. Gen. AEW Harman's ADC is away on leave, and the fellow who was acting as Intelligence Officer left about three weeks ago, so I am to go at once and start right away. I rode over to the Brigade this morning and they were all most awfully nice. 'Puggy' Howes, an old House man, is Brigade-Major. Of course I know him very well and like him immensely. He is also extremely efficient. He said this morning, 'I am very glad you are coming. We want somebody who will really take an interest in the Intelligence. I will try to get you on a course as soon as ever I can; and as regards learning Staff work, there is any amount of stuff I shall be able to give you to do, and it is the best way

to learn. Also', he said, 'remember that the General is a man who is likely to get on, and if you do well here, naturally a general prefers to have fellows round him in his new job whom he knows, in preference to fresh faces'.

Howes showed me the application the General had sent in for me. The things he said were kind, but untrue, but you have to lay it on thick when you apply for somebody.

I shall never actually be in the trenches now, but live at Headquarters. My job is to read through all the Intelligence reports, collect all the information, get new information for myself with regard to our sector of the Line, keep the maps marked up to date and bring things of importance to the notice of the General. It all sounds rather vague, and I am indeed vague about it at present; but like you, though, I recognise it is a good chance, and mean to make the most of it; still I hate anything new.

I am taking four horses to the Brigade and my two servants. Unfortunately both my servants are new at the job, but I hope they will do all right.

Everyone who comes from Paris says peace is very much in the air, and Geoffrey tells one the same thing is true in London. I am following the papers very carefully. The only thing I am doubtful about is that this time last year was very quiet too – and we thought peace was coming. How I wish peace would come. All the chances in the world of learning Staff work don't reconcile me to this life.

The Brigade History is finished.

PS. I trek in a motor now in style, and my four horses and two servants follow on behind!

A second letter next day describes the start of his new work, as he rides round his new area to get the hang of it.

While Burgon is elated, Julian is the very opposite:

I cannot write much, as I am too sad to tell you more than that my old Battalion, the Rangers, has been broken up and scattered to the winds. It is all part of the new scheme of reorganization of the British Army which is taking place. I have seen many sad sights out here in France, but I have never witnessed anything sadder than the destruction of a battalion of battle-comrades. It is not good to see strong men weep.

Personally it has taken from me a large slice of my interest in this division. I only consoled myself with coming to this job at Divisional

HQ by the thought I was near to my first and only love in the Army – the Rangers. Now that they have disappeared, things seem rather empty. There is only one job for a chaplain in France and that is with the battalion. They are the fighting men, the men who bear the brunt of war, who get wounded and recover, return to the trenches, and get wounded again until their time comes and they die. It is good to live with dying men – dying men who are in the full vigour of health and strength, whose comradeship is something past understanding, but sacred and wonderful.

These are the men who are always treated worst. They are the worst paid; they live in greater hardships; they are more away from their homes; they live in greater danger than any other man who wears the King's uniform. It is they who by their lives, their heroism and splendid unselfishness live very close to their God. They have one consolation in the midst of what most people know to be a hopeless existence, and that is their comradeship, their friendship. It is this fact alone which helps them through – the comradeship of men who have shared countless hardships and dangers together; and now even this has been taken from many of them as their little knots and gatherings of friends have been broken up and destroyed. 'Good-bye, chum, let's hope we'll meet in Blighty – some day when the war is over'. 'Keep a good heart, boy, it won't be long now'. 'Cheer up, mate, I'll write and tell you where I get to'; and many similar sayings, accompanied by hearty hand-grips and eyes brimming with tears, are heard as the various contingents formed up to march away – the majority never to meet again on this earth.

And then the country expects the 'morale' of the troops to be kept up!

*　　*　　*

Meanwhile the new Brigade Intelligence Officer is settling in:

Everyone has been extremely kind about my new appointment – in itself of course not much of a job, or rather it has the reputation of being a soft thing; but the point is it does get you out of a rut, and brings you in touch with new people and new interests.

He writes to his brother Geoffrey about the lecturing he hopes to do:

I want to lecture on the different ideals of *Welt Politik* for which Germany, France and ourselves stand, of the German war aims, dividing them into East and West – West: Belgium and the coast, intimidation of France; Gibraltar, retention of Alsace and Lorraine; the way Germany simply possesses Turkey now; and also Africa in the light of Smuts'[17] speech. I am very emphatic in not bringing a general indictment against the German people, but state the aims as being those of the Pan-German party. I shall then give some idea of the majority and minority socialists, and leave them to talk it over as to what they estimate the forces of democracy in Germany to be . . . I feel you want to state the case clearly and not be a Jingoist – in the same way with regard to lectures on social subjects, we want to state the case and not suppress the right socialist ideas, if indeed that were possible, which of course it isn't, as a good deal of socialism is talked, but it is unbalanced and ignorant talk.

After dining with the new CO of his old unit he writes:

I was of course the only officer who knew him well. We did our first MG course together, so it would have been a little trying to serve under him as a subaltern two and a half years later.

Julian spent the last day of the existence of his beloved Rangers battalion with them:

I found I still knew nearly every man in the battalion and I went round with the chaplain, who succeeded me, and shook hands with every man of the party going off. They were soon in the buses, and then with the band playing 'Auld Lang Syne' and the occupants cheering as each bus reached the band, they drove off. I slept the night with the battalion, staying at the old curé's house. I don't know how many men were put to bed. This is a singularly British characteristic – to sink one's troubles in beer, even if it is only French beer! Sad, you will say – yes, but I am giving you the facts. The soldier has not become a pious saint because he may die tomorrow, the reverse is the truth. 'Let us eat and drink for tomorrow we die'. There is no good to be had from hiding our heads in the sand and pretending that things are all right. Personally, I am quite sure that war and all its attendant evils have lowered our moral standards to a terrible extent. I see the bishops in Convocation mentioned something about the immorality at the Front. They have not spoken too soon or too forcibly. It is rampant.

We had the following from Julian this morning, dated 13 February, 1918:

We have had a wonderful day and such an inspiring Confirmation Service. The Bishop was as delightful as ever, but very tired. His work is truly colossal. To have but one bishop for all this Front is really typical, I fear, of our lack of organizing power as a Church. Our church, St Stephen's, looked really beautiful with its rood and great Crucifix, its circle of lights before the Altar. The church was used all the evening before and the morning before by various chaplains for confessions. I think nearly all the candidates made use of this Sacrament before their Confirmation. I am sure more and more chaplains are finding this is just what the men need. I know that is my experience. Of my candidates only three did not use the Sacrament of Penance, and of these three two were non-conformists, who were prejudiced beforehand against it as a Roman 'dodge', and the third, I fear, really funked it. Nothing could be more impressive than the Service of Confirmation itself. A finer lot of young Englishmen you could never want to see. Among them was a Sergeant-major with a bar to his Military Medal, two of my candidates who had won their decorations at Ypres and Cambrai – when the British Army did not run away in its pyjamas, as seems to be the universal belief in home circles and which is a gross calumny and wants refuting every time it is uttered. The reason for the 'breaking-up' of various regiments of which you have heard has nothing to do with the morale of the Army, but is due only to the failure on the part of the Home Government to comb out the civilian population of England, which contains still thousands of shirkers. But all this is by the way, as I was describing the Confirmation.

The Bishop's address was excellent, though rather long, and he was tired. However, the candidates listened to every word in absolute silence. We thundered out 'Come Holy Ghost our souls inspire' on our knees. It is good – and an unusual sight to see Tommies on their knees. Kneeling is not popular in the Army. Then two together in turn knelt before the Bishop.

A chaplain who had just joined us from a home parish said what an amazing contrast a Confirmation at the Front presented to a home service of a similar nature. Certainly we almost felt the sound of the rushing mighty wind, and our hearts were aflame with the fire of the Holy Spirit. Please God, some at least of those splendid lads may be spared to go back to England and help in her regeneration.

*   *   *

Rumours *(writes Burgon on 16 February)* are beginning to fly around about the German offensive. Some say it will not come at all. At any rate I don't really know much more than you about it, and if I did I could not tell you . . .

You will be glad to hear my transfer back to the regiment came through last night, so I am no longer seconded, but once again on the strength of the Royal Dragoons. I have taken down my MG badge and put up the eagle on my cap; and the Colonel and everybody were very nice and said they were glad to see me back. As a matter of fact, of course, it does not mean I really go back and live with the regiment, as I stay at Brigade Headquarters and live with the General. I am glad to be out of the MG Squadron as it has changed a very great deal in two years, and the type of officer in it now is rather poor. So I am well content, if anything happened and I ceased to be Brigade Intelligence Officer, to be able to go back to the Royals. The great thing about living at Brigade is that one gets to know lots of people, not only in the Division but in the Corps. Enormous numbers of people come to meals, which though it swells one's mess bill, does at any rate increase one's acquaintances.

Today I began my aerial photography course. It was most interesting. The lecturer first gave us the main principles of photography reading, and then with photographs of the aerodrome and surrounding country in our hands, we went out and saw the relationship between the actual thing and the image as it appeared on the picture. Our cameras are good, but the German are better. Whenever we capture a German camera, it is installed in one of our machines, and cases have occurred of a camera changing hands four or five times in this way.

VOLUME VIII
FEBRUARY – JULY 1918

Julian on leave – Burgon learns his new job – Ludendorff's March offensive –
the Royals in action as cavalry; Burgon gallops his messages – Julian also in
the thick of the fighting – the brothers meet again, longing for the war to end
– birth of Julian's god-daughter – Burgon in hospital; flies again.

1 March, 1918, 'Julian is home on leave', *writes the diarist,*

and as usual got through a wonderful amount of things; he went off
yesterday to Rugby. Father was in the gallery of the House of Commons on Wednesday, but it was dull and he left early to find later to
his great disappointment that he had missed one of Balfour's[1] finest
speeches. But he met him by chance in the Park yesterday and they
had a talk.

Crauford Monier-Williams, who had served with Julian, came to see
us today. Such a splendid man and now a Lieutenant Colonel and
Assistant Director of Signals in the Second Corps. He says he thinks
neither side will break through, but as the offensive is with the Germans
they must lose heavily, and when we have killed enough Germans the
peace will be in our favour!

Burgon has been flying again,

The first time I've been up since that crash on the Somme, so I was glad
to go up and see if I should mind it. I didn't a bit, and thoroughly
enjoyed looking over the edge all the time and trying to make out the
country. . . . As we landed (that crash had been on landing) my heart
rather went into my mouth, but quite unnecessarily.

Yesterday, I received from John Buchan two very interesting memo-
randa, one of them on German war-aims. . . . You said Julian writes he
is a revolutionary about the Church. There is much that wants altering
in our system, but the more I see of the matter the more convinced I am

that the man is everything, the system, or rather the Church as a system, nothing. A narrow, a stupid or a lazy padre will ruin people's opinions of the Church, however many self-denying ordinances it may pass about bishop's palaces, wives and other luxuries. The man is all that the average layman sees of the Church, the average private soldier at any rate – a wide-minded, efficient, hard-working padre will get a sympathetic hearing for any doctrine he wishes to preach, and the system (with all its shortcomings) will live again in its very best light in his life.

3 March, 1918. 'Another delightful letter from Burgon', records the diarist 'shows how full of interest is his new work':

I have tonight read the aims of the Allied Labour-Socialist Conference very carefully. However idealistic and impracticable they may be in some respects, I think it is a noble document.

The prominence given to the idea of the League of Nations, though I admit the practical working-out of the scheme seems beyond the capacity of the human brain, is surely to the good. I firmly believe that a statement like this must find an enormous amount of sympathy in countless Germans, though we can never know it till peace, or negotiations for peace, have allowed us to get together.

Each year that the war goes on things seem to become more and more perplexing. Certainly no one has ever been witness of more amazing world-events than this generation, so we ought to be thankful we are living now. I know I am.

A little about my doings. I am really very occupied. I am going round this sector to get a knowledge of the OP's[2] and other things I shall need to know if we go into the line.

I have always a lot of writing work on hand. The Brigade History is now back from the Regiment, and I have much to re-write and correct. I am trying to get out a list of practical German phrases for the men – the sort of things that might be useful to them on patrol. In addition to this there are always the small odds and ends to be done; maps to be issued, registers to be kept up, information to be tabulated so it can be got at, and many other small things.

Yesterday a long thing came in about lectures on demobilization, agriculture, disabled soldiers' plans, reconstruction in general. Officers selected are required to have done public speaking before, and to be keen on the idea as a whole. Both these qualifications I fulfil. I think I shall be able to work it in with my intelligence work – and of course if the Boche really pushes, such things as lectures would go by the board till he had been stopped. These preparations for demobilization have come to stay though. I am certain of it.

Yesterday Winston Churchill was dining with a regiment in this division. I am told he did not entertain any very sanguine ideas about the end of the war.

5 March, Canterbury, telegram from Monier this morning to Julian:

'Your god-daughter born 6.45 last night. Both splendid. All so happy'.

We are pleased to have another grand-daughter, and she is Julian's god-child. We saw Julian off by the Staff boat from Folkestone. After lunch at the Royal Pavilion Hotel we walked on the Lees watching the shipping and the endless soldiers collecting ready to embark for France. I think this is our twentieth parting from a son going to the front.

* * *

The diarist comments:

The Germans are treating the Russians and poor Roumanians abominably. The Turks meanwhile are massacring all the remaining Armenians they can find in Asia Minor, putting to the sword all 'men, boys and male infants.' The world seems given over to the devil at the moment. The hopeful signs are that we seem confident we can hold the Germans in the west, our Palestine troops are nearing Shechem, Japan is going to stem the German advance in Siberia, and America is speeding up all she can to help us in Europe.

We found the following from Julian awaiting us on our return from Margate, written from Boulogne:

6 March, 1918:

We left punctually at 4.45 pm. The first person I met on board was Howes, Burgon's Brigade Major, who was at the House with us and was returning from leave. He greeted me most warmly and we found deck chairs together on the boat deck. He told me how much they appreciated Burgon or 'the Bishop' as everybody, he said, calls him. When the vacancy occurred, the Brigadier suggested taking on Burgon and

Howes said how delighted he was to have someone really keen as his Intelligence Officer.

Crossing with Julian was his DACG F.R. Barry[3]:

He has had some interesting interviews while at home, including one this morning with the Archbishop, whom he saw in bed, and who was most sympathetic, saying to him, 'I know all you chaplains think I am very hard to move and "sticky"; yet I want you to know that I am keen – far keener on the projects you have at heart than you have any conception of, and am prepared to go to almost any lengths at the right time; but to get any legislation through Parliament as long as the war lasts is quite impossible and wouldn't be worth the trouble of trying. Your job – that of the chaplains – is quite clear. Create such a public opinion in England and among your troops against the anomalies of our position in the Church, that when we do try to get legislation, the country may be behind us. Meanwhile go on "slanging" us. Write as many "Churches in the Furnace" as you like – it will do us all good'.

Barry came away greatly cheered by the sympathy and foresight of the Archbishop. . . . This opinion of the Archbishop's is not to be quoted please anywhere, and a word to this effect should be put in the Diary if inserted there.

Meanwhile, Burgon is happy and busy:

I fear I have not written for three or four days – four I think. But yesterday was impossible as I was out all day with the Colonel reconnoitring ground just behind the Line and putting in things on the map which were inaccurately marked.

The Colonel, as he rode along, turned to me and said,

'Bishop, do you know what I intend to do? I intend to teach my children to hate the Germans, and to teach them to teach their children to hate the Germans'.

What is one to say or think? I really don't know. Faced on all sides with the handiwork of the Huns, damage some of it necessary from the military point of view, much of it merely spiteful, it is difficult to take any sane view. 'Well then, Colonel,' I said, 'if you do that, what is to be the future of Europe? It all depends on whether we have a changed Germany to deal with or not. If you decide now to hate the Hun, whether the people of Germany get the upper hand or not in the next ten years, you and your children will still be living on the edge of a volcano – Europe will still be divided into two gigantic camps, the people armed to the teeth and high taxes and eventual bankruptcy, an intolerable burden and a constant menace'.

Julian eventually got back to Divisional Headquarters from his leave, his car having had no less than three 'blow-outs' causing him long waits by the side of the road each time, and the rueful comment 'I am just a little inclined to think that the old way of travelling by train is better'. Both brothers refer to the coming 'German Attack'. Thus Julian, 10 March:

We expect an offensive any moment, and are absolutely ready. The Germans have no chance of getting through here – of that I am quite sure. Burgon's lot are expecting an attack too, but not more than we are. In fact everyone is on the alert and all possible precautions have been taken.

Burgon, 18 March:

It is impossible to say what we shall be doing any day now. Every week the war goes on I seem less capable of coherent thought on any subject. I am extremely happy here, and for the army (and my rank in it) my life could not be more agreeable or interesting; but there is only one thing really to live for and that is a return to the pursuit of peace.

Meanwhile despite the scare ('the enemy has become very aggressive, but still the attack has not come'), 150 chaplains have gone back behind the line to an old French barracks for a two-and-a-half-day conference. 'The second half was better than the first, a Quiet Day' but, sadly for Julian, without the accustomed Holy Communion service to start it off:

13 March. At our last meeting on the previous evening, Harry Blackburne, the ACG of the Army had explained why his committee has settled to have no Holy Communion with which to start the Quiet Day. The first proposal of a joint communion was negatived; the second proposal of having two Holy Communions in one room for the C of E and the other in another for non-C of E was also negatived. The first way only presented a short cut to Reunion which would not help – the second was felt, he said, to be equally unsatisfactory and would

introduce the only discordant note of our gathering. In everything we should be able to join together heartily except in this. So the committee felt bound to cut out the service altogether. I feel personally that if the omission of the Sacraments is to be the price we pay for Reunion, even in a small gathering like this, it is hardly worth while. It will be, and can so easily be said later, 'Oh we met together in worship, prayer and discussion, very happily without any Holy Communion. Surely Holy Communion can't be so important an obstacle or so important in itself after all'.

Anyhow, one or two of us felt that to start a Quiet Day without a celebration of Holy Communion was quite wrong, so we went to the local Cathedral to Mass at 8.00 am.

But Julian's disappointment over the concessions on Communion did not prevent him taking trouble to meet

as many non-conformists as possible. There were one or two very fine men – notably Professor Mackintosh, a Presbyterian Minister of Edinburgh, who lectured to us, and G Evans the YMCA leader of the 1st Army, who is a Baptist minister from the North of England.

* * *

The long-expected German attack, on a 50-mile front between Arras and the Oise, began on 21 March. No fewer than seventeen German Divisions were thrown into the fray on one section of the front alone in this 'great battle', which, says the Daily Telegraph:

the enemy hope will yield them the final victory in the west which is to give them the triumphant peace promised to the people.

'It is hard', comments the diarist, 'to think of anything else except that the greatest battle the world has ever known is in progress, accompanied by every devilish modern scientific invention'.

But Burgon, writing on 17 March, is still deep in the final of the Inter-Squadron Football match; '. . . between the 3rd Dragoon Guards and the Machine Gun Squadron. The Machine Guns, I am glad to say, won, and after the match (which I was running), General Harman presented the medals, I giving them to him and reading out the names of the team. I was awfully pleased at the Machine-Guns winning, as of course, I knew every man'. Earlier he had been to the Holy Communion, 'one other man (a private) there besides myself'.

'Once the battle had been joined', writes the diarist, 'the seriousness of it all became evident; the German aim was to cut a way between the French and the British, and drive back the British right and the French left. The German Crown Prince was himself in charge of the German advance; undeterred by enormous losses, his troops were making limited progress only, after five days, and the British and French lines were still firmly joined'. On 27 March Julian wrote quietly confident, but there was no news from Burgon ('surely' says Julian, 'they would not allow cavalry units to be swallowed up in the enemy's advance, but rather use them to harrass the advancing Huns and cover our withdrawal')

Certainly with every day that passed, British confidence both at home and in France grew. 'That we shall be defeated in this battle occurs to nobody out here', writes Julian. Immensely morale-boosting was the King's unexpected visit: 'I simply long to go out there, and see those splendid men and shake some of them by the hand', the King is reported to have said when the battle was eight days old; go he did, on a destroyer across the Channel, and spent two days driving round the front talking with everyone he could; and the soldiers loved him for it.

On Easter Eve 30 March, the diarist's entry reads:

Before going out to the early Holy Communion we had two field post cards from Burgon. One dated 22 March, the day after the battle had begun; the other Sunday 24 March. He merely says, 'I am well' It is true that since then the cavalry has been engaged, but we trust no news is good news. In the evening paper Haig praises the gallant part taken by the cavalry, both mounted and unmounted, in 'stemming the advance of the enemy'.

On Easter Tuesday 2 April, the following came from Julian, showing as his family had thought that they were attacked on Thursday 28th:

We became involved today – in other words, the great battle burst upon our front. The bombardment was terrific. The enemy levelled our front trenches and still came on, wave after wave. Our machine guns never had such targets and mowed down the enemy in thousands [sic !]. Our infantry, firing till their rifles were too hot to hold, held them. Part only of our front system was captured, but the victory lay with us. It has been a day of terrible fighting, but the enemy attack has been broken for the moment. I must get a little sleep, having been up since 4 am. Where is Burgon?

The answer to that question was partly in the cryptic Field Post-Cards, and now at greater length in this letter of 27 March, after six days of the battle:

I hope you got the Field Postcards. This is the first moment I have had to write you a line. We have been living at tremendous pressure and still are. I have had a most amazingly interesting time. It is open warfare at last. We have been split up into all kinds of parties – just living and fighting as we could. Part of my Brigade were with one infantry division and part with another. General Harman has been commanding a sort of composite party, mounted from the first. They did a charge, killed over one hundred Boches, took 140 prisoners with few casualties. We have been living from hour to hour. For four nights we practically had no sleep. I lived and slept at the HQ of the French Division with whom we were operating – had a car at my disposal and went backwards and forwards all day and all night. It was a very responsible job. I took the French General's orders down, translated them and flew off in a car to my General, who then ordered the various dispositions of his troops and MGs. It was a thing you could not afford to make a mistake over.

There was a most dramatic scene on 25 March about noon – when the Boches were pushing us over the Oise only about three miles off – and we ourselves were forced to move our HQ. A message was brought in saying the French were retiring over the Oise from the north to the south bank. The old General got on to the 'phone, and amid the absolute silence of all the Staff Officers in the room, said to the Colonel at the other end. 'Do I understand some of your men are withdrawing', 'Yes'. 'Well, I don't think you quite understand my orders. It was that no man, French or English, is to cross the river under any pretext. They are to hold out to the last extremity. As to the bridges, they will not be blown up till the last moment, and then under my direct orders'.

As a matter of fact, several of the bridges had direct hits on them. I don't know how I got across one of them myself in the car – it was almost gone. My chauffeur was a Canadian from Edmonton! Well, they are exciting times – and I don't think we are finished yet. The whole manoeuvre is a vindication of the use of the cavalry; now we are getting going in our proper role. Some who were in the trenches are as keen as mustard, having killed any number of Boches and ready now to have a go on their horses.

I wonder how old Julian is getting on? I wouldn't have missed this time for anything. The scenes one witnesses daily are amazing. One afternoon I watched French troops going into action, French cavalry on the flanks – English batteries galloping up and opening fire – German batteries on the hills beyond – villages in flames – dumps being fired by us – the roads a block of horse transport – three German balloons brooding over the whole affair – and shells dropping here and there.

I think of you all constantly. Surely this will be the end of the war?

Two days later, resting briefly, he wrote again, having seen The Times *almost every day since the attack started:*

It now turns out that our battalion, i.e. the dismounted men of this brigade, put up a magnificent show. A personal letter from the infantry general arrived yesterday, full of thanks for what they did. I only wish I had been with my Machine-Gunners. They got some wonderful targets, one corporal shooting down the road of a village waited till the Boches were about eighty to a hundred yards off and crowding down the road in a mob, and then let off. He killed fifty in much less time than it takes me to write this sentence. It is all a little difficult to reconcile with Good Friday – a day which of course it has become totally impossible to recognize in any way.

Julian writes:

1st April 1918

All goes well – will write a large letter tomorrow. We are away from the strain of battle for a short time and are much enjoying the rest, but we live from day to day only. Don't worry about not hearing from Burgon. You mayn't hear for three or four weeks, seeing that all the organized system of postal service must have been totally destroyed in his part of the battle.

On 3 April, still resting: 'Please cut out the bit in The Times *of 2 April on the leader page, telling of our Division's exploits in the battle last Thursday, and insert it in the Diary'. The Diarist did just that, it describes how 'it was largely owing to the fine way in which the Third Division held the left of our line that the German attack as a whole fell so far short of its objective'.*

Burgon got to Holy Communion on Easter Day itself:

We have been up since 5 am standing-to at an hour's notice. We all stood up round a very dirty kind of room for the service, at which there were three generals and some officers and a dozen men or so. . . . We find it difficult to get a wide view of things here, being much occupied with what lies immediately before us. . . . I am feeling very fit, but my goodness, when it is all over won't it be great?

Julian is confident (29 March, Good Friday):

The victory remains with us. Our casualties in the battalions who bore the brunt of the fighting are heavy, as had to be expected, but those glorious men know they have not died in vain – at least I hope they know. Each battle removes from the Division some well-known face – some officer who has lasted all through. Today we mourn the death of one of our bravest doctors, who earned the VC a hundred times, but who had received only the MC with a bar. He was frail of figure and delicate in health, but as brave as a lion. He simply did not know what fear meant. Everyone knew him and to know him was to love and admire him. They managed to get his body back, and he was buried today. Quite a few other officers well-known in the Division have 'gone' this time and many a humble fellow in the ranks besides. We feel a momentary pang of regret and then turn our attention to other things. We dare not let our minds meditate upon these sorrows, or we simply could not carry on. So what appears as callousness is really only common sense. . . . At one of our cemeteries, on Easter Eve, I was carrying out several burials, and while waiting for bodies to be prepared I saw three Gunner officers, with their general, carrying one of their officers to his last resting place. It was unusual to see a general lifting a stretcher, but splendid to know that he liked to pay his last respect to one of his subalterns.

He managed two Celebrations of Holy Communion on Easter Day. After the first:

I then bicycled over to a camp two and a half miles away to the Queen's Westminsters and found that in the absence of any C of E Chaplain in the Brigade, the Wesleyan chaplain had arranged a church parade for the battalion, or what was approximately a church parade.

I discovered he was going to celebrate Holy Communion afterwards for anyone who cared to stay, but when he heard I had come to arrange Holy Communion, he cancelled his own altogether. I went back to our village and managed to get a car for half an hour, returning just in time, as his service was coming to an end. I was particularly anxious to take a service for this battalion, as it was one of the three which had borne the brunt of the fighting on the 28th – and they had always been our best Church battalion. Even now, after very heavy losses, there were 120 communicants. I wonder what you will think of my action; the Wesleyan chaplain at my request administered the chalice. He made no sort of request to do so, but as there were one or two non-conformists communicating, and he was their own Chaplain attached to this battalion, I felt it was fitting. He was absolutely reverent and used the words of our prayer book. Let me know what you feel about this. Non-conformists and C of E men had fought and died side by side two days before. Surely we were not wrong to kneel together on Easter morning and partake of the same cup[4].

On Easter Monday Julian had to deal with a shell-shocked chaplain, the only mention of such a happening in the whole diary:

I went over directly after breakfast to the Corps Rest Station to see one of our newest chaplains who came to us on 1 January last, but had collapsed with nerves badly during the battle, and who even after several days was no better. Fortunately Barry, our DACG was himself in hospital at a Casualty Clearing Station only 200 yards from the Corps Rest Station, and I was able to consult him as to what had better be done. I'm afraid we both came to the same conclusion that the nerves were sudden wind-up more than anything else, as no shell had burst near this fellow and he was due to be married in a fortnight's time. In spite of all persuasion, nothing would induce him even to express a desire to go back to his battalion. He had left a Dressing Station during the battle with no chaplain although he had been especially stationed there. So I wired to the ACG of the Army, asking for his instant transfer to the Base.

Afterwards, I walked back four miles along the valley to our divisional HQ and enjoyed the lovely country to the full. All the land was green with the young corn – almost as vivid a green as the paddy-fields of Ceylon. All the trees are sprouting and there are signs of Spring everywhere. The dull roar of distant guns was, however, incessant. The great battle still goes on. How many more Springs will come before the world knows peace again?

I stopped and spoke to an industrious French peasant sowing potatoes. He was anxious to know whether I thought him wise or foolish, to plant laboriously where the enemy might any day over-run his fields, and others than he, would reap the harvest. I reassured him and told him of how the German hordes had been kept back only last Thursday and would be kept back in the days before us, and that he could go on planting with an easy mind.

In the afternoon I went off to the other end of our divisional area to arrange services for our pioneer battalion who had been moving on Easter Day. While I was waiting for a lift in a car on my way back, I saw a remarkably fine feat by a German airman. He flew down our line and 'did in', i.e. set on fire, no less than four of our observation balloons, one after the other. He was surrounded by a barrage of anti-aircraft shell-bursts, but kept serenely on his way, firing incendiary bullets into each balloon as he came along and setting them on fire before they had time to be lowered. The occupants in each case escaped in parachutes, but although he was, I believe, himself brought down later on, it was no mean achievement and a very plucky thing to do.

His last Easter Service church parade was on the Tuesday for all the Royal Engineer companies of the Division:

The RE companies are nearly always in the line, and it is eight or nine months since I held a parade for them. This time all three companies were present, and all the officers and the CRE himself. They formed up round the courtyard of a somewhat strafed château, and there was excitement at one moment because the enemy put a heavy shell just over our heads into the village beyond. When we discovered he wasn't firing at us actually, no more notice was taken, though regularly throughout the service at three minute intervals a shell screeched overhead and burst with a crash 200 to 300 yards beyond us. It is not the first time that I have taken a service under shell fire. No one minds if you can be certain the enemy are not going to lengthen or shorten their range.

During the week Julian sent his god-daughter Mary, aged one month, a four-page letter about the war:[5]

It is fine, isn't it, for a little girl like you to have great big men, hundreds and thousands of them, giving their lives daily that you may grow up free and strong . . .

One day, dear godchild, you will learn all about the great deeds and noble ideals of those fighting men . . .

*   *   *

Burgon continues in the thick of it, writing on 6 April after two days continuous fighting. He must have sat down to write the account of it immediately afterwards for:

On the morning of 4 April (we were just in reserve behind the line) the Boches made a determined attack. I was actually with the Divisional General when the bombardment was on – and took down his orders for my General. Our three regiments were some way off from our head-quarters – so I galloped to them without drawing rein with the orders in my pocket having one moment of doubtful hesitation as to whether in the fog I was going in the right direction. One regiment was moving to its appointed position about thirty minutes after I left the HQ; it was a matter of vital importance I got there in time. Thereafter I was con-stantly moving backwards and forwards between the line and the three Generals about two miles back – the Infantry Divisional General, my Divisional General and my Brigadier. The situation offered all the well-known features of an old-fashioned battle scene. Men were galloping about – bullets whistling all round and shells bursting, our men lying down firing at the enemy with machine-gun and rifle, and the German infantry gradually melting away. The Colonel of the Royals (who did extraordinarily well) and I actually rode right up to our posts and along them. I kept on marking my map with the dispositions as far as possi-ble and, most important of all, our points of contact with the troops on our flank, and then returned to the Generals. Shortly after, my Brigadier and all his staff were ordered to move right up into the sphere of oper-ations, so that he could personally take command of an extremely complicated situation – and for forty-eight hours we did not have a wink of sleep. It simply deluged with rain the whole of those two days (I think the rain undoubtedly helped us) – the going for horses over open coun-try was absolutely fearful.

Yesterday I got caught in a very stiff bombardment with heavies and then a machine-gun indirect fire barrage. We expected the attack and were all quite ready. But the enemy merely advanced a couple of hundred yards nearer and began to dig in right on the sky line in the most ridiculous way. I had a shot at them with a Vickers gun. I could not resist it. I saw literally scores and scores of Boches – of course we got our guns on to them as quickly as we could. I had many other exciting adventures, and I shall begin my usual long detailed letter as soon as I can. If we get a couple of days here I might get it finished. Some record I must have of these days. They are the most remarkable I have ever lived through. You would not believe how fit I am – my servants and horses though are pretty well done. We have had fairish casualties both in officers, men and horses, but nothing unduly large considering the immensity of the struggle.

One's little world is even smaller than ever at these times.

This was the first time in three-and-a-half years' service that he rode a horse into battle. He comments:

Personally, I probably had a more interesting time than most people on this show – as I was nearly always at the chief seat of information – and always knew exactly what was going on. I lost nothing in the retreat except a hunting saddle and a good walking stick! So I am lucky. Others have lost everything in one way or another. . . . I think there is a certain elation in taking part in such a gigantic struggle.

He evidently got a letter from Julian somehow or other, for the latter writes on 8 April:

I heard from Burgon today that he was well and having a fiercely interesting time.

Julian himself had had a quiet interlude:

Last night I went into the little local church, which up to the present has not been hit by a shell. The old Curé was ringing the bell for Benediction himself, and soon one or two villagers dropped in and quite a number of children. In the growing dusk the old church looked beautiful, its tawdry ornaments had lost their tawdriness, and their gleam of candles from the altar was its only light. The singing of the children was really beautiful and as the service progressed we seemed to be in another world. The old priest had a strong voice, sweet-toned, and he led the singing without accompaniment all through. There was something strangely moving in the service, the kneeling priest with acolyte at his side, the incense rising in the light of the altar candles and disappearing into the dark shadows of the roof, the sound of children's voices and the bowed backs of the women kneeling on their chairs – all made me forget the war and its horrors; but every now and then the whole church would shake with the reverberation of one of our heavy guns going off nearby and the present would return with all its awful reality. But the children still sang on and I am sure the angels' song does not cease day or night though the world be bathed in blood.

One of our new chaplains, named Sheppard[6], is a splendid fellow, of Radley, Lincoln College Oxon. and Cuddesdon. I persuaded Army HQ to let him, there and then, transfer to this (3rd) division although he had been on the strength of the 31st.

The 6th Cavalry Brigade continue to be on the move, but Burgon is not in action. His 16 April letter has a PS:

Mother says she felt low the other morning – she must not be that. To be quite honest, the impression all this business leaves on my mind is the almost laughable triviality of this world.

And the diarist comments, 'In this letter Burgon sounds absolutely worn out.'

Julian does too, but remains equally determined:

My feelings about the need of carrying on now are that we must, even if every man dies at his post. But the war may take a lifetime, or should I say ten more years at least. On Sunday 14 April some Canadians invited the General and three of us to dine. We went, and found it was a guest night quite in the old style – a good dinner, a band and afterwards a concert. Are not these contrasts extraordinary so near the battle?

Julian has the chance to create a church in some caves

which when finished will be quite unique. The RE's are building a high wooden reredos, an altar and steps. New Zealand tunnellers, who are putting supports across the caves to secure the walls, are putting up a rough rood screen. Quite close there is a prophet's chamber, where one chaplain will always live, so that we can have daily services.

He achieved five services there on 21 April.

That same week-end Burgon writes two lines about his future at the end of a letter:

I can't make up my mind what I am going to do after the war, if I live through it. I think about it a lot.

Both brothers now experience a peaceful month. The fury of the German attack in March and early April is spent: 'I do not think', writes Julian to one of his brothers in England, 'that the enemy can break through now, though he may bend back the line a good deal more'.

Map preparation takes an increasing amount of Burgon's time as Brigade Intelligence Officer; Julian's responsibilities at Divisional HQ give him less chance to be with the soldiers in the line, and more organisational work with the chaplains:

But I have a splendid horse now, and much enjoy riding round my various units. The chaplains are up to strength. We hope to have another Confirmation in midsummer.

Burgon comments:

Things remain fairly quiet, but how long they will remain so, no one knows.

Julian, still within the sound of guns, has an almost peacetime Ascension Day (9 May):

Such a beautiful day for Ascension Day, glorious sunshine giving us our first really warm day this year, but tempered by the softest breezes. Only fleecy clouds in the blue sky, and all the fruit trees bright with blossom. The old men, women and children all go off to the fields every morning soon after the break of day, only to return for the midday meal and again in the evening, after filling all the hours of sunlight with strenuous toil. It is sad to see the growing crops being cut through by an elaborate and ever-growing trench system, so that even if the enemy do break through our front system, they will only find themselves up against further fortifications and defences.

There are two villages close together, both with good churches served by the same village priest. He says Mass in one and walks to the other for a second Mass, for the people prefer their own church even though they would, none of them, have to walk more than 1000 yards. We have troops in each village, and my friend the Curé and I often pass each other on the road between the villages, each having taken one Mass and proceeding to take the second. It was so this morning.

He was beginning to come in for some social life:

Yesterday evening the ADMS⁷ who is in our Mess, invited five sisters from the nearest Casualty Clearing Station, to dinner. They came over in an ambulance. We got the Divisional band to play in the garden outside the windows, and a specially choice little dinner was prepared. A little female society was a pleasant change. I think the nurses enjoyed their outing. We gave them armfuls of lilac to take away with them. The band played very well and it was a perfect night, so that we were able to sit out after dinner in deck chairs.

* * *

After ranging round the situation in Russia and Japan, the Zeebrugge expedition⁸ and political affairs at home, the diarist comes back to Burgon, still 'standing-to' and pretty fed-up:

16 May. Just a line to tell you I have no news at all. Everything at present remains tolerably quiet. Yesterday I had quite a long ride in one of the tanks, which was extremely interesting – but beyond the bare fact that I did so, I am afraid I can give you no details. . . . This life is really fearfully trying and I wish to goodness the Boches would do something and get it over. . . .

He comments:

I think Father is wrong in imagining that the average man out here does not fear death. The daily existence under desultory shell fire naturally leads to indifference. But before an attack or waiting for an enemy barrage, the ordinary man is thoroughly afraid. Before the Zeebrugge affair (i.e. on the way over) it must have been a wonderful man who did not have the wind up, but those fellows who got on to the mole did not have a moment's fear when once the business had started. This has been proved over and over again. If one dies, one dies in great company and at a great moment; death as faced by the average man at home in his bed must at best be a lonely affair. I do not think Christianity has proved ineffective because the stay-at-home Christian does not exhibit wonderful bravery as the time for him to die draws nearer. It seems to me to have fallen short in so far as it appears to have been totally unable to raise any intelligent interest in the great facts of life and death in the mind of the average soldier. I say 'appears' because the Englishman is so reserved that the ideas and opinions may be there all the time – but I doubt it. If they are, they seem to be quite unformed and unduly childish.

The waiting continues, 'the battle may start at any moment', writes Julian. Burgon says:

Any big attack would affect us, but meanwhile we hope to have ten days in the park of this lovely château, with – to-day because of a ceremony to present medals – a band playing under the trees and the whole valley dressed in all the glory of the first spring green. Not much horror of war about this.

Julian on 21 May writes:

I am convinced the war cannot help lasting another two or possibly three years. In twelve months Germany will have organized Russian wheat, and in another twelve she will be getting from that vast country all she wants [in the way of] every kind of supplies.

Two days later he writes again in happy mood because the brothers have met. He had 'borrowed a car' and eventually got to Amiens

along the exact road on which I struggled on a pushbike two years ago when I eventually found Burgon; and this time too I eventually did the same. He was in his office and jumped up to greet me and introduced me to another officer who was with him, and to the Staff Captain who had brought me in. He 'on'd with his coat and took me up to his room where I washed and got a brush, as I was covered with dust. The first question Burgon asked when we were alone was whether I was a Roman Catholic yet! Whereat much laughter. . . . Everyone seemed to know him – they all call him 'the Bishop'. . . . He told me about his amazingly interesting experiences . . . I hope he may get a French decoration for his excellent work.

Burgon writes enthusiastically:

we lay on the grass in front of the château and exchanged information about the battle and talked of you. . . . Julian thinks there may be a cleavage in the C of E after the war. What I think both sides fail to realize is that the vast majority of laymen stand aside from these controversies and view them with the utmost indifference. They value the man much more than the doctrine. The curious thing is that out here the representatives of both sides fondly imagine that when they are made welcome by officers and men (as they are), it is because religion is making headway.

29 May, Julian indeed thinks that there is certainly some headway being made:

The number of communicants in the Division is really good. I am convinced that the Holy Communion has made a real impression on the men of the Army. Don't forget that the majority had really never heard the term used, or if they had wouldn't know to what it referred and understood absolutely nothing about it. Many men to whom I have spoken and asked if they were confirmed have shown by their answers that they hadn't the least idea what I was talking about. But now practically everyone knows that Holy Communion is a service to which some few men stop after Church parade, that the Chaplains are always making appeals to them to do so, that the Church parade which is the only church service they have ever been present at, or are at all familiar with, is not the most important form of worship possible, but that there is something else from which they find they have been cut off; and they want to know what this thing is and how it is they are excluded. I have some wonderful examples of men who have come and wanted to make their communion knowing very little about it, but obviously feeling within themselves a hunger for the 'Bread of Life'.

It is more than a privilege to help feed such as these. I am also much impressed with the value of a daily service in a village where troops are billeted. I always get a congregation at Evensong, fresh fellows overcoming their shyness and dropping in. We have hymns, and the harmonium – which I bought last year – is invaluable.

On 1 June, after describing in a long letter home the funeral of a much-loved chaplain killed by shrapnel a few days before, he writes very wearily – his 'two or three years more of the war' have trebled:

The war becomes more terrible and soul-corroding as month succeeds month. I cannot bring myself to write of it in letters – that is why my letters are so often dull, short and stupid. It has lost all the romance of some years ago. It is now a perpetual round of dull, prosaic murder, with one desire in the hearts of all – to keep alive a little longer and to see a speedy end to the business. No one has any heart in it. Authorities in the field and in the newspapers at home try to flog us, jaded as we are, into fresh energy, and teaching us to hate the Germans; but men don't and won't hate the Germans – they only hate the war, and so it goes on. One day in the far future it will end – for a short time – to give belligerents the chance to get a 'breather' before they start again. I really feel now that very few of those who survive the war, whichever way it ends, and who are now in the Army, will ever be out of it. We must settle down to the prospect of an army life all our days. Every day the Germans advance further we find ourselves with more land to regain. A summer offensive takes us to a depth of five miles. Three days by the enemy takes him twenty.

Still, it is always easy to look on the pessimistic side too much. I often wonder, however, whether we shall teach Germany to be purer, gentler and holier by beating her by force in the field. Such qualities are not taught by the rod. However, it is useless to start discussing this now. We are in it and we can't get out of it – and we shall have to go on, even if it costs the lives of all who are now in France. Quite frankly, I don't see any end for the war under nine or ten years, unless we break – which to the proud Englishman is unthinkable.

Yes, my work as Divisional Chaplain is interesting. The ACG paid me the compliment of saying that ours was, he thought, the best-run division in the Army from the chaplains' point of view, but he added 'Don't dragoon your chaplains too much – don't be too severe with them'. I was a little amused at this, because of his own reputation. What he says is 'law', and he loves discipline. However, we are a very happy family, and they are all readily falling in with my way of getting the Division properly organized. Just on seventy services in the Division for Whitsunday and over 500 communicants, when all the infantry except two battalions were in the Line, needs some organizing, but no man in the whole Division now can say that he does not get repeated opportunities for Holy Communion and other church services.

So the summer goes on – each day more glorious than the last. Sunshine and cool breezes and the green corn tall enough to look like the waves of the sea when the wind plays upon it. Only war is vile.

* * *

Burgon is being besieged by enquirers who want to know the latest phase of the situation:

No one can deny that it is a big advance – an extremely fine perform-ance by the Boches – but everyone takes it very calmly. I expect the extraordinarily rapid advance took even the Boches by surprise and must have thrown their calculations a little out – so perhaps we may have to wait rather longer than we had anticipated for developments elsewhere. I do not think the Boches will find it so easy to advance fur-ther against us. What perfectly tremendous times to be living in.

I believe the great result of this gigantic struggle will be to prove the uselessness of war. I feel absolutely confident myself that after peace comes and passions have time to subside, we shall see a great rap-prochement of all the peoples of Europe one to the other, and thus will rise a thing far greater than the old narrow 'Internationale' – it will be something approaching the ideal of a league of nations. I believe it is for these things that Morris has laid down his life. I know Father will say these things cannot happen till the Hohenzollerns have been beaten back. Certainly at this moment they do not look like a beaten force. But I think in one sense they are.

On 6 June Julian describes in a twelve page letter how he spent a whole day in pastoral work, his morale high again after the pessimism of the week before. It began with him bicycling a short distance at 7.20 am to his chapel, where one lad from the Queen's Westminsters was with him for Communion; there was shelling at noon when he was with a Scottish battalion; he then had 'as good a lunch as you could get anywhere in the world', beautifully served in a mess which had been a thirteenth cen-tury monastery crypt; after that he then took some soldiers' funerals, followed by a ride ('I had ordered my horse to meet me at the cemetery at 4 pm') of three miles to the Divisional Rest Station; he visited troops there before riding back to HQ for Evensong (twelve present); then a confirmation class of fourteen men; finally back to his billet where he dressed for dinner. He finished up with a 'good hot bath' at 10 pm and went to bed. Most days seem to be as full.

All the time everyone at home and at the Front seems to be waiting for the next German attack – to let them attack is obviously Allied policy – so that they wear themselves out.

Meanwhile Burgon writes: 'Off on a ten-day Intelligence course', and is 'not at all keen to go',

but I daresay I shall like it when I get there. I am getting more and more fed up with this War every day it goes on.

The Australians did an awfully good show here two nights ago – did I tell you about it? They advanced 750 yards, took several officers and over 200 men prisoners, and captured 20 machine-guns. The noise was deafening as our corps artillery co-operated – and the uproar did not die down till midnight.

A Boche plane came down near Villers Bocage the other day and landed at one of our aerodromes. It contained a Sergeant-Major as pilot and a Corporal as observer. They were absolutely unharmed, and it looks very much as if they had meant to be taken prisoner.

I heard from Julian yesterday – very keen about these educational schemes – all part of a bigger demobilization idea. There has been some more discussion of it here this last week, and the General has given me all the correspondence on the subject to manage. But we can really do nothing till the winter.

Burgon went to bed on the third day of the course with a sharp attack of 'the 'flu, which is so prevalent out here now'. It left him 'pretty groggy' after four days in bed. The diarist says that the Germans have the 'flu badly, 'which possibly accounts for the delay in their offensive'.

The gorgeous summer weather helps Burgon to recuperate:

This is my fifth June in succession in France (June, 1914 saw me in Paris), and I never remember such a profusion of wild flowers and such glorious colour.

On 28 June he writes to his parents in almost the same terms as he had the year before:

Tomorrow is the day, every hour of which is graven on my memory. It is two years ago tomorrow that Julian, Morris and I met together in the old farm in the main street of Bus-les-Artois.

After more than six hours together Julian left us and Morris and I rode on into Acheux. I can see every inch of the way. In Acheux we decided Morris had better turn back. We shook hands, each of us leaning forward from his horse, and then as we turned in opposite directions, Morris gave me one of those wonderful smiles which lit up his whole face, and said, 'Good luck old boy'; I said the same, and we parted.

There are certain days in my life which stand out – about half a dozen I think, but this one comes easily first – and our children and grandchildren must be taught to hand on the story of the great honour Morris has conferred on our family.

Two days later he went flying again, this time with the French:

In the morning I went up to a French Flying Squadron not far from here, and liaised with some of the officers. They promised to take me up in the afternoon and accordingly at four pm I rode up there again with my groom. The machine was ready, with a little French pilot (who used to be a jockey before the war) and an observer. I put on the usual fur clothes and helmet, and climbed in. It is a night bombing squadron and the machines are huge. It was a perfect afternoon. I had my own maps with me and followed every yard we went – and found no trouble in looking right down over the sides of the machine which were somewhat frail and not very high. It was amazingly interesting to follow all the main trunk roads – and to see the white cliffs and breaking waves – and our own shadow moving slowly across the blue water. When we were over the sea, the pilot turned jokingly round and yelled, '*A l'Angleterre?*' and I yelled back '*Oui*'. But of course it would never be allowed.

I wished so much you could have been flying with me. I believe it would fascinate you.

Julian writes (17 June):

I ordered my fine black horse at 10 am. I call him Nick, an appropriate name for a chaplain's steed, and rode over to Corps HQ to see the

DACG to ask him to arrange a meeting of our confirmation candidates in the Division Corps area. It is so important to keep in touch with these men, who need all the help we can give them to keep their vision clear. I must say,[9] I think, without undue prejudice, that the boys whom I have found do best from the point of view of the Christian religion out here are those trained in the Catholic parishes at home. They know what they want, and are not ashamed of their faith.

On 3 July there is a different experience described by Burgon:

There is not much news here. Last night I dined with my French flying friends. It was the first time I had dined in a French Officers' Mess under more or less peaceful conditions – and they did me very well, sending a car for me, giving me an excellent dinner with many kinds of wine including champagne, and sending me back by car. I watched '*le depart*' at 10 pm for the night bombing. It was a most picturesque scene. The machines, with their lights on, starting off with a tremendous roar of the gigantic engines – a beautiful summer evening – the bells of the neighbouring church ringing for Vespers – large bombs hung on each machine – a '*drole de vie*' as one of the pilots put it to me, and certainly if one comes to think of it, the life is an extraordinary one. To sit round a table and have an excellent dinner with amusing vivacious talk and within half an hour of drinking one's coffee to don a fur coat, a fur cap and fur boots and sally out to the *terrain d'aviation* where, in the dusk, the outline of these huge machines is just distinguishable, to supervise the placing of the bombs (the big ones carried up by four men) into their proper position, to climb into the machine, to start off into the heavens now bright with stars and travel through the dark many miles, and then having sent the bombs hurtling to the earth by the turn of a handle, to return home and then possibly go through the whole performance again, hurrying back just as dawn begins to break – all this I think might properly be called a '*drôle de vie*' for the twentieth century.

Julian (8 July) describes a successful raid:

Tonight, one of companies of the Queen's Westminsters did a highly successful raid on some old gun-pits used by the enemy as an out-post. They killed sixty of the enemy, took three prisoners and several machine-guns and thoroughly bombed the Huns' dug-outs. I had taken a special service for this company the day before they went up, and gave them God's blessing. They only had eleven wounded men and these only slightly, no one severely wounded or killed.

The long-heralded enemy attack ('We hear the German offensive has begun') finds Julian in delightful billets:

I sit in the parlour of a little old-world cottage – roses everywhere – waving corn as far as the eye can see – the moon shedding a soft light over all as it grows dark, and owls hoot in the copse close by.

Burgon has been 'addressing padres'; there is no record of what he said, other than 'I spoke for about half an hour, and then many of my points were discussed. The General seemed pleased. Julian's useful notes reached me just in time'.
Later:

This new German offensive seems to us here to be rather a failure so far. . . . There is really no news of any importance; but the French push is splendid, and I can't help thinking will have far-reaching effects.

*   *   *

There the diarist ends her eighth volume, after recording the quietest three months her sons had experienced at the Front; they had got bored with the war, like millions of others.

VOLUME IX
AUGUST – NOVEMBER 1918

The Germans in retreat – Burgon's horses killed and his servant wounded –
another Confirmation – Burgon on leave – Julian buries seventy men –
Geoffrey married – Ralph invalided out of the Army – Burgon distinguishes
himself during ten days' battle and wins the MC; then enjoys luxurious
leave in Paris – the advance continues – abdication of the Kaiser, and
the Armistice is announced – jubilation in London and Canterbury –
Burgon describes the Cease Fire.

*Burgon continues with his work as Brigade Intelligence Officer, but has
been attached to Divisional Headquarters:*

The Senior Staff Officer here is very keen I should put my name down
as a staff learner. Everyone has to pass sixty days of doing this before
he has a chance of getting a job. I would be attached to various brigades
and divisional staffs. Then I may or may not get a job. I am not very
keen, but I daresay my name will go in to the General. . . . It would
mean never having a fixed home, and being among strangers. . . . The
only reason I entertain the idea at all is that I am clear I ought not to
remain as Brigade Intelligence Officer much longer, as I am not really
pulling my weight, and everybody ought to do that. The solution to this
and many other problems is 'Let the war finish'.

*At least the Germans are retreating 'in the most orderly fashion',
records the diarist: and Burgon says (2 August, 1918), 'I really think
there is a good chance of the war ending in a reasonable time, say during
the coming winter, don't you? All this fashing about getting on in the
Army seems rather absurd, when one hopes never to see the Army again
after not too long a period'.*

*The contrasts of the war strike Julian again (31 July), along with
some attendant dangers:*

263

I have been busy all week riding round to visit the various units of the Division. But the time each day is so fully occupied that it is almost an impossibility to get hold of the men until quite late in the evening. Everybody is engaged in intensive training, and any time to spare is given to recreation, football, running, boxing etc. On Thursday I rode over to my old brigade.

On my way back to Brigade HQ I stopped and watched a thrilling football match between two battalions of my old brigade, each player straining every nerve for his side amid shouts of a large crowd of onlookers. War seemed forgotten, but on my way through the camp to the Brigade HQ I met a party going out for night operations, and the look on their faces was in striking contrast to the laughter and excitement of the football ground.

I had a very pleasant evening with the Brigade Staff; the Brigadier, for long now a sincere friend, could not have been more pleasant. A great moon rose behind the trees, reminding him, he said as we strolled about after dinner, of some hill station in India.

I left at 9.45 pm after having a talk with most of the officers at the Brigade HQ, hearing all the local gossip and local worries. All was quiet, as I rode off. But after going two miles on my way, I saw a beam of searchlight shoot out across the sky and soon heard the unmistakable hum of aeroplanes, which grew louder and louder, and it was evident not one, nor two, but a whole 'flight' were in the air, coming rapidly towards our lines. I began to wonder how far they were going, whether they had intentions on some far back railhead, or on the camps and billets close behind the lines. I rode on slowly, and had reached a village about four kilometres from where I am billeted, when the aeroplanes seemed almost overhead. One feels somewhat defenceless on a horse – so high off the ground. I had just reached the very centre of the village when I heard an unmistakable whizz followed by a terrific crash, not apparently a hundred yards away. A second followed almost instantaneously, and my horse leapt in the air and got very excited. Bits fell all round me and I turned my horse as fast as I could in the opposite direction from where I took it the bombs had fallen. I had not gone twenty yards before another fell, this time only fifty yards away and it became a little alarming. Judging, however, that the 'plane was circling round the village, I determined to make directly along the road where the first two bombs had obviously fallen, thinking I might have time to get clear of the place before the 'plane got round again. I had only just done so when two fell almost immediately behind me, and a second later one fell in a field 200 yards to my right. I was glad to get into open country.

On the fourth anniversary of the outbreak of war (4 August) Burgon recalls to his mother where they were that day – in an Exeter hotel, where they regarded two or three Territorial Officers in an almost sacred way . . .:

Our position today is surely good. The retreat of the Germans to the Aisne may give them more divisions to play about with, but it will be difficult to explain to their people. In their wireless yesterday they paid much attention to the total area captured from the Entente during the war, thus seeking to minimize the ground they are losing at present. That they will shortly attack in force elsewhere I am certain, but I am equally sure they will have no further successes comparable to those of March 21–29. The summer is wearing on – and their prospects for next year can hardly seem bright.

Julian has been entertaining the new allies:

I took a keen young American officer all over the Cathedral and round the City the day before yesterday. He is a graduate of Yale and attached to one of our brigades for instruction as an Intelligence Officer. It was the nearest he had been yet to the War and he was very interested. These Americans are splendid stuff. I have only seen officers so far, but they are so alive and quick on the up-take, and yet so absolutely free of self-conceit.

But Burgon is in action[1] – on 14 August the diarist had a Field Post Card from him dated 9 August, just stating he was well; and Julian wrote on the 12th

very anxious about Burgon. I do not see how he can have failed to be in the battle. If he was, I long to know that he is safe and well. The cavalry seems to have done splendidly. How pleased he will be that they have had such a chance.

The diarist had simply recorded (12 August) that 'the Allies were pressing forward' . . . and on 14 August 'our advance seems to have stopped'. On 16 August there is a letter of the 11th. Burgon was indeed in the thick of it:

A lull – and so I write just a few lines to tell you I am extremely well. From the papers you can judge what a time we have had. The first day was a great day. It was quite wonderful. The second day we had a pretty heavy time of it till the afternoon, and yesterday we had one of those days when you get shelled and have nothing much to show for it. It took us two days to get into position – so we have been five days away from our former billets. The first three nights we had practically no sleep at all, moving by night and at the end of the first day's fighting holding by night the objective we had reached during the day – this alone was an advance of fifteen kilometres in one day – and we expected very strong counter-attacks which never came. I must give you details later. In a wood we reached at the end of the first day we found huts where there had evidently been a Machine-Gun school – everything left by the occu-pants as it was – and we were able to send back some good maps and papers. We lived in German huts, drank German beer and the men fit-ted themselves out with any German equipment that came in useful. Yesterday we had a very bad shelling, both my horses (the new one from the Life Guards and my dear little African pony) were killed outright (at least I had to shoot the Life Guards horse), and my servant who was holding them had a fearfully shattered leg. I am extremely well, but I hate war and blood and stench more and more. Perhaps inasmuch as we do not see so much of it as the infantry, it is all the more revolting when it comes. On these occasions I always want some of the never-sheath-the-sword type out here – not to see a victorious galloping like Thursday last, but to see men and animals dead, and smell the stench of blood and gunpowder and hear the crump coming and lie flat on the ground wondering whether a great jagged bit will tear your stomach out.

Then the fuller account (14 August):

I really do not know how much I am supposed to tell you about the 'show' which is just finished. For us it was a successful and amusing time – especially the first day. The business had been kept a great secret, and owed its success to this fact. The attack went well from the first. Zero was at 4.20 am on Thursday. A few hours later the whole coun-tryside was covered with advancing troops. Tanks by the score were snorting along by the side of the cavalry.

There was a good deal of resistance by late afternoon – coming from Le Quesnel and Beaufort, and we were ordered to hold a line where we were for the night. So with the Canadian infantry we did our best to consolidate, as we were certain a heavy counter-attack would come either at dusk or dawn. It was here that the General was overcome by fatigue and had to hand over his command. The night passed comparatively quietly – though of course there was little sleep. It was an eerie business. But the light brought no attack.

During these hectic two days I have had three prisoners to interview – one a Boche Officer, an extraordinarily nice fellow I thought. He would tell me nothing except his regiment and division. He was good-looking and well-dressed and perfectly calm and collected. During the second night, about 3 am two Boches arrived guarded by a stalwart Dragoon Guard. I got from them their division and regiment and sent them on to the Division. These two men proved to be the first identification of the 14th Bavarian Division, and therefore it was an important find.

Our aeroplanes were extraordinarily good throughout the show, dropping messages one after the other, giving very accurate information. They circled in hundreds right over our heads. We hardly ever saw a Boche 'plane except late in the evening – and then it was wiser to move the horses. Our work throughout Saturday 10th consisted in patrols watching the progress of the infantry, and on the look-out for any opportunity of exploiting some local success. In the evening the Canadian cavalry charged a low hill on the Roye road – but could not hold it when they got it. Another squadron galloped round to the right flank and took Villers-sur-Roye and forty prisoners. As they entered the village a huge supply dump went up. The French, in whose area this village really was, thought it was a devil of a show and were awfully bucked.

Two days later he writes again:

I am sorry to say that my servant has had his right leg amputated. I do not know at which Base Hospital, so I cannot write to him which troubles me very much. He wrote me such a splendid letter. I am taking immediate steps to start trying to get a vacancy for him at Roehampton. His name is Private W H Furness (10th Hussars), servant to Captain E A Fielden (10th Hussars) and temporarily mine. It is the third time he has been knocked out – this damnable war! How unequal it is. I was only thirty yards off at the time.

By the 20th he is talking of leave in about a fortnight, but the letter had hardly come before a telegram to say he was on his way. His parents hurriedly booked a few days' holiday in the King's Arms Dartmouth, and by the evening of the 26th he was there with them. 'After dinner we sat and talked on the Quay'.

Burgon went to London for the week-end. His mother writes:

He is going to see Mrs Ratcliffe, the widow of his great friend Captain Ratcliffe who was killed. He had risen from the ranks and Burgon is very anxious to see about the education of his little boy Freddy.

2 September, 1918. Garlants Hotel. Father and I arrived here at 5 pm to find Geoff and Jean having tea with Burgon. Later we went with him to Queen's Hall to hear a Wagner Concert. Burgon always finds music refreshes him most on leave.

We have broken the Queant-Drocourt Line, and I think the Londoners have had a big hand in it.

Julian's division is in action again. The indication was as always a Field Postcard (*27 August*).

A letter came very soon:

30 August, 1918

We are having a terribly strenuous time. I cannot write more. Sleep is banished. Work continues with wounded day and night. The dead are many. Peace is forgotten. When will this grim butchery of unfledged boys, German and English, end? For whose glory do we mangle the bodies of our splendid youth – God's or our own? Or that the Northcliffe Press can sing of another triumph? God only knows.

All those confirmed two Sundays ago have gone, with one or two exceptions, and under the most awful conditions.

To get the wounded from forward positions is increasingly difficult as the battle tightens. There are very few German dead. The cry goes up, 'How long, O Lord, how long?'

Forgive this outburst of weary bitterness, but 'my heart is heavy, my heart is heavy'. God bless you and your holiday with Burgon. I hope Dartmouth and its peaceful surroundings may help you and Burgon to forget that war ever existed, the invention of all the devil loves and the negation of all Christ taught. Pray for our lads lying in shell holes.

The diarist comments:

This last letter shows how Julian suffered at the loss of his dear lads. The chaplains have far the worst time at the Front. They see their men return wounded or dead, they also help the doctors with first-aid, they search the battlefield for wounded and see awful sights, and then they have to bury bodies in hundreds. . . . Burgon is still with us, and is turning over in his mind what to do after the War. He is very keen on politics and may possibly stand for Parliament.

Julian has had a bad time:

I have been out of bed most nights for over a week, and must get some sleep. I have got the two Chaplains who were before me on the list off on leave, so that I am next and if we are out of action by 21 September I shall hope to get home, but if the Division is still fighting I cannot come. I know you will understand that.

I am so delighted over Geoff's happy prospect. You don't know what a delightful contrast it is to let one's thoughts fall back on a future of sheer happiness, out of the midst of this welter of blood and tears.

I am very well and try to keep a brave heart, but I sorrow for these lads and their mothers very deeply. Perhaps I am not altogether wrong to do so, for the Christ could weep with those that wept as well as rejoice with those that rejoiced.

The diarist writes (8 September, 1918):

We had some delightful quiet days with Burgon. He left us this morning at 8.30 am. . . . Will this be the last parting before the end of the war? I almost think it will.

There follows a seventeen page letter from Julian. Burgon adds later at the top. 'This is a vivid account of a Chaplain's life when in action'. He reflects in it as well as describing what happened:

All the Division was on the move towards the battle. I rode my black horse along the fourteen kilometres which separated us from our next Divisional HQ. We were in the cornfields, with the corn ready cut and stacked for carting away. It was hot and the distant views were misty, but as I approached my destination unmistakable signs of the back of the battlefront began to show themselves. Many lorries, much movement of guns, camps hurriedly erected, often right in the cornfields, the main roads blocked by traffic of all kinds, and always men marching in column towards the noise of battle, and ambulances hurrying back with their loads of helpless wounded.

I could not help thinking of the lads with very little prospect of sleep that night, save what they may snatch by the roadside. For a good many it was their last sleep on this earth. The man in the ranks of the infantry is the only man out here who is worthy of the fullest possible consideration, and he gets the least. The man behind the Line has time to make himself moderately comfortable, whereas the man with the bayonet has none. Provisions are always more plentiful the further back from the Line you proceed, the pay is higher, less danger to be found even in these days of night bombing to those behind. When the man comes out of the trenches he has to put up with what accommodation he can find, after all the back-of-the-line people have found themselves comfortable billets. The infantryman of the trenches has huge long marches, is often expected to fight without sleep or food, and cursed heartily if he fails. I am more than ever convinced that it is absolutely impossible for the Staff Officer to have the least idea of what the man in the Line has to go through. Often a General will order his men to do things which if he knew the 'forward' situation he would not expect of them. When the infantryman dies, his body receives scant attention, and protests are always met with, 'Oh surely you wouldn't have us neglect the living for the dead', which would be a reasonable remark if the living were considered more. Moreover these modern battlefields are strewn with the dead bodies of mere boys – and I am convinced we are using more boys than the Germans.

I was up early and made my way at once to the Corps Main Dressing Station. The Guards had evidently had a stiff fight. . . . We were soon inundated with a large number of stretcher cases, some very bad, though the wounds were mostly from machine-gun bullet, much easier to deal with than shell wounds. Still only a few of our Division came through, though I was glad to see one of my Scottish Confirmation candidates come along with only a slight head wound. Two of our officer confirmees passed through during the morning, one badly wounded having lost an eye, but the other only slightly. At 4 pm I could stick it no longer, but went forward. I handed over to Holland, and there seemed to be plenty of chaplains about. The news was everywhere good. All our objectives seemed to have been gained . . .

Sunday 25 August
Sunday services were out of the question. The Division was very nearly up against the famous Hindenburg Line, and the fighting had stiffened at once. I went forward soon after breakfast with the Burial Officer. There were a certain number of German dead lying about. We came upon one party pulling German dead by the legs out of dug-outs, to make them habitable for themselves. We chose some sites for forward cemeteries . . .

Monday 26 August
I rode back to the Corps Main Dressing Station and took several funerals. The Dressing Station was in the process of becoming a Casualty Clearing Station. Some sisters had already arrived, and more marquees were going up – all indications of our rapid advance. Then I went forward to search for dead and attend to burials in the forward areas. A long and tiring day ensued. I buried seven or eight of my machine-gunners, five of whom had been killed by one shell. Many of the boys confirmed eight days before were killed or wounded . . .

Wednesday 28 August
It was a glorious day with a strong breeze, which blew away quickly some of the evil scents of the battlefield. As we reached the last ridge before Croisilles and were preparing to descend the sunken road into the village, we came across an artillery officer lying dead on the track. He was quite an oldish man though only a subaltern, and had chevrons on his arm which indicated that he had been out at the front since 1914 – such a fine-looking fellow. I could do no more than cover the face and whisper a prayer for him. I noted the spot, however, so that we could give his body a decent burial later on.

We were about to proceed when we stopped to see what the enemy were shelling so heavily. It appeared to be the road along which we were proceeding! They were sending over 5.9 after 5.9 shells into the village. We decided therefore to strike off to the left towards the Hindenburg Line, and made our way along the now comparatively safe 'summit' trench. . . . I watched with great interest the attempt to bring up the guns into action. It was the first time I had ever seen artillery galloping into action under machine-gun fire; the Battery Commander, however, decided to wait for half an hour until the forward area had been mopped up a bit. There was a certain amount of shelling going on, but little compared with some battles I have been in. Presently my attention was diverted from the artillery, who were still trying to work their way down into the coveted dip, by two or three [London] Scottish coming up and saying they had discovered six men of the 2nd London Regiment who had been lying out for two days and they wanted to get them in. So I got one fine little stretcher-bearer belonging to the King's Liverpools to accompany me with six stalwart German prisoners. Of the six prisoners, two were men of thirty-five to forty, the others mere boys, but great strong boys from Saxony and the only trouble I had was from the latter, as shall presently be related. Securing two stretchers at last, back I went. I was glad to notice on my way that the battery had got to their objective and were unlimbering.

It was now late in the afternoon and I was anxious to get the work done before dark, as I did not like having six German prisoners working with myself only and a small, very tired little British stretcher-bearer so near the Line. In such fighting as this it was impossible to know after four days fighting just how the Line does run, and there are always snipers left behind unless the 'mopping-up' has been perfect, which is well nigh impossible over this awful terrain. So I urged on my little party; one of the prisoners began fumbling in his great-coat pocket just after we had got some little distance from the Aid Post and I instantly made him put his hands up, but he was loud in his protestations that he had nothing in his pockets. However, knowing how easily a bomb or a revolver can be concealed, I made them turn out their pockets before we proceeded further. We were able to bring in the three remaining wounded men, the others had already been collected by the Scottish. One or two were very bad, so we set the Huns to work. All seemed willing enough except two of the Saxon boys, who, in spite of strong shoulders and large frames, feigned inability to carry. The other prisoners were quite different and worked willingly. The splendid little stretcher-bearer of the King's Liverpools had been carrying for thirty-six hours, and was a shrimp compared to the stalwart Germans, yet he carried manfully and was disgusted with the whining Huns.

Presently I lost all patience with one German who was making as if he would let one of the stretchers fall, and I threatened him with my stick. Even his companions expressed disgust. Eventually one of them let the stretcher fall at his end, and the badly wounded man gave a cry of agony as it jarred on the ground. Clasping my stick as firmly as I could I brought it down with all the force I could gather across the shoulders of the lazy youth. He yelled with pain and writhed about as if shot, but the lesson had been learned and he carried better. To some astonished gunners who were passing as I smote him, it must have looked as if a padre had turned slave-driver, but no blow I had ever given gave me as much delight as that one – my only regret was that it was not twice as hard. When we got back to the Scottish post I borrowed a revolver from one of the officers, and made some significant signs with it to my young German. Even more than the blow, this had the desired effect, and we completed our task just as it was getting too dark to see, having carried these wounded men about a mile and a half to a spot where they were later picked up by horse-ambulance. I then handed the prisoners to a guard who was taking more down.

I went straight back to where forty or fifty stretcher cases were lying in rows waiting to be taken away – all cold and rather miserable – many in great pain. A Sergeant-major (RAMC), who was in charge, said he had sent down messages asking for motor-ambulances. So I told him I would go down to the ADS and see what was the matter. By this time the moon had risen and I walked down into the valley to try and get motor-ambulances. Eventually a colonel, who had been fast asleep, promised to send up motor-ambulances as well as horse-ambulances; and half an hour later, when they had at last got the traffic going again, I went up with the first motor-ambulance to the spot where the wounded were lying, and after that a pretty continuous stream of them got up the hill, and by 2 am we had cleared the large group of lying cases, who were waiting patiently in the cold to be taken away. I had an exciting day, and as we got the last case away I began to realize how tired I was. Still four miles from my tent, I was lucky to get a lift near the Aid Post from a motor-lorry and got to my flea bag by 3.30 to 4.00 am.

Next day the battle continued. We soon began to get stretcher-cases, and once more I pressed German prisoners into service. One of the stretcher-cases, I discovered, was a lad named Godly of the Machine Gunners, whom I had prepared for Confirmation only a few days before, who was badly hit in the leg. He had only just been found after lying out for thirty-six hours, but his pulse was good and he did not look too bad a colour, so I had hopes all would be well. I got four stalwart Germans on to his stretcher.

All the rest of the day I was backwards and forwards with wounded, and far into the night, and made no attempt to get any rest during the hours of darkness. Dawn found us still hard at work, but by 8.00 am things were quieter. I found a divisional car on its way back to Div. HQ and, taking advantage of it, I jumped in and was back in half-an-hour at the camp, where I had breakfast and went to bed.

30 August, Friday
I slept on till lunch time – being very tired. Think of the difference between myself, let us say, and a man in the Line who has no opportunity of going back to rest and must stay on without sleep day or night in a battle zone. But even my little excursions put me into closer touch with the sufferings of the infantry than was possible for the Staff Officers, who could only think of how far we had advanced or the success or failure of this or that attack. Returning from the battlefield to this atmosphere always makes me unhappy – because I see so clearly the cleavage between those who direct operations and those whose duty it is to carry them out. This is as true in civilian life, of that I am sure. The employer of Labour, however sympathetic, can never really appreciate the sweat of the men, let us say, in the iron foundry, until he lives their life. A visit to the foundry is as much use to initiate him into the feelings and attitude of the worker as a Staff Officer's hurried and periodical walk round the trenches is. I assure you Socialism or socialistic ideas grow apace in such an atmosphere as that which I have lived in recently.

Next afternoon I was with a doctor in charge of the 'bearer posts', and we had quite an exciting time. One 5.9 shell burst within a few yards of us, but fortunately we were in a trench and so only got the descending shower of earth and bits after they had gone up. We visited every relay post and the aid posts of the battalions, mostly situated in old German pill-boxes made of reinforced concrete.

The attack had gone well, we discovered later. The CO told me that Monday was the day fixed for the next attack. Sunday had been chosen, but the General, who is the Canadian Corps Commander, had refused to fight on Sunday, and the C-in-C had acquiesced.

Sunday, 1 September
The battle being for the moment comparatively quiet, I turned my attention to burying, and went out all day till the evening with our Divisional Burial Officer and a large party, collecting and burying dead. We were clearing up from the back area forwards, and as a party were engaged in burying horses as well, our progress was naturally slow. However, there was no difficulty in identifying our dead, as we could follow up soon after the battle. It is piteous work this collecting of dead and committing their poor bodies to the earth. After three or four days in the forward area too, it tries the nerves and causes a curious kind of irritability which was quite infectious – all the party being cross and out of

temper, and it was quite easy to find oneself heatedly arguing some trivial point for no apparent reason. I buried about seventy of our lads today – such fine-looking fellows many of them so young. Oh! what a debt England will owe to these lads when the war is over and we can settle down to enjoy the peace which they have won for us by the sacrifice – yes, cheerful sacrifice of their young bodies. I returned just before dusk to bury two of the Queen's Westminster officers, one of whom I had known well, only married three months ago, whose bodies the battalion had managed to get away from the battlefield. I took no services today – how could I? Two delightful London Rifle Brigade boys, however, came over to see us – their brigade being round about Divisional HQ having been relieved the night before, to see if they could find any service. None being possible, I had Evensong in the bell-tent with them, much to their satisfaction and mine.

Friday, 6 September
The Corps Commander came round today and made most complimentary speeches, telling the men the enormous importance of the job they had so successfully accomplished.

Sunday, 8 September
I managed to celebrate Holy Communion for our Divisional HQ at 8.00 am in an old Nissen hut riddled with shot. I went over after breakfast to our new area, on the main Arras–Cambrai road, to have a look round. I lunched in an old shell-hole with the Staff Captain who was busy fixing up his brigade in their new area. I then lorry-hopped into Arras, which is now far from the front Line, but the enemy shell it heavily daily, and more of its beauties are endangered. I got back to our Divisional HQ in time for Evensong.

Monday 9 September
I thought of Father this morning on his birthday, but did not have time to do more than start a letter to him, as the Division was on the move.

Sunday, 15 September
I had begun a service in the open air for the London Scottish when an enemy aeroplane came darting out of the clouds and attacked an 'obo' as the men call an observation balloon and brought it down in flames, the two observers jumping out and floating down not far away. What could a preacher do amid such distractions? I simply turned round and

said, 'Now we will watch the balloon' – a thing everybody was already doing!

Three nights later he was in Boulogne en route home:

At the delightful French villa where the Deputy Chaplain General lives I found Pat McCormick, who was Senior Chaplain of the Guards Division and is now ACG of Boulogne, also staying the night. We dined at eight, the Bishop getting in just before. We had a most interesting evening. It is delightful to have the opportunity to talk on vital subjects. How absurdly trivial is so much of our conversation in Messes in the Army. The failure to educate is more and more brought to me as a fair criticism of the public schools. The knowledge of the world, too, of the ordinary public school man is extraordinarily limited. Of great Labour Movements they know nothing, except what the press intends them to know.

The weather fortunately is lovely, and open-air life quite comfortable in consequence. I cannot write at length. I have not the power left to concentrate. Letter-writing has become an abomination, so don't measure my love by letters.

I have been all over the ground of our fierce fighting, searching and finding our many dead. How we ever took such an appalling bit of country beats all comprehension. It is simply a mass of shell-holes, half overgrown, with dead bodies a year old lying about or upturned, and with fresh dead lying about all over the place. I will spare you the worst details. But our casualties on the whole were not heavy when you take into consideration the 15,000 yards advance our lads accomplished.

On 16 September the diarist writes:

We heard from Burgon today. He says how much he enjoyed his leave, but he feels things are very perplexing just now, with the war wandering on. Life seems unproductive and useless. It is a world crisis we are passing through and almost every department of life seems completely dislocated.

But he is glad about Mrs Ratcliffe's letter:

I will start writing round to get the money at once. Do not stint in anything he ought to have and let nothing be inferior, as other boys are quick to see it. I shall long to hear how everything goes off on the 19th. Poor little fellow, I fear he will be miserable to start with. But I am sure it is right.

He revelled in a stimulating evening with the war correspondents:

Last night Wallace and I went over to dine with the war correspondents, which I always enjoy. We had a most interesting talk. Beach Thomas had just come in from the Somme area. Philip Gibbs was full of interest about Milner[2], whom he had tremendous regard for; Perry Robinson of 'The Times' was full of Campbell, the great bayonet-fighting expert out here. I have described his 'hatred' lectures to you before. But apparently he is a much bigger man than this – and his School at Hardelot is a wonderful exhibition of the manner in which he aims at humanizing again the dehumanized man from the trenches.

The diarist permits herself a page of praise of Burgon:

When Burgon was in the advance on 8 August he lost his horses through the bursting of a shell. I asked why he did not go back for the things in his saddlebags. He replied, the spot was being shelled so badly it was not worth the risk. I learnt afterwards from a letter sent to him by the servant Furness (which came after Burgon had left for France) that this danger did not prevent his going with the doctor to help to dress this man's wounds under the same heavy shell fire, and get him safely out. Furness wrote:

I am pleased that you came out all right. Hope that the Brigade did not suffer very heavy. I will not try to thank you for your action in getting me out of that place, and also the Doctor. But I thank God that we still have some brave men left. I am going on fine. The leg is in straps with weight on to stretch the skin over the stump, it has started to heal very nicely. . . . I am in a very nice place with nothing left to be desired, plenty of attention and also very good food. I am well off and not in need of anything.

I cannot help, *writes the diarist,* adding an extract from a letter I received from Miss Ethel Gore Booth on 6 September, 1918:

The advance is wonderful and one does not know how to be thankful enough for the better news every day. The rapidity of it is so grand and so surprising and our own troops have done marvels, and the French give them all the praise for overcoming such tremendous obstacles.

I felt I must write to you this evening, because I have been talking to one of our wounded about Burgon. As you can imagine, he gave him the highest praise he could.

*   *   *

Geoffrey was duly married on 23 September in the University Church, Cambridge. Burgon writes about the wedding:

I am thinking of Julian arriving in London today, and envy him very much. I hope you will all have a thoroughly good day. I should not have been allowed to come on leave now – so it is a good thing I came when I did. It is a very good rule never to refuse leave when you can get it. Still it is a dreadful disappointment to me not to be there on the 23rd; I shall try and picture it as best I can.

He writes again on the 27th having heard the news of the day:

Father's letter of 23rd, telling me the wedding had gone off well, reached me yesterday – and curiously enough it found me within a stone's throw of the actual house where Julian, Morris and I met thirty-six hours before the Battle of the Somme started. In fact I actually read the letter standing on the same ground where Julian and I stood watching Morris at the head of his Company that afternoon, when the Divisional General came and addressed the battalion.

On 30 September he writes:

There is an extraordinary feeling of optimism in the air, quite undamped by the deluge of rain last night.

The new mood continues three days later:

We have done nothing yet, and perhaps may not be called on for some little time. It is difficult to tell – but we are ready and not far off. The news of Bulgaria's giving in caused tremendous satisfaction out here – and certainly it is the end of *Mittel Europa*. Now if the Channel ports go, the Pan-German programme will go too. We have not had much time to think of all the results, direct and indirect, of the surrender of Bulgaria. But our terms as given in '*The Times*' are crushing enough, and to-night there is a definite rumour that Turkey has chucked her hand in. I made time to read every word of Wilson's speech on the League of Nations, and thought it was a fine one. I shall write to Ralph directly if I can. If there is anyone who has done his bit, it is he, and I am not saying that just to cheer him up[3].

Between 3 and 13 October, Burgon saw almost continuous action. There is a brief account of part of it written on 6 October, and then fifteen pages ten days later; it was for what he did then that he won the MC.

On 3 October at 12.30, the General, who, with Wallace, had been to the Divisional Conference, ordered me to patrol into Joncourt to find out the situation there. I started at 12.45 with my servant, my corporal and six scouts (intelligence) men. We were all mounted. We rode straight up to Joncourt, which except for occasional shells at the cross-roads was quiet. The village was deserted, and I could find no officer and no responsible person who could give me any information. With the greatest difficulty I extracted from a corporal that he thought there were two battalions holding a line somewhere in front of the village – but that we had been driven out of Montbrehain an hour or so ago, and the Boches were now massing for an attack on Ramiecourt. It was clear that this was not the kind of information I could send back to the Brigade, so leaving my horses and men up a side street in the village, Corporal Harding and I made our way on foot along the road leading to Montbrehain.

We reached the point where the railway crosses the road – on either side of the road there is here an embankment on the northern and eastern side (i.e. towards Montbrehain) which was lined with a number of tired listless-looking infantrymen. I walked along the railway line looking for an officer. Seeing none I shouted for one. After a short delay, two curious-looking objects, subalterns, white-faced and somewhat helpless shuffled to their feet. I asked them where their Battalion HQ was. 'There', they said and pointed to some figures hurrying back towards the slope behind the village which I had crossed on entering it. 'But there are no senior officers left', they added, 'they have all been killed'. I asked what men all these were. They replied they were elements from the whole brigade – they did not know how many there were nor to what battalion they belonged. They were just beginning to explain how they had taken Montbrehain that morning at 8.00 am, liberating over 200 French civilians who had welcomed them with coffee and food, and how then the Boches had counter-attacked and driven them out, when a man shouted, 'Here they come'.

I looked over to the right and about 400 yards off I saw the Boches advancing in a long straggly line and in little groups. With my glasses I could see their faces and their equipment very clearly. Our infantry seemed to take no interest in the matter at all. The enemy were not immediately to their front, but half-right, and whether they considered they were only concerned with what was immediately in front of them, or whether they were bored, or what it was I don't know – but they did nothing. Corporal Harding and I were astounded. I said to one of the subalterns. 'Aren't you going to get your Lewis guns on those devils?' 'I don't know the men', he said, 'they are not my men. I can't well alter my front'. 'If you don't do something', I replied, 'they will soon be in Ramiecourt and behind you'. Still he hesitated, 'Quick', I said, 'get everyone lined out half-right towards the cemetery – tell the men to fire and get the Lewis Gun into action'. He gave a feeble order – most of the work was done by the sergeant, who seemed a stout fellow. The men rather meekly obeyed – though without much enthusiasm. I helped, and soon they were lying on the grass facing the Boches, and their rifles began to crack, and a couple of Lewis Guns to rattle.

The effect was instantaneous. The Boches seemed to scuttle into a ravine which lay halfway between us and them. It was, as a matter of fact, a sunken road. We waited a little – they did not come on. I then suggested to the two subalterns that they should keep the men where they were, and should be prepared to take up any front. The Boches were not keen to fight and would give no trouble. I then went back into the village and sat down to write a message. What impressed me was the utter lack of any controlling hand. All the colonels and seconds-in-command may have been killed during the morning, and here were elements of three battalions of a regiment with no idea as to who were on their flanks, if anybody, very vague as to where the Boches were, out of touch with their Battalion HQ, let alone the brigade, with apparently no reinforcements, not frightened but hopeless, not sullen or unwilling to obey, but uncertain what to do and badly led – indeed not led at all.

I sent back a message to the General by motor-cyclist, giving him as much of the situation as I could, and saying that I thought cavalry could do useful work, that the country was thoroughly open (I had been over a good deal of it to the right and had explored the rest thoroughly with my glasses), that the infantry would cooperate in re-taking Montbrehain.

Having done this, there was nothing to do but sit and wait – I or a couple of men were looking out with glasses the whole time.

At about 3.45 in the afternoon the Boches suddenly began to crump Ramiecourt, and I only just moved my horse in time. I sent off another message to say that the shelling had become very heavy, and had to choose a circuitous route for my two scouts, so that they might have a better chance of getting back. Just before 5 pm came a message from the Brigade Major saying that the Brigade was moving up to a point S. of Joncourt and that the 3rd Dragoon Guards had been ordered to seize the high ground SE of Montbrehain. I was to meet the General at the SE exit of Joncourt. Accordingly I went off with my servant and two men – and having found the General and Brigade Major brought them up to the high ground near Swiss Cottage from where the General made a personal reconnaissance.

We were now having casualties. Several men were killed and a number of horses. MG fire was very strong from the ridge by Montbrehain. We saw Boches moving about; it was clear that they had brought up a number of guns – and all prospects of a cavalry advance, especially as it was now nearly dark, seemed at an end. . . .

Next morning we heard the first talk of an armistice – but no one believed it.

On the morning of 8 October we had reveillé at 2.30 am. As we were marching up to our concentration area, the barrage started. The eastern horizon, which it was now light enough to see, was alive with the bursting shrapnel and the glow of HE. The attack appeared to be going pretty well; the Americans had taken over from the Australians. The French were attacking Fontaine Uterte. During the day we kept in touch with the attack, and moved by bounds to the high ground.

I saw one striking example of the fighting. About a hundred yards from where our Brigade HQ was established, there stood a German machine-gun in a shell-hole cunningly placed, from where our infantry coming over the ridge could be raked with fire. Round the gun in different postures lay a Boche officer, his NCO and four men, all dead, having fought till the last. They appeared, all of them, to have been shot, not bayoneted, so probably we must have got into action on their flank and knocked them out. But these machine-gunners are brave men. The Germans are holding up our advancing troops almost entirely by machine-gun. Their infantry will not fight. Machine-gunners cover their retreat – and in most cases fight till the last.

As it was getting dark, we moved back and Brigade Headquarters was established in the Bellenglise Tunnel. In many respects this is one of the most remarkable nights I have ever spent. The St Quentin Canal runs under a tunnel from Vendhuile to just south of Bellecourt – a distance of 5,000 yards and more. It also runs through a tunnel for about 1,000 yards at Le Tronquoy. These tunnels were opened by Napoleon III, and during the war had been of tremendous value to the Boches, who have closed up the ends with doors, stored ammunition there in barges and using them as a basis, have dug a huge tunnel system, creating a hundred feet below the earth a vast town, served by railways, lit by electric light, aired by shafts and mechanical contrivances and capable of housing an army of men entirely immune from the heaviest of our shells.

These tunnels, of which we had often heard tales, formed one of the chief features of the Hindenburg defensive system. The entrance was unassuming. Steps led down about forty feet as into any ordinary dugout. At the bottom of the steps one found oneself in a long passage, doors opening out on either side into different rooms. The air was somewhat musty, but not so as to be unpleasant. Mess rooms for officers and men, kitchens, offices, telephone exchanges, long rooms full of bunks succeeded one another. After walking forty or fifty yards we came to more steps – about forty – and descended still more into the earth. Here one found the same thing – more passages, more rooms, turning to the left and to the right, sign-boards 'Nach Magny-La-Fosse', 'Nach Bellecourt', and a light railway with sidings. We were allotted two rooms by the OC tunnel – a Scottish captain, who told us that the engines for the electricity were still manned by the four Boches who had worked it when the tunnels were German. When the tunnel system was taken, it was found full of booby traps – apparently both electric light engines had been tampered with, so that the whole place would blow up when our engineers tried to use them. Fortunately our men caught the four Boches before they could get away; and their unwillingness to start up the engines was after some hesitation admitted to be due to the fact that they were mined. They were made to dismount the engine and remove the booby traps. Imagine what the taking of this subterranean town must have meant. Groping one's way along a maze of passages, every moment expecting to be blown up or meet a band of the enemy. Personally I think that the taking of the Hindenburg system by our troops is probably the finest exploit of this war.

On the morning of 9 October the men had hardly managed to get some hot tea (it now being light) when the order to move forward came

– and it was whispered that the Boches had gone. Our infantry had lost touch with them. Then began a steady advance over open country which a couple of hours before had been held by the Boches. We trotted steadily along, keeping south of the road leading due NE to Le Cateau and moving in a north-easterly direction ourselves. The Royals were in front, and I was one 'bound' ahead of the General all the time, keeping him and the main body in touch with the Royals. We passed through Maretz, the inhabitants crowding to the doors and waving flowers and shouting good wishes. The Colonel of the Royals decided to send on a squadron in advance to make good, if they could, two copses near the railway just this side of Honnechy village. This was 'C' Squadron, and I decided to go with it. My role on these occasions is undetermined, and I and my servant, my corporal and six scouts are fairly free to go where we wish, so long as we carry out our premier duty, which on this occasion was to keep the General supplied with information. I went on and found 'C' Squadron in a quarry just short of the copse and the railway; they had come under pretty heavy MG fire getting there – and so did I and my men – so much so that I galloped down the slope into the quarry.

I went on with my corporal and two men, dismounted, and found the Intelligence Officer of the Royals. On scrambling up a railway embankment and crossing the line to a shelter of a railwayman's house, we ran the gauntlet of bullets. The house was two-storeyed, of brick and fairly solid. I at once went upstairs and found the window facing the Boches had been covered with corrugated iron and straw. We pulled down enough to leave us space to observe – below the embankment on the other side there was a ditch and then a grass field at the top of which, about 500 yards off, we detected Boche machine-guns. We could actually count three, each served by a couple of men, and we could guess pretty accurately where the others were. An outpost of our own infantry was just below the embankment, having been driven back from the top of the grassy slope, and it now looked a pretty ugly place to take on. The captain of the infantry had been killed. It was hell to show yourself round the corner of the house, and communication with the infantry in the ditch below was difficult. The large amount of wire all round the village made any advance for cavalry an extremely perilous, if not impossible, job.

I therefore sent back information to that effect, and suggested they should send up a Vickers to the house and also get our artillery on to the ridge.

All this took time. About then, quite a young boy in the Sherwood Foresters ran up the embankment into the shelter of the house sobbing like a child. 'They have killed my captain', he kept saying. He was wounded in the arm and completely unnerved.

I could see that the Boches were walking about just over the brow of the hill (thinking they were unseen) with the greatest impertinence. I shot several times at them but without effect. Shortly afterwards I caught sight of about fifty Boches filing back through the orchards at the south-west corner of the village. At the same time the machine-gunners on the brow of the hill began to melt away. We sent back immediate word of this, the difficulty being to stop the artillery, which was to open on the hill where the Boches had been in about ten minutes. This was successfully done and everybody having been acquainted with the fact that we were going to advance, we started off. I was riding at the head of the Regiment with the Colonel when a tremendous barrage began – and what was more, the air became black with Boche aeroplanes, which came down and fired at us as we advanced, – gas shells, so that everybody was sneezing, high explosive and shrapnel and bullets from the air, the noise was terrific.

The Colonel decided to recross the road a bit further up and then seize the high ground due east of Reumont. Two or three of us ran across the road into a farm, and Corporal Harding and I got up into the loft and through a broken tile we could see straight up the village street. In the farm there were a few South African infantry – and they could not get on. There were also a crowd of civilians there – an old man with a grey beard had picked up one of our rifles and was peering cautiously out of the yard gateway to get a shot if he could see a 'Salle Boche'. Just imagine what an experience these people had been through in twenty-four hours. From here I sent back a long careful message, saying where we were, what the South African line was, and what the Colonel's plans were. By then the Regiment had crossed the road further back, and had galloped up towards the high ground. The horses were left just below the brow of the hill, and we walked up to the top. Our reception soon brought us all to our stomachs and we crawled into some old disused trenches and shell-holes. The rifle fire and MG fire was very strong and one could hardly show one's head. It was a wonderful view towards Le Cateau.

About 4 pm a large number of enemy aeroplanes appeared, and of course spotted our horses. The consequence was that about a quarter of an hour later shrapnel began bursting just over our horses and we had casualties. My servant was wounded. Our ridge too was pounded with a large number of tear-gas shells and a certain amount of heavy stuff. Ellis, who had brought his two Vickers guns up to consolidate the position, was in the next shell-hole to mine, with a corporal, a private and a gun. The Boches got a direct hit on them and killed all three. I did not realize this for about a quarter of an hour and began calling out to Ellis. No answer – and then I caught sight of his body thrown half out of the shell-hole. I crawled across to the hole and found him, one half of his head entirely blown away. The corporal had his left arm and side entirely blown off – there was no sign of his arm at all – and Pte. Harris lay there just breathing, a thick red slime welling out of his throat. He died while I was crouching in the hole with them. Having taken papers and paybooks off their bodies, Corporal Harding and I wriggled down the hill, and found General Peterson had arrived up.

It was decided that it was now too late to push on. . . . In a farm where we had established our HQ for the night, we secured the use of one room – perhaps this gives the wrong idea. The room was half full of refugees' furniture and also refugees themselves. Mattresses, chairs, boxes, clothes were piled high against the walls, and a crowd of women with small children at their knee stood round in a half-dazed sort of way – anxious to show their pleasure at the arrival of the British by ministering to our wants. Into this room we managed to get, and at the only table ate bully and drank coffee and wrote orders and dealt with a hundred and one officers and orderlies and liaison parties who came in one after the other. I got a good deal of information from the civilians about the possible German lines behind, especially with regard to the Le Cateau-St Souplet Line. This I sent back to Division.

About midnight, I lay down on one of the mattresses which I pulled down from a pile in the corner, and covered myself with an old table-cloth and tried to sleep. Almost at once an orderly from the 3rd DG arrived with a very scared-looking German. I questioned him in the kitchen by the light of one guttering candle and surrounded by French-women, some of whom I noticed spoke German fairly well. The man proved to be a batman and had been sent out to recover his master's kit in Reumont. Unaware of the situation, he had ridden up the Le Cateau road and had blundered into our patrols on the further side of the village; he was terrified. I had to make arrangements for sending him down to Division, and then tried to sleep again.

Next day, the Canadian infantry had got a long way ahead of us. There was even a band which came marching through the village, leading a battalion. There is something inexpressibly moving in a military band swinging proudly through a village, which till shortly before was in enemy hands. An advance is a great thing.

That night, 10 October, we moved into a village called Montigny – or rather the Brigade was bivouacked in the fields outside – and we got a small cottage as our HQ. The woman and her daughters were absolutely delighted to have us, and out of their poverty gave us all they could – and helped our servants to prepare food. There were hundreds of Russian prisoners in and around this village till a few weeks ago. Then they were all removed. There have generally been a number of English prisoners too – chiefly employed on the roads. She once attempted to give one of them some soap, and was sternly reprimanded by the NCO in charge. She said the men were all filthy and verminous. This woman also told us that yesterday afternoon the Boches were in such a hurry that, the wind being favourable, they cut several captive balloons loose, instead of hauling them down in the usual way, and the balloons presumably went solemnly floating back to Germany.

The next day (*12 October*), the Divisional General and his staff, having been shelled out of where they were, came and lived in the same house as we in Elincourt, and that night we sat down fifteen to dinner, with General Harman (our old Brigadier) there – and had the greatest fun. There was a good piano and pretty well in tune too. No doubt it has whiled away many an hour for German officers. We had a riotous sing-song.

Stuck loose, years later, in the diary at this point is a long and very friendly letter beginning, 'My Dear Bishop', and dated 20.3.56 from Lieutenant General Sir Wentworth Harman KCB, DSO, the very same general Burgon has mentioned several times in these pages. The letter describes what had happened to him, a regular soldier of course, since 'the old 3rd. Cav. Div. was broken up in the Spring of 1919'. He ends: 'All good luck from one who owes you quite a lot; particularly to the day when I worked on the information you sent back'; and Burgon adds, 'The reference is to a reconnaissance which I was ordered to make in October 1918, and for which I got a bar to my MC[4].

On 15 October the diarist records: 'Many thousands of prisoners are being taken in our advance. The German Government is negotiating for peace; President Wilson's wise reply seems just right, and I could hardly eat my dinner in my excitement'.

286

Geoffrey comments the same day:

These are the most extraordinary days to be living in – the most important and critical in the history of man. God grant Burgon is kept safe till the end, which will come before Christmas, I think. I have always said German morale would never stand defeat. History shows that autocracies can only exist on wars and successful wars. The German Empire will have been a fifty-year wonder like the Babylonian. As for Austria, she will exist no longer at all, has in fact ceased to exist. I must say that the man of this war is Lloyd George. He staked his all and won, and deserves full credit, and has yet years of his life before him. Although the USA seem to be running things, make no mistake, it is we really, and the British Empire who will emerge far and away the most powerful, political and economic combination the world has ever seen. What a responsibility!

But Julian is not sure:

You will be excited by the latest news from Germany, but we are very sceptical here at the Front. I don't believe for the moment we shall stop yet. This morning Foch starts a major attack on Belgium, which should bring the end appreciably nearer. Germany is done but wants to crawl out before all is lost. And this, I think, we cannot afford to let her do, or the war will start up again in ten years time. I long for news of Burgon.

  You ask what a pip-squeak is – it is a small German shell, which generally comes so quickly that you have no time to hear it coming.

By 16 October he is near Arras and has had an interesting time visiting Cambrai, a city not so damaged as Arras,

but the central square is one vast wreck of broken stone and rubble and quite burnt out. . . . The city is practically deserted now. . . . We made our way first to the Cathedral, the nave is three or four feet deep with debris . . . some Hun has wantonly fired two shots through the central door of the Tabernacle . . . we went out and sat on comfortable garden seats and ate our sandwiches – the war might have been, and really is, of course, now far away. . . . no one, however, has any doubt now as to the issue. We all know that Foch has the Germans beat and that it is really only a matter of months – some people say weeks – before they cave in completely. . . . Peace will not come before Christmas, I fear, but soon afterwards, if the next few weeks of fighting go well.

But by the 19th he is happier:

The German retreat is coming more pronounced every day, and truly remarkable. Where it will end, I have no idea. There is scarcely any fighting, it is simply marching, marching, marching towards Germany. I have been busy as usual the last two days, fixing up services for the Division. We had a Chaplains' Meeting yesterday, when we had an interesting discussion about after the war and what the Church of England should try to do.

Two days later, Burgon writes from Paris, where he and a friend had been given some unexpected leave. It is the first real jaunt he has had since the war began:

Voici les changements de la guerre! Two of us arrived yesterday afternoon, in an express train just as fast as in peace time, and we actually crossed the country where we had been fighting, or rather billeted, just before the fight, and saw the woods where we had fought – further on passed a field where I had slept in the open. We could not get in at the Ritz and so came here (Hotel Mirabeau). Of course everything is the height of luxury. Last night we dined at the Café de Paris, and went to the Folies Bergères.

Julian's division, west of Arras, was still moving forward:

Our real trouble seems to be that the enemy is retreating too fast to be able to be caught up for satisfactory engagement. How far he intends to go, nobody knows.

On 25 October, the end is not yet certain:

The war will now last well into next year, is the general opinion out here. There is no doubt we have severely shaken, not beaten, the enemy's main army, and that his withdrawal has been absolutely masterly.

'This is true what Julian says', comments the diarist. 'At the same time in the Le Cateau -Valenciennes battle under Haig, which has been going

on since Wednesday last, we have taken 10,000 prisoners and 150 guns'. Burgon is still in Paris:

For three days we have been living a life of utter lavish luxury, and I must say that it has been thoroughly enjoyable. Tomorrow morning we go back to our huts in the wood. Here we have a private suite of rooms with our own bathroom, hot baths any time we like. We have had our private motor, and practically live at the Ritz which is just opposite. Every night we have dined at one of the restaurants where occasionally, when my purse would run to it, I used to go in the old days – such as Henri, Voisin, or the Café de Paris – and then go on to a box in the theatre. The Ritz is a sort of meeting-house of everybody, and I have met scores of people I know.

On the last day of the month the diarist writes excitedly:

Thursday, 31 October, 1918. Burgon has a Military Cross – an immediate reward for valour in the field. Burgon has deserved the MC several times before[4], in fact has been recommended for it, and it is splendid it should come now the way it has. Perhaps the Croix de Guerre and Palm may follow for the work he did in the Retreat earlier in the year.

Burgon wrote on 27 October:

We got back from Paris an hour ago. The visit has been an unqualified success, and I am extremely glad I went. I feel absolutely fit again and the change (what could be more of a complete change) has done me the world of good.

You will be glad to hear that I have got the Military Cross – an immediate award – for my work on 4 October at Ramiecourt and also on 9 October. It is very satisfactory to get it for a specific piece of work. Everybody congratulated me when I arrived back here today. The General did so to me at once – and you can have no idea how kind everybody has been. It came through the day after I went to Paris – so I did not know till I reached Amiens, and several officers going on English leave rushed up to congratulate me. I feel all the men (and especially Corporal Harding) who worked with me deserve a decoration more than I do. I have not put the ribbon up yet, but shall do so tomorrow I expect.

*Julian (29 October) has been to Lille, enjoying the ecstatic welcome of
the citizens:*

It was only yesterday, as you will see from our papers, that the British
troops made their official entry into the grand old city, and the excitement and happiness of yesterday's historic march pervaded the whole
place today. The novelty of being free was not yet worn off, and though
the faces on all sides are thin and often haggard there is no doubt as to
the light in their eyes. '*Gloire aux libérateurs*' hastily printed on red,
white and blue posters all over the town, as well as various messages of
congratulations from the Lord Mayor of London and other cities. It is
a moving sight to see the wonderful display of flags. I don't know where
they got them from; they were nearly all Belgian, English or French, and
there was scarcely a house in the whole city which didn't display three
or four, and some many more, in the sidestreets as well as in the main
boulevardes. Children waved to us, and the women looked pleased as
we passed. We went up the Rue de Postes to the Place de la République.
As we stopped by the curb, up rushed a dear little girl with her arms
outstretched. She was just made to be kissed. Anyhow she seemed to
expect it, and she was indeed kissed, much to her joy. As we walked
along the street, other children would rush up and seize you by the hand
and ask for a souvenir. Everywhere were British Tommies belonging to
the Division which made the triumphant entry yesterday, walking about
looking smart in belt and side-arms. To make the picture complete, a
party of fifty Boche prisoners passed along the street under a British
guard, much to the joy of the numerous '*garçons*' who took great delight
in getting their own back by running by their side crying '*A bas les
Allemands*', words which not one of them would have dared utter a few
days ago.

On All Saints Day, Burgon writes to Ninny:

If all these nationalities in Austro-Hungary get freedom, and Russia and
Germany herself learn from us and adopt democratic ideas of government, I think Morris will have died in a great cause. I cannot tell you
how paltry any little decoration one may receive seems, in comparison
with what has been given by those who laid down their lives in this
Great War: and indeed the sorrow of their relatives would seem hopeless if we did not believe they are alive in a far fuller sense than we are.

These words of Burgon's, writes the diarist, 'make one think of the text in Wisdom (W. 14) "The righteous live for evermore; their reward also is with the Lord, and the care of them is with the Most High".' She records the swift movement of events:

Sunday, 3 November, 1918. Canterbury

Father is at Folkestone today and it is drenching with rain. The prisoners taken now number 80,000, and 1,600 guns. Prince Boris of Bulgaria has abdicated after one month's reign, and a Republic has been declared. The Kaiser, who had been in Berlin for some weeks, but never daring to show himself, left secretly by night a couple of days ago and went to his Army Main Headquarters, where he is meeting Ludendorff, Hindenburg, the Crown Prince and Prince Max. Rumours abound that the Reichstag means him to abdicate. The Emperor Carl has fled with the Crown Jewels.

The influenza epidemic seems to be abating a little, but the deaths from septic pneumonia following influenza have been hundreds, all over England.

Five days later Burgon's waiting continues:

We are not doing much here at the moment. I think we are rather biding our time till the Armistice terms are published. Much will then depend on whether they are accepted or not by the Boches. Last night the Divisional General (Harman, our old Brigadier) dined with us and congratulated me so warmly again when he saw I had my ribbon up.

The diarist's excitement is mounting: 'The allied armies are pushing victoriously on, sweeping the Germans before them'.
Julian's division is involved. He writes (All Souls' Day, 2 Nov.):

A long motor journey brought us back again the day before yesterday into the proximity of the operations, and we found ourselves tolerably comfortable quarters; but the filth and the flies were unimaginable. Not the filth of a week or so, but the accumulated filth of four years occupation by the enemy; there is garbage and refuse feet high in the streets and gardens everywhere. It was All Saints' Eve and I foresaw but little chance of arranging any services for the Feast. However, next morning, All Saints' Day, I discovered that none of the Division would move for twenty-four hours, so off I went to the next village four miles away, lorry-jumping to find my old brigade; there I discovered them all in the same village, and saw and routed out the C of E chaplain; so together we spent the morning finding a place for a service, getting it into order and putting up notices thick all over the village. The place was packed with troops, and a good many French civilians being left and a good number of houses being destroyed, no accommodation could be found for a church service. At last we fell back upon the Salle des Concerts or local concert hall, which was, however, filled with troops as a billet. However, we arranged to use it for three-quarters of an hour that afternoon. Later in the morning I returned to my billet and to my delight, found Burgon standing outside it; his car enabled me to put off my departure for half an hour, so I gave him lunch and then we went on together to my service.

You can imagine my surprise and joy when he took his overcoat off and disclosed his bright and shining MC ribbon. So at last his splendid work had been recognized. I made him tell me the story of the act. Apparently he took command of two companies of infantry at the moment when they were being counter-attacked and reorganized the men to resist it, over the heads of two frightened and incompetent infantry subalterns. With this he combined the sending back of accurate messages to his General. The Corps Commander said that these were the only messages he got all day. There was also another occasion on a later date when apparently he did extraordinarily good work, but he dismissed at once talking about himself. I must get a full report later from him. We filled our brief time to the full, you may be sure.

He took me in his car up to the door of the Salle des Concerts, where I found a group of men waiting for the service. It was really splendid to get a glimpse of Burgon and to be able to congratulate him in person on his Military Cross. Now we must look forward to going up together to get it from His Majesty.

The service was well-attended and it was really worth all the trouble of arranging it, and we had seventy communicants. I had some tea with the London Scottish and hurried back to take my Machine Gunners' service, which was held in an estaminet, deserted by its owners, and turned for the moment into a very tolerable church. I had fifty or sixty to Evensong, and twenty communicants. So we had been able to keep All Saints' Day after all. Then today we moved forward again and are close up to 'things' now, living once more in French farms, damaged it is true by war, but still providing cover for our heads, although the flies are intolerable.

We expect great things very shortly and shall hope to be ploughing our way through Belgium at no very distant date.

'The same post', writes the diarist, 'brought us one from Burgon, dated the same day as the meeting, 1 November, 1918':

This is just a line, as it is very late, to tell you that Julian and I met this afternoon. I have never seen him look fitter – and he was very jolly and full of energy. He seemed to know nearly everybody. I really think he is a wonderful padre; if the DSO is given for real sterling work, as it is, he ought to have it!

He is delighted to have given such joy to his parents:

Your letter written after hearing about my Military Cross came today. I am very glad you are pleased. I am genuinely pleased myself – everybody's congratulations have been half the pleasure.

The same day (5 November), Julian writes that the momentum of advance is being kept up:

All goes well. We are back in the thick of it again, but the enemy opposition is very uneven. He generally runs away at night, and we follow up in the morning to find him gone and the opposition stiffens again in the afternoon while we are bringing our guns up. I slept last night in a bed occupied the previous night by a German officer. Today we hear of still greater successes further south. By tomorrow we expect to be well within the Belgian frontier.

'This', says the diarist:

shows that the Germans are nearly driven out of France, but I wish Julian were not in danger just at the end of hostilities.

Last night Geoffrey telephoned to me, and incidentally mentioned that the Americans are sending over no more troops. It is supposed that the Armistice may be signed today or tomorrow. It must be signed by 11 am on Monday or rejected. Foch gives them seventy-two hours, but in the face of the Revolution which is spreading over all the Naval Bases, Germany has no option. The entire German fleet seems to be in the hands of the soldiers and workmen's councils, and Bavaria has declared herself a Republic.

Today I heard from Private Furness, the man who was wounded when holding Burgon's horses. He says, dated Nov. 6th 1918:

'I was pleased to hear that Mr Bickersteth had got some recognition. I would have trusted myself with him anywhere, and that is the feeling of all who had the good fortune to serve with him.'

The Kaiser refuses to abdicate, saying if he did so, the German Empire would be given over to Bolshevism. Meanwhile Prince Max has resigned.

Monday, 11 November, 1918. Canterbury.
A memorable day. Yesterday it was announced that the Kaiser and the Crown Prince had abdicated – also the King of Bavaria and the Duke of Brunswick, and all the chief German towns are in the hands of the Socialists and of soldiers and workmen's councils. This morning there was a rumour that the Armistice was signed at 5 am today and that hostilities were to cease at 11 am. I was glad to have a friend with me, for I broke down after the long strain and anxiety. Then I pulled myself together and put a French flag and the Union Jack on Morris's picture, and flowers underneath, and with the help of the servants hung out all our flags. The bells are ringing, and all Canterbury is coming to a Thanksgiving Service in the Cathedral at 3 pm. We lock the house, and the whole household will go.

Burgon writes in a letter dated 6 November:

It has been a soaking day and we have all been travelling since early breakfast.

All morning we have marched through mile after mile of dreary country, every inch fought over half a dozen times, covered with thick coarse grass, cut by trenches, interminable belts of wire, dug-outs over-run with rats, cemeteries, and literally thousands of crosses, singly or in groups of two or three together. Derelict tanks, overturned lorries, aeroplanes which have crashed, heap after heap of shells of all sizes, and all the refuse of war meet the eye everywhere. Even the wretched camps of timber and corrugated iron, which follow a few miles behind the battle, are deserted and broken down. The war and even its most distant followers have passed on. There is no sound of guns – no sign of life except a few scurrying rats, not a living being of any kind in the villages, which are merely a shapeless mass of shattered walls, twisted girders and

rotting timber – sheer stark ugliness seen through a mist of driving piti-
less rain. Surely there can be no more dreadful place on earth, no more
convincing argument of war's utter wickedness, no greater monument
to the heroism of man, whether British or Boche, than this vast waste
known as 'the Somme Battlefield'. We are fortunate tonight in having
a roof over our heads. There is a roof on part of this house, though the
wind blows through it – but we have contrived to make one room fairly
comfortable – and upstairs the floor is dry. Tomorrow we move on
again and shall be clear of this foul country.

No rations yet (6 pm) and therefore no mail. But the letters and the
food will come soon and I shall hear from you both. My thoughts wander to Morris constantly. The freedom being won today by so many
people must lessen your sense of loss. It is a solid satisfaction to feel that
these thousands of crosses are not the real memorial of those who lie
buried underneath them. There is now assured to them a far more
lasting monument.

The diarist adds:

We also had the following from Julian, showing how at the Front a
Division may only know its own bit and nothing of the general situa-
tion. Still it was a curious letter to receive actually on the day the
Armistice was signed:

7 November 1918
Our battle still continues and we are pushing the enemy back step by
step. He is, however, fighting a very clever rear-guard action and I do
not see how we can hope to get him moving any faster. The difficulties about our communications as we advance are appalling – with
bridges blown up and roads ruined, our progress is of necessity very
slow, and the enemy has plenty of time to get back and form new
machine-gun posts, which cause us heavy casualties as we advance. I
am sorry not to give a rosier account, but don't please anticipate peace
before it is likely to come – it only causes endless disappointment. We
all, except perhaps the Staff Officers who don't see anything of the
fighting or of the morale of the Germans, anticipate another six months
of fighting at least.

Only two days later, he is more cheerful (9 November):

We have got the enemy on the run at last. The Germans have gone so fast we have practically lost touch with them. How far he will go before he puts up another fight seems doubtful. Today I have followed up the division on the move, after staying behind to bury our dead – a sad but necessary task – I buried some thirty today, a very heavy job as it means carrying the bodies a long distance to the nearest authorized place of burial. We have lost some splendid fellows in this last battle -- especially in the Queen's Own Westminsters and London Rifle Brigade. The inhabitants of those freed villages cover the graves with flowers and show every possible mark of respect. Everyone thinks peace is certain to come within a day or two. Personally I am not so sanguine, though we must be near the end of the war now.

He continues on:

Sunday 10 November
The battle moves still further and further away and we cannot keep pace. What days we live in! This race suicide is about to stop after all, it would seem, and peace is really close but we still hear our guns hammering away in the distance. We are close now to Mons. It would be strange if the war ended for the British Army close to where it began. Sedan also has been captured we hear. That too is a name which the French would like to associate with happier memories. No time for more now.
    PS. It is great being in at the death.

'It is true', writes the diarist, 'what this letter foreshadows. Our troops entered Mons before the Armistice was signed'.
    She goes on:

The Kaiser is in Holland, having run away, it is said; he wished to give himself up to Haig, but his own soldiers turned him back. The terms of the Armistice are very severe, so as to prevent any fear of future fighting.
    The scenes in London yesterday are past description, but the most wonderful thing was that the instinct of the whole people is to worship and give thanks. Cathedrals, City Churches, little village churches, all were packed with impromptu congregations. There was not standing room in any church building. Geoffrey, knowing I was alone,

telephoned to me last night and told me of the ovation the King and Queen had, the crowds round Buckingham Palace all day being a sight. People were packed like sardines shouting 'We – want – King – George'. Of course they appeared on the balcony. What a contrast to the humiliated skulking figure of the Kaiser. Today the King and Queen go to St Paul's for a Thanksgiving Service. We see the cavalry were in action on Sunday and long for news. Alas, Hugh Aglionby[5] was killed on the 7th, only four days before the cessation of hostilities.

Monday, 18 November, 1918
On Saturday 16th, Father and I came to London, as he is preaching at the Chapel Royal in the morning and at Westminster Abbey at night. It was a magnificent occasion on which to preach at the Abbey. The Chapel Royal was full too, and the dignified people who form the congregation listened very intently to a sermon from Father on 'This God is our God for ever and ever, even to death'[6]. At night the Abbey was packed, people standing in every aisle close together right up to the pulpit. Father preached on 'They shall mount up with wings like eagles', and used 'aviation' as an illustration to this sermon. Geoff said he felt it was a sermon worthy of the occasion. He and I walked in the Mall after lunch, where in two rows on either side right up to Buckingham Palace are arranged huge guns of every kind and calibre taken from the Germans. There are others in many places. Trafalgar Square and the streets are packed every night, but there has been little or no drunkenness.

Julian wrote:

Laus Deo! The great news was brought to me by my clerk while I was dressing – that hostilities would cease at 11 am today. There was a heavy bombardment all along the line this morning, but the sound of guns gradually died down and although there was some gunfire audible after the hour of 11 am, that has been caused by Battery Commanders being out of touch with their headquarters on the telephone – a not unusual experience during these last few days of furious pursuit after a beaten and flying enemy.

The relief is astonishing, although everybody here has taken it very calmly indeed. Only a quiet look of happiness on the tired faces of the men, and a ready smile when one speaks to them, show how they feel. We are at least fourteen miles from the line, because we really couldn't stand the pace. All the roads and bridges have been mined and blown up, and the fords unable to stand our traffic. It became a serious problem to feed our troops. The enemy were running so fast it became impossible to catch up with them.

The satisfaction of the Belgian peasants is most marked. Their kindness to us all is delightful. They cannot do enough for us and they have suffered terribly in the four years of German rule.

. . . I feel too that the joy of the news cannot be unalloyed. The thought of the cost of the war is almost uppermost in my thoughts today, though sometimes I think thankfulness has driven out every other thought.

I know how you feel and how our darling Morris claims today a very large part in your thoughts and prayers. Surely he knows about it all. Surely all Paradise today will be happier for the happiness on earth. Thankfulness for the end includes thankfulness for the splendour of his self-sacrifice, and the glory of his life so nobly laid down to achieve this end. He must be allowed to share in happiness over the peace for which he fought and for which he died.

Burgon wrote:

Today, the 11th November 1918, I must send you and my dearest little mother a word of love.

We have been living in historic days so crowded with unforgettable scenes that I do not know how to describe them.

For the last week we have moved continuously – getting in late at night and moving early. But we are all very fit. At present we cannot realize hostilities have ceased. It is impossible to alter one's habit of mind of four years in an hour or so. On the whole our men have taken it all very quietly. They took the memorable days of March 21–25 very quietly too. Perhaps that is the secret of our strength.

I have thought of you both over and over again, and all of my five brothers. Morris has lived with me all day. Geoff's letter and telegram came, and at least a dozen letters of congratulation. Thank Geoff and Monier and Ralph for all they say. My dear, dear love to the dearest of parents.

Burgon wrote again, dated 13 November, 1918:

It is all like a dream. Apparently we are to march eastwards into Germany. We start about the 17th and we march by easy stages (twenty miles one day and then rest three days) – at this rate it will take us three weeks or a month before we arrive at the Rhine. We are to go with Plumer's Army. I believe the route takes us through Luxembourg. I only hope we do not find the Rhine provinces '*en pleine revolution*', when we arrive there. I am going to work at my German for the next two or three weeks, as we go along. Your letters have reached me. I am glad to hear of Father speaking and preaching on Sunday, 16 November – what great days!

At this juncture I do not think I could come home and stand for Parliament. Besides, the great fact remains that I am not clear what I want to do. It is impossible to rush into things – my mind is in almost as much chaos as the world.

By 15 November Burgon knows roughly what is to happen:

We leave here on Sunday and by about 27 November we are on the Liège line and by the first few days of December we are then on the Belgian–German frontier, where we wait a little and move forward again, and I should say be well established on the Rhine by Christmas. We march from here with great pomp – swords drawn through all the villages, and guards mounted when we arrive in billets, trumpet calls – and headed by regimental standards which have been specially sent for from England. We are moving forward to impress the people, and especially Boche land, when we get there. It is all very extraordinary – this reversal of everything. Personally I pray that England may not become arrogant.

Julian had attended a solemn Te Deum *in Mons Cathedral, and witnessed the march of 12,000 troops in brilliant sunshine. He wrote on 17 November:*

We are busy now tidying up and getting ready for our journey to Germany. Our numbers are terribly low. Our Division fought until the very end. We had a sergeant and private killed only a few minutes before 11 o'clock on Monday, the day of the Armistice. We are to have reinforcements. We are all rather suffering from the reaction to these tense and terrible years. There was no demonstration of any kind on the day itself nor subsequently. The Army took it absolutely quietly. In fact we are almost stunned by what has happened. The collapse of Germany has been so complete and rapid.

We have received the following from Burgon – he is evidently very busy:

18 November, 1918
Our progress can only be described as regal. This morning, on entering Saintes, a small town between Brussels and Enghien, the town band, headed by the Mayor, met us with crowds of people. We passed through cheering people under triumphal arches, and drew up in the Market Place. Here we formed a hollow square and the three National Anthems were played – British, French and Belgian. Then the Mayor, a huge tri-color-coloured sash round his waist, mounted a chair and pronounced a most terrific discourse, which had it been understood by any of the soldiery would surely have made them blush. After this, the General from his horse replied by means of a Belgian interpreter – and endless rounds of cheers closed the proceedings.

This afternoon we have been serenaded by the band – and also by the Mayor, who paid another visit. Tomorrow there is a dance and a concert. Our billets are splendid. Nearly every man has a bed.

In spite of these festivities our work goes on. I am probably the busiest man on the staff at the moment, reports have to be written on the roads, on the railways, on mines, on prisoners, on munition depots, on Belgians friendly to the Boches and many other matters. This afternoon you might have seen me walking down the Enghien-Brussels railway line with the Station-master of Saintes, examining bridges and sidings, with two sappers as expert advisors. This morning after the ceremony, I interviewed the Mayor, the local gendarmes, the Secretary of the Town and others, and have already written several long reports.

Everywhere people line the roads, and flags and triumphal arches greet us at every point. It is an amazing experience. Last night our host supplied lunch and dinner and twelve bottles of his best wine.

These are wonderful days and I would not miss them for anything. I am very well.

Long letter it certainly was, running to 23 pages of typescript:

In the great central '*place*' a band of pipers and drummers were strutting up and down, a massed band with three magnificent drum-majors throwing such a chest I thought they would burst – the pipers' cheeks balloons, and the drummers flourishing their sticks as they never had before. The crowds were huge and the enthusiasm impossible to describe. As soon as the Scotsmen stopped, a brass band started up in another corner of the square. Such scenes are historic, and everyone knew they were. It simply brought a lump to one's throat.

But intelligence work was still to be done, and as Burgon was about the only officer in the Brigade with good French, he was kept very busy: 'There are German deserters to interrogate; Belgian Mayors to be negotiated with, and Belgian suspects to question; new maps to draw up and issue'. And he marched – i.e. rode – with his regiment within a stone's throw of the battlefield of Waterloo:

A few guides rushed at us and held picture post-cards and badly translated guides of the battle. I wonder whether the man, who offered to the Colonel of the Royal Dragoons marching at the head of his regiment a copy of '*Waterloo: Special Ter-centenary Account of the Battle*', realised what a historic scene he was witnessing. Here were the Royal Dragoons marching as victors over the very spot where, in conjunction with the Greys and Inniskillings, they had charged over just over a century ago. Both then and now they have played their part nobly. It was a scene to bring tears to the eyes, and I think we all felt the extraordinary coincidence by which this particular day's march took us right over this very piece of ground.

He took over German guns:

The next morning (23 November) a German officer and a gunner from the Cavalry Corps arrived in a car; the officer was dressed in an ordinary field-grey uniform, and was allowed to carry from his belt a very small bayonet. He talked as good English as I do and told me he had spent a long time in England. We three went carefully through all the guns, taking all particulars – number, date, calibre. There were four heavy French guns among them and three Russian – altogether forty-three – of which twenty were heavy and twelve field guns. Nearly all had had their sights removed. The German said the civilians had done this but I doubt it. At any rate, in various places in the village we found sixteen brand new sights for field guns, each worth fifty pounds sterling and various other sights. After taking over the big dump of guns, the Corps gunner got back into the car in front with the driver, and the German officer and I sat side by side behind, and went down to the station. Here we took over the naval guns and a tractor.

He dealt with evacuees:

There they were, fifty-six people, middle-aged men, and old and young women with children, and their worldly belongings done up in sacks and other weird-looking pieces of baggage. As luck would have it the lorries arrived about midnight – as soon as they had unloaded rations and forage, they backed down to the school and we bundled out the people with their baggage and began loading up. It was a glorious moonlight night and extremely cold, but the people did not seem to mind, though they realised they were in for three days of extreme discomfort. The courage they show is marvellous – especially the women . . .

He attended a Solemn Mass of Thanksgiving on Sunday 24 November, with the General and his ADC:

We were conducted to red plush *prie dieux* not ten feet from the High Altar. It was all really embarrassing. . . . there was not an empty seat. . . . Everyone seemed pleased.

Julian is obviously disappointed that the 56th Division now is not to be marching into Germany:

22 *November, 1918*
Just a line to let you know that, after all, we do not go to Germany. Why, I cannot say, except that the whole Corps (22nd) is not going. I believe the difficulty of feeding, and the acquiescence of Germany may have something to do with it. So our lot now is to remain in almost the same area where we are now – a little to the east – due south of Mons town itself. Here we spend, I expect, the winter in cottages and farms. How to keep the men contented will be a real problem.

The Army is suddenly waking up to the fact that the man has a soul, or at least a mind, and we are being inundated with educational and recreational schemes all to be run by the 'G' Staff, who now that 'operations' are at an end have nothing else to do. Their amateur efforts at dealing with educational problems are not a little amusing. Their interest in securing footballs and football grounds, and their astonishment at how hard it is to find recreation rooms and make other similar comforts for the troops, is a little laughable to us chaplains, who have been labouring at similar tasks all along without any official encouragement.

My time is fully occupied, and I think we chaplains shall have a busy winter, though to keep the men contented will be no easy task. The area is a poor one for general comfort, and the men are in cold barns and not allowed fires.

No time for more now, as I am just off to the other end of our divisional area, ten miles away, on my horse, to lecture on Australia.

Burgon writes on 27 November:

The Divisional General wants me to go to Division permanently to run education in the Division. I cannot say I am particularly keen to do so, and I think I shall try to get out of it. The authorities have selected the most dreadful fellow as Corps Educational Officer, under whom I shall be working. I do not believe that the educational programme can ever be carried out satisfactorily in the cavalry, who are scattered all over the country and who take not the slightest interest in the subject. I shall do my level best to get away, playing any card I can by February or March. The main principles of demobilization have got to be explained to the men at once, and I expect I shall have to do a great deal of it.

I went out riding this morning and one of my horses bucked me off – a thing that hasn't happened for a long time! I have got a very good mare now, which won some jumping competitions at Bath before the war. She is ten years old and a beautiful hack, and would do awfully well for Father after the war. I don't quite know what I am going to do after the war without a horse. Of my four horses I should like to keep two.

*   *   *

But this 1914–1918 Diary must end with Burgon's experiences on 11 November:

The Royals, that day leading regiment of the Brigade, were moving forward into action and had got to the small town of Leuze in Belgium. It was about ten o'clock in the morning when the Brigade Major arrived in his car with a report that it was all over, but they were to go on. We knew then that we were not likely to get into a real fight, but hardly liked to pass it down the column to all the men, though I think most of them knew from our faces what was in the wind. And then just as we were reaching the central square of Leuze a motor dashed up the column and pulled up when it reached us riding at the head. In it was the chief RE of the Cavalry Corps and he handed the General the following historic telegram *(see opposite)*:

    The column halted. The head of it was actually in the centre of Leuze. The news spread like wildfire. We went into a house which we made our temporary HQ, and sent out copies of the message to all concerned. The chief thing was to get the news to the advance regiments and to the patrols. This was eventually done, though it was 1.30 pm before the message reached one of the patrols who were nearly in Enghien being fired at from some woods near Bassilly. It was 10.30 by the time the messages were sent out, and we had half-an-hour to arrange a little ceremony.

    Drawn up in the square was an infantry battalion with its band. They were at once asked to take part and to supply the music. Representatives from all our regiments and various units were summoned, and just before 11 o'clock struck, we were all drawn up; mounted men formed three sides of a square and the infantry the fourth. The General and his Staff were mounted and by his side stood the Mayor. The civilians crowded round and every window had its onlookers. As the hour struck, the trumpeters played 'Cease Fire' and then the band[7] crashed out 'God Save the King'. The infantry presented arms, and every cavalryman sat on his horse at attention, the officers saluting. Then followed the *Marseillaise* and after that the Belgian National Anthem. There was a great deal of cheering and waving of flags and handkerchiefs. The General then dismounted. The Mayor, an old man with a grey beard, made a speech about '*nos vaillants defenseurs*' and the '*prouesse incroyable des troupes alliées*'; and

Prefix.............Code..............m.	Words.	Charge.	This message is on ale of :	Recd. at........ m.
Office of Origin and Service Instructions.		Sent		Date ....
....	At...............m.		.......Service.	From ....
....	To			By ....
	By............		(Signature of "Franking Officer.")	

TO	1st Cav Div
	3rd. Cav Div

Sender's Number.	Day of Month.	In reply to Number.	
* G.C. 303	11		A A A

Hostilities will cease at
1100 today Nov 11 troops
will stand fast on
positions reached at hour
named aaa line of
outposts will be established
and reported to Corps
HQ aaa remainder of
troops will be collected
and organised ready to
meet any demand aaa
all military precautions will
be preserved and there
will be no communication
with enemy aaa further
instructions will be issued
aaa acknowledge
Cav Corps

received LEUZE 11/11/18
1030

0810

The above may be forwarded as now corrected. (Z) G Reynolds Major then the General and he wrung each other's hands amid the greatest enthusiasm. The ceremony ended, and the infantry marched off through a lane of mounted men, the cavalry giving cheer after cheer for the infantry. We then formed the column again and moved off to the eastern side of Leuze.

*   *   *

A little over fifty years later, in July 1969, Burgon, then eighty years old, was on holiday in France with Ralph and Frances (Ralph's second wife), staying the night of 8 July in Tournai. Next morning, they drove the ten miles to Leuze and bought a picture postcard of the centre of the little town, to put in the appropriate page of the War Diary. On it, Burgon wrote:

It was deluging with rain, but I got out of Ralph's car and stood in La Grande Place where, at 10.30 am on 11 November 1918, we had received that historic message that hostilities would cease at 11 am.

EPILOGUE

There are two more large volumes of the diary, packed with newspaper cuttings, and Armistice memorabilia. They also contain many letters from Julian and Burgon, who remained on the continent until the spring of 1919. They record, too, their father's preaching in Westminster Abbey on the National Thanksgiving Day for Victory, and include long descriptions of the handling of the Treaty of Versailles.

On 23 June, 1919, Julian and Burgon, both now civilians, went to Buckingham Palace to receive their Military Crosses together from the King – a day of immense pride and joy for Ella and Sam, who accompanied them. A few weeks later, the four of them crossed to France on a family pilgrimage to visit the place on the Somme where Morris had died, and to lay flowers by the wooden cross still standing where Julian had planted it in 1917. In the years that followed, Julian and Burgon would arrange their home leaves from Australia and Canada to coincide, and many a family trip to the continent took place, always including a visit to Morris's grave, which was by now in the beautifully ordered Queen's Cemetery at Hébuterne near Arras.

Hardly had Julian been demobilised in June than he was appointed Headmaster of St Peter's Collegiate School, Adelaide. Here he spent fourteen years, making many notable innovations, and exercising a profound influence upon a rising generation of young Australians. He established an Australian Headmasters' Conference on English lines, and was largely instrumental in the foundation of St Mark's College, the first residential college in Adelaide University. To this day, our own second son, another Julian, living in Sydney, is constantly asked whether he is related to 'that great headmaster St Peter's had after the First World War?'

Julian's reputation had reached England, and in the early spring of 1933, despite being too far away to attend any form of interview, he was selected by the governors of Felsted School in Essex for the headship, out of a field of fifty-five. It comes as no surprise to find that he at once began to raise academic and sporting standards in this long-established school, and soon put it more firmly on the educational map. He started a new building programme, including the conversion of a large mansion – the Bury – recently given to the School, making it a centre for the boys' leisure activities – and drawing much on Burgon's experience and achievements at Hart House in Toronto (see page 309). From his memories of Rugby, he introduced a tutorial system whereby housemasters chose two members of staff to assist with the pastoral care of every boy, between them following each in his progress up the school. Despite initial mutterings of 'too high church', he introduced weekend Retreats for his confirmation candidates – his deep conviction of the importance of thorough preparation having its roots in his experience as an Army chaplain. He also established an annual conference for public school chaplains, which is still held. His brilliant operation to move the school by lorry across England to several large houses in the Wye Valley in May 1940, was a masterpiece of administration, achieved largely through his forethought and realization that, should war come, compulsory evacuation of the school would be a near-certainty.

It must have been with sad feelings that he felt he had to bow to the insistence of his old friend Archbishop William Temple in 1943 and leave Felsted to become Archdeacon of Maidstone and a Residentiary Canon of Canterbury Cathedral, like his father before him. In Craze's *History of Felsted School* (Cassell 1955), a thirty-page chapter, headed 'Julian Bickersteth', concludes:

His dynamic personality, his teeming imagination, the strength of his influence in spiritual matters, give him a high place in the long line of Felsted Headmasters.

He threw himself into his new duties with all his customary energy – not only with the life of Cathedral and City but also as a tireless visitor of the clergy and their parishes throughout the diocese. Meanwhile he never lost his interest in education or in the Christian teaching of young people, being in great demand at Retreats and as a counsellor, not least in the King's School where the old Bickersteth home, Meister Omers, had by then become a house for boarding boys.

At about this time he was closely involved in the siting and funding of the new university for Kent. In 1953 he became a Chaplain to the Queen, and so like his father before him began to preach annually at the Chapel Royal in St James's Palace. A further interest arose from his conviction of the importance of family life as the foundation of

Christian civilisation, in that he encouraged one of his godsons to establish in Canterbury an Institute of Heraldic and Genealogical Studies. It seemed an almost impossible brief; but against all the odds, the founder Cecil Humphery Smith rose to the challenge and to-day, thirty years later, the Institute flourishes, having gained international recognition. In Julian's memory, the Bickersteth Medal is presented to a person 'who has made a notable contribution to family history studies' – the recipients including so far Earl Mountbatten, the Duke of Norfolk and Sir Colin Cole, the last Garter King of Arms.

In 1957, now retired, Julian became the Chairman of a new county school in Canterbury, the Archbishop's School, and saw it successfully through the first five years of its existence. He continued to be in great demand, preaching, hearing confessions and conducting Quiet Days and Retreats in schools and parishes. It was a time greatly-enhanced by the fact that Burgon was living so close. They worked together on a number of local projects, not least the funding and restoration of Greyfriars, the 13th Century Franciscan chapel off the High Street in Canterbury – now a centre of pilgrimage for Franciscans the world over. A bust of Burgon by Oscar Nemon and a tablet to Julian on the stairs records the brothers' involvement in a task which meant much to them both, and has given the Franciscan movement a spiritual home again in Canterbury.

* * *

Burgon's life between the two World Wars had been a full one. His story in the First leaves no doubt about his natural ability and courage as a leader nor about the strength of his personality, which clearly earned him the respect not only of his peers but also of the senior officers under whom he served.

Returning from France in March 1919, he proceeded to take up the teaching post in Alberta University that had been held open for him; but after a couple of years, he decided that it was not the life for him; and he was actually in Toronto, on his way home, when he was approached by the University and asked to become Warden of Hart House, a two-year-old venture designed to be the cultural hub of the whole place. He accepted with alacrity, and for twenty-five years he devoted his life to it, creating a fine library and art gallery, organizing lectures by public and international figures and, importantly for him, converting a room into a chapel to become the spiritual core of the entire community. His huge contribution to Hart House is described fully in *An Uncommon Fellowship* by Ian Montagnes (University of Toronto Press, 1969).

A personal friend of the Prime Minister of Canada, Mackenzie King, Burgon became a considerable force behind the scenes in Canadian politics in the years leading up to the Second World War. In 1927 King invited him to be his personal assistant, which would lead to being secretary of his Cabinet. But Burgon's attachment to his Toronto undergraduates and the sage advice of Sir Maurice Hankey, the Cabinet Secretary in London, led him to decline. Nevertheless, his close involvement with the Royal Tour of Canada in 1937 resulted in him becoming an unofficial adviser to the King on Canadian affairs for some fifteen years, – enabling him to have fun with the family in his letters with the throw-away line 'had tea at the Palace with the King and Queen today' – something that I remember impressed me mightily as a boy!

At home when the war broke out in 1939, Burgon returned at once to his post in Canada, but the pull of home in adversity was too strong and he obtained permission from the University to return to England for the duration of the war. He joined the Local Defence Volunteers (later the Home Guard) and, truth to tell, thoroughly enjoyed the excitement of nights on duty in the Canterbury area, even though he was by then in his mid-fifties.

As Canadian troops began to arrive in England, General McNaughton, their commander, invited Burgon to become his Director of Education, to which he readily agreed and was soon travelling to every corner of the country where Canadian soldiers were to be found. Before long, his work came to the notice of an old friend, General Paget, the C-in-C Home Forces and this led him to be invited to become Director of Army Education, an invitation he felt bound to accept although he declined to take military rank. Here, as in so many aspects of his life, he soon made his presence felt. One of his measures was the creation of the Army Bureau of Current Affairs (ABCA) whose pamphlets were distributed to troops throughout the world as part of their preparation for the post-war years. These pamphlets contained plenty of controversial matter, and there are those who hold that they influenced the landslide victory of the Labour Party in the 1945 election!

The war over, Burgon returned to Toronto where he soon found that the needs of a university population containing a high proportion of ex-service people, impatient of the kind of authority he had wielded so effortlessly between the wars, were better suited to a younger man; and so, in 1947, he resigned and left Canada for Canterbury amidst moving tributes from the highest in the land. In 1967, the University of Toronto reprinted *The Land of Open Doors*, which Burgon had written sixty-two years earlier and had become a Canadian classic of the pioneer days. In 1974 he was appointed a member of the Order of Canada.

Canterbury was, of course, the only place to which he could retire. Ella, his mother, was ageing and Julian lived only yards away from her. Here, in addition to the activities which he and Julian shared, Burgon became a prison visitor, travelling round most of the prisons of England, where he became renowned and respected by both the prison authorities and the prisoners themselves, whom he served with such diligence and understanding. But he also completed a year's study at London University, learning enough about palaeography to enable him to do valuable work in the Cathedral library of which his father had earlier been Canon Librarian. Friends from all over the world, especially of course from Canada, streamed into his home, and he was their indefatigable guide round the Cathedral – to which he was a generous benefactor. He took great delight in his voluminous visitors books which would tend to show the name of the Archbishop of Canterbury immediately below that of some old lag just out of Dartmoor!

Just short of her ninety-sixth birthday, on St. Andrew's Day, 1954, Ella, the diarist, beloved mother of six sons died suddenly, quite *compos mentis* that morning when she had received the Sacrament of Holy Communion in her home. Her eldest son, Monier, my father, was the celebrant, and both Julian and Burgon were there. Her death meant what Burgon described to me as 'a total revolution in my life'. Indeed it marked the end of an era for the whole family but especially for the two bachelor brothers, who had lived within walking distance of their mother for so long and had called in on her almost every day.

The diarist always seemed old to us, the grandchildren, partly because of the slowing effect of her blindness I suppose (she had hardly any sight from 1928 onwards), but also due as every grandchild finds to the very fact of her being two generations removed from us. I remember her very clearly, and the way she kept up into her nineties an intense interest in how we were and what we were doing. It was never a duty, always a pleasure to go and see her. This is borne out by a friend who, like me, was a schoolboy in the mid-1930s. His home was in

Canterbury then; and, in response to my invitation, he writes with evident enjoyment at reliving the friendship they had over a period of some twenty years:

I found Mrs Bickersteth a quite enchanting person from the first summer evening when my father took me to meet her; her lovely animated voice was like no voice I had ever heard before. We became great friends, and I often visited her in the school holidays. I used to read aloud to her, and we talked a lot. Her merry laughter is something I can still hear. When the war came, and I was on active service overseas, I wrote to her from time to time – and I believe some of my letters are in the Bickersteth War Diary to this day![1] Then, in 1952, I had the satisfaction of taking in to her the girl I was going to marry. I recall the news of her death took me by surprise. Someone who wrote to us after the birth of our son in early December 1954 said, 'I saw in yesterday's *Times* that your old friend has died. It is as if she were making room for him.'

Another, slightly younger, Canterbury schoolboy of the late 1940s says of Julian and Burgon:

What I remember about the brothers was their idealistic enthusiasm affirming people, and especially young people – where the affirmation was in reality a bit premature. Over half a century, the self-revealing acclamation 'Splendid', in which they both delighted, echoes into a time when it is not usual to come across such examples of dedication, assured in its own position, yet always eager to help others. In a Canterbury still recovering from war and blitz, it was a glimpse of the City of God.

More than sixteen years passed between the brothers' deaths. Julian died in 1962; Burgon survived into his nineties, as did my father Monier and my godfather Ralph. Archbishop Ramsey preached at Julian's funeral, Archbishop Coggan at Burgon's in 1979. I loved 'the uncles', as we always called them, and it was a joy to me to see that my wife and children came to do so too. From childhood, my generation had been captivated by the romance of their lives. They lived in the far 'dominions'. They always seemed to have plenty of money. They had both 'done well in the war'. They were always such fun to be with, teasing us – and each other – unmercifully, but always interested in what we were doing. They would look us up on holidays and make sandcastles with our offspring as they had with us. Later, their half-crown tip to us of earlier days would be transformed into a fat cheque for school fees. Here, we instinctively knew, were two believers of the old school, whose sheer example of Christianity in action we would always remember. Of course, countless other steadfast lives over the centuries have testified to the truth of the Christian faith; it was simply my privilege to have known two such men whose experiences, eighty years ago now, in an appalling war, helped to shape their characters as nothing else could.

* * *

The Bickersteth War Diary itself must have the last word; and it can, thanks to two typescript pages that I found loose in Volume XI. Burgon had written them at the time of his parents' Golden Wedding. So the brother who had written the first fifty pages of the Diary now contributed the last two. For all its wishful thinking – 'a new faith', 'the League of Nations', and what today we would call its blatant racism ('even the Russians have the right to live as they desire'), his piece must stand as the intended conclusion of their mother's painstaking and faithful enterprise:

'I write these closing words of the XIth and last volume of the Bickersteth War Diary on 4 August, 1931. The keeping of this diary was, I think, my suggestion, and I myself wrote the first few pages of it. But it is to Mother that must go the credit of carrying through an undertaking which proved to be far vaster than we had ever anticipated. She it was who had our war letters typed and tabulated, linked them up with a running commentary on family affairs at home, and set down all that Father and she heard about the conduct of the war. The result is a human document of considerable interest, and it is possible that in years to come it may be thought worthwhile to reduce the mass of material in these eleven volumes to a size suitable for publication, so that future generations may learn how the Great War affected an average English family.

'Seventeen years ago today, war was declared between England and Germany. To the rising generation – our nephews and nieces for instance – that stupendous struggle which lasted for four years and three months is far more remote than the Napoleonic campaigns. Ella (aged 19) and Edward (aged 16)[3], both said to me this summer that the Battle of the Somme was far less real to them than the Battle of Waterloo. This may be our fault. Perhaps we do not talk enough about our experiences in France and Flanders. But if that is so, it is because we are afraid of being bores, and also because we realize how hopeless a task it is to attempt even the simplest account of those stupendous days. This very indifference of the younger generation creates a bond between all those who fought. We are conscious of belonging to a fraternity of all those who had common experiences in the trenches. It is a blessed fact that the mere lapse of years serves to extinguish the anguish and bitterness of those experiences, and that we tend to remember the good times, the friendships and humour of the soldier's life. We are perhaps more cynical in the years immediately succeeding the Armistice than at any other time in our lives. Most men returned to civilian occupations, if indeed they were lucky enough to find occupation, sick at heart and conscious of a disillusionment which had begun long before November 1918. But as the Great War recedes into 'history', we begin to see that out of the maelstrom has come a new faith; the injustice and mistakes of the Peace Treaty at Versailles are now patent to all; the appalling economic troubles of almost every country in the world in this year of grace 1931 bring home the futility of war with its resulting financial chaos; we admit the right of people, even the Russians, to live as they desire; and we wish well to the League of Nations, Toc H or any other movement, great or small, which stands for a better and a saner world.

'These things are not yet clear. We are too close to the gigantic struggle which shook the very world to its foundations. But it may be that, a century hence, the Great War of 1914–1918 will be viewed in its right perspective and will be seen as a great dividing line in the long history of mankind, as not only the end of one epoch but the beginning of a new and better age. In that case, Morris and all those great souls who fell on Flanders' Fields will not have died in vain.'

J. M. B.

APPENDIX
ANOTHER DIARY

———————

Burgon was a prolific, not to say almost compulsive writer. In addition to the frequent long letters home from France, often two or three a week, which his mother put intact into the War Diary – I have only used a fraction of them in this book – he was, for three of his four years on active service, engaged also on a personal diary. He was writing, contrary I am sure to all kinds of King's Regulations, a detailed account of his doings in diary form, using eventually three volumes of Army Books 152, over the period February, 1916 until his demobilization in March, 1919. There are more than 150 pages, all written in pencil, remaining entirely legible nearly eighty years on because of the clear hand which he retained all his life.

In 1989 my brother Ted decided, with the family's full approval, to offer these three notebooks to the Household Cavalry Museum; and the Royals having become part of that amalgamation of cavalry regiments, the gift was gratefully accepted by the Regimental Colonel.

I have not drawn at all on the mass of material in that diary, for the reason that it has always been quite separate from what my grandmother was doing in her *magnum opus*, of which this present book is a précis. There would of course be very considerable overlap. But Burgon's private diary is still intact and unedited, along with a mass of newspaper cuttings, photographs, orders and so on stuck loose into the pages of those three 152's.

So Combermere Barracks, Windsor, now houses them; and Churchill College, Cambridge my brother's set of the eleven volumes of the Bickersteth War Diary. Future students of First World War history can take their pick!

NOTES

INTRODUCTION

1 Peter Simkins, *Kitchener's Army* (Manchester University Press, 1988) p. xiv.

2 Now part of the Household Cavalry, by amalgamation with the Royal Horse Guards and Life Guards. In November 1918 (see p301), Burgon had the excitement of passing with his regiment very close to the battlefield of Waterloo, where on 18 June 1815, the Royal Dragoons captured the Eagle of the French 105th Infantry Regiment.

3 Total military enlistments, 1914–1918 (all voluntary, since Australia refused to adopt conscription) out of a population of 4.9 million: 412,953
Total sent overseas: 331,781
Total casualties (officers and men): 214,360
Total deaths: (2,826 officers, 55,306 other ranks): 58,132

4 Official History, *Military Operations in France and Flanders 1916* Vol. 1 p.473.

5 An extensive bibliography would certainly include: Gummer, Canon Selwyn, *The Chavasse Twins* (Hodder & Stoughton, 1988). Harcourt, Melville *Tubby Clayton: a personal saga* (Hodder & Stoughton, 1953). Pursell, William, *Woodbine Willy* (Hodder & Stoughton, 1962). Raw, David, *'It's only me': The Rev. Theodore Bayley Hardy* VC DSO MC. [Hardy died from wounds received when winning his VC].

6 Admiral Alfred von Tirpitz (1849–1930), the creator of the High Seas Fleet. 'Slaughter of innocents' almost certainly refers to civilians lost at sea due to German submarine warfare.

7 A characteristic passage, from a mid-1915 letter when the Royal Dragoons moved to otherwise pleasant new billets refers to 'a large number of cases of drunkenness – due, I think, partly to the fact of coming to a new place, when the men try all the *estaminets*, and partly to the fact that they are heartily sick of this peace soldiering – inspections, schemes etc. I wish to goodness we could do something. The trenches would be greatly preferable to this.' It was a running refrain.

8 Paul Nash, *Outline: An Autobiography and Other Writings.*

9 Viscount Chandos, *From Peace to War: A study in contrast 1857–1918*, p. 182.

VOLUME I

1 Then C-in-C Northern Command. Later Field Marshal Viscount Plumer: GCB (1857–1932).

2 Former Governor General of Canada (1904–11). He had written the Foreword to Burgon's recently-published book about life in the Far West – *The Land of Open Doors.*

3 Cosmo Gordon Lang (1864–1945). Archbishop of York (1909–28), Archbishop of Canterbury (1928–42). He and Sam were friends from the days when both were curates.

4 Later the Earl of Harewood KG (1882–1947), a lover of the arts and interested in Freemasonry and horse racing. Sixty years later, in a typically generous way, Burgon added to that page of the diary: 'A very wrong estimate of Lascelles by me. He did magnificently with the Grenadiers, wounded, refused staff jobs which he could easily have had, and returned to duty each time with his regiment. His DSO was for bravery in the field.'

5 Randall Davidson (1848–1930) had married Edith Tait, whose father became Archbishop of Canterbury.

6 The reference is to Leeds Parish Church, still a centre of excellence for church music.

7 The Music Hall was at the peak of its Victorian and Edwardian popularity, and the war kept it going; it provided an anchor of normality and recreation for the troops on leave.

8 Cecil Rhodes (1835–1902). English imperialist and benefactor. MA(Oxon) 1881. Prime Minister of the Cape by 1890. In his will he endowed some 170 scholarships for students from the Colonies, the United States and Germany.

VOLUME II

1 The fifth earl (1847–1929). Prime Minister (1894), missionary of imperial ideas, advocate of House of Lords reform and successful owner of racehorses.

2 This hymn, only now tending to be dropped from modern hymnbooks, had been written twenty-five years earlier by Burgon's grandfather, then Vicar of Christ Church, Hampstead and later Bishop of Exeter (1885–1900).

3 Waterloo Day

4 First Earl of Ypres (1852–1925). Commander-in-Chief of the British Expeditionary Force (1914–15). He resigned in December 1915 in the face of criticism of his leadership after a lack of success of the BEF.

5 Sam was chaplain to this Territorial Force battalion. (see the photograph of him in uniform in the family group on the jacket of this book).

6 Bishop Taylor Smith was the (not much appreciated!) Chaplain General (i.e. head of the Royal Army Chaplains Department).

7 Canon Michael Furse later became Bishop of St Albans.

8 Dragoon Guards.

9 Dr 'Tommy' Strong GBE (1861–1944). Later Bishop of Ripon and then of Oxford. Clerk of the Closet to HM the King and Chancellor of the Order of the Garter (1925–37).

10 Vice-Chancellor of the University; he was following a beadle (known in University terms as his 'poker').

VOLUME III

1 There are many accounts of Rupert Brooke's death; this one may not have seen the light of day elsewhere. It clearly meant much to the diarist.

2 Royal Engineers.

3 First Earl of Balfour KG OM (1848–1930). Philosopher and statesman. Prime Minister 1902–05. Inaugurated Franco–British *entente*. First Lord of the Admiralty 1915. Foreign Secretary 1916–19.

4 That is, of Victoria.

5 His old nurse, Elizabeth Peters, known to all as 'Ninny', who remained with the family

for fifty-two years. Not dying until 1936, she was a great feature of my own child-hood, always at Meister Omers, the diarist's home in Canterbury, to welcome us.

6 First Earl of Oxford and Asquith KG QC (1852–1928). Prime Minister (1908–1916).

7 My mother and older sister, then aged three.

8 The country house which the diarist and her husband rented in the Yorkshire Dales for some years as a bolt-hole from Leeds Vicarage.

9 He was to be its Headmaster within four years.

10 Third Baron and first Viscount Chelmsford (1868–1933). Viceroy of India (1916–21). He had been Governor of Queensland and then of New South Wales.

VOLUME IV

1 Bishop Llewellyn Gwynne CMG OBE (1863–1957). Later the greatly loved Bishop in Egypt and the Sudan.

2 His first cousin, Clare Monier-Williams.

3 Army Service Corps. Later the Royal Army Service Corps and now part of the Royal Logistic Corps.

4 A reference to the fact that Sam had been Vicar of St Mary's Lewisham before they moved to Leeds.

5 The Rev., E.N. Mellish VC MC. His was the first VC won by an Army chaplain in the Great War.

6 Three traditions of Methodism amalgamated in 1932 – the Wesleyans, the Primitive Methodists and the Methodists. The Wesleyan branch was nearest theologically to the Church of England.

7 The Edict of 1598, which had allowed freedom of worship to the Huguenots, was revoked in 1685.

8 Wearing moustaches was a 'Low Church' practice, much looked down upon by Catholic-minded priests. It remains rare in these days of much less rigid divisions of churchmanship.

9 G. A. Studdert-Kennedy, later awarded the MC, was a controversial figure. He acquired the nickname 'Woodbine Willie' because of his enthusiastic sharing of cigarettes with the troops.

10 After 1920 they were called Chaplains to the King (or Queen). There are thirty-six of them at any one time in Her Majesty's College of Chaplains.

11 The young poet Charles Sorley (1895–1915) was killed in action. In 1918 his sister Jean was to marry Geoffrey, the diarist's second son.

12 The first Earl Kitchener KG (1850–1916). Secretary of State for War from 1914–16. When he was on passage to Russia on board the SS *Hampshire*, the ship struck a mine north of the Orkneys and he was drowned.

13 Lord Bradford was patron of my father's living at Castle Bromwich, outside Birmingham. His house was in the village.

14 The first Earl Haig (1816–1928). Field Marshal and Commander-in-Chief of the BEF (1916–19).

15 To coincide with their Golden Wedding in June 1931, Morris' father published a 155 pp memoir of his fifth son, entitled: *Morris Bickersteth 1891–1916* by His father the Rev. Samuel Bickersteth DD TD Canon Residentiary of Canterbury and Chaplain to the King. It was printed For Private Circulation Only at the University Press Cambridge 1931.

16 At the time of the battle, he was off sick in England. On 1 July, Major (Acting Lieutenant Colonel) Neill was commanding the battalion.

17 A fellow chaplain in 56th(London) Division.

18 Royal Army Medical Corps.

19 Advanced Dressing Station.

20 Assistant Provost Marshal (of the Military Police).

21 Although it is a third account of the meeting, which was a watershed in the war for Julian and Burgon, this is deliberately included. It was two days before Morris' death; different aspects of the encounter are brought out by each of the three brothers.

22 Bishop of Bath and Wells (1894–1921).

VOLUME V

1 The Church of England's Men's Society, a great force for good for many decades. Outliving its usefulness, it did not actually cease to exist until the 1980's.

2 This refers to the ancient liturgical practice of the priest not giving wine, but the bread only, previously marked with wine – obviously a much easier way of communicating in the field.

3 His friend the *Daily Telegraph* war correspondent, already mentioned, was knighted for his work in Flanders.

4 'More active work' never materialized. He remained in Canterbury, retiring in 1936 – his deafness having got progressively worse over the years.

5 Second Lieutenant Gordon Jelf, The Buffs (1886–1915) had been killed in action after only four months at the Front. He was one of my mother's brothers.

6 Casualty Clearing Station.

7 The King's Own Yorkshire Light Infantry, which became part of the The Light Infantry in 1968.

8 The war correspondent, already mentioned on p. 86 and 112.

9 Poet, novelist, critic and devoted Roman Catholic (1874–1936).

10 Later, first Earl Lloyd George of Dwyfor OM (1863–1945). Prime Minister (1916–22).

11 Llewellyn Gwynne. (See Vol IV Note 1)

12 Throughout the war, all chaplains were volunteers.

VOLUME VI

1 Our two year old brother Edward (Ted).

2 Her uncle, Gordon Jelf, already mentioned. (See Vol V Note 5 above)

3 He refers to the Chaplain General, Bishop Taylor Smith.

4 New South Wales.

5 Canon B. K. Cunningham, later a notable Principal of Westcott House, Cambridge, *alma mater* of more bishops in the Church of England than any other Theological College.

6 Trans. 'Thirteen brave Englishmen'.

7 An informal soldiers' concert, often arranged at company level when out of the line, at which beer and tobacco featured on a generous scale.

8 He retained it, many regarding him as having a charmed life.

9 'The Baron' was, of course, the famous air ace Baron Manfred von Richthofen, the

legendary and chivalrous hero of many a war story in the years to come.

10 This was Burgon who, as recounted in the Prologue, captained Oxford University at Association Football in 1911.

11 A mural tablet of Limoges enamel and designed by Bainbridge Reynolds, in the War Memorial Chapel, Leeds Parish Church, unveiled by a family friend, Sir Berkeley Moynihan, on 18 June, 1917.

12 *The Spectator* used it complete in September 1991, and in their 1992 Annual. 'As long ago as 1920', wrote the historian Stephen Roskill in a letter to *The Times* on 8 May, 1972, 'that most sensitive and accurate war correspondent Sir Philip Gibbs wrote about the incident in his book *The Realities of War*. Someone commenting on the *Spectator* article wrote to me: 'the simple compassion it expresses, its quiet, gentle statement of cruel fact is unforgettable'.

13 Actually he was awarded the MC for his part in this raid, but much later, in January 1919. The citation does not survive, in common with many others awarded in the months after the Armistice. Meanwhile he had already won the Cross in October 1918, so he later thought of that later award as his Bar.

14 Later Archbishop of York and then Canterbury (1881–1944). He was at Rugby with Julian.

15 In *The Times* letter mentioned in Note 12, Roskill says that he thinks the figure of 187 'about right' for the number of British troops shot for desertion in the First World War. Stephen Hopkirk, in a letter to the same paper on 18 May, 1972, is convinced that the total was much more like 300. In 1995, the subject was aired by HM Opposition, which 'might seek' in office the reviewing of certain cases for posthumous pardon. The Prime Minister is on record as saying that history cannot be rewritten.

16 Confined to Barracks. A mild punishment.

VOLUME VII

1 Christ Church, Oxford – from the Latin *aedes* (house) of Christ.

2 Deputy Assistant Chaplain General; Gwynne had appointed one per Corps.

3 This was none other than (as he became) Prebendary 'Tubby' Clayton, the founder of the Toc H movement. All Hallows by the Tower was his London base for forty years after the war.

4 There had just been a Peace Conference in Stockholm which came to nothing.

5 Leigh Mount was my father's and mother's home from 1915–1920.

6 The phrase used to describe how far into the Rocky Mountains (or indeed anywhere else) a railway line had so far been laid.

7 The Royal Flying Corps did not become the Royal Air Force until 1 April, 1918.

8 Later the first Baron Tweedsmuir CH, GCVO, GCMG (1875–1940) author, and Governor General of Canada (1935–1940).

9 The fifth Marquess (1846–1935), statesman and historian.

10 London had indeed gone wild over General Allenby's entry into Jerusalem on 11 December, 1917.

11 Jean was the daughter of Professor Sorley, who had the Chair of Moral Philosophy in Cambridge. Her brother Charles was the poet, already mentioned by Burgon. (See Volume IV and VII).

12 Commander Royal Engineers, the senior Sapper in a Division.

13 The devoted mother was convinced there was an almost automatic progression from MC to DSO.

14 Later Dean of Canterbury and Bishop of Chichester, (1883–1958). Lover of Christian Unity.

15 Later Viscount Cave (1856–1928), lawyer and statesman.

16 This work was indeed finished. It was published in 1919 with the title *History of the 6th Cavalry Brigade 1914–1918.*

17 Later Field Marshal Jan Christian Smuts (1870–1950), CH, OM, FRS. Lawyer, soldier and statesman. Prime Minister of South Africa (1939–48).

VOLUME VIII

1 See Vol III Note 3.

2 Observation Posts, from which artillery fire was directed by field telephone.

3 Deputy Assistant Chaplain General. He was later Bishop of Southwell.

4 Julian was ahead of his time in extending what would now seem to us to be an obvious courtesy.

5 The letter was obviously meant to be kept for her teens, but my sister says it never came her way.

6 This was the Rev. H.R.C Sheppard – Dick – who went on to become Vicar of St Martin-in-the-Fields and the father of religious broadcasting.

7 The Assistant Director of Medical Services. Responsible for the control of all medical units and staff throughout each division.

8 On 23 April, 1918, a naval force commanded by Admiral Sir Roger Keyes made an historic raid on Zeebrugge in an attempt to block the U-boat base. Although the ships' crews and demolition parties displayed great gallantry and much damage was caused, the raid was only partly successful.

9 Julian had said this before. This repeat emphasizes the conviction he had arrived at on the Somme (p.92, 93).

VOLUME IX

1 On 8 August, 1918, General Rawlinson's Fourth Army had attacked on a broad front in great strength, the infantry being supported by some hundreds of tanks and the Cavalry Corps being held in readiness to exploit any breakthrough. A crushing defeat was inflicted on the Germans, and the Hindenburg Line penetrated. Later, General Erich von Ludendorff would describe 8 August as 'the black day of the German Army in the history of the war'. Now known as 'the Second Battle of Amiens', it marked the beginning of the end for the Germans.

2 Lord Milner KG (1854–1925). Statesman whose chief contribution to contemporary political thought was his conviction of the need for imperial unity.

3 The reference is to Ralph being invalided out after three years home service due to ill health, the legacy of the peritonitis he had contracted in the trenches in 1915, very soon after he arrived at the Front and from which he very nearly died. (See Volume II page 31). He recovered fully and, later, pursued a successful career in the City. Twice married, with two silver weddings, he died at the age of 94. A much loved godfather to me.

4 See Volume VI Note 13 for the unusual sequence of his awards, recorded in the Christ Church, Oxford Roll of Service: MC 1 February, 1919, Bar 1 January, 1919. The reconnaissance to which Burgon refers is the one described on pp. 279–284.

5 Major Hugh Aglionby MC was one of the five serving sons of the diarist's brother-in-law, Canon Frank Aglionby, an American episcopalian priest who married Amy Bickersteth, one of the sixteen children of the Bishop of Exeter.

6 These words are now engraved on the steps of the Chapel of St Nicholas, in the Undercroft of Canterbury Cathedral. The brothers restored the chapel in 1956 in memory of their father and mother.

7 At no stage of the war were regimental bands far from their fighting units. As stretcher-bearers, the bandsmen were often in the thick of things and performing with heroism.

EPILOGUE

1 True; there are several of them in the seven volumes the diarist put together during the 1939–45 war.

2. J. R. Mallory, *Mackenzie King and the origins of the Cabinet Secretariat* (p. 256 Canadian Public Administration); and Stephen Roskill, *Hankey: Man of Secrets* Vol II p. 302 (London: Collins 1972).

3. My older sister and my brother, later known as Kay and Ted.

INDEX

National Mission, 80, 81, 117, 188, 196, 215
Neill, Colonel, 99, 318
Nemon, Oscar, 309
Neuve Chapelle, 153
New Guinea, German, 11
New South Wales, 161, 318
New Zealand, 11
New Zealanders, 252
'Ninny', 54, 96, 290
No-Man's-Land, 109, 168
Norfolk, Duke of, 309
Northcliffe Press, 268
North Somerset Yeomanry, 30, 39, 68, 173
Norwich, 70

Observation Posts, 321
Offra, 87
Oise, River, 243, 245
Okell, Padre, 67
Old Rugbeians, 67
Olympia, 209
Ontario, 2
Ordination, 225
Orkneys, The, 318
OTC, ix, 2
Owen, Wilfred, xiii
Oxford, 34, 64
Oxford, Bishop of, 317
Oxford Blue, 182, 319
Oxford, Christ Church, 9, 20, 34, 64, 125, 240, 320, 321
Oxford, Lincoln College, 252
Oxford, St John's, 226
Oxford, Town Hall, 64
Oxford, Trinity College, 67
Oxford, University of, xix, 34, 43, 317
Oxo, 2, 106

Paget, General, 310
Palmer, Padre, 98, 106, 109, 110, 111, 141, 142, 145
Paradeniya, 62
Paradise, 2, 98, 175
Paris, 5, 72, 214, 233, 259
Paris, Opera House, 164
Paris, Ritz Hotel, 288, 289
Parliament, 212, 269, 299
Passchendaele, xiii, 199, 226
Patriotism, ix, xi, xiv, 2, 11, 14
Peckham Rye, 73
Peckwater Quad, xx
Peronne, 148
Peters, Miss Elizabeth ('Ninny'), 317

Peterson, General, 285
Phillips, Derek, xx
Plumer, Sir Herbert, 2, 6, 10, 316
Plumer's Army, 299
Poland, 150
Polo, 45
Pompeii, 38
Pope, The, 72, 202
Poperinghe, 207
Port Phillip Bay, 8
Port Said, 60, 64
Prince Max, 291, 294
Prussia, 149
Public Schools, x, xiv, 63, 76, 79, 83, 276
Pullman, 66
Punch, 27, 47
Pursell, William, 316

Queen Alexandra's Hospital, 103
Queen, HM The, 15, 90, 296
Queen Victoria, ix
Queen's Westminsters, 221, 247, 258, 261, 275, 296
Queensland, 318
Quiet Day, 242, 243, 309

Radley, 252
RAMC, 52, 78, 106, 138, 173, 273, 319
Ramiecourt, 279, 280, 281, 289
Ramsey, Archbishop, 312
Rangers, The, xi, 73, 76, 98, 136, 170, 200, 210, 233, 234, 235
Ratcliffe, Captain, 268
Ratcliffe, Freddie, 268
Ratcliffe, Mrs, 268, 276
Raw, David, 317
Rawlinson, General, 321
Recruiting Officers, ix
Red Cross, The, 61, 64, 116
Regular Army, ix
Reichstag, 15, 291
Religion, ix, 156, 182, 193, 210, 261
Retreats, 181, 309
Reumont, 284, 285
Reunion, 197, 242, 243
Reynolds, Bainbridge, 320
RHA, (Royal Horse Artillery), 30
Rhine, The, 298, 299
Rhodes, Cecil, 317
Rhodes, Scholars, 18
Rhodes, Trustees, 17
Rifle Brigade, The London, 275, 296
Ripon, Bishop of, 317